Death of an Angel

The Inside Story of how Justice Prevailed in the San Francisco Dog-Mauling Case

by

Joseph Harrington

Published by

QE

Quantum Entertainment
LLC
Creating the word, the sound, the sight of entertainment since 1992

FIRST EDITION
Printed in the United States of America
by Thomson-Shore Inc.

Library of Congress Cataloging-in-Publishing Data

Harrington, Joseph
    Death of an Angel;
        The Inside Story of how Justice Prevailed
        In the San Francisco Dog-Mauling Case

ISBN 0-9718899-0-2

For information about reproducing
selections from this book, write: Permissions,
Quantum Entertainment
228 Commercial Street, Nevada City CA 95959
email QEangel@Netshel.Net
www.deathofanangel.com

This book
is dedicated
to
the memory of

Diane Alexis Whipple

and
all members
of

Law and Order

This is the story of a horrific event.
Out of respect for the memory of Diane Alexis Whipple, this effort
touches only lightly on her life and no photos arc included.

Cast of Main Characters
(age at time of the incident)

Diane Whipple (33). Mauled to death by the dog Bane
on January 26, 2001. Lacrosse coach at St.
Mary's College, Moraga, California.
Weight: 110 pounds.

Sharon Smith (35). Diane Whipple's roommate and seven-
year domestic partner.
Regional vice president at Charles Schwab &
Company.

Robert Noel (59). Tax attorney and self-proclaimed legal
activist. Co-owner of the dogs Bane and Hera.

Marjorie Knoller (45). Tax attorney and wife of Noel.
Co-owner of the dogs Bane and Hera.

Henry Hunter (54). General Work lieutenant for the
San Francisco Police Department (SFPD).

Bane (3). Male dog, a Presa Canario, an unusual mixture
of Canary Island cattle dog and English
mastiff. A hybrid on the verge of extinction.
Weight: 123 pounds.

Hera (2). Female dog, also a Presa Canario.
Weight: 112 pounds.

Paul "Cornfed" Schneider (38). Inmate at Pelican Bay
State Prison, life without possibility of
parole. Robbery; aggravated assault; attempted
murder. Ranking member of the Aryan
Brotherhood.

Dale Bretches (44). Inmate at Pelican Bay State Prison, Life without possibility of parole.
Murder. Ranking member of the Aryan Brotherhood.
Partner with Cornfed in raising 'killer' dogs.

Michael Cardoza (57). Sharon Smith's lawyer in domestic partnership legislation and wrongful death suit.

Sarah Miller (24). Diane Whipple's successor as head lacrosse coach at St. Mary's College.

Inspector Rich Daniele (44). General Work Division field investigator, SFPD.

Inspector Mike Becker (44). General Work Division field investigator, SFPD.

Sergeant Paul Morse (56). Stationed at Northern Precinct. Ranking officer at the crime scene.

Terence "KO" Hallinan (62). Controversial district attorney of San Francisco, following a career as a high-profile defense attorney, an amateur pugilist and member of a notorious family in the City.

Paul Cummins (54). Second-in-command of the San Francisco district attorney's office.

James Hammer (41). Assistant district attorney, co-prosecutor in the case.

Kimberly Guilfoyle Newsom (32). Assistant district attorney, co-prosecutor in the case.

Acknowledgements

The author would like to thank all those wonderful people who helped him find substance and answers to this story.

The Police

Police Chief and Mayor Frank Jordan, ret.
Deputy Police Chief Diarmiud Phillpott, ret.
Deputy Police Chief Kevin Mullen, ret.
Officer Sidney Laws   Officer Leslie Forrestal
Sergeant Paul Morse   Sergeant Steve Murphy
Investigator Rich Daniele   Investigator Mike Becker
Animal Care & Control Sergeant Michael Scott
Animal Care & Control Lieutenant Vickie Guldbeck
Animal Care & Control Officer Andrea Runge
Criminal Investigator Dave Parenti
Polygraph Inspector Julie Yee-ho
Criminal Investigator Joe Long
With a very appreciative nod to Lieutenant Henry Hunter
       for his insight and firsthand knowledge, as well as his
       supportive foreword

The Lawyers

District Attorney Terence Hallinan,
Assistant District Attorney James Hammer
Chief Assistant District Attorney Paul Cummins
Attorney Michael Cardoza
Attorney Garry Graham
Attorney Herman Franck
Attorney William Fazio
Tax attorney Jim Sullivan
Tax Attorney Sandy Westin
With eminent thanks to Assistant District Attorney
       Kimberly Guilfoyle Newsom, for her personal
       commitment to this case

St. Mary's College

Sarah Miller
Melissa Boyle
Megan Bryan
With special appreciation to the entire 2001 lacrosse
      team, who played their collective hearts out under very
      difficult circumstances.

Others

Sharon Smith
Robert and Virginia Nurisso
Doctor Julie Duff
Tim and Janel Harrington
Dave and Joanne Kragen
Dr. Leo Harrington
Patti and Jack Foster
Devin and Damon Epidendio
Steve and Sabrina Busher
Bob Cooksely
Jack and Erica Young
Julia Katherine Harrington
N.Y. AKC Ambassador Ann Letiss
Jeff Rhoades

Julie Rameriz
Jennifer Krusing
Theresa Ewins
Pam MacDonough
Charley Mike
Elizabeth Faulkner
Dr. Bob Harrington
John Kruger
Amory Graham
Greg Semans
Tucker Spolter
Kathleen Kiernan
David A. Parker
Erin Harrington

And to Russ Vorpagel, FBI ret., co-founder of the department's
      Behavioral Science Unit, for insight into the pathology of
      sociopaths.

Publication

John Burger, computer graphics
Charles Felix , graphic design
Robert Burger, marketing
Steve Cottrell, editor
And especially to Doctor Iline Kroll Kittredjie, for her very
      insightful remarks pertaining to this case.

TABLE OF CONTENTS

TABLE OF CONTENTS

TABLE OF CONTENTS

Foreword

Lt. Henry Hunter

San Francisco Police Department

At dusk on Friday, January 26, 2001, I received an emergency police call from Sergeant Paul Morse. I was directed to 2398 Pacific Avenue where I noticed police cars, ambulances, emergency vehicles, fire trucks and animal control units jamming the intersection. I quickly learned what had tragically happened: a young woman had been killed... by two dogs.

It became known internationally as "The San Francisco dog-mauling case."

This highly-publicized crime of a preventable tragedy sent shock waves throughout the country. Rightly so. My men and I, as police officers assigned to investigate this crime, could have adopted a traditional criminal investigative approach to this kind of case. We could have agreed with the conventional wisdom that no one, no matter how reckless, can be considered a murderer because of the actions of an animal. Instead, in cooperation with the district attorney's office, we decided to take a stand. As a result of the successful investigation and prosecution of this crime, reckless dog owners have been put on notice. Never again can we treat dog ownership cavalierly, nor jump to the conclusion that all animal attacks are tragic accidents.

Perhaps this is the positive side of a horrific tragedy.

Through the patient accumulation of efforts, large and small, we help forge a just society. As a policeman, I am proud to be a part of that process. At the same time, I well realize, as this powerful book so dramatically reveals, that the effort of the police is only the first act in a succession of hard work by the dedicated women and men in law enforcement, public service and criminal prosecution.

I recommend this excellent book not merely as a story of meticulous police work and thorough prosecution, but as a very human account, about people you want to know.

Mr. Harrington has put a human face on events that the media in general have, at times, dealt with in a sensationalistic way. This is a passionately documented record of what really happened and what it's really like on the front lines of justice.

Henry Hunter
San Francisco, Ca
May 2002

Author's Note

In a work of this nature, which is not a biographical effort, only a few sample events from a person's life can be included. Diane Whipple lived life for each day, grabbing the moment. In this book only a few examples of the spirit, joy and laughter that she brought to her life and those around her have been included.

The trial involving her murder changed California law. Her death not only raises the stakes for all dog owners, it sends the human message that the uncaring, the selfish and the arrogant can and will be held accountable for their actions.

It is my hope that you will come to understand why Diane Alexis Whipple's tragic criminal case needed to be told.

Death of an Angel may seem a pretentious title. An atheist thinks there are no angels among us. A theologian thinks angels can't die.

Yet, a philosopher would argue that while angels aren't saints, they *can* commit sin, and by that act experience a sort of death when condemned.

Can a human be an angel? Of course not, but a human can certainly try to emulate one. And that is what Diane Alexis Whipple did. She had flaws, as do all of us. The author is not trying to canonize her. But she did have a vibrant joy of life that reverberated with, and encompassed, all who met her.

Cops, for the most part, are very adept at keeping a mental granite block wall between themselves and the victim. Not for motives inhumane, rather for psychological protection. Most of us have enough grief in our own lives to not import traumatic sorrow from others.

Diane Whipple's death was different.

The 33-year-old women's lacrosse coach at St. Mary's College, in Northern California, struck many a chord of friendship, love and admiration with those she met in her short life.

She continues to do so in death.

Time after time, the author experienced the following anecdote in one form or another from police officers and prosecutors involved in this heart-rending case.

March 20, 2001, the Plush Room, York Hotel, San Francisco. A benefit was thrown for The Diane Alexis Whipple Foundation at the York Hotel on Sutter Street, a few blocks west of Union Square in San Francisco. The foundation was created to continue some of Diane's most passionate charities: children's education, cancer research and resources for abused children.

Many years earlier, an obsessed Jimmy Stewart followed an elusive Kim Novak to the York Hotel in Alfred Hitchcock's psychological thriller *Vertigo*. Tonight, the hotel was the setting for a memorial for a woman whose death was part of a tangled story more bizarre than anything Hitchcock could have imagined.

The benefit was held in the very aptly named Plush Room, a popular venue for cabaret singers. The doors opened at seven. The room rapidly filled. There was a wide variety of people in attendance: Young men in suits; older men in Pendelton shirts; women, from the very young — representatives of the lacrosse team — to the elderly.

Plus the inevitable presence of TV cameras and reporters.

Sharon Smith spoke briefly, thanking everyone for coming and participating in the Diane Whipple Foundation.

A piano player, a bass player and the female vocalist Paula West took the stage. They played and sang Cole Porter and Irving Berlin songs. The trio chose upbeat and humorous numbers.

At the rear of the nightclub, the author sat next to Sergeant Paul Morse of the San Francisco police department.

Paul, like so many other police officers involved in the case, was a veteran with over 30 years on the force. He was not the first cop to arrive at the scene almost eight weeks prior, but he

14

was the ranking officer and he arrived just minutes after the attack ended. Two young female patrol officers, Sidney Laws and Leslie Forrestal, had the unfortunate distinction of being the first members of law enforcement to see the devastating carnage wrought on Diane by two ferocious Presa Canario dogs.

When he entered the hallway of the sixth floor of the apartment building at 2398 Pacific Avenue, Paul Morse immediately saw that it clearly was not an accidental death. He phoned homicide and was told to call the General Work Detail. He spoke to that division's boss, Henry Hunter, an old friend. Then Paul called the forensic lab and the crime scene photographer.

All investigative police officers who know their jobs realize that you only have one opportunity at a crime scene. You can never recreate it. Once tampered with it opens the way for a clever defense attorney to raise all sorts of doubts in a jury's collective mind.

Paul had done his job, like the pro he was, preserving evidence for later study and analysis by the DA's office.

His work ended weeks earlier, yet he attended the benefit. He sat in the Plush Room, a burly, balding, lantern-chinned, middle-aged man with his thick arms crossed.

Paul had the kind of face you never wanted to see waiting for you if you were led manacled into an interrogation room.

One tough cop.

During his career he had been in the old "S" squad — Special Investigations. He had served in narcotics. He had seen some very gruesome scenes in his years on the force. Part of that past horror showed in his eyes.

Megan Bryan, a member of the St. Mary's lacrosse team, came over from a nearby booth and affectionately patted him on the head. She smiled and went back to her other team members.

Paul Morse said to the author, "I haven't slept properly since walking into that hallway. I can't get the images out of my mind."

Sarah Miller, new head coach of the lacrosse team at St. Mary's, gave Morse a warm hug.

15

The cop watched her return to her seat. He said, "I've met so many incredible people on this case. But the images are still raw. When I got there it was a charnel house."

Paul breathed deeply a few times, trying to regain his composure. "I saw her. Her clothes were shredded off. She was still trying to crawl towards her apartment. I started bawling like a little baby."

The cop sat very still, staring at the stage where a dozen white roses sat in a vase on the piano.

Paul spoke once again to the author, this time in a very quiet voice. "You know, I really would have loved to have met and gotten to know Diane."

*　　*　　*

The author has heard that last sentiment repeated over and over from those whose lives were touched by Diane after she died — cops and prosecutors, and even members of the general public.

This book is about the tragic and senseless death of a human being. Also, it is a book about who that human being was and how joyously she embraced her life and the lives of others.

Diane Alexis Whipple cherished and celebrated living; with her family, her friends, her colleagues, her teammates, and the love of her life.

Orson Welles' movie *Citizen Kane* begins with the famous death scene and a single word, "Rosebud," spoken inside the vast citadel Xanadu mansion of a famous newspaperman. Charles Foster Kane is dead, yet we know nothing of his private life. A reporter is assigned to discover who this man really was.

That's exactly how the author started on this case — knowing nothing about the victim, Diane Whipple. People like Paul Morse helped him understand the tragedy that happened.

Most books on the subject of crime begin with the crime. This book will begin with a prologue involving three-dozen white doves and a memorial service for a very extraordinary woman.

Prologue

Sunday, March 11, 2001, St. Mary's College.
Lacrosse coach Sarah Miller felt as if she had been kicked by an ornery mule. A large aching knot, deep in the pit of her stomach, manufactured bile.

She had not slept well the night before. She had not slept well for many nights before — back to when she first heard that her boss and dear friend was killed.

She drove up the long lane that gave entrance to her place of employment, St. Mary's College, less than an hour's drive east of San Francisco.

The lacrosse game wasn't scheduled to begin until one o'clock. As head coach, Sarah had much to do before then.

She parked by the athletic department's building.

Sarah was pretty and petite and a lithe athlete. She had played soccer while getting her degree at UCLA.

She was now far closer to her roots, having been born and raised in Lafayette, a town a few miles down the road.

She knew that most of what she had to do that morning was routine and rote: Get the locker room open; make sure the towels were out; make sure that those who needed knees or ankles or elbows taped received the proper protection. But, she wondered, what am I going to say to twenty-six students now grieving the loss of their coach?

She glanced at the sky.

The mid-March weather in Northern California had been sly; first teasing with a glimpse of the sun and its warmth, then immediately ambushing an early spring's expectations with torrential downpours of rainfall in the flatlands and blistering blizzards of snow in the mountains.

The fickle sky seemed unable to decide between storm and balmy. By ten in the morning there was a slightly gray tint to an atmosphere devoid of direct sun. Nature vacillated for an hour

17

before spots of blue began to appear over the low foothills that surrounded nearby Mount Diablo.

St. Mary's College could not have been in a more pastoral setting — a direct juxtaposition to the evil represented by the name of the nearby mountain. The Catholic seat of learning nestled in the Moraga hills, a bucolic harbor for its students and teachers.

Except now was a time of sadness, a time of remembrance, a time of closure.

The sun won against the ambiguous grays and soon the clouds dispersed. It was noon.

The lacrosse team silently got ready for the game.

Tears began to gently trickle from Sarah's eyes.

Stop it. Be strong. For the team. You're their leader.

She led her players out onto the field.

The backdrop elements for future drama were there — the sky blue; the sun warm with life; the field below, emerald green. The young female faces of the lacrosse team, now all seemingly older from the tragedy they experienced in the last month and a half, waiting for the moment.

The grandstands started to cradle spectators.

The lacrosse team from North Carolina went through its pre-game ritualistic warm-up maneuvers. Zigzagging in figure-eight formation, they hurled a yellow ball back and forth in a seemingly endless repetition of perfection.

On the other end of the field the St. Mary's team sat in a semi-circle in front of their coach.

Sarah had only been introduced to lacrosse in January, two months earlier. Her sponsor/mentor/friend Diane Whipple had cajoled her into accepting the position of assistant coach with the throwaway line of, "Don't worry, you'll pick it up in no time. And I'll help."

Diane, you're not here to help, Sarah thought. I'm alone with over two-dozen women as my responsibility.

Why did you have to die?

Don't think of the letter about friendship Diane gave me the morning of the day she died.

Don't think of the broad grin on Diane's face that last morning when she said, "You're late."

"A couple of minutes."

"Late's late."

Then the letter of friendship given, accompanied with the grin. That happy, infectious grin. The same smile that had appeared, when? Less than two months ago. Those weeks felt like years.

Diane and Sarah had gone down south to run in a marathon. It was mile 16 in the San Diego Marathon when Diane decided to pick up the pace.

She sprinted away from me. It was your thirty-third birthday. You were nine years older than me. And you sprinted away from me, like you were the younger one, flashing an impish grin over your shoulder.

We had beers that night, and laughter and candy.

"The perfect combination," Diane said, "to celebrate."

Then the inevitable pause, the twinkle in the eye, and the gentle jab. "What was your time today?"

"Three hours and fifty-four minutes."

Diane nodded.

Sarah said, "Say your time, I know you're dying to tell me."

"Let's see, it was around—"

"Three hours and thirty-two minutes."

"Don't worry," Diane said in a soft, modulated voice. "This was your first marathon. You'll do way, way better the next time."

That's how Diane always was, Sarah thought; first the friendly banter, then the encouragement and support would inevitably follow. And quickly.

Except five days after her birthday she died, died so horribly.

The twenty-six members of the St. Mary's lacrosse team looked expectantly at their coach.

Sarah went over things she could say. Rally cries, emotional pleas. She knew the sadness in her heart and the

19

sadness in her players' hearts would not allow it. She simply said, "Play your best, that's all Diane ever asked."

A man and a woman, both dressed in black, protected boxes sitting on the sideline; boxes containing white doves.

The doves were imprisoned, held captive in three wooden-slatted crates. They nestled with each other, cooing, unaware of the symbolism of life and death they were about to impart.

The three boxes of doves were carried to the center of the field. The St. Mary's lacrosse team gathered to meet the classic symbols of love and peace.

Each lacrosse player received a bird and cupped it in her hands. Each player followed a teammate in an ever-growing, majestic-looking circle. Finally, the circle was complete. The last to receive the birds were the coaches, a few members of the teaching staff, and Sharon Smith.

Over the stadium's loud speaker Julie Duff, who umpired many of Diane's games and played club lacrosse with her, spoke. Her amplified words came strong and clear: "I want to express our love and support for the St. Mary's lacrosse team. We also want you to know how much we admired and respected Diane Whipple. As a player, a coach, a leader and a friend she was a gift to our community.

"Diane put her heart out to make a difference to lacrosse in California. She has touched many of our lives forever. It is with much love and deep respect that we have organized this tribute to her honor. We love you Diane and are committed to keeping your spirit alive."

Sharon Smith stood in the center of the field. She was slight of build, with dark hair encompassing her attractive face. She cupped a small white dove in her hands.

Recorded music written by Andrew Lloyd Webber began to play over the loudspeakers. Sarah Brightman's unbelievably pure voice sang lyrics translated to Italian in throbbing music that soared and swooned, expressing deep passion and haunting loss.

At a breathtaking moment — when the chords of music had risen to an intense crescendo — the soprano's words turned to

English and she sang, her words resonating in sadness, "Time to... say good-bye."

Sharon set the first dove free. She opened her cupped hands. The bird spread its wings but failed to fly off. She moved her hands upward in a gentle motion. The bird tentatively flapped and gained a few feet of altitude.

The twenty-six members of the lacrosse team, a few of their teachers and their coach, held white birds aloft — then freed them. A column of small white bodies soared heavenward.

Sarah Brightman stopped singing.

The incredibly gifted tenor, Andrea Bocelli, his voice rich and full and aching, sang his echoing refrain, "Time to... say good-bye."

Three-dozen doves, as one, rose above that green field of combat. They soared as a single entity — wings beating in time to the melodic music.

In the center of the field all those young faces looked aloft. They watched the birds of peace and love spin in a spiral toward heaven.

The birds headed north. The pulsating music continued, as if the notes themselves were crying.

The music stopped, but the hush of silence that embraced all present continued.

As if not wanting to depart, the birds momentarily returned to the northeast end of the field. There they paused, then flashed, again as one unit, white against the azure sky, then hurriedly soared away.

Away... to their future... shunning the sad and tearful past they left behind. A sad and tearful past for those who had to go forward.

The birds disappeared into the distance. Their pure white bodies eventually became so small that the immensity of the blue sky swallowed them.

Sarah looked at her team. Some were sobbing. Some were rubbing their eyes. All still looked up at the vast sky, thinking the three-dozen doves might return.

The doves are gone.

Like Diane.

Sarah glanced at Sharon Smith, back straight, face immobile, as always demure and regal at the same time, except for eyes that shimmered with the pain of loss.

Sarah's heart bled. What must Sharon be thinking? What must she be feeling? I lost a friend. She lost a soul mate. I lost a mentor. She lost her life's singular love.

Six weeks had passed since the unbelievable tragedy happened in that San Francisco hallway, and still the question echoed hollowly about in Sarah's mind without an answer: Why?

Why did Diane have to die?

Part One

The

Investigation

Chapter One

An Angel's Death

Charles Schwab & Company, San Francisco Branch, Sharon Smith's office, Noon, Friday, January 26, 2001.
Sharon Smith's phone rang. Diane Alexis' familiar voice floated over the phone. "Why don't you come home?"

"It's only noon."

"Come home."

"I have to work."

"I'll cook dinner."

"Alexis, my car is buried in the garage. There's no way I'm going to get it out."

"After dinner I'll treat for a movie."

"If you'll come pick me up, I'll come home."

"No. I'll go to the grocery store. I'll get stuff. I'll make tacos, and we'll go out to a movie tonight."

Sharon worked until four. A thought flashed through her mind: *I should leave.* She packed up her laptop and some work she needed to finish before Monday. She went to the office building's garage at twenty-to-five.

She lived 2½ miles from her office. She immediately ran into gridlock.

Friday afternoons. I should have left at noon, like Alexis wanted. I should have called a cab. I hate sitting in traffic.

The line of cars inched forward.

What is it about time and motion? A jet can travel 3,000 miles and cross the country in 5½ hours. Alexis just ran a marathon in 3½ hours; twenty-six miles, 385 yards.

She glanced at her watch. I'm in a car that can do more than a hundred miles an hour and I can't get home in a half hour.

Alexis will be worried.

Alexis. I love calling her that, instead of Diane. I think it's a much more beautiful name.

The traffic inched forward.

This is ridiculous.

Using her cell phone, Sharon called home. The answering machine came on. She said, "Stuck in traffic, Alexis. Where are you? Call me on my cell phone."

Pacific Heights is located northwest of the center of the city. To the south was the Civic Center and municipal buildings, to the north the Marina and San Francisco Bay.

Sharon crossed Van Ness Avenue. She phoned home again and got the answering machine. She said, "I don't know what's going on. I can't get through. Where are you?"

When she was two blocks from home, she called her mother back east. "Stuck in traffic, mom. Don't know what's going on. I can't get through. Alexis and I are going to... There's some vans blocking the street. Down the block, near our apartment. Mom, I can see cop cars down the street. One, two, three, four, five. And a fire truck. Good God, there's a SWAT team van parked in front of..."

She got out of her car, leaving it double-parked, oblivious to the angry sound of horns from the people stuck behind her.

She went down the street. She saw a van marked Animal Care & Control.

Animal. Dog. *Dogs*.

She glanced at her apartment, her lights were off.

Why are the lights off?

Dear God, it's Alexis. I know something's happened to Alexis.

She asked onlookers. No one knew for sure. Just lines like "Dog attack," or, "Someone got hurt."

Sharon saw her apartment manager and friend, Aleta Cerdido, standing across the street with her domestic partner Heather. She ran up and asked, "What's going on here?"

Aleta's face was ash-white. She said, "My God, I thought it was you."

Sharon knew. It's Alexis.

She heard a tinny voice. She looked around, confused, then realized it was her mother on the cell phone she still clutched in her hand. She said, "Mom, it's Alexis."

Her mother said, "What's happened? What's wrong?"

It dawned on Sharon that she hadn't asked.

"Aleta, what happened?"

"She got bit by a dog. They just took her in an ambulance to the hospital."

Sharon thought, I know which dogs. Those monsters that live down the hall from us. "Mom, I have to go. She's at the hospital."

Across the street, two men from animal control led a dog out of the building using come-alongs.

"Aleta, Heather," Sharon asked, "how bad? How bad is she?"

Heather answered, "The cop told me Diane's going to San Francisco General Hospital."

"I'll drive you," Aleta said.

Aleta and Sharon got in the front seat. Heather got in the back. They drove toward the hospital.

Sharon prayed, thank you dear God. She's alive. They're taking her to the hospital, not the morgue. She's alive. Thank God.

A dog bite. What are we talking about here? "Aleta, how serious is this?"

Aleta continued to inch her way toward San Francisco General. The Friday traffic was snarling the entire east end of the City.

"Heather," Sharon asked, "how bad? I have to know what to expect."

Heather said, "Critical."

Critical?

That bad?

Just how bad did she get bit? Bad enough to be taken to a hospital with sirens screeching.

Bad enough to be called critical.

Her hand?

Like when Bane bit Diane only a couple a weeks ago. Right on the wrist.

No, that wasn't critical.

Her arm?

Heather said critical.

Not her leg. Oh God, I pray not her leg. She loves to run. I'd give *my* leg to save *hers*. So she could still run.

She's so beautiful to watch when she runs. Like a gazelle. Free. And her face. The joy radiating from her eyes. The smile. The smile that explodes, driven by the joy from within.

They drove across Market Street and headed down South Van Ness. The major thoroughfare held cars and trucks and buses, each moving in agonizing slow motion.

Sharon begin to rock back and forth in her seat, willing the car to move faster.   She thought, I could *run* there faster than this.

I love to watch Alexis when she runs. Like when she tried out for the Olympics. The 800-meter race. That's when we first met. Or the marathon in San Diego. Distance didn't matter, the freedom of the run did.

She was like the runners in the movie *Chariots of Fire*. When the Scotsman, what was his name? When he raced the hundred-yard dash in the Paris stadium his elation burst forth, his body and mind unable to contain the pure wonder and joy.

Not her leg.

Please, God, not her leg.

Let her still be able to run.

I played sports in college, but not like her. I wouldn't miss it like she would.

I *like* to run.

Alexis *loves* to run.

Sharon looked out the window. Finally. They were in front of San Francisco General. She saw her neighbors from

28

across the hall, Hank and Ginger Putek, standing in front of the hospital.

What are they doing here?

Hank waved both arms and pointed at the red zone in front of the emergency entrance.

In a daze, Sharon entered the hospital. She asked the admitting nurse where Diane was.

The nurse looked away, unwilling to meet her eyes.

"Where?" Sharon repeated.

"In the emergency operating room."

"How bad?"

"The doctor will tell you."

"Did you see her admitted?"

The nurse's eyes shifted nervously about, still unable to focus on Sharon.

"Tell me," Sharon said, voice breaking. "How bad is it?"

"Very bad," replied the nurse.

*   *   *

Just before nine o'clock that Friday night, Diane Alexis Whipple died.

Chapter
Two

An Incident Report

**Lieutenant Henry Hunter's home, two blocks from City
College of San Francisco, Saturday, January 27, 2001.**
Henry Hunter was the officer in charge of the San Francisco Police
Department's General Work Detail. His command handled all
felony animal killings.

He was not your Hollywood version of a police officer. No
Dirty Harry saying, "Make my day." No affectations like Sherlock
Holmes' Meerschaum pipe and syringe filled with a seven percent
solution. If Hunter was to be compared to any fictional character,
it would have to be Agatha Christie's Hercule Poirot.

Unassuming. Mild-mannered, pleasant face.

He was the antithesis of the public's mental picture of a
seasoned cop. If he sported anything unusual, it was suspenders, a
half-size-too-small fedora, and a once-in-awhile tendency to wear
slightly garish ties.

Years earlier, his pleasant face had been an asset when he
worked decoy. In less than three months, he and his team wiped
out muggings in San Francisco. The muggers moved elsewhere
when they learned an impossible-looking cop was nailing them.

Henry Hunter did not normally take his work home with
him. As head of the General Work Detail his function was
administrator rather than investigator. He monitored hours and
overtime, turning in payroll. He assigned teams to different
investigations. At this point in his career he spent most of his time
in front of a computer screen, rather than at a crime scene.

An Incident Report

But this Saturday morning Hunter had made an exception. He brought home the Incident Report filed by the first officer on the scene of the dog-mauling death — Officer Forrestal.

He read: "On Friday 01/26/01 at approximately 1605 hours Officer Laws #1520 and I were sent to 2398 Pacific Avenue regarding a well-being check on the 6th floor. Dispatch advised us that there were two large dogs running in the hallway. Dispatch received a second call from a CHP cellular transfer reporting a woman screaming for help from the same location.

"Upon our arrival we entered the apartment building lobby and were met by a maintenance worker who told us he heard dogs barking and a woman screaming from several flights up. I took the elevator to the 6th floor and upon exiting the elevator I saw V — (victim) — Whipple lying face down bleeding severely from the left side of the neck. The victim was naked and I could see multiple dog bites on her limbs, head and body. There was shredded clothing, blood and human hair covering approximately 20'-30' of hallway floors and walls. I immediately called for a code 3 ambulance and additional assistance.

"Officer Laws had taken the stairs up to the 6th floor and told me she saw a dog run past her, away from the victim; however, she did not see where the dog went. Officer Laws and I protected the victim from further attack until we saw the owner of the dogs, Knoller, exit her apartment. Knoller told us that she had secured the dogs inside the apartment.

"Knoller was also covered in blood and her clothing was torn and stained.

"…I spoke with Knoller regarding the incident and she told me the following: She had just returned home with the dogs from a walk and was entering her apartment when her neighbor, Whipple, came home carrying grocery bags.

"Knoller stated that her male dog, a large bull mastiff (sic), ran down the hall and attacked the victim. Knoller said she tried to control the dog after the attack began, but was unsuccessful. Knoller then attempted to place her body between the dog and the victim. However, each time the victim tried to move toward her apartment the dog renewed its attack.

"Knoller also stated that her other dog, a female bull mastiff (sic), did not initiate the attack, but was pulling at the victim's clothing.

"I then spoke to E-W Ester Birkmaier who told me the following: She heard the owner of the dogs yelling, 'Stop it. Stop it.' She looked through the peep hole and saw the dog attack her neighbor. Whipple was trying desperately to enter her apartment to get away from the dog, but could not."

Hunter thought, an eye witness.

Except that E-W in front of Ester Birkmaier was a flag. E-W was shorthand for Elderly Woman. Elderly was unfortunate. It was amazing what a good defense attorney could do to an elderly person's memory. He would have to have an inspector interview Ester and see what kind of witness she was.

He turned the page on the incident report and continued to read:

"Birkmaier also stated she was stunned for about 3-5 minutes before she was able to call the police. Birkmaier said that she has been deathly afraid of the dogs for several months.

Hunter thought, she called the police. 911. A taped message. Have to get that.

Except... Usually a judge wouldn't allow it as evidence. Hearsay. He went back to the report.

"Officer Laws was able to locate identification for the victim from a purse found on the floor just inside the victim's apartment. The door to the victim's apartment was open and her keys were in the lock. There was a ripped grocery bag just inside the doorway and groceries strewn about the hall near the victim's door.

"Sergeant Morse contacted Ops Center. I spoke with Inspector Lew at Ops Center regarding the incident."

Hunter put the Incident Report file in his briefcase and opened the *San Francisco Chronicle*.

The newspaper carried the story of the tragic dog-mauling death. Things jumped out. Like how neighbors referred to the dog Bane. "Killer Dog." Or, "Dog of Death."

An Incident Report

Item: Robert Noel stated he had adopted the dogs about three months ago after suing, pro bono, on behalf of a client to have them released from a breeding facility that was leaving them chained up outside.

Hunter wondered, if you sue for a client and win custody of the dogs why do you adopt them instead of turning them over to the client?

Item: Robert Noel and Marjorie Knoller are known for their pro bono work, particularly on behalf of the city's homeless.

Item: Noel stated, "Bane and I had encountered her (Ms. Whipple) at least four or five times in the past month. He never showed the least bit of interest in her."

Hunter finished reading and thought, what would the DA do? Usually, in tragedies like this, the law was very understanding.

But it is always better to be over-prepared than under-prepared. A woman had died.

Henry Hunter's home, Sunday morning, January 28, 2001.
Hunter was as excited as a Bible-thumping tent revivalist giving a sermon in a church with a real roof.

Actually, he corrected himself, I'm acting like a young groom pacing a maternity ward.

Except it's two months early for the maternity ward.

His son Russell and his daughter-in-law, Imelda, were expecting a child near the end of March. It would be his second grandchild. His granddaughter had arrived months earlier.

He already knew that his next grandchild would be a boy. He also knew that starting to worry two months early was ridiculous.

In the front room was the rest of Hunter's family. His wife Cindy, his daughter Sandra and her husband Hicham Senhaji and their seven-month-old daughter Isobel, and, lastly, Henry's other son, 15-year-old Harry.

My daughter-in-law, Hunter thought, with a phrase from the Bible rattling in his mind, looks great with child.

Death of an Angel

Super Bowl XXXV was about to begin. Ravens versus the Giants.

A Super Bowl without the 49ers. The cop shook his head. Terrible. No Steve Young. No Joe Montana. Just Jerry Rice from the legends that Bill Walsh had been a part of creating, and both the former coach and the wide receiver were watching the game instead of playing in it.

What kind of name was Ravens? At least the Giants sounded like a football team.

He watched Ray Lewis, Ravens middle-linebacker, run onto the field to screams of appreciation from the fans gathered at Raymond James Stadium in Tampa.

Hunter, who joined the police force a few years after the first Super Bowl was played, remembered, a year ago two guys died outside a club in Atlanta. Then Ray Lewis, football player, pleaded the case down from a murder charge to obstructing justice.

No remorse.

Nothing about the two dead men.

He watched an official toss a ceremonial coin and realized, I haven't heard Noel or Knoller say *anything* to Sharon Smith or anyone else, remorseful or otherwise.

The game was a rout. The Ravens lived up to their pre-game "trash talk" and won 34 -7.

Dinner was one of Hunter and his wife's favorite meals: lamb shanks with all the trimmings.

The family's buttering me up, the cop realized, and ganging up. Full-court press by the whole clan — led by my wife of three decades.

Why?

This is really the royal red carpet treatment.

After the family savored succulent lamb shank, the dishes were bused; baked Alaska, with a full-bodied desert wine, was served. His son and daughter-in-law served Hunter first.

I've been a cop for thirty years, he thought. Longer than either of the lives of these two almost-parents, and they think they can schmooze me into a comfort zone and then blindside me with information.

It must be what they're going to name the boy, my first grandson.

That means it's not going to be "Henry." But why the killing of the fatted calf? Or, in this case, the fatted lamb.

He amused himself pretending he wasn't catching the sidelong glances going on between Russ and Imelda, two young people whom he loved.

His son finally fumbled out that they had decided to name the baby Joshua.

Joshua.

Biblical.

Joshua. I love it. My grandson.

Joshua, successor to Moses. The man God Himself promised to assist.

Hunter gave his blessings on the name of his soon-to-be first grandson.

His youngest son, Harry, asked, "How's the dog case going, dad?"

"Too early to tell. But a crime has definitely been committed."

"Which is?"

"Minimum, owning a mischievous animal."

"Wow," Harry said sarcastically, "like that's the crime of the century."

"Someone died, son."

"I know."

"And horribly."

"I know."

Russ said, "And we all know how you're going to handle the case."

Hunter grinned. His family all too well knew his battle cry when it came to crime. He loved the Bible's Proverbs and could quote from them extensively.

His favorite of all was, "The wicked go where no man pursucth."

He always enthusiastically added, "But *I* do."

Death of an Angel

After his families had dispersed to their own homes, he switched on the television to Channel 7. KGO's attractive reporter Laura Anthony was talking with some of the neighbors of Noel and Knoller.

A woman, whose name was not identified, said about Bane: "The dog lunges all the time. If he's not lunging, he's very intimidating. I don't have anything against animals, but seems like he's the kind of dog that should have a little space to roam."

Wrong tense, Hunter corrected. She should have used the past tense. Bane's not lunging at anyone anymore. He's dead. Executed by lethal injection.

That kind of speed in carrying out a death sentence hasn't been seen since the Gold Rush. Like a hundred and fifty years ago. Pass sentence. Get a rope. Say your prayers.

What do I have to do tomorrow? I know what the DA's going to want. No one's been charged, but I'm going to have to find out if the owners knew the dogs were trained or had a history of scaring or biting people.

What level charge?

Criminal negligence?

Manslaughter?

Or, on the low end, owning a mischievous animal?

On the high end, second-degree homicide?

Let the DA's office figure it out.

My job is to assemble facts.

On the TV a resident of the Pacific Heights building, Ed Lewis, said, "I personally have friends who have been growled at and snapped at. No one I know wants to be near those dogs. The lawyers always defended them to a fault."

The reporter said, "Those two dogs came from somewhere. And the fate of one is still in the air."

Hunter watched a woman respond to the question of how she would feel if the dog Hera returned to the apartment building.

"This is outrageously disrespectful to the woman just killed. It's very dangerous to the people in the building."

Hunter knew that Hera was at the pound, awaiting trial at dog court. But if by a miracle she gets a reprieve, would the

36

lawyers really bring that dog back to the apartment? An apartment two doors away from where the victim lived?

Must be a mistake.

Noel and Knoller can't have so little empathy as to even consider bringing the dog back to the apartment.

I have to ask Sharon if she's planning on moving. Of *course* she's planning on moving. Wouldn't I move if this happened to *my* wife?

That hallway must feel like a sepulchre.

Like living in a mausoleum of memories.

The news on TV shifted to a spokesperson from Animal Care and Control.

Sergeant Judy Choy explained that reports of dangerous dog situations have gone through the roof. "People are just afraid."

The officer was replaced by a woman identified as Judy Massey. Her daughter was coached by Diane Whipple. "She was full of energy. She had a passion for lacrosse. And so many girls would come out for this sport they had never heard of. It was infectious."

Henry knew that tomorrow, without a doubt, Paul Cummins would want to see him.

He and Cummins went back to their college days. They both attended the University of San Francisco.

Jesuit educated.

Hunter went into police work, Cummins into prosecution. Both men brought to their jobs the perception and logic for which Jesuits are famous.

And both their jobs often involved homicide.

Homicide. The killing of one human being by another.

And the weapon could be anything. A gun. A vehicle. A knife. A dog.

Hunter decided not to put off thinking about the case for too long. Obviously, the media had latched onto the story. One of his job descriptions was liaison between his command and the press.

Hunter had assigned General Work field investigators Rich Daniele and Mike Becker to conduct the case.

Both investigators had twenty years experience on the police force. General Work handled all cases not specifically assigned to another investigative unit. Its primary cases were weapons, assaults, threats, kidnappings, non-domestic stalkings and all felony animal cases.

Chapter
Three

Rashomon

San Francisco Hall of Justice, General Work Detail, Tuesday, January 30, 2001.
Henry Hunter arrived at work early that Monday morning. He reread the Incident Report involving the death of Diane Whipple.

Focus, he thought, do what you always do on a case. Get into the mindset that served you so well while running the city's polygraph division. He had spent ten years hooking up wires to people and listening to them lie.

The best liars, Lt. Hunter knew, are the ones who steer closest to the truth.

Over the years, he had developed a habit while reviewing the statement made by a witness or a suspect. He'd gotten the idea while watching the Japanese movie *Rashomon*. In Akira Kurosawa's compelling classic tale, four people are involved one way or another in a rape that takes place deep in a woods. There is a married couple, a Samurai warrior, and a peeping Tom woodcutter. The four are brought to a courtroom and a trial begins. Each tells what he or she saw or did. And each tale is very, very different from the others. The woman thinks she's alluring, the husband thinks he's heroic, the Samurai also thinks he's heroic, and the woodcutter sees what they all really are: the woman vain and both men cowardly.

Each eye forms its own view, Hunter reminded himself.

The habit he had developed was to visualize the person's statement with a motion picture playing the scene in his head.

Then, if he saw a discrepancy, he would replay the movie with this new information.

Images formed in Hunter's mind. He visualized the hallway on the top floor and the relative positions of Diane Whipple's and Marjorie Knoller's apartments to the elevator and stairway.

There was, he recalled, a garbage chute to the right as one exited the elevator.

He ordered himself to couple the police incident report with the statement Knoller made to Becker. The mental motion picture began.

*   *   *

Marjorie Knoller took her dog Bane for a walk. The neighborhood immediately around the Pacific Heights apartment was fairly level, but soon dropped steeply toward the San Francisco Bay. The panorama was sometimes enshrouded in fog and sometimes gloriously revealed the complete spectrum of the bay's beauty.

Nearby Alta Plaza Park was a favorite for dog owners and dog walkers alike.

Marjorie entered her apartment building and rode the elevator to the sixth floor. She went to her door, inserted the key in the lock, and opened the door.

She heard the elevator door open and saw her neighbor Diane Whipple exit, turn away from her, and walk toward her own apartment. She carried two grocery bags. Diane opened her apartment door.

*   *   *

Wait a minute, Hunter thought. What's wrong with this scene? Knoller stood in front of her doorway with Bane and watched Whipple walk down the hall, put her key in the lock, and open her door?

He rummaged in his desk and took out inspector Mike Becker's report. He scanned the paperwork.

1) Incident Report = returned home from a walk and was entering her apartment when her neighbor, Whipple, came home carrying grocery bags.

2) Becker's report = Knoller opened the door to her apartment. Then Knoller was going to throw away the dog droppings.

40

Hunter had remembered correctly. It was thirty feet to the left from the elevator to Whipple's doorway, and about thirty feet from the elevator to the right was Knoller's doorway.

So Knoller stood there and watched Diane for how long? Ten seconds? Fifteen? Try it, don't guess.

Hunter got up, paced off thirty feet, glanced at his watch, and walked back to his starting point. About ten seconds. Then Diane had to get her key in the lock and open her door. She's holding two grocery bags and her purse.

Awkward.

At least another five seconds either placing the bags on the ground or balancing — no, her keys are in her purse. She had to put the groceries down. Then open her purse. Find her keys. Then open the door.

At least another five seconds.

Fifteen seconds, minimum. Marjorie stood in front on her own apartment door, by her own admission, for at least fifteen seconds and watched her neighbor walk down a hallway and open a door?

Why?

Why didn't Marjorie just put Bane in her apartment? Why stand by an open door? An open door that allowed the other dog, Hera, access to the hallway?

Maybe to put the dog droppings into the chute.

But the chute is closer to the stairwell or the elevator than Marjorie's apartment. Why carry dog droppings to the apartment door, open it, then retrace your steps back to the garbage chute?

Didn't make sense.

Henry jotted the problem down in a notebook.

The movie in his mind began to play again.

*　　*　　*

Marjorie opened the door to her apartment, then turned to the garbage chute to dispose of the bag. She felt Bane tug mightily on his leash.

Hera appeared at Marjorie's open apartment door and came out into the hallway.

The large female Presa Canario passed Marjorie and Bane and ran down the hallway.

Bane raced down the hall toward Diane.

Knoller ran down the hall and placed herself between her neighbor and Bane, shouting, "Stop it, stop it!"

Bane, thinking that Diane was assaulting his mistress, attacked. Hera stood by and watched.

Diane tried to crawl toward her apartment door.

* * *

Hunter thought, I've been around a lot of dogs in my life and they don't act this way. Why would the female race by its master if the master was just standing there holding the companion dog?

A dog might come out in the hallway to see what's going on, but why take off — and then stop?

It *was* logical that Bane would follow after Hera.

But what catalyzed the attack?

Knoller running down the hallway, shouting, "Stop it!"

Why would the dogs attack after being told to stop?

Not enough information, Hunter told himself. Wait.

Then, despite having warned himself, he visualized the results of what happened after the attack was over:

When it ended, Diane was naked, except for one sock.

Her throat had been so savagely attacked that her head was skewed 180 degrees from a normal position.

All over the floor and on the walls were blood and flesh and bits of hair. Diane Alexis' body was riddled from head to foot with bite marks.

The phone rang. Hunter listened as one of his investigators, Rich Daniele, said, "Found out where the dogs came from. Pelican Bay State Prison."

Hunter said, "Impossible. The owners are Robert Noel and Marjorie—"

"The dogs' owners are two convicts in Pelican Bay State Prison. Names: Paul Schneider and Dale Bretches. The dogs were boarded at a Janet Coumbs Ranch."

Chapter
Four

Noel and Knoller

San Francisco Hall of Justice, General Work Detail, Tuesday, January 30, 2001.
Convicts and Pelican Bay. Robert Noel and Marjorie Knoller. Paul Schneider and Dale Bretches. Paul and Dale. Robert and Marjorie. What's the connection between two lawyers in San Francisco and two convicts at Pelican Bay State Prison?

Hunter doodled, writing the two names and encasing them in circles and squares and triangles and rectangles.

As he drew random geometric figures, random thoughts raced through his mind.

The media is all over me.

I'm not a politician. I'm not a diplomat.

I'm a desk jockey. A payroll bookkeeper.

Things could be worse.

He smiled. Over the years he had developed a way of diverting himself from of any negative thoughts that invaded his mind.

I could be a victim down at San Francisco General, the survivor of a four-car crash and a quadriplegic.

I'd rather be me.

I could be Tom Cruise. Handsome. Rich. A super star. Going through a vitriolic divorce from Nicole.

I'd rather be me.

I could be Timothy McVeigh, sitting in a cell in Terra Haute, Indiana waiting to pay for killing 168 people.

I'd rather be me, behind a desk, mundane work, files, payroll and all.

As he usually did when first arriving at work, Hunter opened the *San Francisco Chronicle*. Many years earlier he had discovered the media had its purposes. They sometimes asked different questions than a policeman. And sometimes they happened to be in the right time and place when something broke.

He had become adept at scanning for information. He rifled through the paper.

An article jumped out at him. The California Department of Corrections was investigating whether the dogs were being raised for the Mexican Mafia, for guarding methamphetamine labs.

Hunter rubbed his temples. The CDC's involved. This can't get any more bizarre. Or can it?

He opened the *Chronicle* to another page. He zeroed in when he saw the heading: Controversial Dog Owners Defy Convention, by Marriane Costantinou and Peter Hartlaub.

As he read the article he made notes, writing down a couple of quotes:

Noel: "I don't think anyone even knows me anymore. I'm sure there are people who don't want to know me."

Knoller: "I don't fit any stereotypes. People can never figure us out."

Mike Daniele and Rich Becker walked in to Hunter's office. Mike said, "Had a good day yesterday." He handed Hunter a file. "Here's the log."

The investigators left. Hunter read the Chronological Report of Investigation:

0715: I phoned Janet Coumbs at her residence. Janet told me she was raising the dogs until April of last year. Janet said she had a lot of problems with the animals. Janet was willing to give me a statement at her residence. She has documentation regarding the dogs.

Hunter decided Becker and Daniele were definitely going to Hayfork on Thursday.

0800: John Schnieder (neighbor of Diane Whipple) called. He is willing to give an interview.

0845: Daniele received a telephone call from Rhea Wertman-Tallent. She related an incident involving a man and a woman walking two dogs that looked a lot like the two dogs in this case. The dogs were acting very aggressive. Standing on their back legs growling and barking.

To Rhea, the dogs were waiting to attack the two boys who were walking alongside her. The dogs were not able to attack because the man and woman physically restrained the dogs with leashes.

1121: Daniele and I went to Sharon Smith's apartment. She was not there. We met Diane Whipple's mother, Penny Whipple-Kelly. She was born August 8, 1949. She lives in Norwalk, Connecticut.

1130: Sharon arrived back home. I conducted a taped interview. In summary Sharon told me about a prior attack on Diane by one of the dogs. Diane was bitten on her left hand. Diane treated the bite herself. Sharon stated that Diane told the owner to keep the dog on a leash. Sharon advised that Diane told the assistant coach at St. Mary's College in Moraga, CA., about the incident.

The log went on to tell of Becker and Daniele visiting the other apartment residents on the sixth floor, including a visit to Noel to see if he still had the leash.

Then the two detectives extended their interviews throughout the rest of the building.

Hunter closed the file. He thought, give me a Becker or a Daniele before a Dirty Harry any day. This log is an example of thorough police work. Not flashy, like in the movies or on television, but methodically precise and productive.

Hunter's phone rang. It was his friend and source at the morning newspaper. The source said, "You asked for background on the lawyers. I got it. Be coming out in tomorrow's paper."

"Like?"

"They sued two San Francisco police chiefs."

"Which ones did they—"

"They sued their landlord. For years and years."

Hunter asked, "For what?"

"Things like scalding water coming from the shower."

"Any background on either lawyer?"

"Noel and Knoller met in 1987. Both were married at the time. They went on their first date the day after Thanksgiving. They moved in together a week later."

"Any deep background?" Hunter asked.

"Noel was born in Baltimore. His dad was a pipe fitter and his mom a beauty parlor owner. He graduated from the University of Baltimore Law School in 1967. Then on to the Department of Justice in D.C., tax litigation. Then he moved to San Diego and got a job as an assistant U.S. attorney. Then to a private firm here in town."

"Knoller?"

"Knoller was born in Brooklyn. Dad a dentist, mom a housewife. She went to McGeorge School of Law in Sacramento, graduating in 1983. She didn't get a license until 1992."

"Anything else?"

"You'll love this. They sued four cops."

"Why?"

"Some wife was getting beat up. Noel said the cops didn't listen to her. Husband burned her house down."

Hunter said, "I knew about suing prison guards, but cops?"

"Oh, they're not particular. After suing the four cops, they sued the department for a cop who wouldn't shave off his mustache."

"You can sue for that?"

"Beats me. Noel sued for discrimination based on the cop refusing to shave off the handlebar."

Henry Hunter's reporter/source finished with, "You owe me one," and hung up.

"Nothing more can happen," Hunter muttered, with a mind on prayer rather than supposition.

A courier from the DA's office, one floor below, entered and handed the lieutenant a file containing a single piece of paper. The guy grinned and said, "You're not going to believe this."

Noel and Knoller

"Why?"

"Read the letter and find out."

The courier left.

Now what? Hunter thought as he opened the file and began to read:

"From: Robert Noel

"To: Terence Hallinan, DA of SF.

"January 30, 2001.

"Via messenger.

"RE: Diane Whipple

"Dear Mr. Hallinan:

"The purpose of this letter is to make a formal request upon you, your office and those working with you in connection with the investigation into the tragic death of Diane Whipple to do the following to preserve evidence in the matter:

"One: Insure that an examination is made of the body and clothing of Ms. Whipple to determine if there is present on her person any phermones or scents or perfume containing phermones;

"Two: Insure that examination is made of Ms. Whipple's blood and/or tissue to determine the presence or absence of steroids or steroid use by her. Examination of the bladder and urine should be included;

"Three: Preserve the brain of the dog Bane in order to determine the presence or absence of any pathological cause for his behavior;

"Four: Secure from Ms. Diane Whipple's residence and her locker at work all dietary supplements and perfumes, scents, shampoos and cosmetics that might contain phermones and steroids.

"We have been advised by knowledgeable dog trainers that the presence of phermones in perfume scents and steroid use produce scents on the human body which trigger aggressive behavior in male dogs. The presence of either of those substances would also explain Ms. Whipple's behavior at the time of the incident in leaving the confines and safety of her apartment and

47

coming into the hall to confront the dog after Ms. Knoller had
secured it.
"Sincerely
"Robert E. Noel"

Hunter put the letter in his ever-growing file marked
"Diane Whipple Case."

Nothing can happen, he prayed again, to push this any
further into Bizzaro's world.

Besides the fact that this letter was the obvious first salvo
in anticipation of a future civil lawsuit, there was something wrong
with the letter.

An itch began, deep inside his mind where he couldn't
scratch.

Not physically.

The only way to take care of these kinds of itches, the
lieutenant knew, was to scratch them intellectually.

He took the letter out of the file and reread the contents.

Phermones looked wrong.

He opened his dictionary. The correct spelling was
"pheromone."

Henry studied the definition of pheromone: *Biochem.* Any
of a class of hormonal substances secreted by an individual and
stimulating a physiological or behavioral response from an
individual of the same species.

Bane and Diane the same species?

Hera and Diane the same species?

Hmmm. Fairly sure what species means, but why not? He
looked up the word.

Species: A class of individuals having some common
characteristics or qualities; distinct sort of kind.

He nodded. Humans and dogs share some common
denominators: eyes, ears, nose, mammals.

Next he read the biological definition. *Biol.* The major
subdivision of a genus or subgenus, regarded as a basic category of
biological classification, composed of related individuals that

resemble one another, are able to breed among themselves, but are not able to breed with members of another species.

So, he decided, Noel's letter doesn't make any sense despite what a bunch of dog trainers may have suggested.

Unless.

He reread the letter a third time.

I can't be right, he thought.

He reread the letter for a fourth time.

Noel can't be blaming the victim for the attack.

I must be wrong.

What a monstrous and preposterous notion.

I have to be wrong.

No one blames the victim

Do they?

Chapter
Five

A Meter Reader's Nightmare

Charley Mike's home, City of Los Gatos, Santa Clara County, Wednesday, January 31, 2001.
The figure sat in the shadows of the living room. It was noon, yet the drapes were drawn. Only a small Tiffany-style lamp on the end table provided illumination.

Charley Mike opened his newspaper. The dog mauling was still front page news.

He thought, maybe Whipple's attack is front page news in the *San Francisco Chronicle*, but my own dog mauling is still front page news where I'm *sitting*.

He read that the San Francisco DA's office was getting numerous phone calls demanding that the "book" be thrown at the dogs owners.

The director of Animal Care and Control stated, "I get sick when people hurt animals. I get sicker when animals hurt people. It's such a tragedy."

I know, Charley Mike thought, I've been there.

He read a statement by Carl Clapp, director of athletics at St. Mary's College. "Shock, disbelief. A whole range of emotions. Particularly for the young people. Diane was a mentor, a coach and a friend for the student athletes. They've lost somebody who's very special and important."

Charley noticed another article titled: Presa Canarios All the Rage with Shady Characters. By Steve Rubenstein.

The article stated: Loraine Kelly, owner of Show Stopper Kennels in Middlesex, N.J., said she is often approached by the "wrong kind of people trying to buy our dogs."

A Meter Reader's Nightmare

"We try to screen them," she said. "We don't want to sell to drug people or dog fighters. Being so close to New York City we have to be careful."

Any decent dog breeder, Kelly said, can easily spot trouble.

"You can tell right away from the questions they ask," she said. "Like, 'Can your dog kill a pit bull? Have you ever rolled (fought) your dogs?' We know what to listen for."

A Presa Canario, she said, is a loyal, hardworking and protective animal that, properly trained, is never a problem.

She said the Presa Canario is a territorial animal that, if kept in an apartment building, may not understand that the territory is only one apartment and not the entire building.

"To that dog, it's possible that the whole building would be its territory," Kelly added.

Charley Mike remembered the monster that almost killed him. That dog wanted the whole neighborhood as his territory.

Ever since the attack on Diane Whipple occurred, he could not get Sharon Smith out of his mind. Should he tell her? Would it hurt or help if he did?

What happened to him was similar to what happened to Diane Whipple, except he survived.

*   *   *

Charley's route took him past many kinds of structures; apartment buildings, residences and a few retail storefronts.

Being a utility company meter reader was not hard work, but it could be tedious. Charley fought the boredom by being friendly with everyone he saw.

Sometimes people got angry at him because they read their meter and came up with a different figure than he did.

He could not count the number of times over the years he had patiently explained that the numbers on an electrical meter were different than almost any other series of numbers when it came to reading them.

Five circles of numbers had to be read. The first circle of numbers ran clockwise, the second counter-clockwise, the third clockwise and so forth.

Confusing until you got used to reading them.

So, many people knew him as a familiar and friendly face in their neighborhood.

The job was easy except for one thing — dogs.

Like mailmen, meter readers had a high incident rate of dog bites.

Charley didn't worry about it much. He had been a medic in the Air Force. Back then he worked in a neuro-surgical ward and later in an intensive care unit. During his tour of duty in ICU he learned the phrase "Turning it off," and what it meant.

In a moment of danger, "turning it off" meant closing down your emotions. Throwing a switch to turn off the fear that could kill you because it clouded your judgment at a time when you most needed your brain functioning precisely.

But those three years in the military were almost thirty years ago and he had never since come into a situation where he had to practice turning it off.

As he walked down the street toward another meter, he at first did not hear the staccato click, click, click of the animal's toenails on the sidewalk.

When he did, he instinctively turned. A huge brindle-colored, motley-looking dog nailed him in the crotch.

Turning it off was not an option when a fireball of pain erupted from your groin and flooded your mind.

Except this was phantom pain. The huge dog had grabbed cloth and missed meat. Charlie's brain had manufactured the pain in self-defense. The self-defense being, "Do something, you're being attacked!"

That message was the exact opposite of the message of turning it off.

Charlie listened to the first message and punched the dog square on the nose as hard as he could.

The dog let go of the loose clothes and locked onto Charley's upper left thigh.

This time the pain was not phantom. It felt as excruciating as the time someone had accidentally slammed a car door on his hand.

A Meter Reader's Nightmare

The dog shook Charley like a rag doll. The animal tossed Charley to the ground, released off his leg and lunged toward his throat.

Instinctively, Charley threw his hands up and the jaws of the animal locked on his left hand.

With his right hand, Charley grabbed the throat of the dog. His medical training came back and shouted in his mind, cut off the Goddamned dog's windpipe, tear out its carotids, puncture its trachea.

Strangle the son of a bitch!

The dog's throat felt like a tree trunk. Iron hard.

Charley smelled foul odor puffing from the panting dog, whose teeth were a sickly yellow and tongue covered with black-bluish markings. Foaming dog spittle spattered about, spraying the panic-stricken and terrified meter reader's face.

Shock set in as the man and the animal thrashed and wrestled around on the ground, each trying to gain an advantage over the other.

Shock sometimes allows the brain to start functioning again in some semblance of logic.

That was when the phrase "turning it off" from Charley's Air Force days returned.

Turn the emotions off, he ordered himself.

He had an out-of-body experience. He floated a few feet above the scene.

The smell of fear entered his mind.

Never knew what that was, he thought, or how fear could smell. He lazily looked at himself thrashing about with the dog below.

How did fear smell?

Mingle the aroma of fresh defecation and stale urine with a dose of angry skunk, toss in rancid meat and you're close to the odor when you're in absolute terror.

The taste of fear was the sour green bile rising from your stomach and choking your throat.

Death of an Angel

The sound of fear was the unbelievably nasty gnashing of the dog's teeth grinding on the bone of your left hand as the fangs ratcheted about searching for a better purchase.

The feeling of fear was a heart that beat more rapidly than John Coffey's did in Stephen King's *The Green Mile* when, as an innocent man, he was strapped into the electric chair.

Charley Mike didn't have to think about the touch of fear. Those teeth clamped on his hand shrieked the message to his brain.

How do I get rid of the vise-like grip this monster's got on my hand?

Quit trying to strangle a neck harder than an oak tree and use your right hand for something useful.

He let go of the dog's throat.

He was left-handed. His dog repellent/pepper spray was clipped on his belt on the left side. When he let go of the dog's throat, the animal quickly crunched down on Charley's left hand. It felt to him like ripping the raw flesh of a steak from a bone.

Better my hand than my throat.

Despite the pain screeching its message from his left hand, he managed to get his right hand on the repellent. He unloaded the whole six-ounce can into the dog's eyes and nose.

The dog let go of his left hand and stumbled back a few feet.

Charley screamed for help.

The dog zeroed in on his voice and lunged again, missing flesh.

The temporarily-blinded dog withdrew.

Charley screamed again.

The dog attacked again.

A painter, five buildings down the street, heard Charley screaming. He called 911. Then the painter grabbed a hefty two-by-four out of the back of his truck and raced to the sounds of terror.

The painter was big; six-four, six-five. He hit the dog on the snout with the plank as hard as he could. He whacked the dog resoundingly and repeatedly until the animal finally ran off.

A firefighter arrived. Coincidentally, he was a friend of Charley's. He didn't recognize his friend because Charley was covered in his own blood.

Charley spent five days in the hospital. He was a mess physically and mentally. He had an IV in his arm, pain meds in his system, and horror in his mind.

* * *

Charley Mike recalled, while the attack was going on — except for the first phantom agony mentally created from the crotch bite — I never felt much pain. I was in shock. Which is what I think Diane Whipple was in during her whole attack.

Who *wouldn't* be in shock when being attacked by two dogs each weighing more than you do?

Would a letter explaining my experiences help or hurt Sharon Smith?

I'll just explain that I wasn't in pain.

He wrote the letter, then realized he did not know where to send it. Would a letter simply addressed 2398 Pacific Avenue get to Ms. Smith?

He decided to immediately fax it to the police officer in charge, Henry Hunter. He called the SFPD, got the fax number for General Work Detail, and within minutes the letter was being transmitted.

* * *

Henry Hunter received the fax from Charley Mike. He read:

"Dear Sharon Smith: Letter delivered kindness of Lt. Henry Hunter.

"I pray that you are not visualizing Diane's last moments in that hallway. If you are, quit trying to empathize with her death. As horrible as her death was, it was quick.

"As a former military medic who'd worked Intensive Care, a civilian EMT in an emergency room, and later a fireman who learned to disassociate from the agony of heat, fear, and fatigue, I am going to be specific, because I believe knowledge is power. The power to understand. I am not writing this to hurt you in any way, rather to help you understand that your loved one's last moments were not filled with pain.

Death of an Angel

"When the carotid arteries, which supply blood to the brain, and the trachea, supplying oxygen to the lungs are crushed, a person becomes unconscious in literally seconds.

"That's probably what happened to Diane; she just went from numbing shock to unconsciousness, and then, 'walked into the light.' It was a terrifying first few seconds, but then it was over.

"Like the lion does to the gazelle, there is a conservation of energy — the aggressor does what is quickest."

Chapter
Six

The Presa Canario

2398 Pacific Avenue, San Francisco, Saturday, January 31, 2001.

Conservation of energy, Hunter thought, like the lion does to the gazelle.

Hunter understood Charley Mike's fax. He knew Diane Whipple wasn't able to testify as to the terror of what happened in that hallway, but others could. Others who knew the emotional trauma, and had survived the horror of a ferocious dog attack.

Charley Mike, utility company meter reader, had brought the stark reality of this case front and center.

Hunter liked to visit the scene of a crime. He liked to put himself into the minds of various players involved.

He rode the elevator to the sixth floor.

The hallway carpet had disappeared — just bare wood remained.

The walls still glinted from being washed.

He smelt the turpentine used to remove the blood from the hallway walls; from the bare floors where a carpet had been a few days earlier.

He walked into the hall.

Someone had placed votive candles on either side of Diane Whipple's entrance way.

Hunter went to the roof. He replayed the scene. He walked down the stairs, went to the attorneys' door, then went back to the garbage chute.

He stared down the dimly-lit, narrow hallway. Diane Whipple stood there and watched Marjorie with the dog, or dogs.

She stood there. Why? There's nothing interesting in a person dumping garbage.

On the way home, the policeman picked up the day's newspapers.

In his study, he read a statement made to the press by Robert Noel about his wife:

"Marjorie just about had the dogs in the apartment when the elevator door opened and our neighbor came out. Bane sort of perked up and headed down the hallway. The woman had the apartment door open and was just standing there."

Perked up? Bane perked up? Then attacked Diane?

And Diane just stood there? Watching the dog perk up?

A world-class athlete stood there watching a perked up dog and did nothing? No defense? No escape? Just watched the dog?

He continued reading.

Noel went on to state: "Marjorie was telling the women to stay still, but she kept moving and Marjorie would try to cover her again."

Hunter thought, what was Noel trying to say? It read like if Diane had stayed still, or listened to Marjorie Knoller, she'd be alive.

He continued reading the news article. Noel stated, "If Bane had shown any aggression toward people, he wouldn't have been here."

Noel remembered the first time he met Bane, whom he affectionately called "The Big Guy."

"The first thing Bane did was he sniffed me and licked my hand. Then started licking me from my toes up. With women, Bane would usually give a few well-placed sniffs, then roll over on his back so his stomach could be scratched.

"Hera's a very perceptive person. When I'm feeling down, she'll sit next to me and start licking me. She won't stop until she has me laughing."

Laughing? Perceptive *person*? Licking?

Doesn't this guy realize that a woman just died? Killed by these dogs. Talk about insensitive.

The Presa Canario

Hunter read: Doctor Carl Semencie, in his book *Pit Bulls and Tenacious Guard Dogs*, says of the breed, "As a guardian breed with man-stopping ability there is no dog that is more effective that the Canary Dog. This dog will not hesitate to attack anyone whom it perceived as a threat to its family or home. Such an attack could only be a hopeless situation for any man involved."

The cop thought, how was Diane a threat?

He read what Noel felt about bringing the dog Hera back to his apartment.

"I think she'd be fine here. But I don't know how the neighbors would feel."

"What!" Without realizing it, Hunter was shouting out loud.

He doesn't know how the neighbors would *feel*? He doesn't have enough compassion or empathy to know what the surviving partner, Sharon Smith, would feel if the elevator door opened and she saw Hera standing there?

His son Harry appeared at the study door. He said, "I heard you shout out something. Are you all right?"

Hunter explained to his son what he had just read.

Harry asked, "Just what kind of dog is a Presa Canario?"

Good question, the cop thought. Those two dogs came from somewhere. Those kind of fighting machines don't just accidentally wind up in an 800-square-foot apartment.

You didn't, on a whim, enter a pet store and browse by the goldfish and hamsters and canaries and finches and say, "Think I'll take two of those adorable Presa Canario puppies in the window."

Two dogs. Bane already executed and Hera at Animal Care and Control on death row waiting trial.

My kid's right, Hunter thought, time to find out just what kind of dog a Presa Canario *is*.

Hunter said, "Never heard of that breed, son. But time to find out. Let's go online."

Hunter let his son sit at the computer. He stood behind him and watched his child use a search engine to bring up Presa Canario.

Hunter silently read the first article:

"Unfortunately, the history of the Perro de Presa Canario is not so clear as we wished.

"Under the reign of Juba, king of Mauritania, 50 years before Christ, an expedition to the Canary Islands took place and two large dogs were brought to the court of Juba.

"The records from then to 1402 are vague at best. That year the Frenchman Jean de Béthencourt and Gadifier de la Salle conquered a few islands in the Canary archipelago for the king of Castille.

"Legend began about stories of an *unreal* dog that looked like a demon."

Hunter thought, Diane's neighbors were on the mark with their descriptive comments about "devil dog" and "dog of death."

He continued reading:

"A decree was issued in 1515, by the Spanish Government, which forbade ownership of the dogs.

"This edict was followed shortly by another that decreed that butchers could own the dog, but only if they butchered cows.

"The decree went on to state that the dogs had to be chained up night and day, only loosed to solve duties.

"Around 1650 another decree was issued: the dogs were to be killed because of the heavy damage they were doing to livestock.

"The dogs were virtually wiped out. However, the Perro de Ganado Majorero still carried the genetic code of the animal."

For some reason a scene from the movie *Jurassic Park* flashed in Hunter's mind.

The scene with a piece of amber containing a mosquito which had sucked the blood off a dinosaur, thereby capturing its genetic code for later tampering.

The image of a gigantic T-Rex's fangs and the dogs Bane and Hera, with mouths agape, came to mind.

He read on:

"In the 20th Century, on the Canary Islands, as a result of a number of crosses, evidence suggests a great number of dogs as to phenotype.

The Presa Canario

"Dogs like the Perro de la Tierra, Perro Basto, Perro Bordòn and the Perro de Ganado.

"Other breeds from England were introduced into the cross-breeding process. Dogs like Bull terrier, British Bulldog, and the Great Dane.

"Originally, the dogs' coloring was mostly brindle, but the introduction of the Great Dane brought the colors fawn and black."

His son closed the file and said, "Quite a history."

"Yes. King Juba to Spain. Then from Spain to an 800-square-foot apartment in the middle of a metropolitan and cosmopolitan city."

Then, Hunter mentally added, Diane, the hallway, and the lethal charge.

Chapter
Seven

A Much Longer Letter

San Francisco Hall of Justice, General Work Detail, Wednesday, January 31, 2001.

Hunter was ready to call it a day, when his door opened and a courier from the DA's office placed a file on his desk.

"Another letter from Noel," said the courier, "but a lot longer."

Now what? Hunter opened the file and read:

"To: District Attorney Terence Hallinan

"From: Robert E. Noel

"There are several purposes to this letter. I heard a news report last evening as I sat in my living room at #604, 2398 Pacific Ave, that your investigators were searching for me and Ms. Kneeler and believed we were on the lam because they had been unable to locate us."

Hunter asked himself, Ms. Kneeler?

Who was Ms. Kneeler?

Must be a typo.

He continued with the letter.

"With the exception of 15 minutes at approximately 3:45 p.m. when Ms. Kneeler and I left the apartment to go to the post office, we were home all day. I was in telephonic and fax contact from home all day with Pelican Bay State Prison confirming visiting at Pelican Bay on Friday, February 2nd. And making trial preparations for..."

Hunter glanced through the first few pages. Lines jumped out: *"Your office made statements to the press indicating our disappearance in a manner that appeared calculated to inflame an already volatile situation and which makes it very difficult to secure a fair trial and a fair jury in San Francisco or any Bay Area community..."*

"...I had communicated directly with your office in a messenger delivered letter yesterday requesting that you insure steps were taken to preserve certain forensic evidence with respect to Ms. Whipple..."

"...The response from your office was that you would not meet with us unless we were represented by counsel, that you expected to be contacted by a lawyer representing us today and that you would meet with us only if we did not make statements to the media. Up to this point Ms. Kneeler and I have generally declined to discuss the events of 1/26/01, largely out of consideration to the family and friends of Ms. Whipple..."

"...Ms. Coumbs repeatedly represented 'Bane' as being a really gentle animal, who had befriended her daughter's kitten, carrying it around in his mouth..."

"...Bane and Hera were chained next to one another in the yard in the weather. Our information from Ms. Coumbs was that those two and another adult female, Fury, had been kept on a chain for a year in the weather at 2,000 elevation, getting snowed and rained on in the coldest conditions..."

How long is this thing? Hunter thought, as he flipped to the last page. Eighteen single-spaced pages.

He went back and continued to read. The next few pages were about transporting the dogs from Coumbs Ranch to Peninsula Pet Resort and from there to the Holly Street Veterinarian. From there, Hera went to her new home in Pacific Heights. Both dogs were undernourished. Noel and Knoller took them to Pets Unlimited. Bane was kept at the facility.

The next few pages extolled the virtues of the dogs and that the lawyers virtually lived with them 24/7. When they traveled, the dogs went with them. Every day they took the dogs for walks; to Chinatown, North Beach, the Marina, Fisherman's Wharf, Aquatic Park, Crissy Field and to neighborhood parks like Alta Plaza and Lafayette.

More pages described Hera's actions when in heat, when not in heat, and in general.

In September 2000, Bane came to live with them.

They started taking both dogs for walks.

The letter went on to describe various incidents with other dogs.

Something popped out at Hunter from Noel's letter:

"I have heard reports that friends of Ms. Whipple claim that she reported having been bitten on the hand by Bane. Ms. Whipple encountered Bane on only 3 occasions before the 26th.

"1) Bane and I were getting off the elevator on the sixth floor and Whipple was waiting to get on. Because of Bane's size and mine I asked her to please step back from the door so we could pass. She did without comment and Bane and I exited and turned for our apartment as she boarded the elevator. There was no encounter with Ms. Whipple.

"2) Bane and I were getting out of the elevator in the lobby and Ms. Whipple was waiting to get in. Again, I asked her to stand back so we could get by. She again did so without comment and we passed her and exited the building without comment from either of us and with no contact between Ms. Whipple and Bane.

"3) Bane and I were waiting in the lobby to get on the elevator and Ms. Whipple exited the elevator. As I usually did when I had either dog in the lobby and the elevator was coming not at my call, I had Bane over to the side and on a short lead so that whoever was coming out of the elevator could exit the elevator and pass unimpeded by either the dog or me. Ms. Whipple came out of the elevator and exited the building. At no time did she come in contact with Bane.

"Until the events of the 26th those had been the only contacts with Ms. Whipple for either me or Bane..."

He scanned the next few pages. Noel covered newspaper reports claiming that the dogs were being trained either as fighters or guards for drugs. Then he saw his own name.

"I understand from contacts with reporters that Lt. Hunter has announced that he had amassed a large number of incident reports on either other attacks on other people allegedly by Bane

and Hera occurring around the City. In the large number of places mentioned are more than several to which Hera and Bane have never been."

Have to have Mike and Rich check that claim out, Hunter decided.

Pages 15, 16 and 17 of the letter recounted the events in the hallway on the 26th, according to Marjorie Knoller.

He read:

"Marjorie had taken Bane to the roof in response to indications from him that he had to relieve himself."

Hunter thought, the roof? I thought she had taken the dog/dogs out for a walk? He read:

"After cleaning up Bane's scat in a Bags on Board, Marjorie lingered for a short while to make certain that Bane did not need to go again. She heard the elevator arrive at the sixth floor and stop, not starting again during the 30 second period she remained on the roof.

"Marjorie returned downstairs with Bane and upon reaching the 6th floor turned to the right with Bane and walked to the stairs at the north end of the sixth floor to deposit the bag in the trash chute...

"...Bane began to try to come back into the hall and Marjorie, who was partly in the hall, and she and Bane were plainly visible to Ms. Whipple. Marjorie had Bane by the lead and the harness in both hands.:

"This continued for approximately one minute with Ms. Whipple simply standing in her open doorway and making no effort to move inside and close the door. When Marjorie began to tire and Bane was able to overcome her efforts, Bane began going down the hallway dragging Marjorie who had fallen to her knees and was acting like an anchor with him. With his gimpy left rear leg and the resistance of Marjorie, Bane moved slowly down the hall coming in range after fifteen seconds or so had passed."

In Hunter's mind the motion picture began to play, unfolding, in vivid Technicolor, the black-and-white words on the pages of the letter.

*   *   *

The dog Bane was showing signs of distress in the apartment. Bane had diarrhea. Marjorie put on his leash, opened the door and went up the stairway to the roof deck, a simple tar and gravel affair. The building was old, dating to the twenties. No fire doors separated the stairs from the hallways. She waited on the roof for the dog to relieve himself.

It was four in the afternoon and the sun was deep in its winter cycle for early setting. The nearest star was sinking behind the roof tops of the buildings across Fillmore Street.

The view was spectacular. Facing north, the Golden Gate Bridge was off to the left, Alcatraz front-and-center, Marin County gleaming in the distance, and the Marina District nestled below.

Bane sniffed about the coarse tar and gravel before taking care of business.

Marjorie did her best to gather the dog's defecation into a brown bag. She opened the roof's access door and led Bane down the U-shaped stairwell. At the bottom she turned right, toward her apartment.

Her husband, Robert Noel, hadn't returned home yet.

She had her keys and the brown bag in her right hand, Bane's leash in her left.

She opened the door to her apartment, then turned to the garbage chute to dispose of the bag. She felt Bane tug mightily on his leash.

Marjorie looked down the narrow hallway. There was a figure at the far end standing in front of an open apartment door. The light in the hallway was dim; the female figure, back-lit from the light in the apartment, was shadowy.

Bane strained forward and Marjorie strained just as much in the opposite direction.

Marjorie thought, why doesn't she go into her apartment?

Marjorie's arms began to shake from the effort restraining Bane.

Her hands began to hurt as the seconds ticked by.

Move, move, move into your apartment.

The ache went up her arm, spreading from her wrists to her forearms to her biceps.

A Much Longer Letter

As Marjorie stood at her open apartment door, Hera came out into the hallway. The large female Presa Canario passed Marjorie and Bane and went about twenty feet down the hallway toward the immobile figure standing in the dim light.

Marjorie sank to her knees, exhausted. Bane, tugging at the harness, started to drag his mistress down the hallway.

Act like an anchor, Marjorie thought as she slid along the floor.

Why? Why? Why was Bane so anxious to get to that woman?

Bane hauled her the full sixty feet of hallway to the young woman's doorway. It took the dog fifteen seconds to cover the distance.

Four feet a second.

And still the woman did not enter her apartment. She stood frozen, an immobile Venus-like statue with arms holding grocery bags.

Bane arrived at his target. He jumped up and placed one paw to the right of the woman and one paw to the left.

*   *   *

Hunter reread the last statement.

"Upon reaching Ms. Whipple, Bane jumped up and put his paws on the wall with one in front and one behind Ms. Whipple."

He pictured the dog eyeball-to-eyeball with Diane. The dog's breath must have puffed hot, fetid air right into her face.

What must Diane have been thinking? What must she have been feeling? Just how terrified was she?

Large dogs salivate more than smaller ones. Diane was face to face with tongue-licking fangs, and sour panting breath, and foaming flecks of saliva.

Face to face with her worst nightmare.

Hunter had already learned that Diane was twice a college All-American; female player of the year at Penn State in her senior season; a marathoner; a lacrosse coach. Yet she froze for seventy-five seconds; sixty seconds while Marjorie restrained Bane and fifteen seconds while she was dragged down the hall.

Hunter once again visualized what was behind the words written in the letter by Robert Noel.

*   *   *

Bane dropped back to all-fours. Marjorie grabbed Diane and, while trying to force her into her apartment, stumbled. Both women fell into the apartment. Grocery bags went flying.

Bane, thinking that Diane was assaulting his mistress, attacked.

Hera joined in, tugging at Diane's sweat pants.

Marjorie again got hold of Bane's leash and backed out of the apartment. To her amazement, Diane crawled out after her. The attack was resumed, with Marjorie once again throwing herself on top of Diane and shouting, "Don't move. He's trying to protect me."

She again tried to back out of the apartment, pulling Bane with her.

Diane crawled out into the hallway.

Again, the attack was resumed.

The attack lasted for more than five minutes.

*   *   *

Hunter read the last of Noel's letter regarding the attack:

"Marjorie was able to get Bane under control and into the apartment, dragging Hera along with her. Hera's harness had been cut in half during the attack, apparently by Bane when Hera moved between Marjorie and Bane. Marjorie secured Bane in the bathroom and Hera in the bedroom, went back to Ms. Whipple's apartment to retrieve her keys which had fallen there and turned to check on Ms. Whipple. At this point the first SWAT officers arrived and Marjorie told them the dogs were secured. During the next 5 to 7 minutes no one from the P.D. or fire department worked on Ms. Whipple, they simply let her lie where she was."

The last point, Hunter knew, was easy to explain. The P.D. and fire department, unless so trained, were not allowed to work on a victim lest they do more harm than good. They were supposed to wait for someone trained in emergency procedures to arrive, then assist as requested.

A Much Longer Letter

Take the letter point by point, Hunter ordered himself. But first dig out the original Incident Report and the initial statement made to Becker and Daniele by Knoller. Then I'll have Noel's letter to compare with Knoller's initial statement.

He rummaged about his desk, finally found the applicable documents, and settled back in his chair.

He reread the letter from Noel to D.A. Hallinan.

"She heard the elevator arrive at the sixth floor and stop, not starting again for the 30 second period of time she remained on the roof."

Meaning what? Why specific about the 30 seconds?

He read another portion of the letter:

"Marjorie did not see where Ms. Whipple had come from but assumed the elevator because it had arrived 30 seconds before... Hera stuck her head out of the door and upon seeing Ms. Whipple, whom she had never encountered before, barked and went into the hall and stopping about 20 feet from Ms. Whipple. In the hundreds of times that Hera had been inside when Bane was brought home from a walk, Hera had never stuck her head out of the door, suggesting that possibly in the 30 second interval between the arrival of the elevator and Marjorie's reaching the 6th floor that Ms. Whipple may have come down to our apartment door.

"We understand that Ms. Whipple, her domestic partner and the apartment manager, Aleta and her domestic partner are close friends.

"We have had recurring disputes with both the previous owner and the current one over conditions at the building and have required the previous owner to spend $300,000 in making inadequate repairs to the building,

"Aleta has attempted in the past to take action against us and may have enlisted the aid of her friend Ms. Whipple."

So, Hunter thought, the 30 seconds is another red flag waving fault at Diane Alexis. She may, possibly, could have, been in cahoots with Aleta and, instead of entering her apartment, went down to Noel's apartment.

To do what? Listen at the door?

At the door where two dogs lived that terrified her?

A smoke screen. A lawyer's smoke screen.

Next point is the timing. He reread:

"Bane began to try to come back into the hall and Marjorie, who was partly in the hall, and she and Bane were plainly visible to Ms. Whipple. Marjorie had Bane by the lead and the harness in both hands—"

Both hands!

Doesn't jibe with something I read somewhere. Wait, it will come. Hunter went on reading:

"...Bane began going down the hallway dragging Marjorie who had fallen to her knees and was acting like an anchor with him. With his gimpy left rear leg and the resistance of Marjorie, Bane moved slowly down the hall coming in range after fifteen seconds or so had passed."

Gimpy leg? Moved slowly? Marjorie an anchor?

Fifteen seconds to cover sixty feet is not exactly a snail's pace. That's four feet a second.

Hunter went out into the hallway outside his office and paced off twenty good-sized steps. Twenty-times-three-feet equals sixty feet, he thought and glanced at his watch. The second hand reached twelve.

He walked the sixty feet.

Eighteen seconds.

He redid the test, walking faster. Fifteen seconds.

I'm not acting like an anchor and resisting anything.

What else has a stench about it in this statement?

He read:

"Ms. Whipple got to her knees and crawled out into the hallway after Marjorie and Bane."

Hunter picked up the Incident Report. He searched and found what he was looking for. Marjorie told Officer Forrestal, first on the scene with Officer Laws, the following:

"Knoller said she tried to control the dog after the attack began but was unsuccessful. Knoller then attempted to place her body between the dog and the victim. However, each time the

victim tried to move toward her apartment the dog renewed its attack."

The victim moved *toward* her apartment.

What else? Hunter asked himself. Something else jumped out, as he flipped through the letter written by Noel:

"Ms. Whipple, rather than stay still or move back into her apartment, continued to crawl toward Marjorie and Bane.

"When that happened, Bane again moved for Ms. Whipple. Marjorie again covered Ms. Whipple's body with Marjorie's body and Bane stopped the attack.

"At this time, Ms. Whipple forcibly struck Ms. Kneeler in the right eye..."

What? Of course I'm going to duke it out with a woman while her two massive dogs are standing next to her.

Something else is bothering me. The itch. That itch that warns me something else is bull. Something in the text, but I can't put my finger on whatever, whatever...

It will come, the police officer knew, it will come.

What else is bothering me? He flipped through the text. Then, on page 17, the words leapt off the page:

"It has been suggested to us by an expert on dog behavior that Ms. Whipple may have been wearing a pheromone-based cosmetic or scent or that as a serious athlete she may have been a user of steroids which could have triggered the initial interest of Bane in her and would also have had an effect on Hera. We have previously requested that you insure the preservation of all cosmetics and dietary supplements in Ms. Whipple's apartment and work place for forensic examination."

Hunter slumped back in his chair.

He reread the last paragraph. *"...could have triggered the initial interest..."*

Then he read it again. *"...pheromone-based cosmetic or scent... ...triggered..."*

No getting around it. I was wrong when I read the one-page letter yesterday. They *are* trying to blame the victim.

This is going to provoke a reaction out of a lot of people. Wait until the media gets hold of this letter.

Death of an Angel

Damn it, I wear cologne.
Does that mean a dog has the right to attack *me*?
To kill me?

Chapter Eight

Adoptions Normal and Strange

Henry Hunter's office, Hall of Justice, General Work Detail, Wednesday, January 31, 2001.
Hunter folded his hands on his lap. He was ensconced in front of his computer terminal. Prayers may help, he thought, but answers are what I deal with. Answers that lead to the truth.

Truth. What is truth?

Searching for truth in Hunter's profession was essential.

But, unfortunately, if it wasn't absent it was nearly always elusive. Lies follow crimes like greed follows a stock market tip.

He thought of a couple of his favorite quotes:

"It is twice as hard to crush a half truth as a whole lie." Austin O'Malley.

Or Shakespeare's *Merchant of Venice.* "Truth will come to light, murder cannot hide for long."

What a day.

The courier entered, tossed the newspaper on his desk, said, "Latest edition. You're not going to believe it," and left.

Hunter thought, I'm not going to believe it?

Why shouldn't I believe whatever it is?

I believe the 49ers can make it to the Super Bowl.

And without Jerry Rice.

I believe a man will walk on Mars before I die.

I believe that good will someday conquer evil.

With the Whipple case, I'm beginning to think I'll believe anything.

Hunter opened the newspaper and read the Headlines: Dogs' Owners Adopted Inmate Who Bred Dogs.

What? Adopt Paul "Cornfed" Schneider? Wasn't he 38 years old?

I don't believe it.

Must be a misprint.

Or maybe the prisoner had a young kid.

Other article titles jumped off the page at him.

Headline: S.F. Lawyers Adopt Con Who Bred Killer Dog — action by animal's keepers stuns state corrections officials, by Jaxon Van Derbeken.

Headline: Lawyers Adoption of Inmate Stuns Legal Experts — this type of law not often used in attorney-client relationships, by Harriet Chiang.

Henry thought, not *easy* to simultaneously stun the Department of Corrections and legal experts.

He scanned more quotes:

Russ Heimerick, Department of Corrections: "We're a little puzzled by this."

A *little* puzzled?

Robert Noel: "Mr. Schneider is definitely a man of more character and integrity than most of the people you're going to find in the California Department of Corrections administration."

Nice slam against the guards.

Adoption Decree: The adoption will be in the best interest of the parties and the public interest.

Not hard to figure out who wrote *that*.

Adoption Decree: Mr. Schneider could not attend the adoption proceeding, his physical presence being impossible.

No kidding. The only place his physical presence *was* possible was in the toughest joint in the state.

Adoption Decree: The parties shall assume towards each other the relation of parent and child, including all rights of inheritance and intestate succession.

Henry wondered, was that it? Inheritance? Did the lawyers really believe that the CDC was out to kill Paul? He'd heard a few rumors to that effect, but if they're killing him with X-rays, they're taking the slow road. The *very* slow road.

Hunter turned back to the newspaper.

74

Adoptions Normal and Strange

Family lawyer Nordin Blacker: "I don't know what's going on in this dog case. This seems particularly strange."

Talk about an understatement. No kidding it seems strange.

Henry read that the other reasons for seemingly weird adoptions are older men and their mistresses — to insure an inheritance, or a stepparent who wants to adopt but can't get permission from the natural parent. Once an adult, the child signs for him or herself.

What exactly are the ethical ramifications of a lawyer adopting his client?

No itches here, Hunter realized, just mass confusion. How could two New Yorkers of the Jewish persuasion have adopted a 38-year-old member of the Aryan Brotherhood?

* * *

James Sullivan sat in his office in Los Gatos. He was a 60-year-old tax attorney. Although born in San Francisco, Sullivan's ruddy complexion and quick smile revealed his Irish ancestry.

He read the article about the adoption of a 38-year-old criminal.

Sullivan knew the definition of adoption — to take as one's own a child by a formal legal act.

Sullivan's adopted son Scott told him that he had read that Diane Whipple's partner, Sharon Smith, was adopted.

And Marjorie Knoller was also adopted.

Jim Sullivan realized that there was a peculiar similarity between very dissimilar people: Paul 'Cornfed' Schneider, the convict; Sharon Smith, the regional vice president of a financial giant; Marjorie Knoller, the owner of the dog that killed Diane Whipple; all linked by the same phantom legal adoption umbilical cord.

The tax lawyer continued to read the newspaper article. Noel's comment about his adoption of a man seven years younger than his wife seemed very condescending. "At least we'll know where he is at night."

A wise-ass remark, make a joke, or an accusation.

When you adopt a baby it's called love.

You adopt a man old enough to be a grandfather and what do you call that?

An abomination?

Sullivan called Henry Hunter and asked to meet at the Buchanan Bar & Grill. The pub was a favorite watering hole for many of the older Irish in San Francisco because Mike McCourt, who was Frank McCourt's older brother, was the day bartender. Frank had best sellers with *Angela's Ashes* and *Tis;* Mike was a local legend behind the plank.

The pub had a high ceiling. The walls were covered in knickknacks and memorabilia.

The tax attorney waited in the corner stool facing the door. Hunter entered and Sullivan said, "Thanks for coming."

"And I came because?"

"I have two adopted children."

"And?"

"I want to talk about the adoption of the 38-year-old convict. And Noel's claim that it strengthens access to a client?"

"Does it?"

"Not really. Most of the time a lawyer has better access to a prisoner than a mother or father. If it was me looking for a motive, I'd follow the money. Of course, this is all hypothetical, but this is the way I'd have set this up."

Hunter waited for Sullivan to sort out his thoughts as the tax lawyer waved at McCourt, signaling for a beer. He pointed at the cop and raised an eyebrow.

"Ice tea."

Sullivan ordered and said, "We know they *may* have adopted Cornfed because they wanted a 38-year-old bouncing baby who weighs in just this side of 300 pounds."

He drained a third of his beer and wiped the foam from his mouth. "People act for different reasons — no matter how strange to others." He killed the rest his beer and inspected the glass. "Love the way the first one goes down."

"The adoption?"

"Or they may have adopted Cornfed to satisfy some psychological, voyeuristic or exhibitionist coupling between mom and son. And maybe even dad."

Sullivan waved frantically at the barkeep servicing the crowded bar, got his attention, and asked for another beer. He again sucked off the foam and the top three inches of distilled hops and said, "But we pretty much know it wasn't to create a stronger ability to see their client. So, if the motive's not a legal one, what's left?"

Hunter waited for almost thirty seconds, realized Sullivan was waiting for a response, and said, "I don't know."

"Not legal, then fiscal. There are certain things that kick in when you create, for instance, a family trust between family members. Flow of money, division of money, hidden assets or accounts, right of survivorship, that sort of thing."

"And in this case that would mean?"

"Just winging it, making suppositions, of course, but let's say that what the Department of Corrections is claiming about the end use of the dogs is true."

"Guards for amphetamine labs."

"Exactly. Which is the cheapest if you're a drug producer? Hire a few guys to walk your compound carrying Uzi's, or raise a half-dozen dogs — known to love whoever raises them but hate everything and everyone else — to guard your cash and product?"

Hunter nodded.

Sullivan continued. "Once you've trained them as killers, your daily cost is a few cans of dog chow. Dogs aren't going to steal your product, or sneak into your room at night when there's a lot of cash around and put a .38 slug in your ear."

Hunter continued to nod.

Sullivan belted down the rest of his beer. "So, follow this hypothesis. We have a connection from Pelican Bay Prison to the Aryan Brotherhood, drug labs, and guard dogs. Who do you need as conduit?"

"The only people that have ready access to the lifers on the inside — lawyers."

"Bingo!" Sullivan waved his empty beer mug around like a cheerleader waves a pom-pom. "Refill."

Hunter threw a ten on the bar and bought.

Sullivan continued. "This is all speculation on my part like everything else about this case from the beginning."

His beer arrived. He again swallowed, the foam and first third disappearing in one gulp. "So, we have convicts as owners raising dogs on the outside and selling them to fellow Aryans and other brothers-under-the-skin, like the Mexican Mafia."

"You said follow the money."

"Right, that's exactly what I said."

"What else?"

" And I think I read somewhere that these dogs have litters as large as ten. And that the puppies go for around twenty-five hundred bucks a pop."

"That's correct."

"That's 25 G's per litter. Get ten bitches having puppies every year and you've got a nice business going with a gross profit of a quarter-million dollars."

"Quarter of a million."

"Run by two cons that can't even spend the money on cigarettes, now that this state has taken that privilege away from them."

Hunter nodded.

The jovial lawyer inspected his empty glass. "And they can only spend so much on smuggled hooch and drugs. Needs in the hoosegow are minimal at best. At least minimal at best on the needs you may be able to actually get access to."

"So the convicts get some perks. "

"And the joy of having a connection to the outside world. And the lawyers get the cash. But keep in mind, none of this has been proven. When did the lawyers start the adoption proceedings?"

"I don't know."

"Well, I do know they had to start them way before all this terrible stuff started happening."

"Why?"

Adoptions Normal and Strange

The lawyer answered, "Having the adoption finalized a few days after the tragedy was coincidental. Maybe we'll never know the why. Or maybe they're just as weird as the press is making them out to be, and they just view life differently than most of us. Weird."

Hunter thought, if they're weird, they're very, *very* weird.

Chapter
Nine

Pelican Bay

Henry Hunter's home, Wednesday, January 31, 2001.
Hunter ate dinner with his family and settled down in front of the
television. His dog, a cocker spaniel named Babs, settled in right
next to him.

Harry came in, sat on the sofa and said, "Been reading
about your case. The dogs."

"We went over the history of that type of dog already. "

"I know, dad. What I don't understand is how two convicts
could end up owning and raising dogs on the outside of prison."

Hunter wondered, how to explain the mindset of a lifer to a
fifteen-year-old? Various movies he had watched with his son
flashed through his mind, like *Shawshank Redemption*. Had they
watched *Stalag 17* together? Or *Carbine Williams*? Those were
old flicks.

Those movies all had one common denominator — a
convict used his mind to escape the reality of his circumstances.

Hunter thought about Pelican Bay Prison and the convicts
who lived there.

* * *

Pelican Bay State Prison is north of Crescent City in the upper
northwest corner of California, in Del Norte County. The prison
is so close to the Pacific Ocean that the scent of the sea drifts into
the cells. But it is also far enough inland so that the forest
surrounding it has the melodic sound of birds.

One of the most foreboding and secure prisons ever erected
hunches like an immobile monolith in this idyllic setting. Inside
this citadel is an even tighter area, known as the "shoe." The

Security Housing Unit, or SHU, held the toughest of the toughest. Prisoners here could only contact the world beyond through letters or strictly limited visits that were overseen by the guards.

Cells in the "shoe" were concrete. Even the bunks were molded in concrete. The door was steel. Food was delivered via a slot in the door.

The exercise yard was called the "dog run." This area also was made of concrete. It was eleven-by-twenty-five feet. A tiny opening, almost twenty feet above the floor, allowed a single shaft of sunlight to enter.

When it comes to rumors, this prison is no different than any other prison, either minimum or maximum security. Rumors here fly faster than they do on the floor of the New York Stock Exchange.

Fish lines and kites, or even a friendly guard, are used to pass messages.

There are only 68 known members of the Aryan Brotherhood in California prisons. If you are white, it is one of your only options for group protection.

The Mexican Mafia accepts non-Hispanics, but you have to be incarcerated for a drug-connected crime to join.

The rumor mill had flashed that Paul Schnieder and Dale Bretches were enforcers, bought by guards in exchange for allowing them to bunk together.

The guards also looked the other way as the mountain of pictures of the two prisoners' dogs grew from a few dozen to over three thousand.

Photos and paintings. The two convicts-turned-artists used Bic™ pens. The two men scraped the protective coating off medical pills. Pills coated with blue, or yellow gave them some of the pigments they were looking for. They would soak the coatings in warm water and create watercolors. They soaked other things, like magazines. Marlboro ads gave them red.

Rumors at Pelican Bay began almost as soon as the place was completed. Rumors, according to the convicts, of Dark Age treatment of suffering inmates by brutal guards.

Lawsuit after lawsuit was filed.

Death of an Angel

Guards were accused of throwing an inmate into a boiling cauldron of water because the man refused to bathe.

Other rumors oozed out of the grim prison. Tales of inmates pitted against each other, gladiator fights to the death for the entertainment and wagering of the guards.

Pelican Bay, despite its rather bucolic name, is the last stop in California for a violent convicted person. It is the state's version of the fed's now-defunct Alcatraz.

That violence occurred there, whether between prisoners and prisoners, or between guards and prisoners, was no surprise. No matter what the causes — childhood abuse or indifference, bad companionship, or just born a sociopath — the men there were as tough as they come.

And you don't station a lamb to guard a lion.

Guards at Pelican Bay are as tough as the prisoners.

The ones that worked the shoe, the isolation areas, were the toughest. Some guards were realists. Why bother risking a lawsuit, or disciplinary write-up, or a broken hand beating the tar out of someone when you can get someone else to do it willingly, and for next-to-nothing?

Next-to-nothing on the inside, of course, would seem an insignificant luxury on the outside.

Questions of inmate perks pervaded the prison as much as rumors.

Question: How did Dale and Paul, longtime friends, end up in the same cell?

Inmates were not allowed to choose with whom they bunked, any more than a soldier can choose the men beside him in battle.

Question: Why were Dale and Paul allowed to run a business on the outside from their cell?

It is illegal for inmates to run any kind of business on the outside. Yet they *were* trying to run a business.

Paul and Dale's dog-breeding business was common knowledge. No one overlooked three thousand pictures in a small cell. A tiny cell that was shaken down with regularity.

A cell at Pelican Bay measures six-by-nine.

Pelican Bay

Not even Houdini could hide three thousand photos and drawings in that 54-square-foot concrete prison cell.

Why were they allowed this perk?

The scuttlebutt was that the two Aryan Brothers were used by the guards to give "attitude adjustments" to unruly prisoners.

Beat the living daylights out of someone and life in the toughest joint in California could be made slightly easier as long as the guard endorsed the contract.

Life at Pelican Bay could only be described as dismal. Built to house 2,000 inmates, at the beginning of 2001 it held over 3,000.

Over a thousand shared cells, the other 2,000 convicts were held in what the CDC euphemistically called executive segregation — meaning isolation.

For 23½ hours a day, the prisoner sat in his cell. He received a reprieve for a half-hour in the exercise yard. A convict spent 23½ hours a day watching TV. An inert 23½ hours a day staring at a screen that told you what the real world was doing. The real world to a lifer is a daily dose of morning news, breakfast, talk shows, midday news, lunch, soaps, evening news, dinner, sitcoms, and late night wrap-up news.

During the height of the Bastille days in France, prisoners, driven insane from sensory deprivation, sometimes tried to kill themselves by running full tilt and bashing their heads against the stone walls.

At Pelican Bay in the 21st century, some prisoners just stared at a small TV set and atrophied into vegetables.

Paul Schneider and Dale Bretches took a different path. Trapped in a prison they had brought on themselves by their anti-social behavior, assault/robbery/murder, they decided like many before them to liberate themselves from the cement walls that were their home and live vicariously in the outside world.

Pappilon did it with his dreams of escape.

So did the convict Frank Morse, played by Clint Eastwood in the movie *Escape from Alcatraz*, and his painstakingly-planned and dramatic escape from "The Rock;" an escape that eventually led to the closure of that maximum security federal prison.

Death of an Angel

Richard Stroud, The Birdman, did it with his intense study involving the diseases of birds. His contributions to ornithology are well documented.

Paul and Dale chose dogs.

Dogs. Dogs on the outside. Dogs running free. And through those dogs the prisoners' minds would link and they also would run free.

But what breed?

These men were criminals. These men were violent.

Poodles? Cocker Spaniels? Not even thought of. Even hunters like Labradors and Golden Retrievers were not considered.

They used some of the money they had won suing the prison system and bought books.

As Stephen King dramatically illustrated in his novella *Rita Hayworth and the Shawshank Redemption,* monotony was the killer of the mind in prison.

First rote routine, then monotony descending, then the warm and safe feeling of belonging. Result: a prisoner became institutionalized.

There are very few jobs available for prisoners at Pelican Bay. Only a select few are allowed the privilege of cooking, dish washing, doing laundry, mopping floors.

Paul and Dale weren't interested in cooking or washing or cleaning or mopping. And they weren't interested in turning into eggplants from boredom.

They bought books about dogs.

Pit bulls and Rottweillers and Dobermans were studied and considered.

They decided they wanted nothing to do with the mundane.

The two prisoners wanted something special; something that proudly represented strength, power, courage.

During their research they stumbled on the words "Dog O' War."

More books were purchased. In all, the two men spent $1,100 studying their project.

They kept coming back to the Dog O' War — the Presa Canario. A breed with lineage that went back to the Roman Empire.

In the opening scene of the movie *Gladiator* there are a few brief shots of dogs running, and one short moment of a dog attacking.

But Rome had perfected the art of warfare better than Hollywood's rendition.

When you wanted to expand an empire and conquer the known world, you used every practical device possible. A dog killed in battle was far easier and cheaper to replace than a legionnaire who had fought and survived the siege of Carthage.

Breed the toughest dog possible. Breed a lot of them. Breed hundreds of them. Then, as Academy Award-winner Russell Crowe dramatically said, "On my signal, unleash hell." That's exactly what the Roman legions did.

Except, after the catapults and archers delivered their bolts of fire, the infantry did not then attack. The Romans unleashed the Dog O' War.

A warrior waiting to kill Roman legionnaires was first greeted with balls of flaming fire, followed by hundreds of clones of the hound of the Baskervilles.

A man can only swing a battle-ax so fast. Take out one, maybe two dogs before the third had you by the throat.

Paul and Dale found the type of animal with which they wanted to be associated.

Presa Canario. In Latin, meaning violent canine.

Violent dog. A dog so violent that Franco's Spain in the rebellious 1930s outlawed breeding of the animals.

The next step for the life-without-possibility-of-parole convicts was to set out and buy some Presa Canarios. They contacted a few breeders and received the same answer. "Sell to convicts? No way."

They needed a beard — a front. Plus someone on the outside who was legit to board and breed the dogs.

They knew they were never actually going to meet the dogs they wanted to breed. It really didn't make any difference if the

85

beard was close to Pelican Bay or on the other side of the country, but they wanted to feel close to their charges.

So Janet Coumbs' ranch, in nearby Hayfork, Trinity County, entered the picture.

A ranch.

The prisoners imagined the dogs on a ranch. Romping through pastoral fields of wild flowers. And breeding. Making love and having puppies and being free, and making more love and having more puppies and being free.

Doing the things that the two inmates had lost.

What they planned to do wasn't much different than what racehorse breeders do.

Seek pure lineage. Bloodline is everything.

Paul and Dale researched more. Much like the member of the Sport of Kings who found the sire of Secretariat, they knew they had to discover a purebred.

They bought Isis.

A king was needed.

Step by methodical step, the two prisoners sought a mate for Hera. It was a day of relief when a mutual decision was made to buy the male dog they were looking for, and arrangements made to send him to the Janet Coumbs Ranch.

The royal match for queen Isis was called Bane.

Bane: a word meaning blight.

Isis was the most important goddess of the ancient Egyptians. She was the mother of all things, the lady of all elements, the beginning of all time

*   *   *

Hunter glanced at his son, who was watching the news hoping to catch his father on camera.

How to explain to a teenager?

There was no way to explain the desperate need of an intelligent adult to be free from an eternal cage — even if it only meant a mental freedom.

Chapter
Ten

Diane and Christmas

Lacrosse Coach Sarah Miller's office, St. Mary's College, Wednesday. January 31, 2001.
Sarah Miller glanced around what had been Diane's office. It contained so many memories.

She thought, how am I supposed to think about happy things? That's what the grief counselor told me. Sounds easy, but it's impossible.

Sarah wanted to think about Diane in any way other than her last gruesome moments.

The tiny office was located on the second floor of the basketball gymnasium.

Diane Whipple's memorabilia was everywhere. There was a huge poster on one wall with puns involving the use of candy. An example proclaimed, "Mars is a planet," with a photograph of Mars and a Mars Bar in the sentence where the word Mars should have been. Also, there was one stating, "You've got Butterfingers," with a photo of a kid with a broken plate at his feet.

There were aliens everywhere. Masks and dolls — gigantic and tiny. Almost all were some shade of green.

Sarah cupped her head in her hands. Aliens and candy aren't making for happy memories. Not anymore. They're being replaced by dogs and pain.

Jennifer Krusing entered Sarah's office.

Jennifer had luxurious black, shoulder-length hair and classic features including high cheekbones. She was a firefighter in Palo Alto.

Sarah said, "Jenn, I can't believe how much I miss her." Moisture formed at the corners of the pretty woman's eyes. "We trained the lacrosse team together." Now her eyes welled with tears. "We had lunch almost every day together." Tears trickled down her cheeks. Her voice broke when she repeated, "She was my best friend."

Jennifer handed her a handkerchief.

Sarah dabbed the tears away.

Jennifer said, "Think of something positive. Something we did with Diane."

"Like when we all went to San Diego for a marathon?"

"Or last Christmas, with you and Diane and the dogs."

*   *   *

Sarah arrived early and stayed late at the college Christmas party. So did Diane. It was held in the St. Mary's banquet room, called the Soda Center, which was a misnomer that night because the party had an open bar.

Sarah was driving. She was tired. She didn't want to buck the traffic into San Francisco and back. So she invited Diane to stay at her house.

Sarah pulled into the driveway in front of her home. Her roommate, Christie Bard, let them in.

They entered the front room and Diane asked, "Where's the furniture?"

There was a Christmas tree in one corner and nothing else. No couch. No sofa. No TV. Not even a rug.

Diane noticed two dogs sitting side-by-side in the corner. She recognized one as a Dalmatian. The other dog was a mixed breed of something or other.

Christie pointed at a shiny metal track and said, "I ran that around two walls. Then, at night, I leash the dogs to the pole. That way they can move around."

"But why?" Diane asked.

"They were eating the furniture. And the rugs."

Diane said, "I've got to get a dog. What's this one?"

"A mix. Yellow Lab, husky and wolf."

"Wolf?" Diane asked.

"Yes."

"What are their names?"

"The Dalmatian is Bailey and the wolf is Bamboo."

"They're so cute." Diane glanced around the room. "They have to sleep out here all alone?"

"Sure. Why not?"

"Don't they get lonely?"

"They have each other."

"What about human companionship?"

"That's me."

"Maybe if you let them into the bedroom at night they'd stop eating your furniture."

"I let them into my bedroom at night and they *still* ate my furniture."

Diane glanced at Sarah. "Kind of like those two monsters I have living down the hall from me. No way would I keep animals that big in my tiny apartment."

"I thought," Sarah said, "you wanted to buy a dog?"

"I do. I've been researching, reading books. I'm thinking about getting a Jack Russell terrier."

"*Terra*," Sarah said, "from the Latin for earth. Did you know terriers were once used to drive game out of their burrows? Like little rat terriers."

"No," answered Christie and Diane.

"Yes," Sarah insisted. "They started out in England. There are many breeds." Sarah squinted her face up in concentration, "There's a Welsh terrier and Manchester terrier."

Diane said firmly, "I want a Jack Russell terrier."

Christie said, "I'm pooped. Come on, call it a night. I'll show you where to sleep."

"What about the dogs?" Diane asked.

"What about them?"

"They look so lonely," Diane said. "I'm sleeping with them."

"What?" Sarah said.

"Don't want them alone."

Diane proceeded to yank a bedspread and a comforter off the nearest two beds. She grabbed two pillows and headed for the front room.

Her friends followed her.

Near the two dogs, Diane made a nest, first neatly laying out the bedspread, then placing the comforter on top of it.

She snuggled herself under the comforter, arranged the two pillows, then looked at Christie and Sarah and said, "What? You thought I was kidding?"

Diane puffed up her pillow and said, "Merry Christmas, and good night."

As Sarah went down the hall she heard Diane say, "Merry Christmas, Bailey. Merry Christmas, Bamboo."

* * *

Jennifer said, "She never got to buy that Jack Russell terrier."

"No," Sarah said sadly. " She told me she wanted to wait until after the marathon."

"Have the police contacted you yet?"

"Yes," Sarah answered. "They wanted to know if Diane ever had a run-in with the dogs. I told them about what happened in December, before Diane... before Diane..." Her eyes again welled with tears.

Jennifer said, "You told me. Diane said the male, Bane, lunged at her and bit her on the wrist. She got nailed, but not as bad as it could have been."

"She was wearing a sports watch. The band was wide, hard rubber. One of those big things that's easy to read when you're running. That protected most of her wrist. Not that it did any good," Sarah sobbed, "now that the dog killed... the *dogs* killed..."

"I know," Jennifer said sadly. "The *damned* dogs."

Chapter Eleven

Cujo in a Cage

Janet Coumbs Ranch, Hayfork, just off Highway 299, Trinity County, Thursday, February 1, 2001.
The sky was black, a bowl of nothingness, the stars and moon blotted out by an early fog.

Mike Becker and Rich Daniele had left the City at four in the morning and drove to Trinity County. It took them six hours. Shortly after ten in the morning they arrived at the rural four-acre ranch.

The ranch was typical for a remote working residence. A few outbuildings and two fifth-wheel trailers were scattered about the property. A large satellite dish sat in an enclosed dog-run area. The fence was part six-foot chain-link and part jury-rigged board and mesh.

Patches of snow mingled with dirt and grass.

A substantial woman, with salt-and-peppered hair flowing over the shoulders, left a small white house and introduced herself as Janet Coumbs.

Becker introduced himself and Daniele. Janet showed them into a modest but clean living room. The police video camera was set up and focused.

Becker led the interview. "The time, according to my clock, is about ten-twelve." The investigator got the vital statistics out of the way, like date of birth and address. Then he asked, "When did the dogs arrive here?"

Janet Coumbs said, "They arrived, two of them, in June of '98. Then two of them in February '99."

"How did they arrive here?"

"Paul John Schneider told me he would like to purchase me some dogs so that I could have an income."

"Paul John Schneider is presently in prison?"

"Yes."

"Do you know what prison?"

"Pelican Bay. A friend of mine down the road was visiting a prisoner. She said that it says in the Bible that you're supposed to, as a Christian, visit the sick and the infirm and those in prison. As your Christian duty you should do this. And here's this poor guy sitting in prison and he's not been visited. He just sits in his cell for four years. That's not right."

Becker asked, "Paul offered to buy you dogs?"

"He wanted me to become self-sufficient, so I wouldn't have to depend on disability."

Becker walked the witness through how she first met the prisoner, in 1998, through their letters of correspondence.

Janet said, "I'm really gullible. What he said was, 'we're here, we're your friends.' If he was on the outside, he could come and help me fix my house. But 'we' can't do that."

"When you say 'we,' you mean?"

"Dale."

"Do you know the last name?"

"Bretches."

Becker learned that the prisoners sent Janet Coumbs money to purchase the dogs. All they wanted in return were pictures of the dogs so they could do their art work. They told Janet that the dogs would protect her ranch. She had been losing a few sheep to mountain lions and bears.

Janet said, "He said that the dogs would protect my property. Yeah, right." She laughed. "They took care of my herd all right."

"Did they ask you to train these dogs in any way?"

"Bane was pulling my wagon from the wood pile to the porch. They didn't want me to make wooses out of them. They said, 'These dogs are like royalty and you're making them into peasants.' I said, 'But these are dogs. They're like family.' And he didn't like the pictures I was sending him. Like the ones with the cat. It was Bane's cat. He slept with the cat."

"How old were the dogs?"

"Bane was three months old. Isis was nine months old. Those were the two that we got first. Then, later, they kind of bullied me into getting two more because one female would not be sufficient to help you do anything regarding breeding. But I'm not set up for more than one female. But we got two more. They were born in August and we got them in January. That was Hera and Fury. Along with Isis, we had three females and a male to breed."

Becker asked, "Was that their plan, to breed the dogs?"

"But that was for me. To be able to have some money to be able to go see them. That was part of our conflict right away. Isis did not come in heat right away. Paul said, 'You have to get them bred right away. What's wrong with you?' And I said, 'They haven't come in heat.' Then I got this threatening type letter. I got really frightened, and I said this isn't right. It was because I wasn't doing everything the way he wanted. I decided I didn't want any more to do with him if he was going to be this way."

Becker needed clarification. "Wouldn't have any more to do with *who*?"

"Schneider." Coumbs went on to explain that Bretches wrote her a letter explaining that Paul had a short temper, but he doesn't mean what he says. That the dogs were hers. And not to worry.

Becker asked, "When the dogs were here, what were they doing?"

"When we just had Bane and Isis, they'd play in the pond. They were just dogs. And they were loving dogs." She explained how once they knocked down the front door when she was at church and ransacked her home.

Becker said, "I heard that sometimes these dogs attacked livestock?"

"Hera and Fury. They were the two instigators. The two that we had problems with from the beginning. When we went to the airport to get these dogs, the guy at the airport said, 'Lady, you got Cujo in a cage.'"

Becker walked her through the various breeders who had the dogs originally, and how the dogs were transported to her ranch.

Janet said, "I couldn't believe, when we went to the airport, that these dogs were the same as Bane and Isis. The difference was like night and day."

She explained how much trouble it was to bring the dogs home. She had to keep Hera and Fury in a separate area from Bane and Isis. Then she had to separate Hera from Fury. Hera couldn't be contained in the yard.

Becker asked, "They didn't get along?"

"No. This was turning into a nightmare. Then we had ten puppies from Bane and Isis. Only four survived."

"Six puppies died?"

"Yes. Killed by their mother. But animals do that sometimes with their first batch. But then with the four puppies that were left, she got into motherhood."

"Were the other dogs tied up then?"

"In the yard. Bane was an escape artist. We couldn't keep him in a fence. Under, over, around, through. We couldn't keep him on a collar or leash. So we had to do a collar, with a harness and a 25-foot chain, with a stake in the ground. He had a 50-foot radius."

Becker took the witness through Bane's life on the ranch before Hera arrived. Bane did attack sheep, but with Fury.

After Hera arrived, she also attacked the sheep with Fury. All together, they killed a dozen. Janet could not remember exactly how many chickens, except that it was a lot.

She explained that Bane once got hold of one of her roosters. She thought it was dead, but the dog was only holding it in his mouth. Then he let the bird go.

Hera, however, killed the family cat.

Janet said, "That really upset me. My daughter said, 'I don't even want to look at Hera.'"

94

The rancher told the detectives the dogs attacked her sheep. "This was devastating to me because I really cared about my sheep. I kept telling Paul that I don't like this."

"How did he take that?" asked Becker.

"'I'm sorry,' he'd say. 'This is sad. Maybe you need to beef up your fencing.'"

"You did that?"

"Yeah. But I didn't want Hera or Fury. Then Paul and I had the falling out and I was in a holding pattern with these dogs."

Becker took her through how the dogs were fed. The first food was furnished by the convicts through Brenda Storey.

Brenda was the person who had originally arranged for the dogs to be purchased and transported to the Coumbs Ranch

Then the convicts wanted her to give raw meat to the dogs. Janet explained, "I never gave them raw meat because I don't believe in doing that. I've never done that with any dog."

The money for food stopped. Paul was angry at Janet because she would not give the dogs a supplement used for horses to make them grow bigger and run faster. "He has nothing else to think about except thinking about these magnificent dogs."

After Paul and Janet had their blow-up, Brenda Storey told her that she was going to be the go-between because Paul was still interested in the dogs. He still wanted pictures of the dogs. And, after six of the puppies were killed, wanted to sell the other four to families of prisoners for protection, because the men were incarcerated.

Janet said about Brenda, "But she would never give me a name. She said, 'The puppies are old enough to leave mamma. You need to take the four puppies, and the paper work, and take them up there.'"

Becker asked, "Leave them with *who*?"

"I asked where? She wouldn't tell me. She wouldn't give me an address. And I said, what? Am I taking them to a street corner? And what was the price?"

Janet said Brenda explained that Paul had arranged to sell two of the puppies to one person and wanted to give her a deal.

Also, Paul was not satisfied with the pictures Janet was sending him and Dale. Pictures of the dog Bane with the cat. Pictures of the dogs playing in the pond. He wanted more majestic pictures. These dogs were named after gods, like Thor and Isis and Hera.

The dogs were royalty.

Becker asked, "Did you set up an account for the money that came in?"

"The money went out as fast as it came in. And there wasn't that many times he actually sent me any money."

"You were sent legal papers," Becker noted, "by Noel and Knoller."

"Yeah. In October of '99. They said, 'We're suing you for a quarter of a million dollars.'"

"Two hundred and fifty thousand dollars?"

"Two hundred and twenty-six thousand dollars. A thousand dollars is a lot to me. I got the papers and the next day they were on the phone."

"At this time you had how many dogs?"

"The four; Isis, Fury, Bane and Hera. Plus the four puppies."

"What did you tell them about the dogs?"

"I told them they killed my sheep. They attacked my cat. I told them it all. It's too much for us. They said, 'The dogs belong to Brenda.' I said, 'I don't understand how they could belong to Brenda Storey because Paul said he was purchasing these dogs for me.' They said the money went to Brenda; it was in Brenda's hands. Therefore, she can claim the money as hers. That's the way it is. They're her dogs. In the lawsuit, the way it was worded, she had sent the dogs up here for them to be trained. That I had presented myself as a professional trainer with a kennel. I said, none of this is true.

"They said, 'The bottom line is the dogs belong to Brenda.'

"I said I didn't have money for a lawyer.

"They said, 'We can take your house, we can take you car. We can take your animals. We can take everything.'

"If these dogs were Brenda's, how come she hasn't been sending me any money to take care of these dogs? Do you know, if you go through a kennel, how much it costs? I called a kennel. It was between seven and nine dollars a day per dog. I haven't seen any seven to nine dollars a day per dog.

"They said, 'That's because you weren't doing what she wanted.'

"They said, 'Brenda is willing to settle if you just give her the dogs back. We'll go away and leave you alone. And we'll indemnify you.'"

The offer was to pay off all other debts. They would never claim anything against Janet, and Janet could never claim anything against them. Then they would go out of her life.

Janet said, "So I said, 'You're coming tomorrow to get these dogs, right?'

"They said, 'As soon as we can.' I said, 'If these are Brenda's dogs, I don't want them here.'"

Janet then explained to Becker and Daniele that a Saint Bernard had bitten someone in the neighborhood. People were saying the owner of the dog could go to prison. And Janet was afraid if one of the dogs on her property did the same, she would get sued.

She continued. "The other dogs would bark when someone came, like saying someone's here. Fury and Hera had a totally different attitude. They would pull on the end of the chain or bounce against the fence. But when I would walk over there, they would be calm. Like, oh, mom, I love you. They would rub on my leg or jump up and lick me. The same with my daughter."

Janet explained that sometimes the dogs would act friendly to others. But if someone stayed overnight the dogs would bark because that was an intruder.

Becker asked, "When Noel and Knoller arrived here did you tell them about the dogs?"

"Yes."

"About the livestock?"

"Yes. The whole story. I told them when they came, 'I don't know how you're going to unload these dogs. These dogs are bonded to us. These dogs love us.'"

Janet explained that the dogs did not want to go. "One sat down when put on a leash. It was like pulling a mule. They had to physically pick it up and carry it to the transport."

Becker asked, "One dog or…"

"All eight dogs."

"Did they have you sign-off on that?"

"Oh yes. And they signed off, too."

"Did you have an attorney present?"

"No, a friend."

"Did the friend witness your telling them how the dogs were?"

"Right. He even told them. And, as an aside, 'please don't let Hera come back. Please put her down.' I didn't feel comfortable with them even taking her. But they said these were valuable dogs and, 'If you don't you're going to owe us that money.'"

Becker asked, "Did your friend talk to Noel and Knoller when they were here?"

"I don't think he talked to them. But they knew. They talked about giving the dogs tranquilizers to get them out of the crates. So they knew."

"Did anyone else?"

"There was six people who came. There was them and four other people. They came at six in the morning on April first."

"How much did these dogs weigh when they took them?"

"Bane weighed about a hundred and forty pounds. Hera was younger. A hundred, maybe a hundred and ten. Maybe not that much. They were in good health. Isis was a hundred and thirty-five. Fury was even less than Hera."

"When Noel and Knoller took possession of the dogs, was that the last time you heard from them?"

"Yes. "

"When Noel and Knoller took the dogs, did they tell you what they were going to do with the dogs?"

"They told me it wasn't my worry. They told me they had professional trainers. Bane will be taken care of. Isis will be taken care of. Good homes. Basically, that it was none of my business."

Becker wrapped up with the usual qualifying questions aimed at the later possibility that a defense lawyer would one day challenge the statement:

"Has anyone forced you to make a statement today?"

"No."

"Has anyone promised you anything?"

"No."

"You gave this statement of your own free will?"

"Yes."

On the long drive back to San Francisco, Daniele asked Becker, "If you had to pick one line from the entire interview, which would you bet the media would jump on?"

"What are you talking about?"

"The ten-second sound bite."

Becker passed an eighteen-wheeler and asked again, "What are you talking about?"

"If the media were only allowed one line from our interview, what would it be?"

"Easy. 'Lady, you got Cujo in a cage.'"

Chapter
Twelve

An Abandoned and Malignant Heart

Henry Hunter's office, Hall of Justice, Thursday, General Work Detail, February 1, 2001.
Cujo in a cage. Hunter had read Stephen King's classic horror story when it first came out.

He remembered the chill he had experienced when he first read the book. Be interesting to read it again. If I remember right, in *Cujo* King goes into the dog's mental processes.

That's the psychic ability I need right now.

What was Bane thinking?

What was Hera thinking?

Not being a psychic, dog or otherwise, it was time to do some work.

Hunter hadn't reviewed Becker's logs from the day before. He pulled out the file and read:

0800: Met with inspector Daniele and went to Rancho Cordova to meet with CDC Investigator Hawks and Inspector Matthews. Inspector Hawks gave me copies of an investigation conducted by CDC.

Hunter realized that was work by the California Department of Corrections regarding the convicts and dogs and the Mexican Mafia. He continued reading:

1230: I phoned Brenda and Russell Storey at home. Transcript to follow.

Hunter had learned from the California Department of Corrections that Brenda and Russell Storey had originally purchased the male and female Presa Canario dogs. The Storeys' involvement seemed limited; they purchased dogs for clients and then had them shipped to Janet Coumbs Ranch.

The Storeys were just intermediaries, Hunter knew, they weren't the key to this.

Key.

He felt the itch grow in his mind. It wasn't really an itch, more like the shadow of a thought that eluded him every time he tried to capture it. So it wasn't really an itch, just an irritation. Like an itch, but in an unscratchable area.

Keys.

What about the keys?

That's it! That's what caused the itch when I first read Noel's letter. Where Marjorie's keys ended up.

Play the scene again, but with the new information. Start with Bane pulling Marjorie down the hallway.

*   *   *

Marjorie sank to her knees, exhausted. Bane, tugging at the harness, started to drag his mistress down the hallway.

Act like an anchor, Marjorie thought as she slid along the floor.

Why? Why is Bane so anxious to get to that woman?

Bane hauled her the full sixty feet of the hallway to the young woman's doorway. It took the dog fifteen seconds to cover the distance.

Four feet a second.

And still the woman did not enter her apartment. She stood frozen, an immobile Venus-like statue with arms holding grocery bags.

Bane arrived at his target. He jumped up and placed one paw to the right of the woman and one paw to the left.

The dog and the woman were face to face.

Bane dropped back to all fours. Marjorie grabbed Diane and, while trying to force her into her apartment, stumbled. Both women fell into the apartment. Grocery bags went flying.

Marjorie again got hold of Bane's leash and backed out of the apartment. To her amazement, Diane crawled out after her.

Death of an Angel

The attack was resumed, with Marjorie once again throwing herself on top of Diane and shouting, "Stay still! He's trying to protect me."

She again tried to back out of the apartment, pulling Bane with her.

Again, Diane crawled out into the hallway.

Again, the attack was resumed.

The attack lasted for five minutes.

She gained control of both her animals and led them back to her apartment.

She could hear sirens approaching. She put Bane in the bathroom and Hera in the bedroom. She went back down the hall and retrieved her apartment keys.

* * *

Hunter wondered, how did those keys get down the hall in front of Diane's apartment?

Break her statement down. When I first heard it I visualized Marjorie, desperately clutching the leash, being towed "like an anchor."

Now she's claiming she restrained the dog with one hand and held her keys in the other?

Also, she's too tired to control one dog on a leash, but, after the attack, she, "gained control of both her animals and led them back to her apartment."

What else is irritating me? The itch is almost gone, but something is still bothering me.

Oh, yes. She went back to retrieve her keys. She did not call 911. Esther, across the hall in #607, performed that corporal work of mercy even though she was terrified.

I can imagine a completely different scenario that makes much more sense.

Once again the policeman closed his eyes and let a movie play in his head.

* * *

At the bottom of the stairs, Marjorie turned right toward her apartment.

She had her keys and brown bag in her right hand, Bane's leash in her left.

She opened the door to her apartment, then turned back toward the garbage chute.

Marjorie looked down the narrow hallway. There was a figure at the far end standing in front of an open apartment. The light was extremely dim, the female figure shadowy.

The figure was holding two grocery bags.

Suddenly, Bane lunged and the leash came out of Marjorie's hand. The dog charged down the hallway, barking and growling, with Marjorie frantically following. Hera, hearing the noise, left her apartment and joined the chase.

Diane, seeing a 120-pound dog roaring straight at her, devised the best defensive maneuver she could: She froze against the wall, becoming an insignificant threat to the animal.

Bane rushed to Diane and jumped up, placing a paw on either side of her.

Correctly, Diane averted her eyes rather than staring at the animal's eyes. With no confrontation, Bane withdrew to a crouching position.

Marjorie dropped her keys and grabbed Diane. She tried to force her into the apartment and safety. Both women fell to the ground with Marjorie on top.

Bane, thinking Diane was attacking Marjorie, came to the defense of his mistress. Diane got hit in the throat, puncturing one of her carotid arteries.

The two major arteries in the front of the neck are called the carotids because of their relationship to the heart. They come off directly from the artery to the heart and run along the big muscle on the side of the neck. These vessels are the size of a ring finger. At the jaw they branch out into vessels that supply the face and the brain.

Arteries operate under pressure called "systolic." They are so close to the pump source that when cut, produce arrhythmic bleeding — a spurting effect.

Diane's blood began to spray the door, the walls, the carpet, Marjorie Knoller.

Marjorie got control of Bane and backed him out of the apartment and a few feet down the hallway. Hera followed.

Trying to control both dogs, Marjorie shouted over and over again, "Help! Someone help me!"

Dazed, bloodied, at the door of her apartment, Diane heard cries for help and instinctively crawled toward them to give aid.

In the hallway, the dogs saw Diane and, thinking once again she was a threat, launched another attack.

*　*　*

Hunter considered talking with prosecutor Paul Cummins, but he knew Cummins would ask, "This is based on *what*?"

Hunter took out a copy of the crime scene sketch. The majority of blood, flesh and hair was *not* at the apartment door, but in a semi-circle down the hallway.

Esther, across the hallway, said she heard shouts for help. If Diane crawled toward Marjorie's cries for help, that would explain where the most blood ended up.

It would also explain Diane crawling toward the threat instead of away form it.

Except, in her first statement to the cops, Marjorie said that Diane was crawling *towards* her apartment, not away from it.

What else? Marjorie's saying she spent sixty seconds frantically holding Bane back and then got tugged down the hallway for fifteen seconds, acting like an anchor.

And all the time clutching her apartment keys in one hand.

Doesn't wash.

The truth is the truth. It does not change.

So either Marjorie was telling the truth when she first spoke to Officer Forrestal and Inspector Daniele right after the attack, or she's telling the truth now.

But she can't be telling the truth in both instances.

So, one way or the other, she *is* lying.

Northern Station, Thursday, February 1, 2001.
Sergeant Paul Morse was with inspectors Giovannell and Reltor. They had just returned to Northern Station after interviewing

another citizen who had phoned in reporting involvement with the dogs Bane and Hera.

They gave Morse a copy of the statement. He read the signature: Rhea Tallent. Then he read the statement:

"I was walking to work on Fillmore Street, from Jackson, toward Pacific.

"Two school boys were walking abreast of me as well. They looked junior high school age. We heard from a block away the most horrible barking and grumbling sounds I've ever heard before. The boys said, one to the other, 'Those dogs are rumbling.'

"Then there was a high-pitched squeal, screaming and crying as if another dog was being bitten.

"We were walking toward the sounds. At Fillmore and Pacific I looked to my right and saw about a quarter of a block away a man and woman. Each had a huge dog on a leash trying to control the out-of-control animals. There was a man in front of the open garage door and a German Shepherd.

"The two huge dogs were reared up on their hind legs, eyes crazed, baring their teeth, lunging forward, trying to break their leashes and making the most horrible sounds.

"I was so frightened, I just glanced at the dogs, didn't make eye contact, didn't run, but started walking faster. The little boys did too. I didn't look back but headed for Broadway and down the hill to Union Street.

"I was very afraid. I felt that they could have bitten my legs off!"

Paul Morse placed the statement in a file, told his secretary to make copies, then forward them on to Hunter and went outside.

The words, "Could have bitten my legs off," rattled around in Morse's mind.

The memory of Diane in the hallway flashed.

Think of something else, something... anything...

He pictured one of his boats. He loved boats. Boats and the water and fishing.

Fishing was like being a policeman. You stalked the prey, cunningly. The fish tried to elude you, cunningly. Sometimes you won, sometimes the fish got away.

He visualized a rainbow trout, flashing its colors in the rays of the sun as it leapt, spun and danced on the end of the line trying to free itself.

Or, better yet, deep-sea fishing. Out in the Pacific. The boat riding each swell, bracing your legs without thinking about it. The feel of a huge salmon striking the line.

Sometimes you caught fish. Sometimes you didn't.

Sometimes you won, sometimes you lost.

Like Diane.

Her image was back in his mind. And the sadness was back in his heart.

Sharon Smith's apartment building, garage, February 1, 2001.
Sharon and her sister Janet entered the garage. They were headed for the memorial service for Diane at St. Mary's College. Janet had left her husband and family at home and flown out from Colorado,

They went to the car.

Across from them Sharon saw Robert Noel and Marjorie Knoller standing by the lawyers' car.

Noel's hulking stature stood next to his wife's diminutive one, in size comparable to the *Maltese Falcon*'s Sidney Greenstreet to Peter Lorre.

Sharon froze. He sister looked at her, puzzled, then glanced at the couple.

Marjorie Knoller stared back. Not exactly a glare, not exactly a scowl, but definitely not a friendly look.

Henry Hunter's office, February 1, 2001.
Henry Hunter was alerted by an aide that Janet Coumbs had been on ABC's *Good Morning America*. The aide gave his boss the VHS tape. Hunter quickly flicked on the television in his office. Janet Coumbs appeared.

He watched the owner of the Coumbs Ranch explain how she got the dogs. Then she said, "The lawyers were told that I felt they should have been put down before they left my property, because they showed aggression just through the fence."

Hunter shook his head. What an understatement. Unless you consider that eating your young, eating sheep, eating chickens and eating a family cat did not show aggression.

His aide handed him a file. Inside were quotes from neighbors that Sergeant Morse had interviewed while canvassing the neighborhood. Hunter read: Derek Brown, who lives on the fifth floor of the Pacific Heights building, stated, "I'm absolutely speechless. Every time they have crossed my path, they've gone berserk and lunged at me, trying to take a chunk out of me."

Henry read the rest of the statements. All similar. Dogs did this. Dog did that. Then he turned to the newspapers he'd purchased earlier. He had been meaning to get at them most of the day, but something kept coming up.

The second edition of the *San Francisco Chronicle* carried the first salvo against Noel's claim that Diane might have triggered the attack herself.

The headline read: Mauling Death Victim's Fault, Lawyers Say — rambling letter to police says she placed self in harm's way.

Noel had even gone further regarding perfume or steroids, stating, "The presence of either of those substances would also explain Ms. Whipple's behavior at the time of the incident in leaving the confines and safety of her apartment and coming into the hall to confront the dog after Ms. Knoller had secured it."

How, wondered Hunter, did perfume or steroids explain Whipple's supposed behavior?

Was perfume supposed to make you irrational?

Steroids?

What was going on? What possible motive could the two lawyers have for blaming the victim?

He phoned Paul Cummins, second-in-command of the DA's office, looking for some insight.

Paul said, "California's fighting-dog statute is clear that the victim cannot promote or provoke the attack. If the victim did, in any way, then there's no crime."

"Meaning if they can prove Diane somehow caused the attack, then no crime's been committed?"

"No crime."

"What about malice?"

"Get me the proof and we'll see."

Hunter hung up. He turned on his computer and did a search. He wanted to find the exact definition for malice.

The screen filled: *Malice may be expressed or implied. It is expressed when there is manifested a deliberate intention unlawfully to take away the life of a fellow creature. It is implied when no considerable provocation appears, or when the circumstances attending the killing show an abandoned and malignant heart.*

Chapter Thirteen

A Memorial

St. Mary's Chapel, Moraga, Thursday, February 1, 2001.
The statues in St. Mary's Chapel were dedicated to the church's namesake. Various times in the Blessed Mother's life were reenacted in the alcoves.

Those who loved Diane Whipple and the people whose lives she had affected were there.

Sharon Smith and her sister Janet sat in the first pew. Next to them was Diane's mother, Penny Whipple-Kelly.

Air has a peculiar quality, sometimes, of having a feeling of its own. Not the shimmering effect that surrounds a fire. Or the various colors air can achieve depending on meteorological circumstances, like a sunset or a rainbow. Those are physical properties. But the kind of feeling that the air has at a sporting event: *charged.* Or at a party celebrating a special event: *animated.*

The air in the chapel was laden with palpable *grief.*

A large photo of Diane Whipple holding a lacrosse stick dominated the right side of the altar. Only a few flowers were beneath the picture. A lone wreath was in front of the altar.

The chapel was crowded to overflowing, its capacity of 450 exceeded. More than 200 mourners were relocated next door in a conference room.

Instead of flowers, it had been requested that donations be made to the Diane Whipple Foundation.

The congregation contained a conglomeration of people involved in Diane's life: co-workers knelt by Sharon's financial associates; lacrosse players melded with social friends.

Death of an Angel

The president of the college, Brother Craig, took the pulpit. "On behalf of our community, I want to express our condolences to the family and friends that are with us this evening.

"This is a moment that we can come together and support each other. This is a place where broken hearts are repaired. We are thankful to Diane for her efforts to build a community.

"She worked with a fledgling group."

Laughter interrupted the monk. Laughter from the lacrosse team who knew *they* were the fledgling group.

"And raised them out to the outstanding team they are now."

The president of the college went on to extol Diane Alexis' virtues. "If Diane taught us anything, she taught us how important each one of us is to the other. We come together in love."

The priest raised his arms and invoked a prayer: "Shepherd me, oh God, beyond my wants, beyond my fears, from death into life."

The priest celebrated the Mass. Instead of wearing the requiem robes of purple and black, he wore the robes of joy: white and gold.

The priest signaled and the entire lacrosse team stood up and went to the pulpit holding hands. They formed a semi-circle.

Amy Harms said, "The first time Coach saw us play, I thought she'd fall over laughing. Knowledge of the sport got Coach her job. But her friendship made us love her.

"As we remember Diane over these last few days, though our hearts have been sad, we have been filled with warm memories of an amazing friend. Scavenger hunts, crazy dress days, candy, team dinners, unofficial team outings, nicknames, and laughter were simply part of a typical week.

"Conversations which lasted well after practice was over and which touched on a lot of non-lacrosse issues were commonplace. A steady stream of players in and out of her office all day long was requested by her and loved by us."

Megan Bryan, top scorer of the team, stepped forward. "She was a mother, a sister, a teacher, a mentor, a friend and a coach. She would step in and out of each necessary role. We would want to be Diane Whipple.

"She told me, 'Destiny is not a matter of chance, it is a matter of choice.'"

Megan Guiatu said, "There are two things you told me once that I have never forgotten: 'You can't please anyone unless you please yourself,' and 'Life is full of disappointments, don't let yourself become one by trying *not* to disappoint.'"

Each girl had written of how much their coach had meant to them, how she had impacted their lives for the better, how she was the role model that they admired the most, how each wanted be like Diane Whipple.

Nicole Cherry said, "You are a perfect model of a life lived well, to its fullest potential, until now. Happy you were, shining — undoubtedly dreams are what guided you. Inspiration is what followed. Weak people can't do what they dream of most — money, cars, houses, status, popularity — you avoided but most don't. You sacrificed so much to get where you are and I know you are smiling. Your ashes, your closure, your spirit, and attitude were all perfect."

Katy Flood came forward and said, "Thank you for everything you taught me, and why did you have to leave? I miss you, Coach, and a lot of people love you."

The entire team had sorrow burning on their faces and emotions churning in their hearts.

Rosy Iaccino came forward. "How many coaches would allow someone who had never picked up a lacrosse stick to miss practice every Tuesday during the season to go to ROTC in Berkeley? How many coaches could pull a team of unique personalities and diverse backgrounds together to become a tight-knit family?"

Meghan Jones said, "Diane was a gift. She had an amazing ability to instill love in people's hearts. She reminded me that I deserved to be treated with respect even if I wasn't the leading scorer, the fastest sprinter, or the best defender."

One-by-one the lacrosse players expressed their love and admiration for their friend and coach.

The lacrosse team was replaced on the altar by Diane's mother, Penny Whipple-Kelly, along with longtime friend Cheri DiCerbo, Sharon Smith and her sister Janet.

Eulogy after eulogy was given. Diane's attributes were lauded, her accomplishments reviewed, the love of her friends, family and associates remembered.

Sharon Smith spoke briefly, her grief obvious on her face. Diane's mother was so overcome she could not speak for herself. Janet read what the mother had written.

Last to speak, Sarah Miller went to the dais. She took out a piece of paper and said, "The morning Diane died she gave me this letter."

The petite young woman inhaled sharply. She composed herself and continued. "I would like to share it with all of you."

She carefully removed a paper from the folds of her sweater, opened it, and then gently placed it on the pulpit.

She read:

"Dear Sarah,

"Congrats on a great achievement!

"Some only ever dream of finishing a marathon. It was fun and a blast to train with you. Cheers to months of hurting. And nasty hills (yuck) ☹

"People come into your life for a Reason a Season or a Lifetime. When you figure out which it is you know exactly what to do.

"When someone is in your life for a Reason, it is usually to meet a need you have expressed outwardly or inwardly.

"They have come to assist you through a difficulty, to provide guidance and support, to aid physically, emotionally, or spiritually.

"They may seem like a godsend, and they are.

"They are there for the reason you need them to be.

"Then, without any wrongdoing on your part or at an inconvenient time, this person will say or do something to bring the relationship to an end.

"Sometimes they die.

"Sometime they walk away.

112

A Memorial

"Sometimes they act out and force you to take a stand.

"What we must realize is that our need has been met, our desire fulfilled; their work is done.

"The prayer you sent up has been answered and it is now time to move on. When people come into your life for a SEASON, it is because your turn has come to share, grow or learn.

"They may bring you an experience of peace or make you laugh. They may teach you something you have never done. They usually give you an unbelievable amount of joy!

"Believe it! It is real! But, only for a Season! LIFETIME relationships teach you lifetime lessons; those things you must build upon in order to have a solid emotional foundation.

"Your job is to accept the lesson, love the person/people (anyway); and put what you have learned to use in all other relationships and areas of your life.

"It is said that Love is blind but friendship is clairvoyant. Thank you for being a part of my life!

"Love,

"Diane ☺"

Chapter
Fourteen

The Mailman Cometh

Corner of Fillmore Street and Pacific Avenue, Monday, February 5, 2001.
Sergeant Paul Morse showed up at Fillmore and Pacific at 9:30 in the morning. He was a half hour early. The night before, he had swung by the intersection. There were mailboxes on the corner, right in front of the building. Pick up at 10 a.m. every weekday.

He wanted to talk to the mailman.

He parked across the street. He had a direct line-of-sight to the relay mailbox. He thought, here I am, a 31-year pro and I'm staking out a mailbox.

Weird, considering some of the narcotic rings I've staked out before the busts went down. Those were life-threatening, this about as benign as it gets.

He watched a dog-walker pass by, a phalanx of a half dozen animals on leash, headed toward nearby Alta Plaza Park.

He recognized most of the breeds; a couple of coiffured poodles, a sleek-looking Irish Setter, a bouncy Australian Sheep Dog, a mid-sized mutt of indiscriminate breeding with a face that only an owner could love, and a manicured Irish Wolfhound.

My lord, Paul wondered, how much does that Irish thing weigh?

Curiosity got the better of him and he got out of the car, showed his badge and asked the dog-walker.

"One-eighty-five."

"That's more than *I* weigh."

"More than me, too. Thank God he obeys. If he ever bolted I'd be in trouble."

"You have half a dozen dogs there. Have you ever had a problem?"

"Nope. These are all well-trained animals. They obey all the usual commands. I actually think they get a kick out of doing it together. Watch." The dog-walker faced his six charges. "Sit."

All six dogs promptly sat. A half-dozen pink tongues lolled out of a half-dozen mouths. Twelve eyes expectantly looked at the dog-walker. He said, "Shake hands."

Six paws waved at Paul Morse. He reached out and solemnly shook each paw.

"Play dead," the dog-walker ordered.

Six dogs flopped over. They appeared dead except for the alert eyes watching the boss. The boss said, "Sit."

The dogs went back to squatting on their haunches.

"Nice," Paul said and thought, too bad someone didn't yell "sit" to Bane and Hera. Or "roll over." Or "play dead."

What happened to Diane wasn't *playing* dead.

He thanked the dog-walker and watched him head off towards nearby Alta Plaza Park.

It was 9:50 a.m. No mailman yet.

Paul studied the building at 2398 Pacific. Six stories. Rather ornate. Fireplace in the lobby.

Try as he might, he couldn't escape the thought that kept lunging at his memory. Fireplace in the lobby was squeezed away in his mind and replaced with blood bath in the 6th floor hallway.

Diane's blood.

The life's blood of a young, vibrant and gregarious woman who, from what he had learned from her friends, lived each day to the fullest. Who grabbed life by the throat and shook everything possible out of it.

His last thought vaporized into a different image, a huge dog's white fangs sinking into a slim, delicate throat and shaking and tearing and…

Stop it, he ordered himself. Stop replaying the incident over and over.

Incident?

Replaying the *slaughter* over and over in my mind.

Stop letting those images dominate. Stop letting them creep in when I wake up at three in the morning and stare at the ceiling, mouth dry. Stop remembering when I first walked into that hallway and saw... saw...

I have to talk to someone about this, before it drives me crazy. Someone who's a professional. I need trauma counseling.

He had talked to his longtime friend Henry Hunter about his nightmares and about his reoccurring daydreams that felt like nightmares.

Hunter could empathize with the nightmares and gut-wrenching daydreams.

Except Hunter hadn't felt like this for years, not since he was assigned decoy in the city, the police had moved him over to another assignment — playing decoy for the tactical division.

His job then was to try and lure out members of the notorious Zebra Gang. The Zebra Case was black-on-white murder. When the case broke it was learned that members received so many "points" for each killing: A white male, one; a white female, two; and a white baby, three.

Hunter was one of twelve who, worth only "one point," went out and placed himself in harm's way. With backup lurking in the bushes.

"Just great," Henry had told Paul years later when they worked in the "S" squad. "I was bait. I go down, I'm dead, but homicide gets the bad guys. This wasn't setting up muggers by acting like a drunk. This was damned near suicide."

"Were you packing extra?"

"Five guns and two knives." Henry paused, then added, "And if they would have let me, I would have worn body armor from the top of my head to the tip of my toes."

Now, all these years later, Hunter had told Paul that he tried to compare the waiting terror that he had felt on the Zebra Case, walking through "the wrong parts of town," with what Diane had gone through.

"Didn't work," Hunter told Paul. "Try as I might, I could not compare waiting for a bullet to crash through my brain and watching a dog bigger than me charging straight at me. At least with the bullet, it's over in a flash."

Paul thought, stop thinking about the past. Do your job. Fill your mind with the realities of today, not the terror of yesterday.

He looked up and down Pacific Avenue. No mailman.

He walked around the corner and looked up Fillmore Street. No mailman.

Paul studied the neighborhood around 2398 Pacific Avenue. Just a block away were retail stores like Tullys' Coffee, the Mayflower Market, the San Francisco Boot and Shoe Repair, a dry cleaners, a church.

He looked at the six-story apartment building across the street. Two shallow marble stairs led to a recessed, ornate, black wrought-iron-and-glass front door.

Wonderful looking building. Now wrapped in a shroud of grief.

A mailman walked up Fillmore Street.

The policeman crossed the street. The mailman loaded mail from the relay box into his cart. He had a well-manicured mustache and wore glasses.

Paul showed his badge. "I'm sergeant Paul Morse and I'd like to ask a few questions."

The mailman nodded.

"Ever had any trouble with dogs around here?"

The postman asked, "What's this all about?"

"I'm investigating the incident that occurred here on—"

The postman said, "That poor woman that got mauled?"

"Did you know her?"

"No."

"What's you name?"

"John Watanabe."

"Have you had any problem with dogs around here?"

The mailman said, "Yes."

Paul asked, "When?"

"Second or third week of January."

"This year?"

117

"Yes."

"Do you know where the dogs lived?"

"Right here," John said, as he pointed at 2398 Pacific.

Paul removed two photographs from his coat pocket. They were pictures of Bane and Hera. "Are these the dogs?"

The postman studied the picture for a fraction of a second and said, "That's them. Never forget those two."

"When you had a run-in with these two dogs last month," Paul asked, "what happened?"

John said, "I was walking my route as usual..."

*   *   *

Ten years, thought John, and I've never missed my appointed rounds.

He liked being a mailman. He knew his job provided a very necessary service for the community. People took the mail service very casually, if they thought about it all. But John knew how huge the labyrinth-like network of men and women involved was when it came to getting a letter from point A to point B.

His first delivery was at 2600 Fillmore Street.

The mailman entered the apartment building, went to the bank of mail slots and delivered the mail. He nodded at several familiar faces as they entered or left the building.

John crossed Fillmore and parked his cart in front of 2398 Pacific. He reached down to retrieve the mail.

He heard a snarl and thought, what is that god-awful sound?

He looked up. Two dogs were headed straight for him. Two enormous dogs.

Two snarling, growling, unattended dogs.

Every mailman's nightmare.

John grabbed his cart and placed it between himself and the dogs. He kept pushing the cart at them and wondering, why isn't someone coming to get these dogs?

Ten seconds went by.

John saw a woman standing up the block. There was a large man standing behind her.

Another fifteen seconds went by.

The huge dogs kept snarling, teeth bared.

John kept shoving his cart at them, being careful to keep the cart between himself and the two animals.

The mailman's mind roared.

I'm terrified.

I can't breath.

Look at those things.

They're monsters.

Why isn't anyone coming to rescue me?

Then, all of a sudden, the two dogs stopped.

*   *   *

The postman paused, looked at the policeman, then continued his story.

"They just completely stopped. From snarling dogs trying to get at me, they just stopped and went back to the owner. To the lady. The gentleman was a little further back. At no time did they try to stop these dogs."

Paul asked, "Why do you figure the dogs stopped?"

"I figure why these dogs stopped was she finally called them. Why she didn't call them sooner? I don't know. Strange, a very strange situation. I was in fear for my life. After it stopped, they didn't offer an apology. They didn't give an explanation, they just walked off as if nothing had happened."

Paul asked, "How long do you think the incident lasted?"

"Very hard to tell."

"I know what you mean. Get into a situation involving terror, and time sure can slow down."

The mailman nodded.

"Do you know of any other incidents or people who had a run-in with the dogs?"

The mailman shook his head.

Paul said, "This case may go to an indictment. For that to happen, evidence is going to have to be presented. Do you have any problem with testifying to what you just told us?"

"No. When will I have to testify?"

Paul said, "I'm not sure. This is an animal felony case. Which means it will probably end up in dog court."

119

"Dog court?" the mailman asked, a puzzled look on his face.

"Dog court," Paul repeated. "They have a hearing to determine whether an animal had prior incidents of violence before the last attack. It is very important to establish this. It is also very important to establish that the owners knew their animals had demonstrated violent behavior before."

The mailman nodded.

"That's why," Paul added, "incidents like yours are so important."

The policeman got the vital statistics from the mailman: Home address and home phone number.

The mailman continued on his rounds.

Paul decided that to go to Alta Plaza Park and talk to dog walkers, to see if any of them heard or saw anything.

After that he was headed toward Crissy Field, an old air strip that once serviced the now-closed Presidio of San Francisco — former 6th Army Headquarters.

The policeman hit pay dirt at each location: he found two more witnesses attesting to aggressive behavior by the two Presa Canarios.

The evidence mounted that Bane and Hera had lived up to the nature of their breed: protectively ferocious.

Chapter
Fifteen

Police Log and a Press Conference

Henry Hunter's office, Room 411, Hall of Justice, February 7, 2001.
What a grueling week. Hunter felt as besieged as the critter in an English fox hunt.

An image of that sporting event flashed through his mind — a red fox being chased by a pack of bloodthirsty hounds.

Wrong imagery to have while working on *this* case.

Think about dogs that provide a service. Seeing Eye dogs. A Saint Bernard, with the miniature brandy keg strapped around his neck, rescuing an injured skier. The K-9 corps.

Whatever the imagery, everyone involved in this dog story wants a piece of me. The DA, media, people on the street.

How many times do I have to state to the press that my men are amassing evidence?

Amassing, not sharing — except with prosecutors Paul Cummins, Kimberly Guilfoyle and Jim Hammer.

Time to look at the logs. The overtime on the Whipple Case is killing my budget.

He pulled out Mike Becker's log and read:

02/02/01 2035: Inspector Daniele and I went to Neil Bardack's residence. In summary, Neil was walking his dog. A woman was walking a mastiff. The woman had the dog on a leash. The woman's dog dragged the woman up to Neil's dog. The woman's dog bit Neil's dog on the back. Neil grabbed hold of the woman's dog by its collar.

Neil lifted the woman's dog up off his dog. Neil's dog ran across the street. The woman was lying on the ground. The woman was unable to control her dog. Neil helped the woman to her feet.

The woman stated, "Her dog had never done this before."

Neil is aware of the case we're investigating. He has seen pictures of Knoller in the newspaper. He states that Knoller was the person walking the dog that attacked his dog on the night of the incident.

02/03/01 1000: I phoned the Storey residence. I spoke with Russell Storey. Russell advised 1500 hours was a good time to meet with him and his wife Brenda Storey. At 1300 hours Inspector Daniele and I went to Fair Oaks, California.

Brenda and Russell stated they did not know if Noel and Knoller knew the dogs in this case were vicious. They were involved in a civil case with Janet Coumbs. Noel and Knoller represented the Storeys during this civil litigation.

The only time the Storeys heard the animals were vicious was when Janet Coumbs told an animal transport the dog's were sheep killers.

02/05/01 0945: Inspector Daniele and I conducted an interview with Esther Birkmaier. She lives in #607, 2398 Pacific Avenue, across the hall from Sharon Smith. In summary, Esther heard someone screaming, "Help me, help me," in the hall.

02/05/01 1100: Phoned Mr. Mosher at home. He was bitten by the dog Bane. He wanted to think about whether to testify.

02/06/01 0945: I received a video tape from Officer Gene McManus from the Del Norte County sheriff's department. This is a tape of Noel's press conference held in front of Pelican Bay Prison.

Hunter set the log aside. He called Becker on the intercom and asked, "What kind of witness will Esther Birkmaier make?"

"Excellent. She's in her seventies. White hair and all. Very distinguished looking, very intelligent."

"Where's the video of Robert Noel's Pelican Bay press conference?"

"In the safe."

Hunter went to the General Work Detail's safe. He found the video and went down the hall to the polygraph room. He asked Julie Yee-ho if he could use her TV and VCR. When not in use, this room was much quieter than his own office.

He slid in the video and adjusted the sound. Noel appeared surrounded by reporters holding microphones and cameras, sirens could be heard in the distance. Plus heavy vehicular traffic.

A reporter asked, "He was not a vicious dog, in your estimation?"

Noel answered, "No, he wasn't a vicious dog. He had some issues with other male dogs and other male dogs had issues with him. When I say issues, it's like two teenage boys meeting on the street. They start talking with one another. They growl, they bark at one another and they lunge for one another. Bane has never shown any sign of people-aggression."

"He never bit Ms. Whipple?"

"He encountered Ms. Whipple only three times."

A reporter asked, "Are two dogs of that great size appropriate for a one-bedroom apartment?"

"It would depend on the circumstances. If the dogs were left alone for eight-to-ten, or twelve hours a day, while we were off working someplace, I would say yes, that would be inappropriate. However, we spent twenty-four hours a day, seven days a week with those dogs. We worked out of the house. When we traveled, came up here on business, the dogs would go with us."

"Why are you here instead of San Francisco?"

"Because we scheduled a visit with Mr. Schnieder ."

"Was the perfume and the steroids the catalyst?"

"I was contacted by an investigator who works dog cases. I was also contacted by a professional animal trainer who made the suggestion that those two things should be looked at from a forensic standpoint to see if that was a possibility. My suggestion to Mr. Hallinan was to check and essentially make sure that base was covered. It was not made to suggest in anyway that Ms. Whipple was improperly using steroids."

"What was the catalyst, do you think?"

"I really don't know."

"Why do you think she crawled after Ms. Knoller and the dogs like you said in your letter?"

"I haven't a clue, except by examining the photographs of the scene you will find that Ms. Whipple was down the hall by the elevator."

A truck roaring by drowned out Noel's words. Then his voice became audible again. "...She had managed to get that far down the hall, after having been in her apartment. Her apartment door was open when the officers arrived."

"Do you think she was crawling for help?"

"I really don't want to speculate at this point."

"Where was your wife bitten?"

"She was bitten on her arms. Her breasts. Her back. Her clothing was ripped and torn. When Mr. Hallinan says he doesn't buy her story, all he has to do is look at the forensic evidence. You people should ask him, at the earliest possible time, if he had the facts before he started running his mouth and looked at Ms. Knoller's bloody and torn clothing. Ask him if he would check the photographs that were taken that evening."

A reporter asked, "These dogs had eaten livestock." Again a passing truck lumbered by, blotting out the rest of the question.

Hunter fiddled with the dials on the television and punched up Noel's voice.

"Ms. Coumbs identified one dog, Fury, as a dog that had molested her chickens and supposedly done something to her sheep. And that was the only dog. Fury was the dog that was kept separate."

Another rumbling truck passed by. Annoying. Hunter strained to listen.

Noel's voice became clear again.

"Bane and Hera were on the other side of the driveway and chained to another tree. When we arrived to transport, the dogs didn't bark. When we discussed with Lieutenant O'Brien about Fury's behavior, he indicated in his years of experience, that it was completely attributable to the fact that the dog had been chained."

Who's O'Brien? Hunter wondered, as he pushed the pause button. He called Mike Becker who explained that O'Brien was a retired police officer who operated a dog transport company.

Hunter pushed the play button.

Noel stated, "He indicated that as soon as the dog was taken off the chain, that behavior was gone."

Again, passing traffic blurred the words. All Hunter could pick up was a snatch like, "Fury became a completely tranquil dog."

Hunter thought, either Janet Coumbs is not telling the truth or Robert Noel is not telling the truth. The rancher could not have been more explicit in her statement. Bane was a pussycat until Hera arrived, carrying around a rooster or a cat in his mouth. Then, when pack instinct took hold, started killing sheep along with Hera and Fury.

Fury kills chickens and it's called molesting?

Fury had supposedly done *something* to her sheep?

Hera did nothing?

Bane did nothing?

Who lived at that ranch?

Noel or Coumbs?

Who had access to the information?

Noel or Coumbs?

Does Noel really believe the blather he's spewing?

Chapter Sixteen

Good Morning America

Henry Hunter's home, Thursday, February 8, 2001.
It was seven in the morning. Hunter flipped on the TV to ABC News, Channel Seven.

"Good morning America, glad to have you with us. I'm Charles Gibson. Joining us from Eureka, California are Robert Noel and Marjorie Knoller. Good morning."

"Good morning."

Elizabeth Vargas took over the interview. "I want to ask you the question that is on everyone's mind. Were these dogs, in fact, trained to attack and kill?"

"Absolutely not," Marjorie answered.

"How do you know that?"

"Because I've known the history of the dogs," Knoller replied, "where they came from. And we had to sue the individual who was taking care of them from the time they were puppies to get them for the legal owner of the dogs."

"You mean the dogs had been abused by the previous owner? Each dog weighs more than one hundred pounds. According to that previous owner, they had already killed several animals, and she warned you, she says, that they were dangerous."

Marjorie said, "Ms. Coumbs didn't warn us that they were dangerous. She was having problems with one particular dog, whose name was Fury. Fury was on the shortest chain. Away from the other animals who were also on chains or penned up. The animal trainer that came and took the dogs and transported Fury and Hera to Peninsula Pet Resort, said as soon as Fury was off the chain she'd be just fine. And she was."

The show's host asked, "Mr. Noel, had either of these dogs ever exhibited any signs of aggression before?"

"Not towards people," Noel answered. "They would have issues with other dogs on the beach. Other dogs would come up and bark at them. Hera was attacked twice when she was in heat. Bane was attacked once by a Belgian Malanoa on the beach while he was on lead. But as far as aggression toward people, no."

"People in the neighborhood say they nicknamed the dogs 'killer dogs,' 'beast,' 'dog of death.' Several dozen people have called police to say that they have witnessed those dogs trying to attack people," said Gibson.

"That's total fabrication," Marjorie said. "I know that a lot of people like their fifteen minutes of fame and come forward with outrageous stories. Hera was the dog I trained to walk off-lead. She never had any problem with people at all."

The anchor took Marjorie through the events leading up to the attack, then asked, "Why did Bane lunge towards Ms. Whipple?"

"He didn't lunge towards Ms. Whipple at that time. What happened was, he noticed her, I noticed her, standing by her doorway with two packages on the floor behind her. Her door was open. She was watching me with Bane walk towards my apartment door which is about fifty feet away from where Ms. Whipple was standing near her open apartment doorway."

"Why did Bane attack Ms. Whipple?" Vargas asked. "What happened to spark this attack?"

"Basically, Bane became interested in Ms. Whipple standing down at the end of the hallway. He wasn't making aggressive moves. He was just becoming increasingly interested in her presence. I was trying to get him back into the apartment and was pulling on him. He wasn't doing any aggressive moves. He was just really, really interested. I wasn't sure whether he had smelled something in the bags that he wanted to check out. I didn't know what was in those grocery bags. Or whether there was something about Ms. Whipple herself that was attracting him."

Hunter thought, now Bane was "interested?" A dog goes berserk. Next it's, "Sort of perked up" Now it's, "Became interested?"

The reporter asked, "At what point, Ms. Knoller, did he stop being interested and start being aggressive?"

"When he became more and more interested, he pulled me off my feet.

"He didn't attack her.

"What he did was unusual behavior.

"He had never done it before.

"He jumped up and put both paws on each side of her as she was standing by the wall near her apartment door.

"Then he jumped down.

"I'm on my knees.

"I grab him.

"I get up and I push Ms. Whipple into her open apartment hallway. I tripped.

"We both fall down.

"I'm now on top of her.

"Bane is still on my left-hand lead. I restrain Bane with my right hand. I start pulling him out of the apartment. She hadn't been injured at this point.

"Obviously," Marjorie continued, "she probably was somewhat frightened by what was happening. I'm on my knees and pulling Bane out into the hallway. I had told Ms. Whipple to just stay down. Don't move. As I'm pulling Bane out and myself out of her apartment, she starts to move towards me. At this point she is still uninjured. He seemed to be just really interested — in her. If you have a dog, there's a difference between an aggressive nature and just definite interest. He was trying to get at her. But it didn't seem to me as if it were an aggressive move."

"You already said that he leapt up on her and put a paw on either side, on either shoulder. That's certainly sounds quite aggressive."

"Excuse me. Not on either shoulder of her. He put his paws on the wall."

"So he pinned her to the wall," Vargas said. "At what point did he begin to bite her? To attack? Because her throat was mauled. Her face was unrecognizable."

"What happened," Marjorie said, "was she came out into the hallway, which I didn't understand. I thought she was just going to slam her door shut. And when she does that, Bane starts to get interested in her and go for her. And I get on top of her again. And tell her, don't move. I think he's trying to protect me. I start to pull him off of her again. As that's happening she moves again and he goes for her. Again, I get on top of her. I say, don't move, he's trying to protect me. As I'm pulling him off of her again, she does move again, I'm not sure if it was the second or third time that it was happening with her, but she did strike me with her fist in my right eye. And that's when it changed from overly interested in her to him wanting to bite her."

Hunter thought, Diane struck her in the right eye? I heard that before, but thought it was an error in reporting. I've been misquoted myself the past week or so.

Why on earth, after all Knoller said happened, would Diane hit her?

It didn't make any sense.

It would have been an irrational act. And Diane was not irrational.

The reporter asked, "Do you think, Ms. Knoller, that you bear any responsibility for this attack?"

"Responsibility? No."

The look of Elizabeth Vargas' face was somewhere between stunned and shocked. "You owned the dogs. You were unable to control them. Why aren't you responsible?"

"I wouldn't say that I was unable to control them."

What?! screamed in Hunter's mind. What did she just say? I must have misunderstood. I had to misunderstand.

The reporter said, "You couldn't stop the dog from attacking Diane Whipple?"

"I wouldn't say that it was an attack. I did every thing that was humanly possible to avoid the incident. Ms. Whipple had ample opportunity to move into her apartment.

129

"It took me over a minute restraining Bane from my apartment down to the time that he jumped up and put paws on either side of her. She was in her apartment. She could have just slammed her door."

The TV announcer, her face betraying surprise, asked Knoller, "Can you understand why people might say you weren't able to control this large dog, a dog larger than the victim? The victim is dead after a several-minute-long attack."

"I understand that. But I was on top of Ms. Whipple. I was being bitten as well by the dog. As long as Ms. Whipple was underneath me, he would not bite down. I don't have any puncture wounds, but I was protecting Ms. Whipple. As long as she was underneath me, the dog would not bite down. "

Hunter thought, Marjorie seems to be claiming that it was Diane's fault for trying to get out from under her.

Diane should have stayed under her.

Diane should have gone into her apartment and slammed the door.

Strange defense, the cop thought; it's the victim's fault.

Chapter
Seventeen

A Search Warrant

Stephen Murphy's office, Hall of Justice, General Work Detail, San Francisco, California, Thursday, February 8, 2001.
Steve Murphy was the San Francisco Police Department's liaison with the fed's ATF. He was also attached to the City's General Work Detail.

One of his many job descriptions was preparing search warrants.

He had twenty years in law enforcement. During those years he had investigated thousands of criminal cases: assaults, kidnappings, weapon violations, homicides.

After the Academy, he received training in gang investigation, narcotics investigation, firearms investigation, homicide investigation, SWAT training, forensics training, and the mechanics of both search and arrest warrants.

As a witness, Murphy was recognized as an expert in cocaine, (both base and salt), street gangs, and disguised firearms.

He was a large man, with strong-yet-friendly features and a quick smile.

Henry Hunter asked him to prepare a search warrant request for apartment 604, 2398 Pacific Avenue.

Murphy did so. The search warrant was presented to Judge Leonard Louie. The judge ordered that a special master be present during the search.

A special master is assigned when there is a search of a person or persons involved with the justice system, like attorneys, where there could be a chance of a violation of attorney-client privilege.

Attorney Michael Osborne was assigned the job that involved spearheading the team.

Judge Louie signed the search warrant.

It read:

YOU ARE THEREFORE COMMANDED TO SEARCH:

> *The premises of 2398 Pacific Avenue, apartment #604. San Francisco, California 94109. Further described as an apartment unit with a six-story multi-unit apartment house. The numbers 2398 are affixed above the front entryway to the building. The front door of the building is glass with iron supports. Apartment #604 is located on the 6th floor of the apartment building. The numbers 604 are affixed to the front door of the apartment; and all rooms, attics and other parts within Apartment #604 and all garages, trash containers and storage areas designated for use of Apartment #604, safes or other locked containers, computers and any computer hard drives.*

> *The apartment is in the possession of and under the control of Marjorie F. Knoller and Robert E. Noel, both are attorneys, and use this apartment to conduct their law practice.*

The search warrant was as detailed as possible to prevent entry and search of the wrong premises.

The police and the special master arrived in the hallway of the sixth floor of 2398 Pacific Avenue. The team was comprised of Henry Hunter, Mike Becker, Rich Daniele, Steve Murphy and Mike Osborne.

Murphy's job was to open the door. Hollywood would have one believe that this was accomplished with a kick, or a shoulder blow, or a ram.

Usually, the apartment manager was contacted and opened the door with a master key. Aleta Cerdido could not be found that afternoon.

Murphy used a screwdriver.

Osborne entered first. In the hall he searched a closet. Nothing pertaining to attorneys or their clients. He freed that area for search.

Murphy's job was to oversee Mike Becker and Rich Daniele.

Hunter's job was to oversee everybody.

This duplication, like the checks and balances of the government, was to ensure the law was rigidly upheld.

This process of Osborne being first to enter each room was repeated throughout the apartment. The special master was the only one who searched the office area. There he seized and sealed eleven envelopes and a computer.

The officers waited in the hallway.

Rich Daniele said to Steve Murphy, "I talked to Hank Putek."

"Who is?"

"A neighbor. Lives across the hall in #608. He said he saw Noel and Marjorie leaving this apartment with some boxes."

"When?"

"He's not sure, but he knows it was after the attack."

"Damn it! I knew two weeks was too long."

For obvious reasons, the sooner a search warrant was issued and executed the better.

Osborne finished his preliminary search of the premises. He made a sweeping gesture, like a page waving a courtesan through to a king.

The rest of the team went to work.

Each item seized was tagged as evidence. E-1 was a dog's harness taken from the bedroom closet. Attached was a dog license with the number 34592.

A leash was found.

Then a dog collar.

Then weapons and ammo.

Daniele methodically recorded the evidence as it was found.

E-4 = Highpoint semi-auto pistol, 380, Model CF, serial number P717631, black and silver — loaded with live 380 caliber rounds and an extra box of ammunition.

Also, a black fanny pack, numerous live 380 ammunition inside.

E-10 = Highpoint semi-auto pistol, 380, Model CF serial number P717637, in holster. Live 380 caliber ammunition.

E-11 = Fanny pack — Magazine and extra ammo.

E-12 = Metal box — live ammunition — two holsters.

E-13 = Semi-auto pistol Remington — US property M1911A1 US Army serial number 2387878. US caliber — blue.

Loaded with magazine and live rounds.

One extra magazine loaded with live rounds under the bed.

E-14 = Single-shot shotgun, Hercules, Montgomery Wards and Company.

No serial number. Under bed in case.

Other items were found and tagged. In the kitchen cabinet was found a body-builder for dogs. A dog's leash was found in the hall closet. A spiked dog collar was found in the kitchen.

In all, 22 items were seized as evidence.

The eleven envelopes and the computer would go to Judge Louie. The other items to the Hall of Justice.

Steve Murphy thought his job involving the dog case was finished with this search warrant.

It was only beginning.

Chapter
Eighteen

That's the Law

Michael Cardoza's office, 700 Montgomery Street, Thursday, February 8, 2001.
Sharon Smith had an appointment with Michael Cardoza, former prosecutor for such counties as Alameda and Los Angeles. Now, at 57, he was in private practice.

Sharon entered an old, but immaculately-kept, two-story building. A reception area looked out in two directions at the flow of traffic through the Financial District.

Cardoza shared a receptionist with Angela Alioto, the daughter of former San Francisco mayor Joe Alioto.

The receptionist told Sharon she was expected and that Cardoza's offices were on the second floor.

The lawyer's personal office, like most who had been in law for over thirty years, held mementos of the past. In Cardoza's case, those mementos leaned heavily to sports.

Joe Montana, wearing jersey #16, picture complete with autograph, was next to one with Willie Mays making one of his famous basket catches.

Various newspaper clippings showed legal cases that Cardo, as he was nicknamed by his friends, had won.

The hat rack held a baseball-style cap that had a shark logo with the words "CardoLaw" underneath.

Cardoza introduced himself and said, "Call me Michael."

He was handsome, looking many years younger than his age. A rigorous routine of exercise kept him fit both physically and mentally.

Sharon said, "Michael, I need a lawyer."

"I've followed your story with great interest. I'm heartily sorry for your loss."

She nodded.

He said, "Wrongful death cases involve—"

"I'm not here about a wrongful death lawsuit. I'm worried about the DA, Terence Hallinan. I'm worried because in the past he's, he's—"

The former prosecutor grinned as he interrupted. "Our DA in the past has demonstrated a tendency towards unusual decisions."

"Exactly."

"You want me to make sure that Kayo Hallinan—"

"Follows the law."

"The chief assistant district attorney is Paul Cummins. We played ball with each other in college. I'll talk to him."

"Thank you." Sharon opened her purse and took out her check book.

"That can wait," Michael said. "I want to ask you a few questions." The attorney took Sharon through the events of the fatal afternoon and evening of the attack. She went through the various things that happened: being stuck in traffic, meeting Aleta and Heather, seeing Hank Putek and his wife Ginger at San Francisco General.

Cardoza asked, "Why were they there?"

"They live across the hall. When Hank came home he thought, at first, that it was his wife who got attacked. When he found out she was all right, he discovered it was Alexis."

"Alexis?"

"That was Diane's middle name. That's what I always called her."

"What happened next?"

"Hank called the hospital and told them I was coming. That's why we could park in a red zone out front. Then he and Ginger came to the hospital as support."

She paused, took a deep breath and continued. "Funny, we weren't really close as neighbors until after Alexis died. Now we're very close."

That's the Law

"What happened when you first arrived at the hospital?"

"I was told to go to the waiting room."

* * *

Doctor Isaacs entered the waiting room. He sat beside Sharon. He said, "I'm afraid I have to tell you that Diane lost most of her blood in the hallway."

"Is she alive?"

"She stopped breathing for 23 minutes."

"But now she *is* breathing?"

"Yes. But, the brain after three or four minutes without oxygen loses…" The doctor paused to gather his thoughts.

Sharon thought, I don't want to hear this. This three or four or twenty-three minute business. She's alive. That's what I wanted to know. *She's alive.* I don't care what normally happens in normal people. This is an exceptional person.

The doctor said, "We did the best we could. Her body was basically riddled with bites."

"She's alive."

"Yes, but in an extremely precarious state."

"I want to see her."

The doctor hesitated. He started to say something, paused, started again, and paused again.

Sharon asked, "Is she in ICU?"

"Yes." The doctor pointed at a woman standing nearby. "That's Gloria Young, a social worker stationed here at the hospital. I want you to talk to her."

"I don't need a social worker. Let me see Alexis."

"Talk to Gloria," the doctor said, then added, "I am truly sorry for what happened."

Sharon thanked the doctor, went to Gloria and said, "I want to see Diane."

The social worker said, "Diane was mauled horribly. I don't think that's a good idea."

"I love her. I want to see her."

Gloria nodded and led Sharon to ICU. She opened a door and pointed. "There's Diane. I'm right here if you need me."

Sharon stood at the foot of the hospital bed. Alexis had a white sheet covering her from foot to chin.

Sharon could see just the top of Diane's head.

She started to hyperventilate, gasping for air in quick spurts. She bent forward as dizziness swarmed over her.

Gloria took Sharon's arm and led her back to her office. She put a cold towel, first on her forehead then on the nape of her neck.

Sharon said, "Her face, her beautiful face..."

Gloria sat besides her.

Sharon's numbness was not only in her voice, but gripping her whole body. "She's not going to live, is she?"

"I don't think so."

"I have to go back. I have to see her again."

The two women retraced their steps to the private room in ICU.

Once again, Sharon stood at the foot of the bed.

Only a nearby monitor's needle showing erratic and jagged spikes indicated there was any sign of life.

Someone had been in the room since Sharon was there earlier, moving the blanket. Now Diane's right arm was uncovered.

Sharon stood by the edge of the bed.

The skin looked raw and torn.

There was one spot, on the skin between the thumb and the forefinger, that didn't look violated. One spot, about the size of a half dollar, still recognizable as skin.

Sharon touched the spot.

They were linked for one last time by a connection that started seven years earlier.

* * *

Michael Cardoza asked Sharon, "Did you and Diane ever register as domestic partners?"

"We made a commitment, when we were on a vacation."

"Did you ever register?"

"No."

"One of your options is to file a wrongful death suit."

That's the Law

"I don't want any money."

"Then pledge the money to a charity."

"I've been thinking about setting up a foundation."

Cardoza paused, then plunged on, "Under the current laws, you have no right to even file a wrongful death suit."

"Why not?"

"You're not a member of Diane's family."

"What?"

"That's the law."

"The law doesn't think I'm a member of Diane's family?"

Cardoza pulled out a file and gave it to Sharon. "Assembly Bill 25, recently introduced by Assemblywoman Carol Migden." He pointed at a section.

Sharon read: *"Until the enactment of AB26 in 1999, same-sex couples and their families received no recognition under California law. Even with the enactment of the domestic partner registry with hospital rights and health benefits for public employees, few substantive benefits are available to domestic partners who register."*

Sharon looked up from the file and asked, "What is the law's definition of a same-sex couple?"

Cardoza pointed out another page.

Sharon read, *"AB26 defines domestic partners as 'two adults who have chosen to share one another's lives in an intimate and committed relationship of mutual caring.'"* Sharon said, "That is exactly what Alexis and I had together."

Cardoza continued reading from the bill: *"'…and who file a declaration of Domestic Partnership with the Secretary of State.'* Migden's bill would give domestic partners the right to make medical treatment decisions on behalf of a partner if the partner is in a health facility and is incapable of giving informed consent. So if Diane had lived, but been a vegetable, you couldn't pull the plug. Also, as the proposed bill stands now, among other things, it reads: *'Authorizes a domestic partner to bring a cause of action and recover damages for negligent infliction of emotional distress and wrongful death, to the same extent that spouses are entitled do so under the law.'"*

Sharon mulled on that for a few moments. "So if all of Diane's relatives were dead and Marjorie said, 'Sic her, Bane, kill,' I still couldn't recover damages?"

"As it stands now, that's the law."

"Then we have to change the law."

Chapter Nineteen

Matt Lauer and the Today Show

Henry Hunter's home, Monday, February 12, 2001.
As was his habit each morning before going to work, Henry Hunter flipped on the TV, flopped into his easy chair, and drank his coffee.

On the TV were Robert Noel, his wife Marjorie Knoller and Matt Lauer.

National news again, the cop thought. First, *Good Morning America*, now NBC's *Today Show*.

Noel said, "I advised the district attorney where we were going to be when out of town on trial in Northern California and offered to make available anything that he wanted in respect to the matter. He waited until we were out of town, when he knew we were out of town. His investigators kicked the door down and left the apartment open."

What? Hunter thought. Kicked down the door? Steve Murphy used a screwdriver.

Lauer said, "They took a couple of boxes of evidence with them. What did they take from your apartment?"

"I have no idea," Noel answered. "We haven't been back to examine it."

Lauer asked, "So you have no way of knowing what's missing?

"Not at this time," Noel said.

Lauer said, "Ms. Knoller, on our program Ms. Smith, who is the partner of Diane Whipple, said that they were both terrified of these two dogs of yours — Bane and Hera. That they had had incidents in the past. As a matter of fact, Ms. Whipple had been bitten by one of your dogs in the past. Can you tell me your side of that?"

Knoller replied, "I have had no contact with either Ms. Smith or Ms. Whipple. They are strangers to me. I've never seen them so I wouldn't know what encounters she's talking about. And the dogs were never in their presence when I was in their presence."

Lauer asked Knoller, "The story of Ms. Whipple being bitten by one of your dogs, you're saying, is completely untrue?"

Knoller answered, "Well, it didn't happen in my presence so I can't vouch for anything that happened in Mr. Noel's presence, but it didn't happen in my presence."

"Did you ever have any trouble with either of these dogs in terms of them being aggressive to people?"

Marjorie Knoller said, "Absolutely not. They're just wonderful animals."

Lauer continued. "When these dogs began attacking, or at least one of these dogs began attacking Ms. Whipple, you were taken completely by surprise?"

"Absolutely, completely by surprise. Hera, fortunately, was not involved in the incident, but she was in the hallway. She had no contact with Ms. Whipple at all. It was Bane that I was having the problems with."

Hunter shook his head. Marjorie was still defending Hera. Still claiming the dog did not participate in the ferocious attack.

Lauer recounted statements made in the letter to the San Francisco DA, finishing with Knoller's statement: "Ms. Whipple, instead of what I would have normally done was slam the door shut, followed me out into the hallway again on all fours.'"

Lauer said, "Let me play you a piece of tape. This is what Sharon Smith said on our program last week about that version of the facts."

Sharon Smith appeared on a television monitor next to Lauer. She said, "This is a world-class athlete we're talking about. She probably did everything she could to get into her apartment as fast as she could. To get out of danger."

Lauer again addressed Knoller. "It does sound like unusual behavior by someone who has just been attacked by a dog to go out on all fours and stare down the dog."

Knoller said, "Well, excuse me. I wouldn't say that she was staring down the dog. She just came out of her apartment. And this is significant afterwards on how the event occurred. Ms. Whipple was watching me trying to restrain Bane from a distance of over fifty feet and it took at least a minute for me to restrain him, and another twenty seconds or so once Bane had overcome my resistance and I wound up on my knees with the lead still in my left hand. He jumped up and placing both of his paws — one on the right side and one on the left side of her and then coming down. He had not touched her in anyway, but, just the incident itself prompted me to not know what was going on. Because it was something I had never seen him exhibit before."

Hunter doodled on a napkin. He wrote "Twenty seconds now instead of fifteen," and "Bane had not touched her in any way," and "something I had not seen him exhibit before."

Now it's eighty seconds that Diane stood immobile at the end of the hallway. And Bane went huffing and puffing in a perked up and interested sort of way, towing an anchor-like Knoller who had to weigh — what? One-forty? One-fifty? Whatever, a pretty hefty anchor. So the perked-up dog drags the hefty anchor down the hallway and then just takes a good gander into Diane's face?

The dog expends all that energy just to gaze into Diane's eyes?

Then drops to all fours to do what?

Wait for a command?

What?

On the TV screen, Matt Lauer shifted his attention to Robert Noel. "Mr. Noel, in the letter to the district attorney you suggested that possibly the dogs reacted aggressively because of a perfume or cosmetic product that Ms. Whipple was wearing, or that even possibly she might have used steroids and the dogs reacted to that. It sounds to most people that you are trying to blame the victim."

Noel said, "Definitely not. I had been contacted by a dog expert who suggested that the pheromone-based perfume or steroid use in a world-class athlete might be a possible explanation and all I was doing was asking the district attorney to preserve any forensic evidence that might explain why Bane did what he did. I wasn't saying that she'd done it or used it."

"Were Bane or Hera ever trained to guard or fight?"

"Absolutely not," Noel said, "The dogs have been checked by at least three veterinarians; San Francisco, UC Davis, by professional dog handlers, some of who definitively expressed the opinion that these dogs were never trained to fight or never engaged in a fight."

Hunter wrote in a neat hand, "Absolutely not" and "some expressed the *opinion*."

From an absolute to an opinion in one breath.

The interview continued. "So some of the stories that have come out about these dogs possibly being part of a ring of dogs that were trained by people behind prison walls, you would say what to that story?" asked Lauer.

"It's BS," countered Robert Noel. "Janet Coumbs had the dogs before we got them. She denies ever having trained them. They were never trained in our possession. These dogs just were never near any fights or any training."

Hunter knew that it really wasn't much of a fight when a dog that size kills a chicken or a family cat.

"Is it fair to say," Matt Lauer asked, "that this particular breed of dog does have some kind of history in terms of being aggressive? That others have trained them in the past and noted that they can be extremely aggressive?"

"They can have a hard character," Noel conceded.

Lauer asked, "Were these dogs given any training in terms of obedience to take aggressiveness out of them?"

Noel answered, "Hera was really a gentle soul."

Hunter thought, you didn't answer the question. And if Hera was such a gentle soul, why did your doormat read: "Ask not for whom the dog barks, it barks for thee?"

Lauer wrapped up his interview with Noel and Knoller. "Ms. Knoller, Sharon Smith said she encountered you in the garage of your apartment building. This was a short time after the attack and you said nothing to her in terms of an apology or anything but that you just kind of looked at her and said nothing."

"I didn't know who Ms. Smith was," Knoller answered. "As a matter of fact, the first time that I saw her was on *Prime Time Live*. I had no idea who she was."

"There are possible charges pending. The district attorney is looking into that against both of you. Charges that could go all the way up to second-degree murder. Are you confident that you'll be able to convince him not to bring those charges?"

Knoller said, "I don't know what I can do to convince the district attorney, but I'm confident that in the end I think everything will work out for the best and in our favor. There's been no criminal activity in this incident at all."

"Just a terrible tragedy," Lauer said.

Marjorie Knoller said, "It's a *horrible* tragedy. "

Chapter Twenty

The Fourth Estate

Henry Hunter's office, Hall of Justice, General Work Detail, Monday, February 12, 2001.
The pediatrician predicted March 21 as the exact day the next Hunter progeny would burst gurgling and salivating and kicking into this world.

Everything regarding the upcoming date for the birth of his future grandson was thumbs-up.

Dear Lord, Hunter thought, am I lucky. I feel like a farmer who's never known a drought.

Cindy, a wife I love. Family happy and healthy. Future grandson healthy. And a job I look forward to doing every day.

Over the past few days, information had continued to be gathered regarding the dog case. Tomorrow was dog court, run by Animal Care and Control, for the surviving animal's fate. The female dog Hera would face life or death.

Various factions had rallied on opposite poles of the issue. From "It's wrong to blame and kill the dog," and "There's no such thing as a bad dog, only a badly trained one," to, "Society can't afford to have monsters in its midst," and "Human rights supersede animal rights."

Besides the Whipple Case, other crimes had come across Hunter's desk. Nothing new in that; each day more crimes were committed and other crimes solved.

Hunter knew very well that it was an endless circle of evil being chased by good.

There were more than twenty men assigned to the General Work Detail.

The Fourth Estate

Daniele and Becker had been working exclusively on the dog-mauling case from the beginning, just under three weeks ago.

It had been almost a week since Hunter had checked the growing stack of newspapers on his desk for more stories involving Diane Whipple and the dogs.

He sifted through material on his desk. One of the older news stories led off with the word "Mauling."

He wrote "maul" on a pad and started drawing circles and squares and ovals and rectangles around the word.

Maul. Synonyms were words like claw and mangle and batter. Clawed and mangled and battered. That's certainly what happened to Diane.

When his children were younger, he would play a game with them. Make up a word, then write down as many synonyms as you could think of in one minute.

He wrote BANE in block letters.

Then, quickly, he wrote down: cancer, evil, plague. He paused, felt old brain cells activate, then scribbled: calamity, scourge, curse.

Nice name for a dog.

And in this case, a rather accurate one.

Then we have the dog that didn't get 25 cc's of sodium pentobarbitol. Hera, still alive down at Animal Care and Control, awaiting dog court.

He wrote HERA in block letters on a pad.

Hera, name of the ancient Greek queen of heaven. Wife and sister of Zeus.

Hera, protector of women, in marriage and in childbirth.

Sounds benign, Hunter thought as his brain retrieved an education learned decades earlier. But Hera was also ruthless; ruthless towards the mistresses of her husband and brother, Zeus.

Hunter opened the *Chronicle* dated Wednesday, February 7th and scanned the front page. Above the fold: "Ariel Sharon Crushes Barak in Israeli Election."

Next: "Long Lonely Search in India."

He'd watched that last night on TV. A horrific tragedy. A 7.7 earthquake hit India on the same day Diane Whipple had died. Rampar reduced to rubble.

Under the Rampar article was a story that Robert Noel was angry about the way the search warrant was conducted. He was quoted as saying, "Just another example of the Gestapo kicking down the door of a Jewish home."

What? Hunter thought. Where did this anti-Semitism come from?

Noel went on to elaborate by saying, "The DA chose a time when we were out of town to come over and kick down the doors of a Jewish home."

Hunter thought, back-to-back anti-Jewish remarks. And we kicked Noel's door down? Steve Murphy used a screwdriver because the building manager couldn't be located. Besides, Noel and Knoller had changed the lock and a master key wouldn't have even worked.

Rich Daniele entered and gave Hunter a VHS tape marked: Marjorie Knoller — appearance on ABC's *Good Morning America*.

Watch it again, the cop ordered himself. On the screen Knoller stated, "I wouldn't say it was an attack, and I did everything that was humanly possible. She did strike me with her fist in my right eye, and that's when the dog went from overly interested in her to he wanted to bite her."

Hunter rubbed his forehead. He felt a headache coming on. Phrases like, "wouldn't say it was an attack" and "strike me in the right eye," and "overly interested" were causing a sharp pain behind his temples.

You don't need a litmus test like Pinocchio's nose to know when bull is being hurled.

Knoller went on to state during her *GMA* interview, regarding claims that other people were coming forward with stories about violent behavior regarding the dogs, "Fabrication. A lot of people like their fifteen minutes of fame and come forward with outrageous stories."

Outrageous stories?

Hunter shoved the newspapers aside. He decided, let's take a peek at some of these outrageous stories. He opened a report marked: Bane dog bite — June 2000.

He quickly read the file. He found that Daniele and Becker, after some serious objections by the witness, had convinced a young man, David Mosher, to testify at dog court.

The cop thought, I guess some of us have to be dragged gurgling and salivating and kicking to our 15 minutes of fame.

Rich Daniele appeared in the doorway. He held up a VHS tape. "Interesting stuff. *Prime Time Live* interview of Knoller."

"Talk about the pot calling the kettle black."

"I beg your pardon."

"I just read that Knoller accused witnesses of fabricating things so they could get their fifteen minutes of Andy Warhol fame. Now she's on TV more than Kelsey Grammer."

"Who's Kelsey Grammer?"

"Actor who plays Frasier. Watch this tape with me."

Daniele sat on the couch in his boss's office.

Hunter slid the tape into his VCR.

The interviewer was ABC's John Quihones. He asked what happened.

Marjorie Knoller said, "I really believe that if she had stayed underneath me, and stayed still, that she would be alive today. She was being protected by me. I had the injuries and the blood on me to prove it."

The pause button was hit. Hunter said, "What injuries? The only one I'm aware of is the blow to the eye, but she said Diane did that. Now it comes from the attack itself?"

Daniele nodded. "Seems she can't make up her mind which story to stick with."

The *Prime Time Live* interviewer asked the masters of the dogs, "Was it a mistake to have those dogs living in an apartment building?"

"No," answered Marjorie, "Bane was a people person. A people dog."

Hunter snapped off the television. He gave the VHS tape to Rich Daniele and told him to mark it as evidence and put it into the office safe.

Hunter decided it was time for an introspective chat with himself about Homicide and the Law. He had studied at the University of San Francisco. If the Jesuits had taught him anything it was, when confronted with a problem, to organize his thoughts before plowing ahead.

Hunter thought, let's run through the legal, criminal definitions of murder.

First-degree murder: Death with a destructive device or poison, torture, lying in wait, or while engaged in another crime like arson, robbery, kidnapping, burglary, car-jacking, or rape.

Penalty: 25 years to life. If tried as a capital crime, then life without possibility of parole, or the death penalty.

Like Timothy McVeigh. Using a bomb is one crime. If the bomb kills someone that's another crime. His execution was coming up in May.

Second-degree murder: The willful slaying without any of the prescribed circumstances that qualify for first-degree murder.

Penalty: 15 years to life.

Did this apply in the dog-mauling case?

Marjorie Knoller was not involved in a crime, just walking her dog. But death did occur by a very destructive device.

Voluntary manslaughter: The taking of a human life during the heat of passion, even if there is intent to kill.

Penalty: 11 years in prison.

Like Paul "Cornfed" Schneider stabbing his lawyer in a moment of anger. Except he was already *in* for life.

Involuntary manslaughter: The taking of a life in the commission of an unlawful act not amounting to a felony; or in the commission of a lawful act that might produce death in an unlawful manner, or without due caution and circumstances.

Penalty: Four years in prison.

Walking a dog was the commission of a lawful act. Dog rips someone apart and that produces death and you didn't take due caution, like taking the animal to obedience school training? What degree did that constitute?

Ask a prosecutor. Ask Cummins.

Paul Cummins and Henry Hunter went to the same local high school, Saint Ignatius; and the same college, the University of San Francisco.

Through the open doorway of his office, Cummins saw Hunter standing in front of his secretary, Maria. He waved the General Work officer in and asked what he could do for him.

Hunter asked, "Want to get it clear in my mind what you need to prove certain levels of guilt. I know them by heart if the weapon is a gun or a knife or a baseball bat. But what happens when the weapon is a dog?"

"Manslaughter means negligence by the owners. Murder means evidence of malice. Or, I have always loved the wording on this one, 'an abandoned and malignant heart.'"

Hunter nodded. He had come across the same phrase in earlier research.

Cummins said, "What we lawyers down here on the third floor need from you law enforcement people on the fourth floor is the following: prior violent incidents known by or reported to the owners. Or violence by the animal in the presence of the owner."

"How often are these kind of charges proved?"

"Not often. There's a case going on right now here in California, in Barstow. The Berry case down in Morgan Hill resulted in a conviction. There was a guy in Cleveland who pinned his girl friend down while his dog bit her over a hundred times. He got life."

Hunter nodded.

Cummins said, "Not a lot of cases when you consider there are over fifty million dogs in this country, living in about thirty million houses. According to the Center for Disease Control in Atlanta, there are about four million dog bites reported a year."

"Four million?"

"Four million. And about eighteen a year end up as fatalities, usually among the elderly or children."

"What next?" Hunter asked.

"In a few days we're getting a search warrant from Judge Louie."

"We've already hit the apartment."

"This one's for the convicts' jail cell at Pelican Bay."

Cummins paused, then added, "I need something else from you. Find out if Noel and Knoller ever signed anything stating that they were the owners of the dogs."

"Because?"

"I'm hearing them say that they're guardians, and custodians of the dogs. It might be that they are setting up a possible defense that the dogs aren't theirs; they belong to the convicts. And what do these convicts care if they're hit with a few more felonies? They're already in for life."

Chapter
Twenty-one

Dog Court – Part One

Room 400, fourth floor, San Francisco City Hall, Tuesday, February 13, 2001.
The room where the Animal Care and Control Vicious Animal Hearing would be held, affectionately called by many police "dog court," began to fill very early that afternoon on the eve of Saint Valentine's Day.

Cameramen showed first, busily setting up their equipment, testing sound levels, confirming white balance, focusing their lenses. The cameras, a half dozen, lined the right wall. ABC, CBS and NBC shared space with FOX, CNN and local Bay Area stations.

Shortly before 1:00 p.m., a few members of the press drifted in and took reserved seats in the third row of the large, high-ceiling room usually used for Public Utility Commission meetings.

The first two rows, eighteen seats, were reserved for witnesses. The last four rows contained thirteen seats each, showing that the architect was not a suspicious man, or else he had a strange sense of humor.

At one o'clock sharp, Noel and Knoller showed up, both dressed very casually. They took seats in the front row, to the far right, next to the cameras and photographers.

The judge, Police Sergeant Bill Herndon, arrived almost simultaneously with Noel and Knoller.

The local paparazzi began snapping still pictures of the lawyers.

First, one reporter, then a second and third came over and asked the two attorneys questions.

The public begin to arrive. An older woman and man entered, leading a medium-sized black dog on a red harness. A woman held a magazine called *Our Animals*.

The semi-circled group of reporters around Noel and Knoller grew to a dozen. They were joined by six cameramen. Reporters eyed the clock and scribbled as fast as they could, cognizant of their own deadlines. Cameramen waited, fingers glued to "record" buttons, waiting for ten-second sound and video bites.

The judge called the room to order.

Captain Vicky Guldbech entered. She was the animal control officer presenting the case for the prosecution. The media withdrew to their seats.

She read into the record, "On January 26th, 2001, two dogs, Bane and Hera, owned by Knoller and Noel, were involved in a vicious attack resulting in the death of Diane Whipple. As a result, our department requested this hearing to show the dog Hera to be vicious and dangerous. At this hearing I will be presenting witnesses that will testify to the aggressive nature of this dog.

"I will also be reading statements from people who could not attend this hearing today, as well as any other evidence to show this dog to be vicious and dangerous."

Police sergeant-turned-judge, Bill Herndon, said, "The purpose of the vicious and dangerous dog hearing is to protect the health and safety of the public in the future. It is not to punish for any event in the past."

The judge went on to say, "Information received during this hearing will be the only information used to render a decision on the dog Hera; and any testimony received from the public will be allowed to go forward, and only after will the relevance of that testimony be decided."

The first witness called was David Mosher. He once lived in the same building as Noel and Knoller at 2398 Pacific. He wore a sport coat and slacks. He was in his late-twenties and rather handsome.

Dog Court – Part One

He spoke in an even voice. "I had an incident with the dog Hera in the first few days of June 2000."

*   *   *

The building at the corner of Pacific and Fillmore wasn't ancient, nor was it modern. The elevator was the kind where the door did not slide into a pocket; rather, it opened out like a regular door, complete with doorknob.

David Mosher was carrying a box to the garage. He waited patiently for the elevator to level off with the lobby floor. He opened the door and Noel, Knoller and Hera were standing at the entrance to the elevator.

There wasn't much room to maneuver around the couple and their dog, but Mosher managed to edge past.

A pain erupted in his rear. A searing burn. He jumped away and said, "Hey, your dog just bit me. Bit me on the butt!"

Noel said, "Huh, interesting."

*   *   *

David Mosher cleared his throat, glanced around the packed room and said, "Then the three of them got on the elevator and left, at which point I was just standing there kind of shocked at their reaction."

Mosher went on to say that he returned to his apartment and told his wife, then examined himself to see if the skin was broken and if he needed medical attention.

"Unfortunately, I did not report the incident."

Judge Herndon asked, "Why do you believe the dog bit you?"

"I have no idea."

"Was the dog on a leash? Or was the dog taken away, or did they hold the dog back?"

"They didn't seem to discipline the dog, they didn't apologize for the event."

David Mosher was excused.

Robert Noel walked to the podium. He adjusted the microphone and began. "I recall that particular incident vividly, although in quite a bit different fashion than Mr. Mosher. Marjorie and I were returning from a walk with Hera and were in the lobby waiting for the elevator."

* * *

The elevator at the building at 2398 Pacific would never be confused with an express. It didn't exactly dawdle between floors of the six-story building, but nor did it break any speed records.

In the lobby, Noel punched the elevator button. Marjorie faced the elevator door. To her right was Hera, then Noel.

Marjorie had Hera's leash draped across her arm. The leash was attached to the dog's harness.

Noel heard the elevator start down. He placed his hand on Hera's harness.

The distance from the elevator door to the wall was approximately four feet. The couple had their backs to the wall.

Noel heard a thundering of footsteps on the stairwell.

The elevator arrived at the lobby just as the footsteps arrived at the bottom of the stairs. Mosher appeared. The elevator door flew open.

* * *

Noel adjusted the microphone and continued.

"Mosher was apparently racing this individual. He did not have any boxes in his hand. He bumped into Marjorie, tried pushing between her and the elevator door. When he did, he hit his buttocks on the elevator door handle. I could see that from where I was standing. Hera was between us, controlled by the leash and controlled by me holding the harness when she barked.

"Mosher said, 'I've been bitten.' I didn't walk over and say, 'Huh, interesting.'"

Noel's voice raised slightly. "I said 'bullshit, you hit your ass on the door.'

"He continued running to the garage. He offered no apology to my wife for the assault on her. He apparently was having a race with a friend of his."

The judge asked Noel to elaborate. Noel took the court through the incident again, except this time he finished with, "...having a race with an idiot friend of his."

* * *

Dog Court – Part One

In his office, Henry Hunter listened to the proceedings on the radio. With him was Rich Daniele.

Dog court, Hunter knew, had roots in the Irish contribution to The City. He asked, "Rich, you ever read Kevin Mullen's articles on the history of law enforcement?"

"Couple of them."

Kevin Mullen was a retired deputy police chief and now the Irish Cultural Center's head librarian. He had written a book called *When Justice was Done*, about the history of law enforcement in San Francisco. From time to time he published articles in the *Chronicle* about the history of San Francisco's police department.

Hunter added, "Mullen wrote one a while ago about dog court."

"So?"

"At the turn of the century, before dog court, the cops would just shoot an offending animal out-of-hand. No niceties like a trial and conviction. Just a bullet to the brain."

"Very expedient."

"But not eligible for overtime pay. Cops didn't make much money back then. As a way of making overtime, dog court was created. The job of 'judge' of dog court was an honorary title given to different police officers who needed to make some overtime. A robe was produced, sentence passed on some animal, and a few extra dollars were earned. It was honest work for honest cops."

"What happened to the dog then?" Rich asked.

"After sentence was passed? Still a bullet to the brain."

"Things haven't changed much over the years," Rich said, "at least for dogs."

Hunter continued. "Just as execution of humans evolved from the gallows to gas to lethal injection, dog executions moved from a slug of lead to a needle with enough death in it to fell an elephant."

Hunter and Rich listened over the radio as Noel finished his testimony.

Rich asked, "Do you know who found Mosher?"

157

"Paul Morse," Hunter replied. "What did you think of Mosher's testimony?"

"Fine."

"Morse told me Mosher was reluctant to testify."

Daniele asked, "Why did Mosher change 'bullshit' to 'interesting?'"

"Exactly. If he was fabricating it, 'bullshit' beefs up the color of the story. If anything, Mosher downplayed the incident. His voice never revealed emotion."

"Neither did Noel's."

"A little, when he said 'bullshit.'"

* * *

The dog court's prosecutor called the next witness.

Ron Bosia walked to the podium. He wore a sweater and jeans. He had mutton-chop sideburns. He was slight, but muscular.

The judge asked, "Can you tell me what happened?"

"I'm a dog-walker. I was walking a standard poodle called Bogey for a client in Alta Plaza Park."

Mr. Bosia stopped, started to breath heavily, then told the judge that the cameras were making him nervous.

"Take a breath," the judge advised, "and direct your attention towards me. You'll soon forget about them."

Bosia nodded and continued his statement. "I was walking Bogey..."

* * *

Alta Plaza was a wonderful park for Bogey to stretch his legs. Of course, that day there was more than one dog out taking in the air. There were areas in the park that allowed dogs to be off-leash. There animals could do more than just stretch their legs — they could all-out romp.

Bosia noticed a man and woman with a dog he did not recognize.

Interesting looking animal. And on-leash.

He chatted with the owners and learned they had rescued the dog from a situation. "What situation?" Bosia asked.

The man said, "She was chained up outside and abused by the caretaker."

"She seems to be gentle dog. Want to let her off leash and see if she'll play with Bogey?"

Hera was taken off leash. Bogey went over to check out Hera, as dogs are prone to do. Hera whirled and locked on to the poodle by the skin right behind the ear.

Noel tried to pull Hera away from Bogey. Bosia got Hera in a headlock and pressed his thumbs into the area behind Hera's jaws to try to unlock the rigid grip.

A few seconds later, the dog-walker was able to disengage Hera from Bogey. Hera moved off Bogey without showing any aggression towards Bosia. He examined the poodle and saw that she needed stitches.

Noel gave him his card.

Bosia said, "I'll give this to the dog's owner."

* * *

Bosia continued his testimony. "I got Bogey stitches. I gave the card to my client. As far as I know he never contacted Noel. My client said, 'It's hard to tell who's at fault in a dog fight. I'll take care of my expenses and let Robert Noel take care of his.'"

Bosia explained that later on, with other dogs, he ran into Noel, Knoller and Hera but never saw another attack or act of aggression.

He concluded his testimony. "Bogey, who I walk infrequently, sometimes is a little pushy with other dogs. Bogey's never been in a dog fight before. I'm not sure that Hera was completely to blame for this, but there was an attack and there was aggression."

"How many times after did you see Hera?"

"Three or four, total."

Noel took the podium. "Mr. Bosia's report was factual in nature. The two dogs had been playing together. Bogey had gotten somewhat aggressive. Who did what to who was up in the air, but once we got them separated they were fine. Hera made no move for me or Mr. Bosia when they were separated. And neither did Bogey."

Death of an Angel

The judge called for a short recess.

*   *   *

In his office, Hunter flipped off the radio. He noticed that every complaint about the dogs was rebutted by Noel as being the other person or animal's fault.

That wasn't bothering the former polygraph expert.

In his three decades in law enforcement he had heard all sorts of whoppers. And even, occasionally, the truth.

So Robert Noel blaming everyone except himself for what his dogs did was not bothering the seasoned cop.

Time and motion were bothering the cop.

On a pad, he doodled, "sixty plus fifteen."

Chapter
Twenty-two

Sixty Seconds + Fifteen

Hall of Justice, General Work Detail, San Francisco, February 13, 2001.
Sixty. Plus Fifteen. Those two numbers — 60 and 15 — kept buzzing about Henry Hunter's brain like flies buzz a corpse.

In his hand was a stopwatch. He let the second hand make one full sweep, then let it go for fifteen seconds more.

The former Vietnam search and destroy Army captain thought, how many times has Marjorie Knoller repeated the statement that she tried to restrain Bane for sixty seconds and then was dragged, either as an anchor or otherwise, down the hallway for another fifteen seconds?

Seventy-five seconds. I've been in a fire-fight that lasted *ten* seconds — and it seemed like an hour.

He went to a blackboard on the wall and wrote, in large block letters: SIXTY SECONDS + FIFTEEN. He traced his finger along one of the lines of Knoller's statement: *It was at least sixty seconds before Bane started to pull me down the hallway.*

Why is that bothering me?

He wondered, it's just a minute. Not long. Or is it?

Again he replayed the time-frame in his mind. Sixty seconds is long enough to have people sing *Happy Birthday to You*, blow out the candles and open a present.

Most commercials on television are 15- or 30-second spots. How annoyed would the public become if the commercials were all sixty seconds long?

Sixty seconds.

Long enough for six track stars to run a relay of 600 yards.

Sixty seconds.   Long enough for the chemicals to flow down their respective chutes, combine, begin a chemical reaction and allow deadly gas to begin to fill the gas chamber.

Rich Daniele entered and placed a large file on Hunter's desk. "More information on Noel and Knoller. Mostly law cases. But columnist Patrick May, of the *San Jose Mercury News*, sent up a column he's preparing for later publication.   Lots of great background research on both lawyers."

Daniele left.

Hunter studied the thick files of lawsuits. Too bad you can't arrest a lawyer for overkill.

The sight of the hallway came back to his mind. Overkill was the right word to describe that scene.

Blood on the walls.

Blood on the floor.

Tattered, unrecognizable remains of clothing strewed about.

He picked up the article by Patrick May. He thought, thank God for the press and media on this case. They've given us more information than we've managed to dig up ourselves. But they have different rules for collecting evidence.

And, of course, I don't have the manpower or the finances to send people all over the country.

He read:

"Lawyer says early events led him to fight the system."

The article explained that Noel once worked at the Justice Department in Washington, DC.   That he was present when Attorney General John Mitchell gave the order to arrest the activists in front of the department's building.

Noel told the writer, "I joined to do some civil rights litigation and hopefully kick some KKK butt."

The story went on to relate Noel's move from one coast to the other, ending up in San Diego with the U.S. Attorney's office of Southern California. Since the early sixties, when he married Karen, to the middle eighties, Noel lived the perceived American Dream. Three kids. Home overlooking the Pacific. Good-paying job.

The first marriage fell apart after over twenty years.

The second marriage lasted only briefly.

Then, in San Francisco in 1987, he met Marjorie. He told the reporter, "I knew I'd found the person I'd been looking for my entire existence."

Hunter flipped through the Patrick May file and found material on Marjorie Knoller.

She had once been a lifeguard. She had taught kids to read. She liked helping people.

Noel and Knoller went out on a date on Thanksgiving. Within a week they moved in together.

Noel told the reporter, "I embraced the Jewish concept of tikun olam."

I know what that means, Hunter realized. *To repair a world that has been broken.*

In 1989, in a Jewish ceremony, Noel and Knoller were married.

Noel was alienated, and had been alienated, from his son Rob for years. When asked outside of Pelican Bay Prison about his adoption of the 38-year-old convict, Noel replied, "You don't have to change diapers, or worry about the sheriff bringing him home for underage drinking. At 11 o'clock you know where he is."

The reporter had solicited a comment regarding the strange adoption of a convict from Noel's second wife, who wished to remain anonymous. She said, "It suddenly hit me. He was talking about Rob. What breaks my heart about this whole thing is here's someone who has lost his real son, and this guy in jail has become a substitute. And then it all ends in disaster."

Was that it? Hunter wondered. Not legal access. Not financial access. Just a substitute for something lost?

But that didn't explain why Marjorie went along with it. *She* didn't lose anyone.

Marjorie and those pesky seventy-five seconds.

He remembered that she had bumped the fifteen seconds of being towed down the hall to twenty seconds. Stick with the fifteen, she's used that number almost every time.

He went to his blackboard and drew three lines under the words: Sixty seconds + Fifteen.

Seventy-five seconds.

What actually happened during those 75 clicks on the clock?

Sixty seconds is a very long time for Diane Alexis Whipple to stare at a dog bigger than she was, and do nothing while it fought to free itself from its owner.

How fast does the ball travel in lacrosse?

How quick do you have to be to spin away from someone else's lacrosse racket? Stick? What were those things called?

Fifteen seconds was a long time to watch a massive dog haul its owner down the hallway towards you.

Fifteen seconds was not much time, if you're heating up a cup of coffee in a microwave. Not much time, if you're waiting for your breakfast toast to pop up. But watching a huge dog dragging his owner down a hallway towards you?

You're an All-American and you don't react?

You're an elite athlete and you just stand there?

Hunter needed movement. It helped him to think, occasionally, if he got out of the office. He went to the basement, got his car and began to drive

He passed by a basketball court, kids playing a pick-up game. Hunter took out his stopwatch. Eight seconds for the ball to be brought in-bounds, dribbled down court and a basket attempted.

How long did it take to fling a lacrosse ball down field? Just what shape did you have to be in to play lacrosse?

Any field game with continuous action, such as field hockey, Irish hurling, or soccer meant that the athlete had to be in incredible shape, with snap reflexes.

Just what is the reality, from person-to-person or event-to-event, of how long sixty seconds really is?

I'm at a good movie. Two hours flash by.

I'm at the dentist. Mouth wide open. He's got drill in hand. A minute is an eternity.

Sixty Seconds + Fifteen

He missed a light and stopped, waiting for the signal to change. He knew that stop lights were usually timed for 30-second intervals. Insignificant if you're just out for a Sunday ride. Hysteria time, if, in the passenger seat, your pregnant wife's water just broke.

Maybe I'm obsessing over this, the veteran cop thought, but I know that if Marjorie had simply said, "I came down the stairwell, Bane saw Diane by her apartment doorway, for some reason the dog lunged and I lost control. And I could not, for the life of me, get Bane to quit attacking," then I wouldn't have this incessant itch.

But I'm not the one that stated I fought with a dog for sixty seconds, then wrestled with it while it dragged me for another fifteen seconds.

Probably never find out what really happened in that hallway — either one of Marjorie's many versions, or one of my reenactments.

But sixty seconds, under circumstances that are life-threatening, is an excruciating eternity.

Hall of Justice, General Work Detail, San Francisco, February 13, 2001.
Hunter called Rich Danielle and Mike Becker into his office. The night before, Hunter had reread all the statements that were forthcoming in the dog-mauling case.

Noel had claimed that the police had stood by and done nothing for critical minutes while waiting for the paramedics to arrive.

That accusation had to be addressed.

Becker and Danielle entered.

Hunter showed them Noel's remarks, then asked, "You've both received CPR training?"

Both men nodded.

"Cardio pulmonary resuscitation. And that means that the heart has to stop before being applied."

"Meaning?"

"All police receive the same basic training in CPR. And they are also told not to apply CPR unless the victim has stopped breathing."

"That's Police Academy stuff," Becker said.

"Noel appears to be laying a defense that Whipple might not have died if the cops had done their jobs."

Becker frowned. "We're cops, not paramedics."

Danielle added, "If we cross the line and the victim dies, the department ends up getting sued."

"Exactly," Hunter said. "I remember thinking at the time — what are the cops supposed to do, perform a tracheotomy with a pocket knife? Cops are trained to do CPR. That's it. Some of the officers I talked to said they saw that Diane was still breathing when they arrived. They didn't have any medical training. All they could do was comfort Diane until the paramedics arrived. But a good defense attorney can paint a picture to a jury involving a bunch of cops lounging about, doing nothing, while the victim writhes about on the verge of death. Just remember, what every-one in that hallway did was textbook. Paul Morse told me that his heart felt like it was going to erupt while he stood helplessly by, unable to do anything for Diane."

Becker said, "Not quite everyone in that hallway did what was textbook."

"You mean Knoller?"

Both Danielle and Becker nodded.

Hunter asked his two investigators to go to Animal Care and Control. They were to check on the registration of Bane and Hera with the licensing division.

Danielle drove. Becker scribbled a few reminder notes and sat back in the passenger seat.

Since the horrific attack on Diane Whipple, the two investigators had been assigned exclusively to the dog-mauling case.

The two inspectors had worked for the SFPD for twenty years.

Richard Danielle was raised in the San Francisco Sunset District, attended St. Ceclia's Grammar School, Sacred Heart High School, City College, and San Francisco State.

Fifteen years earlier, Daniele married Teresa Rocha. They had three children: Natalie, Laura and Christina.

Danielle joined the police department in 1981. Over the years he worked at Northern Station, Narcotics, Muni, and now General Work Detail.

He had an identical twin bother, Robert, who was a sergeant with SFPD.

Inspector Michael Becker had amassed a very similar career. He joined the department in September 1982. He'd worked Mission Station, Narcotics, Muni, Taraval Station and now General Works.

Becker also grew up in San Francisco, and went to Thomas Edison Elementary. His family moved to nearby Day City and he attended Colma Intermediate, Serramonte High School, City College of SF, and Canada College in Redwood City.

Becker married 24 years earlier and had four children. Two were in college, one in high school, and one in middle school.

To say the two men complemented each other was an understatement.

They parked on Harrison Street, in the city's Mission District, and entered a two-story building.

Daniele could hear dogs barking. Lots of dogs. He said, "Hera's here. Sitting down some hallway in a cell on Death Row, waiting for Judge Herndon to make his decision."

"What were the odds on life?"

"Thumb up or thumb down? This was one gladiator who's definitely going to get a thumb down."

The two cops went to a counter and met with Mara Camboy. Danielle said, "We're here to check on the registration cards on the dogs Bane and Hera."

The Animal Care and Control officer said, "I remember Noel. He's hard to forget. He came in for the license." She went to a file cabinet, rummaged about, then returned and gave a folder to Becker. Inside were copies of the registration cards.

On the cards involving Hera and Bane were: Robert Noel and Marjorie Knoller — co-owners — dogs Bane and Hera.

The woman asked, "Is that what you needed?"

"Yes," Daniele answered. "If they'd have signed as guardians or custodians, as they've been calling themselves in the media, it might have clouded things under the law."

The two policemen returned to 850 Bryant Street and gave the dog license copies to Hunter.

Hunter filed them in the ever-growing case involving the dog mauling.

Hunter thought, they signed as owners.

Owners.

Not guardians.

Not custodians.

Owners.

So much for the defense, "I was just baby-sitting the dogs. Their real owner is sitting in a cell up in Pelican Bay Prison."

He studied the board and the words "Sixty seconds plus fifteen."

The itch in his brain, the physically unscratchable itch, the itch that could only be satisfied mentally, was rubbing away.

One minute.

Diane Whipple stood at her doorway, at her *open* doorway, holding two bags of groceries, groceries to make tacos before she planned to go to a movie with Sharon Smith; stood there and watched Marjorie Knoller battle a huge dog.

Diane Whipple stood there and watched the second dog race out of the lawyer's apartment; race out and charge down the hallway, only to stop and stare at her.

And still this world-class athlete did *nothing*?

A woman trained to react — react instinctively — freezes?

Doesn't make sense.

Something is very, very wrong with Marjorie's statement.

Chapter
Twenty-three

Dog Court — Part Two

Room 400, San Francisco City Hall, Tuesday, February 13, 2001.

The prosecutor read a statement into the record. "The witness Taylor could not be excused from work. This report is dated January 30, 2001: 'Last Tuesday, when I was in front of their building, I saw Bane and Hera crossing the street with both owners. Hera pulled away from the owners and charged and attacked the dog I was walking. It was seven-thirty AM. I held Hera down until the owner came and got her and took her into the house. On Wednesday, I spoke to Mr. Noel, who was in the elevator with Bane, about the fight. He said Hera was the more protective when the four of them went out.'"

Noel stood at the podium. "Mr. Taylor had been preceding us down the sidewalk as we were coming around the corner. And for some reason unknown to us he had gone up into the foyer area of our building. So when we came around the bushes that blocked the view of the foyer, he and his dog were standing in the middle of the foyer.

"Hera was startled to see Taylor's dog there. He did grab her and she was perfectly satisfied with that."

The prosecutor alerted the next witness. "At this time I would like to call Mr. Neil Bardack, who is here today to testify his dog was attacked by Hera."

A slightly-built, middle-aged man wearing glasses approached the microphone. His hair was salt-and-peppered.

He had already given his statement to the police. Now it was time to tell it to a courtroom full of people. He said, "On September 11th, at about dinner time..."

* * *

Bardack approached the corner of Buchanan and Pacific. His dog tugged, as it usually did, on the leash, anxious for the walk to go on and on.

Neil noticed a woman approaching with a large dog, also on a leash. Looks like a mastiff, he decided.

The woman grew closer. Her dog started to pull her towards Neil. She pulled back. Her dog lunged onto Neil's dog, knocking him over, and sunk its teeth into the back of Neil's dog.

The woman fell and was dragged across the sidewalk. Neil pulled on the woman's dog, which released its grip.

Neil's dog scooted away and ran across the street.

Neil helped the woman up and asked, "Are you all right?"

"Yes, just shaken up."

* * *

Neil Bardack looked up at Judge Herndon. "Never saw that dog again."

"Do you know who this woman is?" asked Herndon.

"I didn't know it before. I know it now. Light brown hair — fortyish. I had never seen her in the neighborhood. Took my dog home. In the evening she was fine. In the morning she was lethargic. Wouldn't get up. Wouldn't move. I called my vet. Took her down. They shaved her side. There was a puncture wound the size of my little finger. The puncture had gone way in, almost to her liver. All kinds of treatments — about seven hundred dollars worth of vet bills when it was all done.

"That was the last of it. Until this incident arose. Someone I know mentioned they saw the dog on TV. I watched the late news and just got a glimpse of one of the dogs coming out of the building. It looked like the breed that attacked my dog."

Judge Herndon asked, "This hearing is about the dog Hera. Do you have any information that leads you to believe that Hera was the dog involved in this incident?"

"I don't know the difference between the two dogs, officer. The dog was a good-sized dog. Big head. I just saw the reddish-brown color and the dark striped marking."

"Why do you believe that either Hera or Bane attacked your dog?"

"Because later on in the week I saw a picture of the woman that looked like the woman I had picked up off the street. And the breed of the dog which has not been seen in my neighborhood the six or seven years I've been around there, led me to believe it was one of the two dogs. Which of the two dogs, I'm not going to say right now."

The prosecutor produced pictures of the two dogs.

The pictures were passed to Neil. He said, "My only concern is, if one of these dogs has been accused of doing something I want to be reasonably certain it is one of these dogs."

He studied the pictures. "This one has the coloration and is the breed of the dog I saw."

The judge asked, "Which dog is that, captain?"

"Hera," answered the prosecutor.

The judge turned back to Bardack. "One last question. Can you identify anyone here in the gallery that may have been with that dog?"

Neil pointed at Marjorie Knoller. "I'd say her."

Neil left the witness podium.

Noel replaced him. "I don't doubt Mr. Bardack's sincerity in testifying the way he did. The only problem with his testimony is that on September the eleventh, at about dinner time, Marjorie was visiting me in the ICU at San Francisco General. Actually, the recovery room at San Francisco General, where I was recovering from an attack, by a Belgian malamute the day before, upon Bane and myself.

"In that attack the malamute charged me, charged Bane, hit me in the face first. I had a lacerated face, cut across the nose, then hit my hands.

"I got knocked to the ground next to Bane and next to the malamute. I was between the dogs. When the dust settled, my finger was almost completely severed.

"The attack ended when Bane returned the bite of the malamute. At the time the malamute had a fang imbedded in Bane's forehead.

"Bane grabbed the malamute once. He released, then Bane released."

The judge asked, "Were the authorities contacted?"

"No." Noel went on to explain that the malamute had previously demonstrated aggressive behavior towards himself, his wife, and both his dogs. And the owner had been warned.

Noel stated, "At the time of that attack, Hera was being walked off-lead. When the malamute hit Bane and hit me, Marjorie told Hera to 'Stay,' and Hera stayed."

The judge said, "Let me ask the Health Department, did you receive any bite report on this?"

"No, we did not."

Noel continued. "With respect to Mr. Bardack's testimony, Marjorie was at San Francisco General at that point in time. And no one else would have been walking Bane or Hera at that time."

"No one was given the authority to walk these dogs?"

"No."

*   *   *

Still in his office, Hunter listened to dog court on the radio. With him was Rich Daniele, who said, "I guess Mike and I are going to S.F. General."

"You're right," Hunter agreed. "To check on the medical records."

"Right. September 11th. Dog bite. Robert Noel. Visiting nightingale Marjorie Knoller."

Hunter nodded. "Except Bardack never said he saw Noel, just Marjorie."

"Too bad guests don't register in hospitals."

"Just Noel's word against Bardack's."

"Noel's and his wife's word."

"Noel always thinks the other guy is wrong."

Hunter said, "That last testimony bothers me. How did Bane bite the malamute if the malamute had a fang imbedded in his forehead?"

Daniele shrugged.

Hunter asked, "You ever see the movie *Liar, Liar*?"

"No."

"It stars Jim Carey as a lawyer incapable, at first, of telling the truth. Very funny. But in the real world, that…"

He trailed off as he heard the tinny sound of the prosecutor came over the radio. "At this time I would like to read a letter from a Donald B. Martin, DVM. It's addressed to Ms. Knoller. There is no date."

*   *   *

The prosecutor held up the letter and began to read.

"The following is a letter written by a Doctor Martin, who is a veterinarian. He writes: 'Enclosed are rabies certificates and health certificates you requested of eight dogs located at Janet Coumbs'.

"'Physically I found the dogs in great shape with the exception of Satan, who had an infection in the left eye. This did not appear too bad. It was probably due to an injury.

"'However, I would be professionally amiss if I did not mention the following so you can be prepared: these dogs are huge, probably weighing in the neighborhood of a hundred pounds each. They've had no training or discipline of any sort. They were a problem to even get to, let alone vaccinate. You mentioned having a professional hauler gather them up to take them to La Puente. Usually, this would be done in crates, but I doubt getting them into anything short of a livestock trailer would work — and if let loose they would have a battle.

"'To add to this, these animals would be a liability in any household, reminding me of the recent attack in Tehama County to a boy by large dogs who lost his arm; was disfigured in his face.

"'In any event, do as you wish, I've given you my opinion.'"

The prosecutor placed the letter back in a file.

Noel stepped to the microphone. "I notice that the letter is unsigned and at the top there is a tag line from the *San Jose Mercury News*. I thought it had come from the San Francisco Police Department."

The judge asked, "Is Doctor Martin the veterinarian who treated your animals?"

"He's a veterinarian that we engaged to vaccinate the animals and issue health certificates so that they could be transported from where they were being poorly kept."

Noel paused, glanced at his notes, then continued. "Dr. Martin declares that the dogs were found in great shape. That was not quite accurate. When we picked up Hera and the other dogs and transported on April the first, 2000, along with retired police lieutenant Jim O'Brien who runs O'Brien Transport Service out of Burlingame...we found the dogs to be in less than great shape."

Noel then told the court about the condition of the dogs he and his wife picked up. How they were kept in a pen with a gate made of four-by-eight sheets of plywood nailed shut.

"Hera was grossly underweight. She was a full-grown female at that point. She should have weighed about 110-120 pounds. When we had her weighed at Pets Unlimited, her weight was 69 pounds."

For the first time since starting to testify, Robert Noel's voice broke slightly. "She had a raw band of skin around her neck from the collar, from having been chained to a tree for a year in the weather in the mountains."

Noel talked about Dr. Martin and the dogs being a problem for O'Brien Transport to ship in crates. Noel said, "There was no problem in shipping Bane and Hera.

"And there was also no problem with Hera at the Holly Street Veterinarian Clinic.

"The staff was so confident of her behavior that they didn't put a collar or harness on her. She was led out on a slip lead, a loop around her neck."

Noel cited other examples of incidents where Hera was in places — such as in the waiting room of a vet with other animals like dogs and cats — where she acted docile.

Noel concluded by telling the court that a vet found a foxtail burr in one of Hera's ears that had been buried long enough that there was concern over her hearing. And even in such pain, she did not react violently to others.

Dog Court – Part Two

The judge called for a ten-minute recess. Cameramen raced out of the double doors and lined up in the hallway in a semi-circle. They waited expectantly, each accompanied by a reporter, for Noel and Knoller to exit.

The two lawyers did not appear in the hallway. The reporters waited in vain.

* * *

Hunter said to Daniele, "Seems to me that I remember, when you interviewed Janet Coumbs, that she said the dogs were healthy. Weighed in at something like 140 for Bane and 100 to 110 for Hera."

"That's what I remember."

"Noel's claiming they were emaciated."

"Guess I'll be checking vet hospitals next."

Hunter glanced at his computer screen. "This case is killing my budget. Seems like I have half the office working it."

"Nothing else going on that has so much pressure to produce from the media."

"The media and..." Hunter pointed at the floor. One flight below was the district attorney's office.

Daniele completed Hunter's thought. "...and those who must be obeyed."

Hunter grinned at the reference to the BBC TV show *Rumpole of the Bailey* and the much-used line referring to the barrister's wife, "She who must be obeyed."

Except Daniele was talking about the district attorney's office and Terence Hallinan.

Prosecutors couldn't do their jobs unless the cops did theirs — a relationship that was truly symbiotic.

Chapter
Twenty-four

The Homeless

The Hall of Justice, Room 411, General Work Detail, February 13, 2001.
Henry Hunter had an itch. He had itches before in his life. They started in the back of his head, a gnawing feeling that he was missing something.

That itch came sometimes because he was missing a fact that was right in front of him, or it came sometimes as a warning.

Like that tour of duty in Vietnam.

He'd been a platoon leader in a search and destroy outfit. With no disrespect to the dead, and a lot of respect towards the weather, soldiers sometimes would "appropriate" a fallen comrade's poncho. One poncho might keep off some of the rain if you were standing up, but you semi-drowned if you lay down to catch some sleep. Two ponchos, cleverly stitched together with a few sticks, made for an impromptu tent. When the flaps were down, the twin hoods protected a soldier's head from getting whipped by wind and soaked with rain.

They were in the field. Hunter jury-rigged his makeshift tent.

He nestled down and tried to sleep.

The escape of unconsciousness would not come. But the itch started in a place he couldn't scratch.

He lifted the stitched hoods and stared at the sky. To the northeast was a break through the dark clouds, allowing a touch of blue to shine through.

Be nice to be under some sunlight. Be nice to be anywhere except where I am.

The Homeless

Not really *anywhere* else. There were worse places than huddling under plastic in a country an ocean away from home.

Think positive. Where else was worse?

How about sitting in the Death Watch cell in San Quentin? Sitting on a bunk thirty feet from the gas chamber. Waiting, within a few hours of certain death by cyanide gas.

Rather be here.

How about being beaten by bamboo sticks by a half-dozen guards wearing black pajamas in a VC prison camp?

Rather be here.

How about standing in front of your doctor when he says, "You have a terminal brain tumor. Cancer Inoperable. Incurable. Your last days will be a nightmare."

Rather be here.

Here was with his outfit the Delta Company, Fifth, of the 46th Infantry Division of the 198th Brigade of the Americal Division. Americal, from the American Forces in New Caledonia — WWII nomenclature.

Americal Division was the largest in our Army's history. A normal division had 10,000 men. The Americal had about 27,000.

Except, Hunter knew, the other 26,985 were someplace else. He and his hacked-down company of fifteen were trying to sleep somewhere in a forward area.

In the Dragon Valley.

And like a dragon, the valley breathed flames and spewed death.

*   *   *

The squad reached its approximate quadrants after the sun went down. It was a cloud-covered night. Pitch black. But the first false dawn was making its barely-perceptible mark on the coming day.

So far, the war had taken some of Hunter's closest military friends. Two had died almost simultaneously when taken out by a machine gun. They had been walking on either side of him.

He'd had the itch moments before the men were hit.

Now the itch was back.

177

A heavy gust of wind slammed the impromptu tent.

Both hoods of the ponchos flopped down.

Hunter started to rise up. Three bullet holes, like magic, appeared in a neat row above his head in the plastic hoods.

Damnation, he thought, his gallows humor bubbling, now the tent will leak.

He and the others in his team battled and killed the ambushers. They had inadvertently set up camp last night in a clearing. In the dark they thought they had 360 degrees of jungle tree protection. There was a large gap that had exposed their position to attack.

But the team had successfully overcome the initial surprise and shock and taken out the ambushers.

The fear hit Hunter later. After he had slept. But fear did come, after the itch had left.

*   *   *

Hunter sat at his desk on the fourth floor of the Hall of Justice. That life-threatening warning itch from long ago was different then the one he was feeling now.

This was the itch that meant he was missing something.

Something involving Noel and Knoller.

Something that didn't jibe with his mental picture of the two attorneys.

He rifled through the stack of *San Francisco Chronicle*s on his desk.

Day One: 26th of January. Nothing except reports of what happened in the hallway.

Day Two: Nothing. Just background on Diane, the victim, the dogs and their owners.

He flipped through newspapers. He found notes that Becker and Danielle had made on the background of the two defendant.

Robert Noel: Family — father and sister died of cancer. Mother remarried, they then moved from just outside Baltimore to a tobacco farm. College — University of Maryland, under-graduate and law. Employment: federal prosecutor for the U.S. Department of Justice, then U.S. attorney in the Southern District

178

The Homeless

Court of San Diego.. This was followed by jobs at two top law firms. Marriage — 23 years to Karen. Second marriage lasted for twenty months.

Marjorie Knoller: adopted by a dentist and a former beauty pageant queen. College — Brooklyn College, McGeorge School of Law. Marriage — once.

While Knoller was studying for the bar in 1987, she met Noel.

After both divorces were finalized they immediately married. In 1988 they started their own law practice.

But deep background wasn't what was giving Hunter the itch. It was more recent — something after they had married and left the law firm.

He opened another file. There it was. The reporter wrote a piece on how the couple were suing everyone.

Except there was a mention that they once represented the homeless.

The itch in his head disappeared.

Pro bono?

Of course, pro bono. What homeless person could afford to hire and pay a retainer to a lawyer, let alone two lawyers?

But who did the homeless person sue?

And for what?

Questions, questions. That's what a cop's job is all about.

Mentally picture the problem. I'm homeless. I'm begging on the street. A retailer gets annoyed at the bad image in front of his business. He gives me the bum's rush.

Can I sue for that?

Noel and Knoller, from all accounts, usually sue the system. Like prison guards. Or, by extension, prisons.

But the homeless?

There can't be any real money in it. By the time the city attorney did her stuff, the ratio of dollar-to-hour pay-back to the plaintiff's attorney would end up the same as a McDonald's employee flipping burgers for minimum wage.

The lieutenant doodled on a yellow legal pad, drawing circles, ovals, squares and rectangles around the word "homeless."

Didn't make sense.

But there it was, in black and white newsprint: The two lawyers represented the homeless.

The homeless.

Not *a* homeless.

Had Noel and Knoller represented a group of homeless?

What? A class action for the disenfranchised?

Give me your poor, your hungry, your homeless and I'll sock it to some social service agency for not doing its job; fast enough, polite enough, or thorough enough.

Hunter studied the rest of the newspaper article.

Interesting. Noel and Knoller apparently mastered the art of burying their opposition under piles and piles of information. Missives as long as novellas.

Discovery on minor lawsuits worthy of a case like the United States v. Microsoft.

Annoy the opposition with enough trivia and they'll eventually settle regardless of the worthiness of the case, just to get rid of you.

A tactic. A legal tactic. A tactic not practiced by many members of the bar.

Noel and Knoller sued prisons and guards on behalf of convicts. They sued prisons on behalf of guards.

If they had an ideology, it wasn't one Hunter admired.

Hunter dropped the report on his desk. I can't get the image of a homeless person— Oops, the homeless *persons* out of my mind.

He knew "homeless" as a search engine wasn't going to get him anything.

He tried: Noel, Robert.

He typed. The computer whirred.

He meticulously sifted through the material.

As he worked, he carried on an internal conversation with himself.

I thought these guys were tax attorneys. Then what's all this prison stuff? They do taxes for the guards like Tim Robbins did in *The Shawshank Redemption.*

The Homeless

Noel and Knoller claim the CDC is subjecting the convicts to hundreds of X-rays. They're suing Pelican Bay, the warden and the CDC on behalf of Paul Schneider and Dale Bretches.

Death by radiation? Slow death by radiation. *Very* slow death by radiation, since they're still alive. Why hundreds of X-rays?

He knew. The guards were looking for metal shanks located in unmentionable places.

Hunter continued his search of Noel and Knoller's legal cases.

In May of 1988 Marjorie Knoller and Robert Noel quit their jobs at a prestigious San Francisco law firm and went into practice for themselves.

They stopped doing tax law.

They represented a guard at Pelican Bay named John Cox. Cox had testified to some of the sadistic goings-on at the prison by guards against convicts.

Cox hired Noel and Knoller. Soon the couple were representing more prison guards with issues against the California Department of Corrections.

They lost the case against the CDC involving Cox. The guard hanged himself.

They defended another Pelican Bay guard who was accused of using the Aryan Brotherhood to give "attitude adjustments" to child molesters.

Their case failed. The guard was found guilty.

A prisoner who testified for the guard was murdered.

Hunter continued researching. He found that in 1992, Noel and Knoller approached a tenants' association at the Geneva Towers. The "Towers" was a public housing high-rise in San Francisco. The Towers' tenant representative at the time was Elzie Lee Byrd.

The two lawyers wanted, on a fee-based contingency, to represent the association.

Elzie told Noel and Knoller he and his two sons were being hassled by security guards at the building. In 1994 Noel and Knoller won the case.

Spurred by victory, Elzie filed a lawsuit against the Towers' management because the apartments were kept in deplorable condition.

Noel and Elzie went to court.

The jury found Elzie's apartment *was* uninhabitable. Then the jury, as juries sometimes do in wisdom unfathomable to those not in on their closed arguments, decided that Elzie owed over five grand in back rent on the pig sty he'd been forced to live in.

The judge ordered him to pay up. Elzie didn't have the money. He and his two sons were booted out.

The next head of the Geneva Towers' tenants association was Marie Harrison. She decided, for whatever reason, to use the same two lawyers and follow the same path as Elzie. It was time to sue. Enter Noel and Knoller, friends of the poor.

Results? She won her case and was tossed out of her apartment for the same reason as her predecessor.

Hunter decided to check the periodicals and do a search on Marie Harrison and Elzie Byrd to see if he could find any follow-up articles.

He found something in *SF Weekly Magazine*. An article quoting Marie Harrison: "I thought Bob was messing up the case so bad that I stood up in court and started talking for myself. The judge told me to sit down, I already had a lawyer."

Hunter shook his head in amazement.

Elzie and Marie. Plus Elzie's two sons. All four end up on the street. Homeless. Two cases, where, when you met your clients they had a roof over their collective heads, and after you're done with them they're living on the street. You claim you represented the homeless that you helped *create*. And then you add, because you didn't collect a contingency fee, that you did it pro bono.

What convoluted logic.

Chapter
Twenty-five

Dog Court — Part Three

Room 400, San Francisco City Hall, Tuesday, February 13, 2001.

The spectators shifted in their seats. The cameramen fiddled with their cameras. The prosecutor called for postal carrier John Watanabe to take the stand. He wore glasses and a neatly trimmed beard.

The mailman said, "I have been a mail carrier for ten years. I have a route right next to where the dogs live. On the second or third week of January, I started my route."

John recounted what he had told Paul Morse earlier. How he was attacked by both dogs and used his mail cart to defend himself. He testified that the dogs would not stop until the owners ordered them to do so.

"Do you recognize the couple?" asked the judge.

"This gentleman right here."

"Mr. Noel?"

"Yes."

"The lady present when this incident took place?"

"Sitting right here."

"Marjorie Knoller?"

"Yes."

"Did the dogs have leashes on them?"

"No."

"Did they have collars?"

"I don't remember that."

"Were you bitten?"

"No."

"Were you afraid?"

"I was terrified."

"Why were you afraid?"

"These dogs were snapping at me. I have never come across a situation in all my years of delivering the mail where you had two dogs of this size and this vicious."

The witness was excused.

Noel addressed the court.

"I was there for that particular event," he said, "and again it did not occur quite as Mr. Watanabe indicted."

*   *   *

Marjorie and Noel parked their Blazer about thirty feet from the front of their apartment building. Hera was in the back seat; Bane in the luggage compartment.

Noel put a six-foot lead on Bane and unloaded him from the back.

Marjorie opened the backdoor. Hera's lead was attached to her. Hera saw Mr. Watanabe's mail cart parked next to a tree.

Hera ran at the mail cart and began barking at it. Marjorie called to her and Hera returned.

Another letter carrier across the street delivering mail to a building called, "Watanabe, is everything okay?"

Mr. Watanabe answered, "Yes, fine."

*   *   *

"Bane was never anywhere near Mr. Watanabe," Noel claimed. "Hera never got anywhere near Mr. Watanabe. I never even saw him from my point of view and I had a clear view of the mail cart.

"We have seen Mr. Watanabe in the neighborhood any number of times; we've lived in that neighborhood for eleven years. Mr. Watanabe's drop box is right on our corner. He never complained to us. He never made any complaint."

The judge had a question for Noel. "The mailman seemed quite adamant that both dogs were very close to him. He said they were being very ferocious, their heads were very big, and his cart was between him and the dogs. You're saying it was only Hera, not Bane."

"That's right."

Dog Court – Part Three

"There was a lead on one of the dogs?"

"There was a lead on both of them. Hera came out of the back seat rather quickly and Marjorie lost a grip on the lead. Marjorie told her to stop and come back. Hera stopped and came back. It was at the mail cart that Hera was directing her interest, not at Mr. Watanabe, because he was nowhere in view."

"Would a mail person normally leave his mail cart unattended? On the sidewalk?" asked the judge.

"Sure. Otherwise, he'd have to drag it up the steps. That building has two steps up to the lobby with the mailboxes."

"He seemed quite adamant to me that he was very close to the dogs, but your perception is different?"

"My perception is very much different. I was back of the Blazer, thirty feet away, with Bane and my wife." Noel took his seat.

The prosecutor rose. "I have a letter from a resident, a Mrs. Ballard, of 2398 Pacific. She wrote: 'My first impression when introduced to the dog Hera by R. Noel, I was taken back by the huge size and powerful built dog. The next time I encountered Hera her demeanor was different. My instincts told me to beware of this confrontational animal. R. Noel had the dog/dogs on leash when they were in the hallway. But Mr. Knoller did not always have a leash on the dogs/dogs. I told her I don't appreciate to encounter the dog/dogs in the hallway in the first place and especially not without a leash. This is irresponsible. Knoller answered, "They won't harm me."

"'How can M. Knoller expect to be able to control two dogs totaling over two hundred pounds, or even one dog weighing over one hundred pounds?

"'I saw R. Noel once in the street with his two dogs and he had a problem controlling them and he is a tall, heavy-set man. These huge, strongly-built unpredictable dogs do not belong in an apartment building.' Dated February 11th, 2001."

The prosecutor put the letter back in its folder.

Noel took the podium and said, "This statement by my longtime neighbor, Ms. Ballard, does cause me concern because I have encountered her any number of times since Hera moved in, and she has never expressed any trepidation about the dogs. As far as I know, she has never said anything to Marjorie.

"In fact, it took some time before anyone in the building realized that Bane had taken up temporary residence, because the dogs did resemble one another.

"It wasn't until the middle of December when Ms. Ballard realized there were two dogs. They were that inconspicuous in the building.

"I did make an effort not to have the dogs get anywhere near her or one of our other neighbors, Ester, because one is rather elderly and has difficulty walking and I would not subject a person in those circumstances to a close proximity to the dogs. Not because I was fearful of the dogs, or anything, but because they were large dogs and I didn't want a misstep to occur.

"With respect to Ester, when I first tried to introduce Hera to her she indicated that she had some childhood problems with dogs that were rather severe and she'd rather not be around dogs. So I made a special effort not to have Hera come anywhere near her. And the same with Bane."

The judge asked, "You felt they were gentle dogs?"

"Yes, they were."

"You feel they would make good household pets?"

"Yes. Hera especially."

"I believe you stated initially that when you picked them up, Bane was the friendlier of the two dogs?"

"Bane was described by Ms. Coumbs as an absolute lover. I've seen reports from her since the incident were she has expressed the opinion that she was absolutely surprised that Bane was involved because he was such a lover. And that was pretty much his reputation in the neighborhood. Hera was somewhat more reserved, but was not the least bit concerned about strangers."

"If Hera and Bane were such friendly dogs why did this incident happen?"

"I can't explain it. I wasn't there for the incident, I can't answer that. Their behavior was totally out of character for either one of them. I saw Hera being led out of the house by animal control officers on the day of the incident. It appeared to me that she did not have any blood on her. My speculation on that would be that since Ms. Knoller was the one who secured her and took her back into the apartment, that any blood on Hera came from Marjorie.

"When I encountered her in the company of the entire SWAT team and the two inspectors on the sixth floor, she was literally covered in blood. Her hair was matted with it. Her face was covered with it. Her sweat shirt was soaked in blood, both front and back. Her sweat pants were soaked in blood. Her sleeve was shredded. She had tears in her sweat clothes. And her hands were bathed in blood.

"If you can, picture Lady Macbeth with her hands covered in blood."

The judge called Jessica Young to the stand. She was in charge of animal care at the control center where Hera was being held in isolation. She began her testimony.

"On the Monday following the impound of the dog, my supervisor, Pat Brown, paged me and let me know that the owners of Hera had dropped some personal belongings; toys, food, some treats, and asked me if I could bring them to Hera. I did."

Jessica explained how she secured the dog and placed the items in the cage. She noticed feces in the run. "When I glanced at the feces I noticed that there seemed to be a foreign substance mixed in with the feces which I assumed to be clothing. There were blue and white fibers. I notified my supervisors. By the time we returned, the feces had been picked up and disposed of. We were not able to examine them more closely.

"This was her first bowel movement since she had been impounded. I was there Friday when she was impounded. I worked Saturday, Sunday and Monday. She had not passed any stool."

"Anything to add?" asked the judge.

"I was there Friday night when the dog was brought in. I could also see blood on Hera's chest. She has a small white star on her chest. Part of the star was red, which I assumed to be blood."

Death of an Angel

The witness was excused.

Noel took the stand. "I do want to note that the person from animal control found bits of blue fiber and white cotton in the stool from Hera. Hera has a blue cotton rug that she uses as a chew toy that was purchased at Cost Plus. And she would sometimes sit there and pull it to shreds. My understanding is that Ms. Whipple's clothing consisted of khaki-colored material and did not contain any blue or white fabric."

The prosecutor said, "Next I would like to call San Francisco police officers Laws and Forrestal."

Forrestal was a Caucasian woman about thirty. Laws was an African American about the same age. Both women were attractive. Both were wearing their uniforms. Forrestal walked business-like to the microphone and said, "On January 26th, my partner, Officer Laws, and I were dispatched to 2398 Pacific regarding a dog complaint. It was a high-priority call. The dispatcher advised us that there were possibly two dogs on the sixth floor, out of control."

She told her part of the story. Then Officer Laws told her part. What happened to them slowly emerged.

* * *

In front of the building, officers Laws and Forrestal were stopped by a man. He said, "I'm a resident here." He held up a cell phone. "I reported it. There are some dogs above the fourth floor. Barking loudly. There's a woman screaming."

The two officers split up on the ground floor, Forrestal taking the elevator and Laws taking the stairs.

Forrestal exited the elevator and saw the victim lying face down, naked. The victim's clothes were shredded.

There was blood. Blood on the walls, on the floor.

My God, the body's riddled with dog-bite wounds. But there was no dog in the hallway.

Officer Laws raced up the staircase. Near the entrance to the sixth floor she passed a dog headed in the opposite direction.

Looks like a pit bull. Maybe involved in the attack.

She yelled at her partner, "Dog just passed me! To my right. No collar. No leash."

"Where did it go?"

Officer Laws saw the victim. She swallowed hard and said, "Don't move."

* * *

The judge interrupted. "Do you know which dog this was?"

"It was Hera," Officer Laws answered. "The smaller of the two dogs."

"Are you sure of that?"

"Yeah. When they took both dogs out of the apartment, I looked at both dogs and it was the female."

"What happened next?"

"I took Marjorie Knoller aside and asked what happened? She said Bane was pretty much the aggressor, but Hera was pulling at the victim's clothing."

The two officers sat down. Noel walked to the lectern. He was asked to explain Hera's behavior.

"I can't explain it. I wasn't there for the incident. Their behavior was totally out of character for either one of them."

* * *

Hunter closed his eyes. Something didn't fit. Forrestal wrote out the original Police Incident Report. Nothing she and her partner testified to in dog court contradicted anything in that report.

Because the truth never changes.

But some of the things they said contradict what Marjorie Knoller said. Like a dog loose in the hallway.

Knoller stated that she had put both dogs away before the cops showed up.

Bane in the bathroom and Hera in the bedroom.

But now we have Hera running around the hallway and stairwell.

The truth never changes. If a statement changes, then either the first statement or the second is a lie.

Only lies change.

Chapter
Twenty-six

Acid and Two Letters

The Hall of Justice, General Work Detail, Tuesday, February 13, 2001.

"Crimes conducted from Prison" was written on the packet Becker delivered. On the outside of the file, in large block letters, was the name: "PAUL SCHNEIDER."

Hunter listened to the radio as Sergeant/Judge Bill Herndon asked the prosecutor to call the next witness. Daniele excused himself and went back to his desk.

Hunter went back to the packet that Becker delivered. On the outside of the file, in block letters were the words: "PAUL SCHNEIDER — CRIMES CONDUCTED FROM PRISON."

The file was being compiled in case Schneider was called in a potential future criminal case against Noel and Knoller.

Another file, Hunter thought. In 30 years as a cop, he had served the city in 21 different capacities for the police department. And always files.

Years giving polygraphs was only a tiny bit of the variety he had seen. His nondescript, seemingly impossible-to-be-a-cop appearance had made him invaluable when he was placed in decoy.

He dressed looking like a bum. He'd act drunk. He'd stumble around. Sooner or later, but usually sooner, someone would think they had an easy mark and try to roll him. His backup team would come out of hiding. The perpetrator was given a quick drive to the Hall of Justice and the team would hit the streets again, looking for the next predator.

Acid and Two Letters

The decoy unit was so successful that muggings in San Francisco dropped to near zero.

They were so successful that the city disbanded the unit. Three months later, of course, the mugging statistics were back to normal.

He opened a file flagged: Background Bio on Paul Schneider. He read:

Height: six feet two

Weight 220.

Blue eyes. Blond hair.

Tattoos: "A" and "B" on right hand — symbol of the Aryan Brotherhood.

Born: 1962 in Cerritos, California.

Family: two younger sisters.

Employment: 16 — worked for Continental K9 – handling protection dogs.

Air force: Strategic Air Command. Crewman KC-130 aerial refueling tanker. Discharged for writing bad checks.

Manager pizza parlor. Robbed restaurant. Robbed Alpha Beta supermarket.

Arrested 1985 — incarcerated New Folsom State Prison.

1987 — stabbed a prison guard in the neck.

1990 — stabbed defense lawyer. Motive — to embarrass the warden. Warden Campbell had bragged about his new security arrangements. About the defense attorney, Schneider wrote: "I didn't like his attitude, his smart aleck remarks, nor his demeanor."

Given life sentence. Transferred to Pelican Bay Prison.

Favorite author — J.R.R. Tolkien.

Favorite pastime — painting, with particular emphasis on runes, the ancient alphabet of early Germanic languages.

Quite a history for a relatively young man, Hunter thought. He read another file on Paul Schneider's crimes in prison and began to visualize what he was reading: How Schneider managed to use a friend on the outside to get him drugs.

* * *

In Sacramento, even a normal day inside the attorney general's office was chaotic. Paul Schneider's outside confidant and helper didn't need to have the honed skills of a master thief. He wasn't sure that what he planned to steal carried even a misdemeanor charge.

Get an AG envelope, were his instructions. Just an envelope. No stationery, just an empty envelope with the attorney general's official return address on it and the Great Seal of the State of California.

Paul Schneider's friend entered the outer offices of the attorney general of California. People bustled about, carrying out the business of serving the citizens of the richest state in the Union by enforcing the letter of the law.

The man waited patiently, pretending to study literature that described the fine job the lawyers working at the AG's office were doing to earn their salaries.

He could see a stack of envelopes sitting on the shelf behind the counter. Too far to reach, unless you had an arm like Michael Jordon, and even then it would have been a stretch.

A pretty girl, mid-twenties, came over and asked, "May I help you?"

The man fumbled in his pockets and pulled out a stub of a pencil. "I need something to write on." He pointed at the envelopes. "Something small, just need to make a note."

She handed him a clean envelope with the return address of the attorney general of California in the top left corner and a reproduction of the Great Seal of the State of California.

The man thanked her and left. Then he went to the nearest Kinko Copy Center and ran off a hundred copies of the envelope.

Cornfed had been right, the man thought, no problem.

He went back to his motel room. From a briefcase he removed a sheet of 8½ X 11 paper and placed it on a table. The paper was one of many legal briefs that Cornfed had mailed him. Cornfed had a stack of legal briefs from the AG's office because of the numerous lawsuits he had instigated against the California Department of Corrections.

He turned the legal brief over to the blank side. Methodically, he placed a small dab of blotter acid in one corner.

Acid and Two Letters

He worked his way across the paper, lining up blotter acid in neat rows and columns.

When he was done there were 100 hits on the back of the legal brief. Should last Paul and Dale at least a few weeks, he knew, and slid the legal brief into the AG envelope.

He neatly wrote out the address of Pelican Bay Prison and prisoner Paul Schneider's inmate number. He placed the correct postage on the envelope and went to the nearest mailbox and posted the letter.

Paul Schneider received mail constantly from the California attorney general's office, mostly responses to his civil rights cases. Cases like abuse of person for being X-rayed hundreds of times, or not paying interest on money held in trust by the prison.

The first mail delivery of blotter acid was successful.

The mail drops continued. Material between the AG's office and prisoners was given only a cursory glance by correction officers.

The scheme worked. Paul and Dale decided that as long as no one was even bothering to look in the envelopes, they should ship in some Humbolt Gold.

Blotter acid was okay, but nothing was a substitute for the marijuana grown in the nearby forests of Humbolt County, Del Norte's southern neighbor.

The correction officer on duty that day arrived and started to hand over the day's mail. The envelope had not been sealed properly; a bud of marijuana rolled out of the envelope and onto the guard's boot.

The guard pointed and said, "What's that?"

Cornfed shrugged. He told the guard, "Beats me. Looks like broccoli."

The suspect broccoli was inspected by the guard's nose. The rich poignant aroma of well-grown hashish was detected.

Cornfed was charged with having drugs in prison. His case went to the United States District Court. His defense? "I don't know why the attorney general was shipping me drugs."

*　　*　　*

Henry Hunter closed the file. Rather ingenious. Like Hawthorne's *Scarlet Letter*, hide something in plain view in a place where it seems the norm.

Hunter turned up the volume on his radio.

The announcer noted that the recess was almost over. Dog court would resume in a few minutes.

Hunter opened another file and read: Letter written to Herman Franck by Dale Bretches

Who was Herman Franck?

A note was pinned to the letter — Herman Franck is a Spokane lawyer representing Paul Schneider and Dale Bretches in the lawsuit involving illegal overuse of X-rays.

Hunter opened the letter from Dale Bretches to his attorney and read:

"Presa breeders are going to have us blacklisted after everything is said and done even though we never did any of the things we are accused of. And since when did dog breeding become illegal?

"Herman, could you tell us who interviewed you about the accident? We understand that they asked everyone who had a hand in helping us with the Presas and since they found out that everything we've done is legal. All money is accounted for and since neither Paul or I have ever been charged with drugs, dog fighting, or cruelty to animals nor hate crimes, they now say that we are conspiring to do all this.

"We try to do something legit and we get treated worse than if we had really been breaking the law. But you know better than anyone how CDC (California Department of Corrections) is about its prisoners wanting to do something constructive with their time. When you wanted to pay us for our art work and they gave us 115s (115 is a CDC disciplinary write-up) and tried to get you into trouble with the Bar. You know that last year the Feds investigated our dogs and they couldn't find how we could be breaking any laws or rules so CDC couldn't do nothing about them."

Acid and Two Letters

Hunter was puzzled. Isn't running a business from prison still against the law? Was last time I checked. He continued to read the letter:

"They couldn't say that Paul and I were running an illegal dog business because we were not the ones breeding and selling pups.

"CDC doesn't have any say on what people on the streets do.

"We just get off on being able to watch the dogs grow up in the photos, hear stories and get to draw them. So what if we don't get to pet the dogs?

"Paul and I have owned dogs ever since we were born — why should it be different just because we're in prison?

"At least we got to see Bane and Hera and we got to see Bane's great grand sire Ch. Arbaco and then when they showed the Mac Harris Presas talking about paying $3,000 plus for CH. Arbaco, he sure was impressive in real life.

"But as far as us conspiring to use our dogs for any illegal purposes that's not going to happen. Neither of us are into fighting dogs and none of our Presas have ever been protection trained.

"If you read the 18-page letter that Noel sent to the DA you'll see that there is an explanation for Bane's behavior.

"No one's trying to blame the victim or be insensitive.

"Noel and Knoller still believe that Presas are the best dogs in the world and are going to do everything they can to save Hera though they feel that there is nothing they can do to save her even though she never actually bit the woman.

"Bane only bit the woman once and never bit her prior to this time.

"This is all stuff that will get proved."

Hunter paused. Only bit the woman once? Never bit her prior to this time? What were the convicts using as their source of information?

He went back to the letter and read:

"Meantime we are looking forward to Bane's daughter Roka having pups any day.

Death of an Angel

"She was bred to our import Menore who is the son of the famous Spanish Canary island champion, Ch. Urco. With Roka being the daughter of the most famous dog in the world right now and bred to Menore, this litter shouldn't be hard to sell...

"...You're right about us not getting to sell any pups since there's only been one litter and you know about it, with Coumbs trying to burn the guy who wanted to buy two pups with his $1,000 deposit.

"By the time we sued for our dogs back the pups were already ten months old and the guy's wife didn't want them."

Hunter smiled a tight smile. Even the convict realizes that this breed is hard to get rid of once it has grown a little.

He read: *"We were able to keep one Roka pup, the best one, but finding good homes for ten month old giants was a bitch.*

"Coumbs stole thousands of the money we got from the lawsuits you won for us plus she tried to lie about us giving her the dogs we spent thousands on, tried to burn us for the pups, starved them near to death.

"We have the paperwork from the vets and photos of their ribs sticking out.

"Two of the vets gave an interview telling how Noel and Knoller rescued them from near starvation and death.

"And that those dogs had never been fought and no scars and no one fights a near-starved and near-dead dogs.

"We can have the dogs personal vets testify our Presas have never been taught to fight nor been fight or attack trained and are the sweetest dogs they ever saw.

"Herman, you know all about Coumbs.

"You might have been the one who sued for us if you hadn't moved.

"As for Hera and Fury killing Coumbs livestock off, if they even did this I couldn't blame them since they had been starved near death.

"You know if it was mentioned that Coumbs was a Mormon inadvertently while talking about her being a lying, cheating, thieving bitch?"

Chapter
Twenty-seven

Dog Court — Part Four

Room 400, San Francisco City Hall, February 13, 2001.
Andrea Runge worked for Animal Care and Control. She was
blonde, with a trim figure. She adjusted the microphone.

"When the elevator door opened, I was facing the victim.
She was naked and appeared to be dead."

"There was blood soaked in the hallway, approximately 20
to 30 feet in the carpet. It was covering the walls approximately
two feet up. All the walls that I could see, from the elevator to the
bedroom doorway, had blood on them."

* * *

Andrea looked away from the carnage. She saw Marjorie Knoller,
who had on sweat clothes. She saw that Knoller was covered in
blood. Her sleeves were torn.

The animal control officer looked closely. No injuries to
Marjorie's face. Wait, there's a small scratch on her cheek.
Nothing else.

Police officers Laws and Forrestal looked at her.

What do they want? Andrea thought. They don't expect
me to go after those dogs until my fellow officers show up, do
they?

No way.

She looked back down the hallway, to where the victim's
body was sprawled.

Where's her clothing?

My God, she's naked and covered in blood.

* * *

Judge Herndon asked, "No clothing?"

"It was just shredded bits of cloth, clumps of hair, and blood."

"When you first saw the dog Hera, what was her appearance?"

"Crazed. I think that's the only way to describe the dog."

"Was there any evidence of blood on Hera?"

"I remember at the time seeing some blood on her."

Officer Runge was excused.

The prosecutor called Animal Control Officer Michael Scott. A thin, well-built man, clean-cut, about thirty and wearing a uniform, approached the microphone. He introduced himself and said, "I responded to the scene to assist Officer Runge."

* * *

Scott stepped out of the elevator and saw Runge. She's shaken, he realized. Then he looked down the hallway and saw the victim. Now I know why. He walked toward Runge.

Officer Runge entered the apartment and saw Knoller crouched in a corner. She said, "Ms. Knoller, I need you to sign this Owner Surrender form for the dog Bane."

Knoller signed.

Runge asked, "Ms. Knoller, has either dog ever been aggressive to humans before?"

"No."

Scott took out a tranquilizer gun from his kit and loaded up a dart. He asked Knoller, "Where are the dogs?"

"Bane is in the bathroom, down the hallway. Hera's in the bedroom."

"Ms. Knoller," asked Runge, "do you think you could bring Bane out?"

"I don't want to bring the dog out."

Knoller's afraid of Bane, Scott thought.

Runge asked Knoller, "I need you to sign a Owner Surrender form for Hera."

Knoller said, "She wasn't involved in the attack. She was only pulling at the victim's pants."

Dog Court – Part Four

Take Bane first, Scott decided. He edged open the bathroom door a crack. No space to maneuver in there. He saw Bane. The dog's not barking or even growling. Just pacing. He's got on a harness and a leash.

Scott glanced down the hall. He heard Hera growling, barking. Suddenly, the bedroom door gave a jump as the dog made physical contact with it.

Hera's the bigger threat. Get Bane first. Get him out of here. Then concentrate on Hera.

Scott again opened the bathroom door slightly, took aim and stuck a tranquilizer dart into Bane.

Runge said, "You're going to need more than one."

No kidding. Scott inserted another dart. He opened the door and shot the animal again.

No effect.

A third dart was delivered into Bane.

No apparent effect.

Three tranquilizers and no effect?

The two animal control officers waited fifteen minutes. During that entire time Hera continued to crash against the bedroom door, growling and barking.

Bane showed no signs of the tranquilizers taking effect.

Come-along time, thought Mike Scott. Come-along poles are steel rods about five feet long with a loop on the end.

Scott again opened the door slightly to the bathroom and studied Bane.

The male dog appeared in a state of punishment. There was defecation all over the bathroom. He wasn't growling. He wasn't barking. His head was down.

Officers Scott and Runge got two come-along loops around Bane's neck. Positioned safely away on either side of the dog, they led Bane outside to a waiting van and got the animal inside.

Scott went back to the apartment for Hera. He stood in front of the bedroom door. It's glass, he realized, and painted over with white paint. He opened the door a crack and saw Hera staring him right in the face.

Hera backed up five paces, leaned forward and gave a deep growl.

No collar, Scott saw. No harness.

Scott closed the door and looked at Runge. He said, "That's a growl I'll definitely remember for a long time. Get a cop."

Runge returned with a police officer.

Scott said, "Draw your weapon, please."

The police officer did so.

Scott, Runge and the cop entered the bedroom.

Hera backed up to the window.

Scott knew he had to keep her from leaping at him. There's blood on her coat.

*   *   *

The judge asked, "Where was Ms. Knoller when this was happening?"

"I believe she was out in the hallway."

"Was Mr. Noel present?"

"He was not present."

The judge studied a piece of paper, then looked up at Scott. "Were you afraid of this dog?"

"I'd like to say that I'm not afraid of *any* dogs. But I was extremely concerned about this dog. I can tell when a dog is going to come at me. That comes from years of working animal control. And I felt that either this dog was going to lunge at me or was going to look for a way to get past me and out the door. That's Hera."

"You mentioned that there was blood on Hera. How much blood and where?"

"I think I saw blood on her shoulder area, not very much. As I was in the apartment I had blood on myself, just from the walls in the apartment. I looked down at my hands and they were covered in blood."

"Just how do you believe the blood got into the apartment?"

"It was on the dogs. Bane was covered in blood."

"Hera did not have as much blood?"

"Not as much blood, no."

"You got the come-alongs on the dog. Then what happened?"

"We took each animal down the stairs — there wasn't enough room in the elevator. She put up much more of a fight than Bane did."

Noel went to the podium. "Regarding the descriptions by the animal control officers about Hera's behavior in the bedroom. Given the circumstances, I think that was probably a natural response for her and anybody else. Strangers invading her house. Her master Marjorie when last seen was covered in blood. Hera not knowing what was going on. I can appreciate her behavior in that respect.

"She did have a harness. I returned to the apartment just before Hera was led out. I had gotten to the lobby just as Bane was being led out. I heard an officer say, 'We think the woman is dead.'

"I thought it was Marjorie that was dead. When I got to the sixth floor, I was greeted by a scene that was pretty much described, although Ms. Whipple had already been transported at this point.

"I arrived in time to watch one of the police inspectors point out to Marjorie that she had, in fact, been struck over the right eye. Her eye was swelling. I directed the photographing of it. Not only of her eye, but the rest of her injuries. And she had handled Hera, getting her back into the bedroom."

The judge asked, "She also put Bane in the bathroom, is that correct?"

"She was able to get Bane locked in the bathroom. That's where animal control officers found him. About Hera's behavior in the bedroom. When I would be working at home and Marjorie would leave to go out, Hera would exhibit some of the behavior that's been described. She would run over and smack the door with her paw. If she couldn't get out she would run into where I was working and look at me and make a sound that could be described as a growl, but it was more of a..."

Noel made a sound that was medium high-pitched, like someone clearing their throat. Then he continued. "Like 'Come, I want to go.' And generally what has to be done after five minutes, I would have to put her harness on and take her out and take her out to the bus stop.

"Hera would just lay there and wait for Marjorie to come back. So I can understand her behavior in the bedroom having been separated from Marjorie under those conditions. She was trying to get to her master."

"If you were to leave both dogs in the apartment would you normally separate them or keep them together?" asked Judge Herndon.

Noel explained that when Hera went into heat they would keep them separated. "But I can count on one hand the times they were left alone. If we went out, they went out. If we went on a trip, they went on a trip. We were with them twenty-four hours a day, seven days a week."

The prosecutor announced, "The next witness I want to call is Jean Donaldson."

Donaldson was a director of training with the Society for the Prevention of Cruelty to Animals. She spoke into the microphone. "I have been called to render an opinion regarding the possible rehabilitation with the dog Hera. I am basing this opinion on reviewing the incident report and discussions with Pat Brown about other incidents at the kennel."

The expert on animal rehabilitation delivered salient point after point regarding Hera's behavior. She listed the incidents of dog-to-dog aggression or dog-to-stranger aggression. "The initial incident report and subsequent letter sent to Hera's guardians was that she was the first to charge Ms. Whipple.

"The degree of under-socialization with strangers in an adult dog (like Hera) has among the poorest prognosis for rehabilitation.

Dog Court – Part Four

"There seems to be some strong denial in Hera's guardians with respect to the potential aggression present."

The judge said, "I want you to give me information from your direct observations of Hera in the kennel."

"I tried the usual things to see if I could develop any rapport with her. Her pupils were dilated. She was throwing herself at the kennel. At one point I raised my arm and she lunged towards my arm. She barked the entire time. She was growling. She was clearly extremely threatening, and did not subside for about five minutes.

"I flipped her some treats to see if it would stop the growling and lunging."

The judge, his voice filled with amazement, asked, "You fed her treats from your hand?"

"Not from my hand. I flipped them in."

The audience, for the first time since the hearing began, laughed.

The judge asked, "How would you feel about working with the dog?"

The director of training with the Society for the Prevention of Cruelty of Animals said, "I don't know anyone that considers this case doable."

Chapter
Twenty-eight

Marjorie Testifies

Court, Room 400, San Francisco's City Hall, Tuesday, February 13, 2001.

Marjorie Knoller stood at the podium and said, "I would like to address some of the statements made by the animal control officers. When I was in the hallway talking to some of the officers, I had stated that Hera had tugged at some of Ms. Whipple's clothing. Hera also tugged at my clothing. This was when the attack was still going on. And Bane was acting the way he was acting. Hera was pulling at the bottom of my sweats and Ms. Whipple's pants leg. And she was barking."

Judge Herndon said, "Hera was pulling on the bottom of your sweats and Ms. Whipple's."

"And Ms. Whipple's sweats." Marjorie's voice began to quiver, "I believe that…" She choked up. She fought for control, then gasped out, "I believe Hera was trying to protect me from Bane. But whatever action she did she was never involved in the attack on Ms. Whipple. She was barking hysterically in the hallway."

"Where were you," the judge asked, "when Hera was biting at your pant leg and Ms. Whipple's?"

"She wasn't biting, she was tugging. There is a difference. On the sweats I was wearing there are no tears or bite marks on the bottom. Bane shredded Ms. Whipple's clothing. Hera was in no way involved."

Again, emotion overcame Marjorie.

The judge asked, "Where was Hera?"

"She was in the hallway. Behind me. Barking. When I finally got Bane to calm down enough to get him back into the apartment, Hera was in the hallway. She had her harness on, but her harness had been ripped. The only way her harness could have been ripped was probably Bane cut it with his teeth. I don't know how it occurred because I was too busy trying to protect Ms. Whipple from Bane. We were both in a prone position. Ms. Whipple was underneath me, I was on top of her trying to protect her from Bane."

"With all that going on, how is it you were aware that Hera was tugging at your sweats and tugging at Ms. Whipple's pants?"

"Because I could feel the pressure on my leg. She was the only other animal in the hallway. I could hear Hera barking and pulling. I knew it wasn't Bane because he was near her torso and I was still battling with him."

"How did you know that Hera was pulling at Ms. Whipple's pants?"

"Because she was just underneath me. And I guess I could... It's a guess, is what it is.... that Hera was pulling at my pants leg and Ms. Whipple's."

The judge said, "You don't really know the extent of what Hera was doing or was not doing."

"Actually, I do know the extent, because she was nowhere near Ms. Whipple's torso. "

"But she was near Ms. Whipple's feet?"

"Yes. Because she was near my feet."

"Do you know how far up the body Hera may have gone?"

"She never got into my peripheral vision when I was turning my head. She wasn't anywhere near her body at all. When my body was on top of Ms. Whipple's, Bane was the animal who was always in my peripheral vision and up near my torso. Hera was nowhere near Ms. Whipple during the attack. She was nowhere near any of the areas on her body where she received any injuries or bite marks. Hera was nowhere near those areas of the body, because I was the one who also had bite wounds, not puncture wounds, but bite wounds inflicted on me in the same areas more or less as on Ms. Whipple's body."

* * *

Hunter sat as his desk and listened on the radio to the testimony.

He doodled. He drew a circle and a square and a rectangle and a triangle.

"I understand," the judge said, "that the clothes were completely shredded off of Ms. Whipple."

"Yes. Bane shredded her clothing."

"Maybe. If Hera was tugging at her pant leg, why do you believe that Hera did not pull any other clothing from her body?"

"I was dealing with Bane and backing him up. I saw what he was doing when I pulled him back. Every time I tried to pull him back he would be tugging at something she was wearing. So the further I pulled him back the more he was tearing her clothing."

Hunter wrote the word "*The*" in the circle.

The judge asked Marjorie Knoller, "What was the condition of your clothing?"

"My right sleeve was shredded and pulled apart. I have tear marks on both the back and front of my sweat shirt. I had bite marks, not puncture wounds, but bite marks, on my arms going all the way up. On my back. On my left arm. There was also some tear marks, not bite marks, on the back of my pants. There were two large tears on the back of my sweat pants. The front of my sweat shirt was also torn in two places. And I was covered in blood. Any blood that was on Hera was from me. Getting her back into the apartment was not a problem, but I did take her by the harness. The harness was cut and left in the bathroom with Bane. I put her in the bedroom."

"If Hera's harness was cut, and you believe it was cut by Bane's teeth, then Bane would have had to have tried to bite Hera."

"Yes," Marjorie said. "Because he was going back and forth over Ms. Whipple's body and my body. That's how I got the blood on my back. He was covered in blood. He was going back and forth across us. I believe one of those times he probably did have contact with Hera."

Hunter wrote the word "*Truth*" in the square.

"So," Judge Herndon said, "Bane would have had to walk all the way across you."

"Bane was a large dog. The lead was still on my hand during the entire incident, but he still had six feet in which to maneuver so that he could easily have gotten down to Ms. Whipple's pants and then gotten up."

"Was there a lead on Hera?"

"No. There was not. Hera had been in the apartment. She was not out with me or Bane at the time. I had opened the apartment door to place Bane inside."

"When you opened the apartment door…?"

"Hera was just standing there, waiting for me to come into the apartment. She looked out the door. That's when Bane became interested in Ms. Whipple at the other end of the hall."

"Why did Hera have the harness on in the apartment?"

"Hera has her harness from the moment of her morning walk 'till after her evening walk. Then we take her harness off. She doesn't have any kind of restraint when she is sleeping at night."

"I'm concerned with your observation that Hera was not involved. If Hera was at the feet of the victim and you were very occupied with the activities of Bane, then I don't know how you can make the statement."

"Because I was on top of Ms. Whipple during the whole period of time the attack was happening. I would know if Hera was biting me or trying to bite me or Ms. Whipple. Because I was the one there dealing with it."

"How did you suffer the tears to the front of your clothing?"

"From Bane."

"If you were on top of Ms. Whipple—"

"Every time I would tell her to stay still and not move, and get Bane off of her, she would move forward and Bane would renew his attack. Every time he did that, pieces of my clothing would get in his way. It was a matter of always trying to fight him, fight her, and try to get her to those areas of safety,"

Hunter wrote in the rectangle the word *"Never."*

207

The judge asked, "How did the dogs get back into the apartment?"

"I took them back into the apartment. I was the one who took Bane back into the apartment. I told Hera to wait. I came out and got Hera. Actually, I got Hera to come with me into the apartment when I was dragging Bane."

"But Hera didn't have a lead on her?"

"No. Hera did not have a lead on. She had not been walked. She had been in the apartment. The way I would take her would be to just grab her by her harness."

"You put Bane where?"

"I put Bane in bathroom and Hera's harness in with Bane and took Hera by the scruff of her neck and put her in the bedroom. So any blood on Hera would have come from me."

Hunter wrote in the triangle *"Changes."*

"What did you do then?" Judge Herndon asked Marjorie.

"I went out into the hallway to check and see where the keys went that were in my sweat suit. They were missing. I knew Ms. Whipple was very injured. I went to see where my keys were. They were in Ms. Whipple's foyer. I picked them up and came back and met your officers."

Hmmm, Hunter thought, big statement. Might explain one thing but it flags two others. If she put her keys in her sweat suit, she would then have had both hands free to struggle with Bane. Then, in the tussle down in front of Diane's place they could have fallen out.

But she is categorically stating that she took Hera by the scruff of the neck and put her in the bedroom.

But the cops said Hera was running loose in the hall.

And the biggest thing, the thing that just rolled my stomach, is she just testified that she went back to find her keys. *She did not call 911.*

Shouldn't the victim's well-being come before the security of your apartment?

Over the radio he listened as the judge asked Marjorie, "Do you feel Hera would be a good pet to have back in your home?"

"She's a wonderful pet. And I do believe she'd do just fine. She's a wonderful animal. She's loving. She's caring. I think of her as a certified lick therapist. Because when you're not doing well, she licks you."

He turned his attention back to the radio and the proceedings going on in dog court.

The judge said, "Even with those positive traits, Hera was involved, to some extent, in this incident."

"From my perspective, she was not involved in this incident in the term of being an aggressive dog. Or being an attack dog, or anything like that. She's involved in this because she was out in the hallway and barking. She was nowhere near Ms. Whipple."

Judge Herndon said, "I really want to clarify a point. You say she was nowhere near Ms. Whipple. But I believe you stated to me that she was tugging at your sweat pants and Ms. Whipple's pants."

"Correct."

"That would place her there at the incident."

"She is at the incident. But what I am saying to you, is she didn't inflict any injury on either Ms. Whipple or on me."

"But you don't know that for sure."

"I do know that for sure."

"How do you know that for sure?"

"I know for sure because I was the one who was near her when she was getting all the injuries. And the only individual who was giving her those injuries was Bane."

The prosecutor asked if Noel or Knoller had any other witness to present. They had none. Then the prosecutor said, "Our department feels, based on the testimony here today, clearly Hera is a vicious and dangerous dog. Hera played an active role in the death of Ms. Whipple.

"Therefore, our department is requesting the destruction of this animal. Carl Friedman, who is the director of Animal Care and Control, would like to make a statement."

Mr. Friedman came to the microphone and said, "Mister hearing officer, thank you. As many of you know, we are in the business of saving lives, not destroying lives. I realize you have a very difficult decision to make. Deciding whether an animal lives or dies is never an easy task. Nobody knows this better than us, because we are put into this situation every day. However, our primary responsibility is to the safety of our citizens. I believe Captain Guldbeck and her witnesses put forth an excellent case showing this dog Hera poses a significant threat, and should be declared vicious and dangerous.

"With this in mind, we implore you not to release this animal back into our community. And ask that your decision is to order Hera humanely destroyed."

Chapter
Twenty-nine

Attitude

Sharon Smith's apartment, 2398 Pacific Avenue, Tuesday, February 13, 2001.
Sharon had still heard nothing from her neighbor lawyers about Diane. Just speeches to the press saying Robert Noel and Marjorie Knoller send condolences to the family of Diane Alexis.

Anonymous people to the two lawyers, anonymous people located somewhere back East.

I'm sixty feet down a hallway from them. Sixty feet over a new carpet, because the old one was ruined by the blood that came from the woman I loved. Blood that stained not only the carpet but my heart.

Stained my heart with loss.

Stained my heart with sorrow.

Stained my heart with anger.

She had a memory flash through her mind from her childhood. A memory from the Catholic teachings of her parents. The memory of the story of Christ driving the moneychangers from the temple.

Righteous anger.

If making money at the wrong location deserved righteous anger, what did a preventable death deserve?

Rage?

Fury?

Vengeance?

I am not a vengeful person, but this is so wrong.

What despicable attitudes Noel and Knoller have.

Sharon sat back in her chair. *Attitude.* Why is that ringing such a bell?

Attitude.

Something to do with Diane Alexis.

She remembered.

Alexis loved a quote from Charles Swindoll about attitude.

Diane once told Sharon, "I make my players read it. I have it posted on my office wall."

Sharon searched through a few drawers and found a copy. She read:

"The longer I live, the more I realize the impact of attitude on life.

"Attitude to me is more important than facts. It is more important than the past, than education, than money, than circumstances, than failures, than successes, than what other people think or do.

"Attitude is more important than appearance, giftedness, or skill.

"It will make or break a company... a church... a home.

"The remarkable thing is we have a choice every day regarding the attitude we embrace for that day.

"We cannot change our past... we cannot change the fact that people will act in a certain way.

"We cannot change the inevitable.

"The only thing we can do is play the one string we have, and that is attitude... I am convinced that life is 10% what happens to me and 90% how I react to it.

"And so it is with you... we are in charge of our attitude."

That was Diane Alexis.

What a lovely attitude she had.

Sharon rummaged about a drawer and found a file.

She removed a certificate from Penn State, Diane's alma mater. The long list of Diane Alexis Whipple's accomplishments was impressive:

NCAA National Champions 1987 and 1989.

NCAA National Championship 2nd place 1988.

NCAA First team All-American 1989 and 1990.

Attitude

Penn State Female Athlete of the Year 1990.

Sharon folded the certificate and placed it in the box. She removed another and read:

USA National Lacrosse Team 1990 – 1991.

USA team vs. Australia 1992; versus England; USA versus Canada, USA versus...

Sharon thought, the attitude of a champion. She reread a sentence from the article on attitude: *I am convinced that life is 10% what happens to me and 90% how I react to it.*

What if Noel and Knoller had lived by those words? They had a choice that day a few weeks ago. They embraced the low road of blaming another, rather than embracing the attitude of remorse and asking forgiveness for what their animals did.

They couldn't *change* the past, but they could have taken responsibility for that past.

The phone rang. It was Sharon's travel agent. She expressed her condolences, then said, "Been going through my records. I assume that you are canceling your trip to Kauai."

"No."

"No? Are you canceling the other ticket? Do you just want one?"

"I'll call back," Sharon said and glanced at the bookshelf.

The urn was on the bookshelf.

The urn with Diane's ashes in it.

A month earlier, Diane had named five places where she wanted her ashes scattered.

*   *   *

Diane said, "Name the places."

"Not again," Sharon said.

"Again."

"Why are you so obsessed with where you want your ashes scattered?"

"Name the places."

"You're young. Not even 33 until next week. Why all this morbid talk?"

"The places."

"The Atlantic Ocean."

"Right. Next?"

"The 50-yard lines of the Manhasset High School and Penn State lacrosse fields."

"Right on numbers two and three. Next?"

"You're going to have me running all over the country. I'm two years older than you. What if I listed a bunch of places for you to go and scatter my ashes?"

"Because it's not going to happen. At least not for me to have to do. Next?"

"A mountain."

"Right. Any mountain."

"Any mountain, anywhere?"

"Your choice. Next?"

"The Pacific Ocean."

"Where in the Pacific Ocean?"

"The beach on Kauai."

"What beach on Kauai?"

"The one out at the end. Past the pavilion, past all those one-lane bridges, way out to where the road stops."

"Right. But what is the name?"

"Out there where the two caves are."

"Past the two caves. Name?"

"Han... Hanoi, or..."

"Hanoi is in Vietnam. I want my ashes scattered at, no, you look it up."

"I will, when the time comes in fifty or so years."

"Don't forget the places."

"How can I when you keep making me repeat them over and over?"

*   *   *

Over and over, she quizzed me. Did she have a premonition? Diane Alexis always lived each day to the fullest, but she did nothing when it came to long-range planning.

That was my department. Me, the financial one. That's what I do for a living. Long-term planning.

When I read her will, I found that she had added a sixth place — the steps of her grandparents' house.

Attitude

Why would Alexis hound me if she hadn't had an inkling?

Most 33-year-old, healthy-as-a-horse athletes don't dwell on where they want their ashes scattered.

Most people don't get so specific as to list six places, even if they know they are dying.

Chapter
Thirty

Legal Privileges

Henry Hunter's home, Wednesday, Valentine's Day, February 14, 2001.

Harry, Hunter's son, turned on the five o'clock news to KGO Channel 7. Announcer Dan Noyes said, "The case is taking more strange twists tonight. One involves nude pictures of the dogs' owner. Also, investigators say that Marjorie Knoller is once again changing her story about what happened that night."

ABC's field reporter Laura Anthony appeared on the screen. "Police tell us that they can use statements made yesterday at the hearing as potential evidence in their criminal investigation."

Young 15-year-old Harry Hunter saw his father, the cop, appear on the screen. He called to the next room, "Dad, you're on TV."

Then he watched his dad's image say, "Their story keeps changing. Her initial statement was that Hera came out and was pulling at the legs or at least the clothing. Now the only reason Hera was out in the hallway was to defend her against Bane. For me this is a problem. The truth doesn't change."

Hunter entered his living room and said with conviction, "And that's the truth."

The reporter said, "For instance, in her original statement Knoller was asked if Whipple hit her. She said no. Now she offers a different story about the attack. "

Cindy Hunter entered and stood next to her husband. The image on screen faded, then Laura Anthony reappeared outside San Francisco's Hall of Justice.

Legal Privileges

With the background noise of passing vehicles, the reporter said, "In another odd twist, sources tell Channel 7 that investigators for the district attorney's office seized nude pictures of Knoller from her adopted son, Paul 'Cornfed' Schneider's jail cell at Pelican Bay Prison."

"Are they serious?" asked Cindy..

"Nothing in this case surprises me," replied Hunter.

That night, after taking his wife out to dinner for Valentine's Day and giving Cindy the obligatory flowers and card, with love, of course, Hunter turned on the eleven o'clock KGO Channel 7 news.

A poll had been conducted. The KGO results regarding Hera were: 89% for death, 10% for being returned with restrictions, 1% returned without restrictions.

The DA's office served Sergeant Bill Herndon an order that no matter what his decision was regarding Hera's fate, either life or death, they wanted the dog kept alive. At least for now.

Noel announced that he and his wife were filing a $100 million lawsuit against the CDC for leaking the confidential news about their adoption of the 38-year-old prisoner, Cornfed.

Reporter Linda Yee said, "The battle today in court was over attorney-client privilege. That it's very sacred in a court of law. One slip-up by the prosecution and they could lose the entire case. At issue: all of the items taken from the owners' apartment. Those items include documents and a computer. In court today, Robert Noel argued many of the papers taken included privileged information on his clients, including convicts Paul Schneider and Dale Bretches.

"Police investigators insist they were careful when they searched Noel's apartment, bringing a Special Master. He's an attorney appointed by the state bar and approved by the court to accompany the police when they look for evidence in an attorney's home or office."

Hunter appeared on the television screen. "We were very careful in obtaining this warrant. We didn't rush to do it. We documented things. Three district attorneys looked at it. The judge reviewed it very closely. He signed it."

Death of an Angel

Hunter flipped to Channel 5, Eye Witness News. Reporter Christie O'Conner appeared. She stood outside Noel's apartment. The reporter asked Noel, "You were in court today. On what basis did you argue? What are the reasons that prosecutors should not have this evidence?"

"Materials that we were arguing about today were covered by attorney-client privilege. Or, the privilege that exists under the penal code for inmates to communicate confidentially with any member of the state bar."

"What about correspondence with Paul Schneider?"

"Some of that correspondence was seized. And that is privileged under both the attorney-client privilege and the attorney communication privilege under the penal code."

"You told me that you had sent Mr. Schneider three or four hundred pictures. What were the pictures of?"

"Of the dogs. Hera riding in taxi cabs. Hera walking around the city. Hera in restaurants where we were eating. Hera on the beach in Bolinas. Hera at Luca's Wharf."

The reporter asked, "Nothing about what we've been told are X-rated pictures? Or anything having to do with showing the dogs fighting or being trained to fight?"

"There are no pictures of any dogs fighting or being trained to fight. These two mutts were just that — mutts. They weren't trained to fight. They weren't protect-trained or guard-dog-trained. They were just urban animals."

"Are you afraid that the evidence might show that your dogs were dangerous?"

"Not at all."

Christie O'Conner continued. "Today, Mr. Noel took us on an exclusive, personal tour of the path the police took. The first thing you wonder about the former home of two huge dogs was how they fit in the elevator. There's not much room for anybody else."

"That's the truth," Noel said. "We wouldn't ride in the elevator with anyone else."

The image on the screen changed to a shot through Noel's open apartment door. Broken pieces of wood lay by the entranceway. The reporter said, "Noel showed us how the police broke into his home. Noel said the police should have seized this."

On camera was a blue and white rug.

The reporter said, "Noel says this explained why blue and white material was found in Hera's stool. Noel says it proves it wasn't Diane Whipple's clothing Hera ate."

A blonde doll, obviously a male, appeared on the screen. The reporter said, "Also left behind was this, a blonde-haired toy doll Hera carried in her mouth. Noel said this is Hera's little prince doll that she had found on the street one day."

The reporter came on the screen standing next to Noel. She pointed at the doll and said, "That's kind of *demolished*, isn't it?"

Noel said. "It's about six months worth of wear."

The scene abruptly shifted to outside the apartment building. Christie O'Conner, over the roar of a passing truck, ended her report. "I couldn't help but think of Diane Whipple when I saw that doll."

Chapter
Thirty-one

Manstopper

Henry Hunter's office, Hall of Justice, General Work Detail, Thursday, February 15, 2001.
Hunter turned on the TV in the General Work Detail's office area. It was noon. Time for the news. Once again he thought of how helpful the media had been so far in the case. To have that kind of manpower all the time would be a dream. He randomly selected a channel and watched.

The reporter said, "You're watching KPIX-TV, Channel 5, Eyewitness News, everywhere. Christie O'Conner noticed a book on training dogs to attack while she was interviewing Noel in his home last night."

The scene shifted to the inside of Noel's apartment.

Christie O'Conner picked up a book and said, "*Manstopper*. A little scary, that title."

The book had a half-dozen pictures of Bane on the cover.

Under one picture: "Bane — el supremo." O'Conner read the words under another black-and-white picture. "Bane — one hundred and sixty pounds."

Noel said, "That's what he weighed at one point."

"What did he weigh when he killed Diane Whipple?"

"About a hundred and twenty-two."

Hunter felt a tap on the shoulder and looked up. It was Sergeant Steve Murphy. Hunter pointed at the screen. He said, "More info. Book called *Manstopper*."

The two policemen watched as O'Conner opened the book and flipped through the pages. She pointed at a woman with a huge arm-wrap. "This woman is obviously wearing protective gear."

"She's an educator."

"So this is teaching *what*? Encouraging the dog to jump on her?"

"Right. "

"So why do you have this book?"

"This is not something we ever intended to undertake. If it were to be done, it would be done by professionals. Such as the fellow who wrote this book. And those dogs would be trained for individuals or police departments."

O'Conner said, "Where did Noel get the *book*? From a friend." She pointed at the book, showed it to Noel and said, "Notice right there? It says 'Bretches.'"

"Right."

"That's the friend?"

"That's the friend."

"A book about Bane and Presa Canarios with the name Bretches on it. Are you surprised that the police didn't take that?"

"Absolutely."

Back in Hunter's office, Murphy said, "We didn't take it because it wasn't *there*. No way did we miss something like that."

The scene on the TV cut to reporter Christie O'Conner. "In the six days since the raid, Noel and Knoller have had unlimited access to their apartment. Was the book there when police searched? Don't know."

Hunter looked at Murphy.

Murphy said, "*I* know, *I* know. You want a second search warrant."

Hunter thought, so far in our investigation we have *not* discovered any specific training or fighting or attacking that these dogs have received. This book could be very helpful.

The cop knew that the FBI was now getting involved. They were looking for any federal laws that may have been broken. They were looking to see if the dog ring was involved in money laundering or fighting.

*   *   *

That night, at home, Hunter settled back into his easy chair in his front room. Flames flickered in the fireplace. His female dog Babs, a cocker spaniel, was next to his chair. By habit, he scratched the dog behind the ear and grabbed the remote. Time for the news. On the TV he saw that the lead story about the book *Manstopper* had taken an unexpected turn.

The reporter said, "The fatal mauling of Diane Whipple has sparked international debate about how dogs should be trained and handled. Tonight, Lance Evans visited a school for dogs to learn how to take the bite out of the bark."

On the television screen appeared a huge dog. Reporter Lance Evans said, "This is a Neapolitan mastiff, a cousin to the dog that killed Diane Whipple. You'd think a dog like this would be automatically aggressive."

The dog trainer, Peter White, said, "All the dogs we have today are designer dogs. Humans created these dogs. None of these dogs are aggressive. Put the wrong dog in the wrong hands and then, of course, there is tragedy."

Hunter looked down at Babs. Designer dog, all right. Pedigreed.

Evans continued. "Peter White owns Olivet Kennel and Dog Training Resort in Santa Rosa. He has trained dogs for a quarter century. He says finding the book *Manstopper*, with the words 'El Supremo Bane' on it, in Robert Noel's apartment, concerns him."

"The book teaches the techniques and the behavior that are necessary to develop aggression in dogs," said White.

"He says since Diane Whipple's mauling death, dogs have gotten a bad rap," injected Evans.

"We should always remember that we have to look at it from the dog's perspective," continued White. "Not what we see as humans. What we see and what a dog sees is two different worlds."

Hunter noticed Babs' eyes were closed, tongue lolling out, tail wagging almost in time to the pacing of his scratching behind her ears. He stopped. Babs stopped wagging. She opened her eyes. There was a gleam in them as she stared at Hunter.

Manstopper

Disapproval, the policeman thought. Or what? Just what do dogs really think? They really do live in a different world. A black-and-white world. A world where a dog got fed everyday, loved, slept in front of a fireplace, and had its ears scratched; or a world where it roamed with a pack of other dogs, fending for themselves, using the power of the pack to overwhelm their next meal.

Like Jack London's *White Fang*. Half-wolf, half-dog. All brains.

On TV, Lance Evans said, "Peter White believes that Robert Noel and Marjorie Knoller made a critical mistake by not having dominion and control over Hera and Bane through months of dog training. His twelve-year-old German shepherd Natia and I bonded beautifully."

On the screen, Lance and the large dog did what humans and dogs have done down through the ages — romped and interacted. Ears got scratched, the dog's tail wagged.

Lance said, "But look how she reacted minutes later to this simulated threat to her and her owner."

Lance had a thick guard on his right arm. Natia had her ears back, her fangs bared. She barked. She growled. She snarled. She lunged and chomped down on the arm guard with a vise-like death grip.

Babs stood up. She snarled softly at the television. Her ears were back.

Hunter said, "It's okay, old gal. Calm down." Babs circled three times, looking back at the screen on each loop, then settled down next to her master.

On television, the owner of the German shepherd gave one command and the attack immediately stopped.

Reporter Evans said, "Natia and I became friends again. White said that's what dog training *should* do. Keep a dog friendly and use them for protection only when there's a real threat. As for Hera *not* attacking Whipple as Marjorie Knoller insists, he says that would go *against* a dog's nature."

Hunter leaned forward in his chair. My kind of witness.

White said, "In my experience, in the majority of cases dogs will assist each other because that's their pack mentality, and that's what they're designed to do."

Hunter flipped to KRON Channel 4. On camera was Phil Matier. He was standing in front of 850 Bryant Street.

Matier? Hunter was puzzled. Matier's a columnist. Matier and his partner Ross. Three times a week. In the *Chronicle*. Channel 4 owned the *Chronicle*. Or was it vice versa?

Matier said, "Investigators here at the Hall of Justice are looking into three key elements. Was it known that the dogs were dangerous? Did the owners of the dogs know they were dangerous? And did they exercise enough caution? It could make a difference, a big difference, when it comes to a criminal case. The law in question is 399.5 of the state's penal code, which makes it against the law for anyone to be in possession of a dog that's specifically trained to fight, attack or kill."

Chapter
Thirty-two

The Cement of Marriage

Sharon Smith's apartment, 2398 Pacific Avenue, Thursday, February 15, 2001.
Sharon Smith drifted off to sleep.

*   *   *

The dream began with nothing but white. Not white clouds; no definition whatsoever, except white.

It was tranquil.

The white changed and took form. Nothingness became random lines and angles. The geometric shapes solidified into place and became the outside of a one-story house.

A house painted white. The door was white. The shutters were white. The lawn was white. The roof was white.

Sharon felt an urgency. Something was wrong. Something was missing. She was suddenly inside. She stood in a foyer that was white. She could see through open archways — the dining room, the sitting room, the library. All painted white.

Her urgency took on meaning.

Where's Alexis?

She went through room after room.

Nothing. Nothing but white walls and white furniture and white floors and ceilings.

Alexis, she called, the sound in her mind.

Alexis! Alexis!

Still no sound reverberated in her mind. Just soundless screams.

Where are you?

She continued to roam. Room after room unfolded before her in a seemingly endless row.

White.

Empty.

She came to a room that had a door that looked outside. It stunned her at first, this sudden burst of green after so much white. She went to the door, opened it and went outside. White sky, one huge green tree, white ground.

There was something on the ground. She could not make out what it was, just a formless mass.

She drew closer.

There was a white blanket over the shape.

Sharon saw the top of a head, only the hair showing, at the edge of the blanket.

Alexis.

Alexis is dead.

Pull the blanket back.

No!

Don't pull the blanket back.

I don't want to see the horror of the marks on her body.

The blanket moved!

Moved!

She's alive!

Sharon bent over and took an edge of the blanket. Carefully she drew it away.

Alexis looked up at her and smiled.

She's fine. She's alive. The mauling was just a dream. A nightmare.

Sharon knelt down and held Alexis in her arms and cried tears of relief onto her partner's shoulder.

She felt complete.

Michael Cardoza's office, 700 Montgomery Street, San Francisco's Financial District, Thursday, February 15. 2001.
Michael Cardoza sat in his office. He had asked his wife, Kim, to print out the complete proposed Assembly Bill 25. He read:

"Key Issues:

The Cement of Marriage

1)   Should the group of individuals who may register as domestic partners be expanded to include opposite sex couples where only one individual, rather than both, is over the age of 65?"

The lawyer wondered, what does that mean?

Before, couples had to be 65? Who wrote the original bill that came up with that logic? And what was the logic behind requiring couples to be 65?

Strange.

He read:

"2)   Should various new legal rights be conferred on registered domestic partners, to the same extent that such rights are guaranteed to married couples."

Michael Cardoza went through the ten-page bill. A number of paragraphs jumped out at him.

"Background: About ten years ago, the legislature appointed a Joint Legislative Task Force on the Changing Family to study the evolving nature of the California family, and to make recommendations to the Legislature as to how the needs of the state's changing families could be better met. The task force found that the traditional structure of the family, as it was known in the 1950s and the 60s, had indeed changed over the years.

"Today, the traditional 'nuclear family' no longer describes the majority of families in California. Instead, the concept of 'family' has extended to include stepparents, grandparents, parents-in-law, and, in many cities, domestic partners.

"Children are relating to multiple families, as their biological parents get divorced, remarry and create new, extended families."

Like Kim and myself, Cardoza realized. I get divorced, we meet, and a new family is created.

He continued reading.

"Recent polls suggest strong support for expanding rights of domestic partners. According to the sponsor, a 1997 Field Poll showed 'a strong majority of Californians (ranging from 59% to 67%) support domestic partners living together in a loving and

227

caring relationship to have many of the same rights married couples enjoy, including medical power of attorney, conservatorship, and financial status granting domestic partners such benefits as pensions, health and dental care coverage, family leave and death benefits.'

"The sponsor also cites a Decision Research poll conducted last year which shows that 'a majority of California voters believe that gay and lesbian couples are entitled to basic protections.' Under this poll, the sponsor claims, '69% of voters believe that gay and lesbian couples suffer obstacles and hardships because they lack the legal protections, benefits, and responsibilities currently afforded by state law to legally married different-sex couples.'"

Cardoza read on to check opposite points of view.

"ARGUMENTS IN OPPOSITION: The position of the Traditional Values Coalition (TVC) is reflective of the principal arguments of opponents of this measure. TVC argues that the bill is an attempt to circumvent the will of the majority of Californians who voted for Proposition 22 which, they claim, 'declared that the rights and privileges of marriage should not be extended to other forms of so-called 'unions.'"

"According to TVC, any domestic partnership is an auto-matic threat of deterrent to the institution of marriage.

The state has no vested interest in advocating or promoting domestic partnerships since they cannot give birth to a family."

Michael wondered, that's the only reason the state has a vested interest in stable relationships? The birth of kids? How about the stability couples bring by the very strength of their union? Power at the top, through all of history, has recognized that a family structure leads to order. Paying taxes, obeying the law.

Besides, does the TVC's stance mean the state should not recognize a legal marriage to a barren heterosexual couple?

Doesn't make much sense. In fact, it makes *no* sense.

Another line jumped out at him form the opposition section: *"Once all the rights currently afforded to those relationships of the opposite sex are granted to those of the same sex, the concept of marriage will have lost its meaning, purpose and legitimacy."*

What *is* the concept of marriage? Cardoza asked himself.

He opened his Random House Dictionary and read: *Marriage: the social institution under which a man and a woman establish their decision to live as husband and wife by legal commitments, religious ceremonies etc.*

Okay, that definition agrees with the opposition. What other definitions of marriage are there? He read: *...and a close or intimate association or union.*

Doesn't that categorically imply people like Diane and Sharon?

The next example: *...the marriage of form and content.*

That's a melding. The melding of form and content. Again, wasn't that what Diane and Sharon had? A marriage of form and content? Their marriage didn't match the traditional definition, complete with the hoopla and festivities that went with the marriage ceremony, but that didn't negate their love as a bond — a union.

For that matter, he realized, almost every marriage consecrated in Nevada is devoid of the religious implications the traditional weddings carry.

How would marriage between Diane and Sharon threaten the meaning, purpose and legitimacy of the more traditional form?

They were good citizens. They both had jobs. They both paid taxes. Neither had a criminal record.

Michael reread all the points made by the opposition.

Confusing, he thought. Isn't love the real cement that binds a marriage?

Chapter
Thirty-three

Bestiality?

Henry Hunter's office, Hall of Justice, General Work Detail, Thursday, February 22, 2001.
Boredom was not exactly a word Hunter associated with the job description for a cop.

Boredom was something found on a manufacturing line in Detroit. Or standing night watch on an empty warehouse. Or checking a column of figures that had been checked by three other accountants before you.

Yet, certain cop jobs were also boring.

Boredom could be rampant in the property room. Or trying to match a set of fingerprints to an endless number of suspects.

Even the Whipple Case was settling into a rhythm: lawyers open mouths; media documents furiously; public is astonished.

Hunter realized he needed something to do.

His time cards were up-to-date; overtime slips inputted into the computer; assignment board healthy.

In one month his grandson Joshua was due to come into the world. His daughter-in-law has just gone for a check-up.

Everyone healthy.

The mother of his future grandson looked radiant. She was anything but bored.

He stared at his blackboard.

The words "Sixty seconds + fifteen" were still there. The words were still underlined.

It had been a month since Diane Whipple supposedly stood immobile while two monster-sized dogs stalked her.

Bestiality?

Stood statue-like for seventy-five seconds.

Marjorie's not telling the truth.

But *why* is she not telling the truth?

His phone rang. Paul Cummins said, "Sergeant Herndon just ruled. Death sentence for the female dog, Hera."

"Not much of a surprise."

"Herndon gave Noel and Knoller the harshest penalty allowed him by law. He forbade them from owning, possessing, controlling or having custody of any dog for a period of three years."

"That's it? Three years?"

"That's the max."

"Then the length of the sentence is not surprising."

"No, but the next thing is. The DA has ordered the animal kept alive, for now."

"Because?"

"Testing. To see if the dog received training."

Hunter thanked Cummins and hung up.

He glanced around his office. Time to catch up on the newspapers. Been awhile.

He pulled a stack out of the bottom drawer of his desk. Top one was dated February 14. Nothing on the front page except more and more bad news regarding California's lack-of-energy problems. The Metro section of the *Chronicle*, called Bay Area, had a story, top of the page. Matier and Ross — Saga of Killer Dog takes on a Racy Turn.

Hunter read: "Just when you thought the twisted tale of the Pacific Heights dog mauling couldn't get any more twisted, it does — and this time the turn is decidedly X-rated.

"For weeks, people have been wondering what lawyer Robert Noel and his wife, Marjorie Knoller, were thinking when they adopted the 38-year-old convicted killer Paul 'Cornfed' Schneider after taking in his two huge dogs at their Pacific Heights apartment.

"Noel has said they adopted Schneider because they had developed a personal relationship with him.

231

"Well, now we find out how personal the relationship really is.

"Law enforcement sources tell us that a recent search of convict Schneider's Pelican Bay jail cell turned up a collection of X-rated photos — featuring none other than Cornfed's new adopted 'mom,' Marjorie Knoller.

"'It was the stuff you would see in a B-rated movie,' said one corrections source.

"The racy snapshots, which were mixed in with Paul Schneider's personal papers, were revealed to San Francisco's district attorney's investigators who had been dispatched to the prison last week as part of the criminal probe into the fatal dog mauling of Knoller's neighbor Diane Whipple.

"So far, however, all the seized photos and any correspondence between Schneider and his attorney-parents are off-limits — even to the DA's office — pending a review by a court-appointed special master hired to ensure that everything about the investigation is done by the book.

"Bob Martinez, spokesman for the Department of Corrections, declined to comment yesterday on the pictures and other correspondence, but he did confirm that two DA's investigators had spent the better part of the day last week at Pelican Bay State Prison.

"'They came and talked to a number of people, and we assisted in giving them whatever information they requested,' Martinez said.

"And what do Noel and Knoller say about the pictures?

"'I'm not going to confirm it or deny it,' Noel told us earlier this week.

"Noel then said, 'There used to be a time when guy-on-guy or woman-on-woman relationships were looked on as unnatural acts. What concern is it of anybody if there is or isn't a personal relationship?'

"If anything, Noel said, the disclosures about the photos only go to show that the Department of Corrections — with which Noel has been battling for years — is 'violating the law again.'

232

Bestiality?

"'If they disclosed any of the confidential materials, then it will be added to the $100 million claim we are going to file for breach of the confidentiality of our adoption.

"One more thing, no matter how strange you might think the couple's relationship is with their new son, Noel once again took the opportunity to remind us that, 'at least he's not a Republican.'"

Hunter thought, bestiality? Was that a misdemeanor or a felony?

Becker entered, gave him a file, and said, "More on Paul Schneider."

Hunter opened the file. Paul 'Cornfed' Schneider was born in 1962. He was raised in Cerritos, California. He had two younger sisters. His mother remarried. His stepfather was a retired Air Force officer.

A lot of the material was a rehash of what he had read earlier: Air Force, bad checks, robbery, then stabbing a prison guard in 1987.

Hunter put down the Schneider file and picked up a newspaper. He glanced at an article. Old news. The female dog Hera to be kept alive — for now.

Robert Noel agreed with the DA's decision. "That's a step in the right direction. We were going to make a demand that she be preserved as evidence for the entirety of any criminal proceedings and the appeals. Animal Care and Control wanted to run their circus."

Circus? Hunter wondered. What circus? He must be referring to dog court.

He read more of Noel's comments. "And they were going to run their circus. They wanted to put Hera down from the beginning as fast as they could."

Hunter snipped out the article and picked up the next one. He read that Sharon Smith was going to file for a wrongful death suit. The article explained that no one had ever successfully challenged the law denying gay and lesbian couples the right to sue.

Kate Kendell was the executive director of the National Center for Lesbian Rights. She said, "It doesn't make any difference how long-term or committed the relationships are, they are vulnerable. The state can't have it both ways. You can't condition a right on marital status, then deny a whole class of people the right of access to be married."

Sharon Smith was quoted: "I want to change some laws so domestic partners have some recourse in the future. As gay and lesbian couples we can't get married. We can't file suit. We are really caught in a Catch-22."

What rights does she have? Hunter wondered as he picked up the phone. He was connected to Paul Cummins. He apologized for bothering him again so soon and asked the chief assistant district attorney about Sharon's rights.

Paul answered, "I'm not a civil attorney, but she might be able to do what Nicole Simpson's family and Ron Goldman's family did in the O.J. civil suit. If Diane left a will naming Sharon."

"Explain."

"There's a state statute that allows the executor of a person's will to sue for loss of companionship, emotional distress and things like economic and medical loss and costs. It's called the survival statute."

"Thanks, Paul," Hunter said. "By the way, what happened in court yesterday?"

"Jim Hammer did an excellent job. In regards to Noel's claim of client-attorney privilege, he said, and I quote, 'The privilege is not carte blanche to plan crimes. If someone engages the services of an attorney, to commit a crime or fraud, those communications fall outside the privilege.'"

Cummins hesitated, then said, "I didn't see Sharon Smith as the sue type."

Hunter said, "She's not. She has publicly stated that any money she receives goes to something she's set up — The Diane Whipple Foundation. It's a non-profit foundation for things like the American Cancer Society."

* * *

Bestiality?

District Attorney Terence Hallinan appointed Jim Hammer and Kimberly Guilfoyle to prosecute the death of Diane Alexis Whipple.

The exact charges they would prosecute had not been determined — yet.

The two assistant district attorneys had remarkably similar backgrounds and remarkably different lives.

Both were raised in San Francisco as Catholics.

She was straight, he was gay.

Both came from an Irish background.

She was once a model for Victoria's Secret, he was once a Jesuit.

They both came from working-class families.

Kimberly's Puerto Rican mother died when she was ten. Her father came to this country from Ireland and worked in construction, was in the military, and served as an inspector for Pacific Gas & Electric Company.

Kimberly went to high school at Mercy in San Francisco and college at UC Davis. She then got her degree at the University of San Francisco Law School.

She went to work for the DA's office, then under Arlo Smith's command. She campaigned for his election. He lost, Terence Hallinan won. To the victor goes the spoils. She was fired.

She moved to Los Angles and became a prosecutor. There she handled over a thousand preliminary hearings. She also prosecuted homicides, armed robberies and sexual assaults. When it came to adult felonies, over the years she had achieved a 100% conviction rate..

Kayo Hallinan was reelected, defeating Bill Fazio in a tough, very close race. Kimberly was rehired.

She created a specialty for herself in the city of her birth. She loved animals, so she prosecuted both those that abused animals and those who allowed animals to harm humans.

She was quoted in the press about the Diane Whipple case. "I think and dream about the case every day and night. I think what resounds about the case is her death could and should have been prevented."

Kimberly Guilfoyle was often quoted as to how much she loved her job.

Jim Hammer's father was a bus driver for San Francisco's Municipal Railway System — the Muni. His mother was a teacher's aide. He graduated from Hastings School of Law. He went to work as a prosecutor in nearby Alameda County.

It was there that the vocational call struck him. He became a Jesuit, but he was still a lawyer. He worked as a public defender in San Diego. While there he taught at a Catholic high school in Watts.

Still a Jesuit, he was transferred to Santa Clara University where he taught law.

In 1995, after deciding that a ecclesiastic life was not for him, he left the order and went to work for the Santa Clara District Attorney's office.

Three years later he returned to San Francisco. In response to a question from the local press, he said, "Almost all crimes seem senseless. But the death of Diane Whipple seems particularly senseless."

Chapter
Thirty-four

Ashes to Ashes

Manhasset Congregational Church, New York State, Sunday, February 25, 2001.
It had been almost a month since Diane Alexis Whipple died, yet the church in Manhasset — just like in the chapel at St. Mary's of Moraga — was filled to overflowing.

Once again people came forward to speak in loving memory of their friend, their student, their relative and their love.

A friend since grammar school, Cheri DiCerbo, said from the pulpit, "She was so animated, so full of energy. She lit up the room. She loved her life. She loved her partner. Even in this craziness a *community* has been created."

Sharon Smith sat in the front pew. With her were her sister, Janet, Diane's mother, (Penny Whipple-Kelly), Diane's aunt Roberts, uncle and aunt Ralph and Joan Whipple, and high school soccer coach Pam McDonough.

A firefighter from remote Trinity County in Northern California, Captain Dan Koneburg, had started a support Internet spot for the bereaved — a place to send condolences if you were unable to attend a service in person.

Leslie King of San Diego wrote: "For Alexis' family, friends, lacrosse sisters and life partner Sharon, we are heartbroken about her passing and praying for her soul to rest in peace. Alexis obviously had a smile and a laugh for you all, and now you have a loving guardian angel looking over you. Sharon, you were a kind and supportive friend to me a few years ago whose words gave me the strength to end an abusive relationship and turn my life around, even though you were very busy In Menlo Park. I am urging you to 'Be strong' as you did for me. May you feel your Southern Californian friends' encouragement, strength, love and prayers as we admire your search for justice and peace."

Another posting on the Internet, from Mechanicsburg, Pennsylvania, was from Tom Samuel. He wrote: "I was fortunate enough to get to know Diane at Penn State. She was full of life and laughter and she will be missed by all who knew her. This tragedy is so difficult to understand but I take comfort in knowing that Diane has a special place in Heaven. The lord has called his angel home and I look forward to seeing her again. Diane's memory will live on for all of us. Her laugh, her smile, and her gusto for living will never be forgotten. God bless you, Diane. You will be missed but, more importantly, forever treasured."

The pastor of the Congregational Church went to the pulpit. The Reverend James Brown Only said, "It is difficult not to be angry that a loving person like Diane should die because members of the Aryan Brotherhood spread their hate throughout the world. That a responsible person like Diane should die because others made reckless choices only compounds the problem. We want justice. But God is not a puppeteer. God is like a coach who puts us in a game where others break the rules."

Coach Pam Monfort McDonough recited the litany of Diane's accomplishments as an elite athlete and finished with, "Diane was a scrawny speed demon."

Barry Allen, from Baltimore, wrote: "I am the husband of one of Diane's closest friends from her college days at Penn State University. I can assure you that this tragic event has deeply affected my wife and many of Diane's college teammates and friends. She was a wonderful person and loved by many. Our deepest condolences and heartfelt prayers go out to her family. I personally came to know Diane and am familiar with her kind and loving nature. Many times she sent warm wishes and gifts to our 2-year-old son, whom she met only once. For those acts of kindness I thank her and will never forget her. Our family prays for her and we know she is in a better place."

The condolences came in from both coasts. People like Sylvia Gentges of Jacksonville, Florida, who wrote: "To the friends and family of Diane, my friendship with her began when she interned at Innisbrook Resort in Florida. She always made me laugh with a funny comment or action. I am flooded with memories of some of our adventures. She was full of spirit that was so quickly spread to those around her. Diane, I'll be digging up old pictures and remembering you with a smile! My sympathies go out to Diane's life partner and her family and friends."

Martina Linar wrote: "Diane was not only the best coach, but also a friend. Her happiness everyday has taught me to live my life to its fullest. She was happy in everything in her life before she left us and I believe she continues to be happy watching over us in another place.

"Diane, I will always remember you and your love of candy and aliens."

One of Diane's lacrosse players, Amy Harms, wrote: "Diane was the most incredible person I ever met. Her love for life, her players, friends, and Sharon should be seen as an inspiration to all of us who had a chance to know her. She was the best coach I ever had. She was enthusiastic, dedicated, and most of all loved each and every one of her players. All that we achieved on the field is a direct result of everything she taught us. I will miss her as a coach, as a teammate, and as one of the best friends that I will ever have the chance to meet. If there is something from her that I can hope to take with me it is her ability to live each day to the fullest surrounded by the people I love. Coach, I will miss you and love you for the rest of my life. Love, Harms."

Sharon Smith said, referring to the social worker Gloria Young — who was with Diane on the day she died — "Even on Alexis's last day, a person who met her for the first time was touched. She told me, 'Diane's spirit was too big for this world.'"

Manhasset High School, soccer field, New York State, Sunday, February 25, 2001.
Sharon and her older sister Janet parked the car at the high school. Earlier they had meticulously divided up Diane Alexis Whipple's

ashes into six separate piles and placed them in six individual containers.

Sharon got one out of the truck. The two women walked to the fifty yard line. With them were the Reverend Only, Diane's aunt Roberts, her mother Penny Whipple-Kelly, and Mr. and Mrs. Monfort.

Sharon opened the container and cast forth the ashes.

Their task completed at the high school field, the two women drove to Diane's grandparent's house. It was the home Diane had been raised in since a baby, only leaving to go to college at 18.

Here she had learned life's lessons from caring relatives.

And here she had asked Sharon to deposit one-sixth of her remains on the steps that led to that home.

Family gathered: Aunts, uncles, mother, friends. Those that loved Diane watched as her life partner completed the second of a six-part obligation.

Sharon cast the ashes on the door steps.

Southampton, New York, Wednesday, February 28, 2001. Southampton was not quite at the end of Long Island. It was nestled next to Water Mill. The town's shoreline faced the Atlantic Ocean.

Sharon Smith stood a few feet back from the surf line.

With her was Diane's best friend, Cheri DeCerbo. She lived and worked in Manhattan, but had grown up in Manhasset and gone to Monday Park Elementary School and Manhasset High School with Diane Whipple. She had driven Sharon to The Hamptons.

The sky was overcast, a slate gray, like the backside of a tombstone. The water matched the ominous colors of the sky. A wind caused the waves to froth and churn.

The two women watched the surf run up and then ebb back on the beach. Together they turned over the small urn holding one-sixth of Diane Alexis' remains. Just at that moment the water receded. Half the ashes splashed down on the wet sand. The other half was swept out with the foam.

Ashes to Ashes

The next wave crashed in and caught the rest of the ashes in its grasp. The water gleamed with an effervescent glow, the half that had originally been whisked away was rejoined with the ashes left behind. The remains swirled in white froth, and then the grasp of the moon's gravity fingers pulled the ashes into the mass of the Atlantic.

DiCerbo said, "She was like a sister to me. This is the most devastating, tragic event that ever happened in my life. One minute you're happy. Your cell phone rings. Next thing you're sobbing and moaning. Not happy anymore, just grieving."

Pennsylvania State University, Thursday, March 1, 2001.
The University was founded in 1855. It has twenty-two colleges scattered about the state.

And it was the one last place on the East Coast that Alexis wanted her ashes scattered — the fifty yard line of the university's lacrosse field.

Sharon's sister Janet drove them out of New York, across New Jersey and to the university.

Diane's request for her ashes to be scattered at six different places was half complete. After Penn State, only the Pacific Ocean in Kauai and any mountain Sharon wanted remained.

They walked to mid-field. The air bristled with the chilling fingers of Pennsylvania weather on the first day of March. Wind-chill factor was zero.

Sharon had never watched Alexis play here in person, but she had watched her play here on video.

Quick, instinctive moves, a flash, a feint, a goal.

Then the exuberance shared with the team.

The stands, then, were filled with enthusiastic classmates and alumni. Now they were empty.

Sharon opened the container. She poured out one-sixth of the remains of the woman she loved.

A blast of winter air swept across the ground. It caught the ashes and scurried them down the field, evenly transporting them in a straight line toward the distant goal. Like a wraith, the ashes spun and twisted and danced until they reached the net at the end of the field. Then the wind died. The ashes settled to the ground.

Diane Alexis scored one last goal.

Chapter
Thirty-five

More and More Search Warrants

Hall of Justice, Steve Murphy's office, Monday, February 26, 2001.

Steve Murphy was in the habit of cleaning up his office around the end of every month.

He separated various cases into piles and filed them. Because it had the most information, he saved the Noel and Knoller case for last.

Murphy had been born on the first day of the year in 1955. One day late for a full year's write-off with the IRS for his parents. And too close to Christmas. Many people had been short-changed by being born near a holiday. Great aunts would say, "I just combined your birthday and Christmas present together and bought you something special."

That fabrication might be understood if you were over thirty, but was very disappointing to a 7-year-old.

But Murphy's easy-going, affable personality didn't wait for adulthood to spring forth, it burst out very young.

He had gone to Robert Louis Stevenson and Mark Twain elementary schools. The two schools named after famous authors foreshadowed a love of books for Murphy.

Following high school, he went to City College of San Francisco. Then off to the US Army from 1973 to 1979. He joined the Imperial County Sheriff's Department at the end of the 70s. Then the police department in San Francisco.

While at Potrero Police Station, he had been a member of Operation "S" — the Red Light Bandit Detail. Afterwards, he worked with the Golden Gate Narcotic Enforcement Team.

He rode bike patrol and walked plainclothes patrol.

He had been stationed in places like the Records Room, the Bureau of Investigations, the General Work Detail. He was now assigned to the joint task force between the SFPD and the ATF.

Along the way during his career he had won the Bronze Medal for Valor, five Police Commission Commendations, two Chief of Police Commendations, two Unit Citations and an earthquake medal, and over 100 commendations from his captains.

And after all that action, Murphy thought, now I feel like a bookkeeper.

There was a stack of search warrants in front of him.

He counted them. Thirteen.

Thirteen times when he had to go out and collect evidence regarding the dog mauling case.

Before filing them he decided he would recreate a chronological table of important events. It helped him to sort out and remember his thoughts while actually serving the search warrants.

He wrote:

January 26   — *Diane Alexis Whipple killed.*
January 29   — *Robert Noel and Marjorie Knoller adopt*
                        Paul 'Cornfed' Schneider.
February 13 — *Dog Court held.*
February 22   — *Bill Herndon rules the female dog*
                        Hera vicious and dangerous.
                        Given death sentence.

Okay, the experienced cop decided, now place the search warrants in chronological order.

The first one was issued on February 8 and served on February 9. That's when we couldn't find the building manager and I had to use a screwdriver to take off Noel and Knoller's front door. We found a bunch of weapons and ammo.

He rummaged through the pile and found what he was looking for. Right, the medical stuff that came up because Noel said he was in the hospital when Neil Bardack said his dog was attacked. That was during dog court.

He found the search warrant issued and served on February 15. It was for medical records at SF General Hospital. When Murphy went to SFGH, he was accompanied by special master Mike Osborne.

They were looking for evidence that the injury sustained by Noel was caused by the dog Bane.

He glanced through the search warrant. There was a copy of a receipt for the carpet from the building manager Aleta Cerdido. The bloody carpets had been removed the day after the attack.

Also in the search warrant were medical records con-firming that Noel had been bitten on the finger by a dog. Among the records was a letter written by Robert Noel to The United States District Court explaining why he was unable to attend a court hearing.

Murphy scanned the letter of explanation and then read the following by Noel:

"On Sunday, September 10, 2000, at approximately 6:45 a.m. at Crissy Field in San Francisco, I and my wife and our 2 Presa Canario dogs were attacked, in what appeared to be a deliberate manner, by a large Belgian Malonois dog who, with its owner, had pursued us for over 150 yards along the beach after being repeatedly told to stay away from us and our dogs.

"The Malonois first struck me in the right hand and then the large male Presa Canario in the face and head. I was astride the large male at the time of the attack in order to restrain and control him by his harness, lead and collar, and as a result of the attack suffered the almost total amputation of the index finger of my right hand at the knuckle joint."

Murphy stared at the page. One dog tried to take out two Presa Canario's?

Deliberately?

Isn't that what Noel is implying? The line — "in what appeared to be a *deliberate* attack" — seemed like a peculiar choice of words.

He went to Hunter's office and asked him if he knew anything about the story.

Death of an Angel

Hunter said, "I read somewhere that Noel thinks the Department of Corrections was trying to kill him."

"With a dog?"

"Apparently."

Murphy went back to his desk. He found a letter written by Noel to a judge, again requesting an excuse from court because of an injury sustained, except this time the dog was described as, "a large German Shepherd type dog."

Confusing. Was the dog a Shepherd or a Malonois?

He picked up the third search warrant. It was a request to search Pets Unlimited for medical records regarding Bane's treatment for injuries from a fight he had with another dog.

Search warrant number four involved the Peninsula Pet Resort — for medical records on the dogs Fury and Hera,

Number five, issued on February 15 and served on the 20th, involved the medical records on the dogs kept at UC Davis.

Six was issued on the 16th and Murphy recalled the wording well. He remembered what he had written: "During the course of this investigation I was told by inspector Richard Daniele that he had spoken to Hank Putek — a resident of 2398 Pacific Avenue, apartment 608. He stated that he had seen Mr. Noel and Ms. Knoller remove several boxes from apartment 604 between the time of the death of Diane Whipple on January 26, 2001 and the execution of the first search warrant on February 9, 2001.

"Based on what I saw on Channel 5, I believe that items listed in the original search warrant may have been removed from the residence before the original search warrant was executed and returned/brought back to the premises after the execution of the original search warrant. I believe the booklet I saw on Channel 5 broadcast and other items listed in the original search warrant will now be located at 2398 Pacific Avenue."

Manstopper. No way did we miss that book the first time around. It wasn't there. And it *was* there when Christie O'Conner interviewed Noel. Therefore, ipso facto, Noel brought the book back. He didn't go out and buy it at a bookstore after the first search warrant — not with a half dozen pictures of El Supremo Bane on the cover and Bretches's signature.

246

More and More Search Warrants

He picked up warrant number seven. It was a search warrant for Channel 5, KPIX. Wanted was a copy of broadcast portions of a videotaped interview of Robert Noel from inside his apartment on February 15, 2001.

He's going to regret that interview. Hell, Murphy mentally added, Knoller and Noel are going to regret *a lot* of interviews.

Search warrant number eight was the same as seven except it called for a search of Channel 2, KTVU in Jack London Square in Oakland.

Number nine was another search of Channel 5.

Number ten was KGO, Channel 7.

Number eleven was KRON, the *Chronicle*'s Channel 4.

Number twelve was WB/KBWB Channel 20.

And number thirteen was for Channel 36, KCIU TV.

Murphy had acquired video footage, both broadcast and raw, from every major television station in the Bay Area.

His motto was leave no stone unturned.

He turned his reports in to Henry Hunter.

Hunter's phone rang, it was the tax attorney Jim Sullivan who asked, without preamble, "Did you go to dog court?"

"No."

"Are the owners still claiming their dog is a gentle, well-bred pet?"

"Yes."

"Maybe the court should ask them to give it a test. Like spend time in the same cell with the animal."

"Those animals are reared to love their owners. The dog Hera knows Knoller and Noel."

Sullivan said, "I'm not talking about Noel and Knoller. But if they are so sure the animal is such a pussy cat, how about letting Hera and Cornfed spend time together."

"They've never met."

"Exactly. Maybe put in a national TV feed to watch the proceedings. Call the show 'Gentle Dog Meet's Mom's Boy.' We could run pools on how long it takes for the dog to sink a fang into Cornfed or Cornfed to sink a shank into Hera."

Chapter
Thirty-six

Cornfed and his Parents

Henry Hunter's home, Sunday, March 4, 2001.
Hunter sat in the easy chair in his front room reading a Stephen King novel he had started the previous night. He was waiting for his wife to finish dressing before going to Mass.

He read, "*He was horribly thirsty but the actual sight of water had driven him into a frenzy both times. He wanted to drink the water; to kill the water; bathe in the water; piss and shit in the water, cover it with dirt, savage it; make it bleed.*"

Hunter's wife called, "Time for church."

"In a sec." He continued to read: "*Cujo screwed his hind quarters down against the ground and waited for her. Urine, warm and painful, ran out of him unheeded. He waited for THE WOMAN to show herself. When she did, he would kill her.*"

Hunter remembered what a top dog behaviorist had told him: "Don't make the mistake of believing dogs think like us. They don't."

Hunter's mind was not completely on the celebration of the Mass that Sunday. It bounced about, invaded by random thoughts.

The priest raised the host.

This is the month I get a new grandson. Joshua Hunter was only a few weeks from coming into this world.

The priest: "This is my body."

What was in Bane's mind in that hallway?

The priest raised the chalice. "This is my blood."

What blood lust was sparked by the sight of Diane at the end of the hallway? Bane saw her, then attacked. No provocation.

And Bane, unlike Cujo, was not caught in the throes of

advanced rabies. Bane's brain was not rotting out from a disease that inevitably lead to death.

Bane went off because he was *bred* to go off — an animal *created* to be a Cujo.

The Mass ended and the Hunters went home.

Henry liked Sunday mornings. He and his wife would don 'Sunday's finest' and go to Mass. Then out to breakfast. Then home. He enjoyed Sunday sports. He liked them all — whether professional or collegiate. He glanced through the TV Guide.

Golf? Tiger Woods was getting ready to try for his fourth major in a row. If he wins, he'll have four trophies on his mantle at the same time.

Basketball? March Madness was around the corner.

Hockey? Never got into it until the Stanley Cup.

There was a nip in the air. March was truly coming in like a lion. Hunter made a fire. As he was gathering old newspapers to get the kindling going, he noticed there was over a week's worth he hadn't yet read.

Catch up. He settled into his easy chair. Babs, his cocker spaniel, took up her position next to him. Her snout gently banged against his calf. He absentmindedly scratched behind her ears with one hand and grabbed a paper with the other.

Headline: Inmate linked to attack defends self, attorney, by Alexis Chiu. Paul Schneider was quoted as saying, "I'm not a damned 'white-supremacist' dog fighter. I do not supply attack dogs to drug labs. I have never been accused of any drug-related crime. I have never been found guilty, or charged with any crime or prison rules violation re: dogs."

Hunter read that Schneider responded, when asked about Noel and Knoller, "They are good people. I care deeply about them. I really hate the fact that they are being vilified by the press and public, not really for the tragedy of January 26, but for befriending and adopting me, and for rescuing two dogs that would otherwise have died from malnutrition or neglect."

Hunter tossed the paper by the stack of firewood. Aren't Noel and Knoller being vilified because they tried to blame the victim? Aren't they being vilified because they have shown an absolute lack of empathy or compassion towards anyone or thing besides a convict and two dogs?

Robert Noel seemed incapable of *not* making statements that inflamed. Like what he said about dog court judge Herndon: "His bias was absolutely obvious. It was a kangaroo court for us and for Hera."

And Marjorie Knoller always seemed to add something equally inflammatory. When Herndon made the statement regarding his decision for Hera to be put down and said, "It's very warranted under the circumstances in which it happened," Knoller responded, "He's full of shit. He wasn't there. I have the blood and the bruises and the bite marks to prove it."

Another passage from Psalms came to Hunter's mind. "The hypocrite with his mouth destroys his neighbor."

Hunter picked up another newspaper. The headline read: Inmate Petitions to Represent Himself.

He who represents himself has a fool for a client.

A few days later, Schneider was granted his request to represent himself. Judge Leonard Louie ordered he be given access to paper and pen. He was also granted unmonitored phone calls from a court-appointed lawyer, David Harrison.

The judge denied a petition for two unmonitored phone calls a week from Noel and Knoller.

The testing of Hera had begun. Kayo Hallinan was present during some of the proceedings. He said, "It is a very impressive dog. A big, powerful dog. They tested reactions with a child, with a woman, and with a man."

Hunter riffled through the stack of papers. It was mostly a rehash of old events. But one article jumped out at him — more on Paul Schneider's background.

The convict was 38 years old.

After high school he married a woman four years his senior. At twenty-two he had a baby son.

About his life of crime he was quoted as saying, "I got hooked on robberies. A major rush."

Chapter
Thirty-seven

The Smoking Gun

General Work Detail, Room 411, Friday, March 9, 2001.
Henry Hunter had requested transcripts of the grand jury testimony
delivered each day as soon as they were transcribed. Becker
entered his office and placed the first file on his desk.

Jim Hammer was the prosecutor presenting the case.

Hunter opened the transcript and read:

GRAND JURY FOREPERSON: *Good morning ladies and
gentlemen, we are now officially on record. I know a number of
you had to walk through a maze of television cameras this morning
just to get into our grand jury room. I want to instruct you that
any media coverage you have heard previously, any TV or radio
reports, should be completely out of your mind when you consider
the case evidence.*

Hunter went through the admonishments to the nineteen-
person jury about letting media influence their judgment. Only
what they heard testified in the grand jury room was to be
considered before rendering their decision.

HAMMER: *We want this to be a fair proceeding. I ask and
instruct you to ignore the publicity outside. Our targets of this
investigation are Robert Noel and Marjorie Knoller.*

Hammer went through the background of the case. He
listed the applicable parts of the penal code.

Hunter then read:

HAMMER: *Does any member of the grand jury feel they cannot
be impartial in this matter?*

GRAND JUROR: *When I was fourteen I was bitten by a dog. It left a scar. I have nothing against dogs. But I do have something against dog owners who are not responsible.*
HAMMER: *I want this to be a completely fair grand jury. Do you think you could be fair?*
GRAND JUROR: *I have some doubt.*
HAMMER: *I would like to ask the grand juror not to be allowed to sit in on this case.*

Hunter read that Esther Birkmaier was the first witness called. Time, he thought, to find out if that flag in the original police report, the E-W for elderly woman, was a worry or not. Hammer took Esther through the background of the case and that she lived in apartment 607, directly across the hall from Diane Whipple. Then he brought the witness to the actual time of the incident.
HAMMER: *Did something attract your attention?*
ESTHER: *Loud barking dogs. Coming from the other end of the hall. The barking got progressively louder. As it got closer I thought, what is going on with these dogs? Then I heard someone cry, 'Help me, help me.' It was a woman's voice.*
HAMMER: *Did you make any effort to see what was happening?*
ESTHER: *I looked through my peephole. I saw a body lying on the floor with a dark object on top of it. The body's head was on the threshold. I remember seeing blonde hair at the top.*
HAMMER: *Did you ever hear the words, 'Get away, get away?'*
ESTHER: *I did, after I called 911.*
HAMMER: *What were you feeling while looking through the peephole?*
ESTHER: *Panic. The banging on my door by the dogs' bodies was very loud. It was crashing. It was so loud that, instinctively, I put the chain on my door thinking, at least if the door breaks down the chain will hold them while I can escape and lock myself in he bathroom.*
HAMMER: *Then what happened?*
ESTHER: *I looked through the peephole, but saw nothing but groceries scattered on the floor.*
HAMMER: *At some point did you hear someone else yell?*

ESTHER: *Yes. I heard the words, 'Get off, get off', 'Stop, stop,' and the words, 'No, no.' I knew it was Marjorie's in a loud shrill voice.*

HAMMER: *How did you know it was Marjorie's voice?*

ESTHER: *They, Robert Noel and Marjorie Knoller, lived in the building for eleven years. I had talked to Marjorie many times, that is why I recognized her voice.*

HAMMER: *When did you first hear Marjorie yell those things out?*

ESTHER: *After I went to the door the second time.*

Hunter thought, first barking, then Diane's voice, then banging, then the phone call, then back to the door, then Marjorie's voice.

How long to call 911? Say a few seconds to get from the door to the phone, a few seconds dialing, a few seconds for the operator to come on — there's usually a message saying if this is not an emergency then call the police directly.

Hunter dialed 911. He heard the lead-in audio auto message. It took about five seconds. When the operator came on he identified himself, told her it was just a test, and hung up.

The cop went back to recreating the scene in Birkmaier's apartment. He thought, Esther, who was looking real good as a very competent witness, despite that E-W flag, goes back to the door, puts the chain on and hears Marjorie yelling at her dogs.

How long was she away from the door? Ten seconds minimum. More like fifteen. He went back to the transcript.

HAMMER: *Could you tell where she was in relationship to your door?*

ESTHER: *Somewhat further away from the door. Marjorie repeated those three different commands at least three times.*

HAMMER: *During this time did you hear the dogs?*

ESTHER: *Yes. They were growling, snarling and barking the entire time. There was no silence.*

HAMMER: *How many times did you hear the other voice?*

ESTHER: *Just the two times, 'Help me, help me.'*

HAMMER: *What happened next?*

ESTHER: *I called 911 again. Now I couldn't hear anything from the hallway. I went to my window and waited for the police to arrive.*
HAMMER: *If you give an estimate from the first time you heard the dogs bark in the hall until the police arrived— how long?*
ESTHER*: Six to eight minutes.*

Jim Hammer took Esther through what happened after officers Laws and Forrestal arrived. Then Hammer showed her a photo of a door with the keys in the lock, and a purse and some groceries on the floor just inside the apartment. He then asked her if he ever saw Marjorie with one of the dogs off leash. Esther had, twice in the hallway. She never saw Noel with the dogs off leash.
HAMMER: *How far away from your door was Marjorie when you heard her shouting commands to the dogs?*
ESTHER: *If she was standing right in front of my door I would have been aware of it. She was down the hallway, between my apartment and the elevator.*
HAMMER: *Based on what?*
ESTHER: *Common sense.*
HAMMER: *How long was it between the time you heard, 'Help me, help me!' and Marjorie Knoller yelling, 'Get off!' and the other things she yelled?*
ESTHER: *Possibly three minutes. My 911 call was in there.*

Three minutes? Hunter thought. Three minutes!
I love this witness. Her testimony changes the scenario. Mental images began to rebound around the cop's mind.
That three minutes is unbelievable. And there's something else itching at me.
Something, he thought, something bothering me. Noel's second letter! The accusation that Diane and Sharon were in cahoots with the building manager, Heather, in an attempt to get the two lawyers evicted.
Animosity.
With the words "what if?" on his tongue, his mind's eye saw the hallway come into focus, and Marjorie Knoller, leading Bane, walked down the stairwell and headed toward her apartment.

The Smoking Gun

* * *

Marjorie deposited the bag of waste into the garbage chute. She turned toward her apartment, but Bane tugged on his leash the other way.

She saw Diane in front of her apartment doorway, one hand with the key in the lock, the other holding a purse, and two bags of groceries on floor,

Marjorie walked a few feet toward her and asked, "Why are you doing this?"

"What?"

"Trying to get us evicted?"

Hera came out into the hallway to investigate the sounds.

Instead of answering, Diane just stared.

Bane, hearing the anger in his master's voice, lunged, broke free and raced down the hallway.

Diane froze and shouted, "Help me, help me!"

A few critical seconds passed while Bane arrived at Diane and jumped, placing a paw on either side of her.

Softly, so as not to further anger the dog, Diane said to Marjorie, "Your dog jumped me."

Marjorie, still down the hallway by the garbage chute, watched as Hera raced by her and arrived at Diane's doorway.

Bane, with pack instinct taking over at the arrival of Hera, started to attack Diane. The two dogs thrashed about, banging against Esther's door.

Marjorie shouted, "Get away, get away!" Then she shouted the command again — to no effect.

She shouted, "Stop it, stop it!" And again repeated this command to no effect.

Finally she raced down the hallway, but by this time the two dogs had dragged Diane away from her own door and down the hall.

Marjorie frantically tried to pull Bane off Diane, shouting, "No, no!"

* * *

Except, the cop thought, that's wrong. According the Esther, three minutes passed between "Help me" and "Get off."

255

What was Marjorie doing during those three minutes?

Let's say Esther was wrong and it wasn't three minutes. Let's say it was only one minute.

What was Marjorie doing during that one minute?

Just watching her dog, or dogs, attack Diane?

What if Esther was wrong about three minutes or one minute? What if it was only thirty seconds?

Why wasn't Marjorie ordering her dogs immediately to stop? Why any delay at all?

"Help me!" should have been followed immediately with "Get away!" and "Stop!"

Also, Hunter thought, Esther's testimony didn't quite square with Marjorie's continued protestations that she tried to restrain Bane for sixty seconds and then was dragged down the hall for another fifteen or twenty seconds.

What else? Esther was quite adamant and specific in her testimony on what she heard. What she didn't hear was what Marjorie told the police, mainly that she had told Diane: "Don't move, he's trying to protect me."

If Marjorie Knoller hesitated at all, even for a moment, in helping Diane, then Marjorie was guilty of homicide. This went from a tragic, preventable accident to much more.

Three minutes between "Help me!" and "Get off!"

It was impossible. No one could just stand there and watch a dog, or two dogs, rip another human apart.

Could they?

Who knew? But there were all those discrepancies, from the very beginning, in Marjorie's accounts of what happened.

Was there any possible scenario that fit Esther Birkmaier's testimony?

What if, when Marjorie was on the roof, a sudden urge to go to the bathroom overcame her?

What if Marjorie hurried down the stairwell with Bane, opened her apartment door, and Hera rushed past her?

What if Marjorie, frantic to go to the bathroom, never noticed Diane down the hall?

The Smoking Gun

What if Marjorie, knowing her bladder couldn't hold it in the time it would take to retrieve Hera, entered her apartment, deciding to round up the two dogs as soon as she relieved herself?

A few minutes later she comes back into the hallway and sees what is happening to Diane. Then she shouts, "Stop it, stop it!"

That would account for the discrepancy involving Esther's three minutes between Diane shouting, "Help me!" and Marjorie shouting, "Get off!"

But why lie?

Why make up that stuff about telling Diane to get into her apartment, about fighting with the dog while being dragged down the hallway like an anchor?

Could the lie be just an initial fear of a huge civil law suit? And the knowledge that this was a criminal act never entering Marjorie's mind?

Too many shadows.

Too many unanswered questions.

Too many "what ifs" and "maybes" to come to any reasonable conclusion, with any assurance, about what happened in that hallway.

Hunter glanced at his blackboard where the words "Sixty seconds + Fifteen" were written.

Shakespeare's line flashed in his mind: "Oh what a tangled web we weave, when first we practice to deceive."

Chapter
Thirty-eight

Wrongful Death and AB25

Sacramento, Assembly Judiciary Committee, Wednesday, March 14, 2001.
Sharon Smith and Michael Cardoza traveled to Sacramento to appear as witnesses for the proposed Assembly Bill 25.

Carole Migden thanked the committee for having a special hearing. She covered the specifics and then explained the need for passage of her proposed bill. Then she said, "That Miss Smith has become an unwitting advocate because of personal tragedy, points to the inadequacy of the law. I'd like to present to you a very important witness for this case. I'd like to extend our deepest sympathy. We often see people when there are tough, challenging times at the darkest hours of their life."

The committee chair, Darrell Steinberg, also extended his condolences to Sharon Smith as she stepped to the microphone.

Sharon said, "I appreciate the opportunity to speak in support of AB 25. A few months ago it never occurred to me that I would be here today. And then the unthinkable happened."

She went through the events of January 26, then said, "As I have tried to absorb the loss, it is clear to me that her meaningless death could have been easily avoided.

"When I was told that current California law did not recognize my right to hold those responsible for Diane's death accountable, I could not believe it. To say that it added insult to injury is a gross understatement.

"Diane and I planned to spend the rest of our lives together. We would have been married if we could have been.

"Despite the lack of legal recognition, we considered ourselves married.

"Current law makes my relationship invisible and disrespects Diane's life and her memory. I am here to request that you acknowledge her and who she was to me. This is not much to ask. Thank you."

Sharon was followed by Lauri Simenson, who spoke of the joy she and her partner brought to friends and relatives when they registered as domestic partners, and how stunned those people were when they learned how little difference that act made in the eyes of California law.

The state still treats them as legal strangers.

The committee chair asked that those in support stand up and register at the podium by announcing their name and affiliation. A long line of people rose and came forward.

A man said, "Bill Powers for AARP."

"Debbie Perry, Gray Panthers."

Others registered: the Berkeley City Council; the California Athletic League; The National Association of Nurses; National Society of Social Workers; the American Civil Liberties Union; all of the West Hollywood City Council; the California Teachers Association; and, lastly, Kate Kendall, Sharon's co-counsel and Executive Director of the National Council for Lesbian Rights.

Mike Cardoza addressed the committee. "I come to you as an ex-acting-prosecutor for fifteen years. Some people would say to you that I come from the right.

"I now represent Sharon Smith.

"I've looked at our laws concerning marriage and I find them awfully interesting. Nowadays people can marry if they're at the requisite age. If they pay a small fee. We don't have any tests before people can marry.

"The only people we do not allow to get married are people who fall in love of the same sex. It's time that ends. It's time we personalize this. That's why Sharon's here today.

"When you get to know people and understand the love that they have for each other, how can we deny them the right to marry?

"I look at my gay friends, I look at the gay people that I work with, and I think, did God make a mistake in creating these people?

"You know the answer to that. Absolutely not.

"I ask that you do pass this bill simply because it's the right thing to do."

Assemblyman Howard Wayne asked, "This bill is not about legalizing gay marriage, is it?"

The sponsor of the bill, Carole Migden, said, "It is not."

The committee chair asked if anyone wanted to voice in opposition to the proposed bill.

Tim Smith rose to speak. "I'm a local attorney in private practice. I'm here on behalf of my family and the people of California who voted for Proposition 22.

"I want to make three points.

"One: The constitutionality of this bill under Article 2, Section 10 that I don't see addressed in the committee analysis. This bill attempts to amend or influence Proposition 22. A long line of court cases, including California Supreme Court cases, say such an amendment affected by an interest group is unconstitutional.

"Two: How this bill is an attempt to undermine Proposition 22, since it just extends rights to certain people."

Mr. Smith started to quote supreme court cases. The chair stopped him and asked him only to summarize the cases.

Mr. Smith continued. "The state's interest in promoting and protecting marriage is inhibited. Unmarried cohabitants receive no solicitous statutory protection, nor should they. Such would impede the state's promoting and protecting marriage.

"The state has a strong interest in marriage relationships.

"This is exactly what this bill attempts to undo.

"Three: I would like to address the personal issue. I represented a lesbian couple here in Sacramento. I looked at the same issue. What it really got down to was emotional distress. People in the very unfortunate situation of Sharon Smith, I have a lot of empathy for her. But there are grandparents in the same situation. There are adopted children in the same situation. There are a ton of very close relationships that are not protected or benefited. If you're going to address the fairness issue, it needs to be addressed on its own merits. Not in the context of a bill that essentially undermines marriage."

The committee chair thanked the speaker. Smith was replaced by Randy Thomason, who said, "I'm the Executive Director for the Campaign for California Families. We represent families around the state. This bill, unfortunately, is an end-run around marriage. It's an end-run around the voters of Proposition 22. It is unconscionable to give eleven marriage rights to persons who are not married. After marriage we see the joy of children progress, the solidity of kinship. Marriage should not be messed with, pure and simple.

"When we look at the benefits suggested in this bill, most of them are completely unnecessary. They are gotten through durable power of attorney. Durable power of attorney for health care. Any responsible two persons can fill out a form. I went to Staples and Office Depot and we got, for less than twenty dollars, the exact benefits that any two people can get. So, in a great sense, this bill is unnecessary.

"In the parts that expands it beyond, it infringes on the rights of businesses. It infringes on the taxpayers. So, for all of these reasons, we'd say please don't undo what the voters have voted. The people voted overwhelmingly to protect the rights of marriage only between a legally married man and a woman."

Art Crony, for Committee of Moral Concerns, was next. "Heterosexual senior citizens can get married if they want to. We oppose domestic partnerships for seniors.

"We believe this is an easy-in, easy-out relationship and there is no place for this in California law. For senior citizens this may be a trap. If they want to get registered as domestic partners, then the federal government in the future could decide that they are the same as married and lower their retirement benefits.

"You can't fix a federal problem with a state law.

"Most of the provisions of this bill can be addressed through power of attorney for health care or a simple will form.

"Diane Whipple's death was indeed a tragedy. We don't want to downplay that, or overlook it. According to the newspapers, though, her friend Sharon Smith was not a domestic partner.

"Should all adult friends and roommates and relatives have standing to sue for wrongful death?

"If you want to deal with that issue, that's finc. We probably wouldn't oppose a general broadening of that standing, but we do oppose any expansion of domestic partner laws.

"Generally, AB 25 supports gay and lesbian relationships.

"We don't think that's a good idea and we're not the radicals here. No major religion or major society in human history ever took such a position.

"This is not just a harmless alternative lifestyle for gay males, this is the most dangerous lifestyle in America.

"For lesbians it's not quite as bad, but it is still far worse than smoking or driving without seat belts. We go to great lengths to promote health for people and teach children to do the same thing. And here we have a bill that would advance the most dangerous lifestyle in America.

"We have sympathy for these folks, but we think it is a bad idea."

The next man opposed was Scott Lively, an attorney, director of the Pro Family Law Center in Citrus Heights, a suburb of Sacramento. He said, "I passed out a book to the members of the committee which addresses the historical consequences in Germany of having embraced homosexuality as a legitimate lifestyle alternative. I offer that to you as a warning of what we can expect as a society if we continue to abandon laws that protect marriage and the natural family—"

Darrell Steinberg interrupted. "We respect the First Amendment here, but start talking about Nazi Germany and somehow implying in any way that gay/lesbians are somehow responsible for the atrocities that went on, is beyond the pale."

Others came forward to register their opposition, like Natalie Williams of Capital Resource Institute. Then the chair asked for comments from the committee.

Christine Kehoe, Democrat from San Diego, said, "It's a privilege to vote for this bill. It's difficult to understand why a simple fairness issue law engenders such ridiculous hostility."

The assemblywoman went on to list the items asked for in the bill. "This is simply an attempt to give some Californians the same protections so many others enjoy," noted Kehoe.

"Despite what the opposition states, the majority of Americans support domestic partners. And they don't support gay marriage.

"There's a Catch-22 here," continued Kehoe. "We're criticized for gay/lesbian relationships for not being more public." She pointed at Sharon Smith. "She wasn't registered. She wasn't taking advantage of the tiny, little avenue we do have. So that's a reason for not to provide a better avenue for gay/lesbians to have public, long-term relationships?

"This weekend my partner and I will celebrate our 16th anniversary. It is one of the happiest aspects of my life.

"It is time to give support to this. The debate should be over.

"Californians support this. We need this. These are not special privileges, these are minimal rights."

Kehoe went on to explain that a similar law in her county did not raise costs substantially.

Hannah-Beth Jackson, Democrat, Santa Barbara, went through some of the history of rights extended over the decades to alternative partners. She cited an example of a woman who, after forty years in the relationship, was denied access to her life partner in the hospital where she was dying. The family swept in, after no contact for over twenty years, and denied this woman any access to her partner on her deathbed.

"When Proposition 22 was introduced," concluded Jackson, "proponents claimed that they did not want to deny any rights to alternate lifestyles, just not for them to be able to marry. This bill allows basic levels of human dignity."

Assemblyman John Longville, Democrat from Rialto, said, "I am disappointed that the people a year ago were telling us that Prop 22 isn't about equal rights, it's about preserving the sanctity of marriage and the unique status it has as an institution called marriage. 'We're not against giving the same rights to people who are homosexual, we just don't want them to have special rights. But we're not against them having same rights that other people have — just not marriage. Marriage is a religious sanctity.'

"To see the same people who, a little over a year ago, were stating those things, immediately afterwards change their tune and say now, 'We're against giving those same rights to the gay community.'

"I was surprised to see an attempt to try and tie homosexuality to Nazism. I'm stunned. It is well-known by all but the most out-of-touch, crazy people; the reality is that the Holocaust was aimed at a number of groups. One of them was the gay community. Countless gay and lesbians were put to death in the ovens because they were gay."

Longville went on to state that in every society a certain percentage was gay. It was genetic, like being left-handed.

"I urge my colleagues, don't find yourself in the situation with your grandchildren that many legislators in states in the Deep South find themselves in today. Having to explain to their grandchildren, how it was, back in the sixties, they could have voted to *not* allow equal rights to all Americans. And now, today, they recognize they were wrong. Don't put yourselves in the same situation. "

Howard Wayne, Democrat, San Diego, said the bill was not about marriage, not about end-running Prop 22. It was about ordinary things that should be available to everyone.

Assemblyman Kevin Shelley, Democrat from San Francisco, expressed his condolences to Sharon. "The environment we're trying to encourage and nurture and promote are expressions of love and commitment amongst people, whether between two people of different sex or the same sex. That's what life is about, encouraging that form of loving commitment. And that is what this bill is about. I find it shocking that the opponents of this bill, while involved in Prop 22, said that was about marriage. 'We're not against rights, and domestic partnership would be okay.' Why did they say that? Because they were desperate about Prop 22."

He went on to say that this was not about legal definitions, it was about hatred. Which was apparent with the comment about Germany. "The opposition to this bill is rooted in one thing: hatred."

Robert Pacheco, Republican, Walnut Creek, spoke to counter Shelley's comments. "A lot of things have been said about sharing love and relationships. I don't have any opposition to what that entails. Miss Smith, I certainly share the grief you have. We have some very distinct legal issues that arise because of this measure that do not apply to other people. When we start making and creating distinctions and not applying the law equally, then we have to look very specifically at a measure such as this.

"Four specific areas that would not apply to the general population:

"Intestate succession.

"Personal income tax deductions."

Carole Migden interrupted. "This bill does not address the issue of personal income tax deduction. I'm happy to show you that there are no special rights."

"On my reading of the bill I have not been satisfied," responded Pacheco.

Darrell Steinberg asked if he could join Carole Migden as a co-sponsor of the bill. He said, "This is about one of the last bastions of permissible discrimination in our society — that against gays and lesbians. It's also about encouraging committed relationships. I'm struck by Miss Smith's comment that the current law makes her invisible. When you think about our society and all the disaffected people in all walks of life, we ought to be doing everything in our power to encourage people to find loving partners. It's good for our society. It's healthy for our society."

The role was called.

The measure was moved out of committee by an 8-1 affirmative vote.

Chapter
Thirty-nine

More Grand Jury Witnesses

General Work Detail, Room 411, Thursday, March 15, 2001.
Hunter had received the testimony given to the grand jury since
March 13, but had not had time to read the statements.

He opened a file. The next witness called after Esther
Birkmaier was Officer Forestall. Her testimony was the same as
she gave at dog court. The next were Andrea Runge and Michael
Scott, who also had testified at dog court.

Next was officer Alec Cardenas. He was a medic on the
SWAT team. His testimony basically affirmed the other officers
on the scene.

Next, Hammer called Sharon Kay Smith.

Henry Hunter took out a pad of paper. His habit of
doodling returned and the squares and circles and triangles and
rectangles began to appear as he read Hammer walk Sharon
through the background of the event.

HAMMER: *Was there an incident sometime in December that
involved Diane and the dog or dogs?*

SHARON: *Yes. I got a phone call at work, around lunchtime.
Diane called me. A brief conversation. She was very excited. Her
speech was very heightened, very loud. She said she had just
gotten bit by that dog. And I said, "those dogs."*

HAMMER: *When she said, "that dog" and you said "those
dogs," what led you to believe she was referring to a specific dog
or dogs?*

SHARON: *That's how we referred to those dogs. I meant Bane
and Hera.*

HAMMER: *Why just, "those dogs?"*

SHARON: *We didn't know their names. We can't believe those dogs are living in a small apartment. Diane said once that she couldn't believe that Marjorie was walking a dog that size. We actually didn't know Marjorie or Robert's names either, and we called them,* "those people.*"*

Jim Hammer took the witness through the time when she went home in December and saw the red marks on Diane's hand. Medical attention was not needed. Then he took her through the events of January 26, 2001. Then Hunter read:

HAMMER: *Was Diane taking any medication?*

SHARON: *She was taking Levoxyl, a synthetic thyroid. She had thyroid cancer so her thyroid is gone.*

HAMMER: *Did Diane wear perfume?*

SHARON: *Yes. Ilbacio. But only some days. It would not be her habit to wear perfume when she was going to coach or workout, to sweat.*

HAMMER: *Did she use pheromone-based products?*

SHRON: *No.*

HAMMER: *Was she using any type of steroids?*

SHARON: *No.*

HAMMER: *Did she use vitamins or nutritional substance?*

SHARON: *No.*

Sharon received the same admonishment as the other witnesses. She was not to speak about her testimony.

Hunter scanned the witness list. Next called was Venus Azar, a physician for the City and County of San Francisco. Azar summarized the injuries that Diane received and a detailed description of the autopsy. Besides having almost her entire body mauled and most of her blood lost, Diane's throat had been punctured and her larynx crushed.

The next witness was Sidney Laws, the police officer who testified at dog court.

Next was Paula Gamick, employed by the San Francisco fire department. She backed up the testimony of the police officers and animal control officers at the scene.

On Thursday, the first witnesses to appear were Janet Coumbs and Ron Bosia, a dog-walker. Then Mara Lamboy,

Death of an Angel

Animal Care and Control officer, who sold dog licenses. On January 3, 2001 she sold a dog license on Bane and Hera to Robert Noel. He signed it as co-owner of both dogs.

Next witness was Lynn Gaines, a dog-walker for four years. She was familiar with both Noel and Knoller. She had told a number of people that she thought the dogs were a hazard and needed muzzles. She once saw Bane barking and lunging at her and a Bernese mountain dog.

Lynn went to the center of the street and called to Robert Noel, "You should put a muzzle on that dog."

Noel called back that she should shut up and called her a bitch. It was her dog causing the problem.

HAMMER: *Were you fearful for your safety and the safety of the dog you were with?*

LYNN: *Yes.*

The neighbor Hank Putek testified, then the lawyer and dog owner Neil Bardack, and mailman John Wantanbe, all of whose dog court testimony Hunter had already read.

The next witness was Alex Lazio. He had an encounter with both Noel and Knoller and the dogs. The male dog was not leashed.

LAZIO: *The male dog started to move toward me. It seemed unusual, this large dog moved in a way toward me with a curious body language. It wasn't conciliatory or friendly. I realized that it had designs on me other than to just say hello. My gut reaction was so strong that I moved back three or four feet. The odd thing about it was Ms. Knoller laughed at the idea that I, a male, six-one and a half was frightened by the dog. I am not a dog phobic. We had large dogs in our family. I'm not afraid to pet a mastiff. I like dogs. I'm not frightened in any respect.*

HAMMER: *You saw her laugh?*

LAZIO: *Yeah. This was not really funny. A normal response to me would have been to get a handle on the dog. The fact that she laughed really resonated in me. She wasn't conciliatory or sorry or anything. I said, "that dog looks like he could do some damage." And the response was, "no, he's a pussy cat." At this*

time she had the dog under control. One word from her and the dog became stationary.
HAMMER: *Did the dog stop in his tracks?*
LAZIO: *Pretty much.*

Diane Curtiss was next. She lived in the Pacific Heights apartment house on the fourth floor. She related an incident she saw out her window between a grandfather, his grandchild and the dogs Bane and Hera — both unleashed — and Robert Noel.
CURTISS: *The little boy went close to one of the dogs and the dog lunged at him and the little boy pulled his arm back. Noel yelled, "No." I could hear it from my apartment window. It was a resounding. "No."*

The next witness was Jill Davis, a tenant in the same building. She ran into the couple getting off the elevator at six in the morning.
DAVIS: *I was eight months pregnant. The dog jumped up at my stomach. Its mouth was open. I ran out of the building.*

Hunter tapped the large stack of papers and thought, how many times did Noel and Knoller tell the press that they never experienced any problems with either dog?

And how many witnesses had appeared in dog court and before the grand jury to testify to the exact opposite?

Chapter Forty

Noel Testifies

Grand Jury Room, Thursday, March 22, 2001.
Robert Noel took the stand and faced the members of the grand jury.

Prosecutor Jim Hammer said, "You understand you are not compelled to testify, only to be here?"

"I understand that."

"Do you further understand that anything you say here today can and will be used in a court of law?"

"Yes."

"You have a right to consult with an attorney."

"I know."

"Do you still want to take questions?"

"Yes, I do."

"Do you have any question regarding your rights?"

"No."

Hammer went through the ownership of the dogs. He asked if the dogs had ever been trained to attack, fight or kill.

Noel answered, "No."

Hammer asked how and when Noel received the book *Manstopper*.

Noel explained that he was interested in an "asinine law" in California where if you train a dog you have a heightened liability. He claimed the statue is counter-productive.

Hammer took Noel through various encounters that other people had testified to regarding the two dogs. Noel rebutted. He also defended his decision to use a harness rather than a choke chain.

Hammer asked if Bane or Hera had ever bitten or lunged at another person.

Noel answered, "No."

Hammer again asked about the ownership of the dogs.

Noel explained how he had first become involved with Paul 'Cornfed' Schneider. He detailed how he had represented the convict, and then, over time, grown to respect him.

Noel stated, "Paul and Dale could have done many things with the money they'd won. They could have invested it in illegal drugs and sold them inside the prison, they could have put it into illegal gambling operations, or they could put it into inmate trust accounts and the Department of Correction could have sold them tooth paste, and cologne and soda crackers for the next twenty years at exorbitant prices.

"What they hit on was, surprisingly, legal. An inmate in the California penal system cannot actively engage in business while he or she is incarcerated. But they are guaranteed the right to own property, sell property, inherit property, subject only to the Department of Correction to restrict sales of property made for business purposes.

"The way the Department of Corrections interprets that is a convict cannot run a business, so they have to run a business through a third party. They can own property that is managed by a third party to their benefit. That's exactly what they did.

"We did not set up the operation."

Noel explained how he and Marjorie became involved, first with shipping them away from Janet Coumbs and how Bane and Hera came to live with them.

Noel then gave examples of how well-behaved his dogs were. He cited the following: "We were waiting for a table, standing outside on Union Street. Hera was asleep on the sidewalk, up against a wall. There was a couple with a very strange looking beagle. The woman was very pregnant, about nine months. Two loud-mouthed, drunken individuals showed up and started harassing her and her dog.

"The little beagle made a heroic stand. Got up and started barking at these two louts. When one of them stepped back to kick

271

the beagle, and he actually just bumped into me — Hera was on her feet barking along with the beagle. And this time it wasn't just a riff, it was a really good bark. But she didn't go after him. It was a really good bark.

"He made a move toward her, and I stepped between him and her and, pardon the expression, said, 'Get the fuck away from the dog.'

"Things calmed down. That's the kind of behavior we had come to expect with Presas in these situations. Purely a defensive, not an aggressive, nature."

Noel went on to explain that what happened on January 26 was completely out of his experience. He then told, from his point of view, what happened on the day.

Hammer asked, "Did you enjoy it when your dogs scared people?"

"My dogs never scared people."

"Would you enjoy that if your dogs *had* scared people?

"No."

"Were you proud of the fact that people were frightened by the sight of your dogs?"

"Not particularly, no."

"Did you ever mock people, in word or writing, when they showed fear about your dogs?"

"Not that I can recall."

"No memory of mocking someone who showed fear?"

"If you have something, show it to me."

"You have no particular memory?"

"No."

Hammer removed a piece of paper from a file. "I'm going to read something to you, sir, and you tell me if it sounds familiar. I'm reading from January 11, 2001, a letter to Paul Schnieder. Skipping to page two."

Hammer read: "This morning was an interesting walk. Getting used to the jail break approach the kids have. Break from the door like horses out of the starting gate. Standing next to the elevator, shifting one leg to the other. Their ferocity in panting in direct proportion to how badly the mutt, he or she, has to go at this point. Elevator comes, hopefully with no one in — otherwise they will knock them down rushing in."

Hammer paused, then asked, "Were there occasions where your dogs knocked people down while rushing in?"

"Never happened. But that particular morning they needed to go to the bathroom."

"You had a fear that they would knock someone down?"

"No, I didn't."

"You wrote that."

"I just wrote that. It never happened and I would never let it happen. If you read further in the letter you will see that when we got downstairs we met two other dogs, one of which started lunging at my dogs. I took the elevator back upstairs."

"How do you refer to those other dogs?"

"I don't recall. They lived on the fourth floor. There was a white one that was always rushing towards people and other dogs."

"You called it a obnoxious, little, white piece of shit."

"Yes I did. And that was what it was."

Hammer picked up the letter again. "I want to read one other part of this to you:

"'This morning was one of those days. We get the elevator after one of our neighbors had been dicking around with it, about a five minute wait for the kids. We got on. The panting is now anxious. When we reach the first floor I see someone standing by the door through the small view window. I tell them to step back. Just at the point the kids hit the door with their snouts, the door blows open. And they are nose to nose with this little collie and the obnoxious, little, white piece of shit. B and H are into a defend mode.'"

The prosecutor looked up at the witness. "What does a 'defend-mode' mean?"

"They just go on point. They go rigid."

"As if they're going to attack?"

"No, not as if they're going to attack. The white dog was snarling. Barking, lunging, and the dog-walker that had it wasn't doing a very good job of controlling it."

"Were your dogs acting aggressively?"

"They were responding to aggression that was being directed at them."

"How old were these dogs? The collie and the white little piece of shit?"

"I have no idea."

Hammer went through a series of questions, asking if Noel thought the other dogs could hurt his, and how big they were. The white one was about fourteen inches tall.

Then Hammer read from the letter:

"'As soon as the elevator got back to the sixth floor, one of the newer female neighbors, a timorous, little mousy blonde who weighs less than Hera meets the dynamic duo exiting and almost has a coronary.'"

Hammer asked, "Who's that?"

"That's Ms. Whipple."

"Are you concerned that she almost had a coronary?"

"Not particularly, no."

"Did you enjoy it?"

"Not particularly, no."

"Did you care how she felt?"

"I didn't know her."

"She looked frightened of your dog, didn't she?"

"Frightened, startled, I don't know."

"You apologized to her?"

"No, not at all. I asked her to step back and walked to the side. The dogs looked at her and just kept walking."

"Were you concerned that she was terrified of your dogs, so, as you put it, she almost had a coronary?"

"Not particularly, no."

"Did you do anything to allay her fears?"

"I took the dogs and got them away from her. She got in the elevator and went down stairs and I assume that the snarling, snapping little piece of shit—"

Hammer said, "Two weeks later Diane died, correct?"

"As it turns out, yes."

"By your dogs?"

"As it turns out, yes."

Noel Testifies

The grand jury foreperson handed Hammer slips of paper with questions from the grand jury. He read a series of questions:

"How much do you weigh?"

"Were you concerned about your own liability?"

"Were there any documents showing that Dale Bretches and Paul Schneider owned the dogs?"

Noel weighed 265, was not concerned about liability, and — besides were the money came from — there were no documents.

Noel was asked if he had any animosity towards either Diane Whipple or Sharon Smith.

He did not.

Chapter
Forty-one

Diane and the Scavenger Hunt

Sarah Miller's apartment, Sunset District, San Francisco, March 25, 2001.
"The call's for you," Sarah said, and handed a cellular phone to Julie Duff.

Julie took the plastic toy cell phone and said, "Diane, how's it going up there in heaven?"

There were four women in the room: Melissa Boyle, a lacrosse player on Diane's team last year; Jennifer Krusing, Palo Alto firefighter; Sarah Miller, Diane's former assistant coach; Julie Duff, sports umpire.

They were part of the A-team — people who had banded together to make sure that Sharon had the emotional support and love she needed to see her through her grief.

Other members of the A-team were Michael Cardoza, Kate Kendell, Jenn and Terry Michele and Teresa Ewins.

Jenn, Terry and Teresa were the ones who organized the show of support immediately after the attack, in front of the apartment building. They showed up with signs reading: "Honk if you love Diane," and, "Justice for Diane."

People honked. People waved. People who had never met Diane or Sharon showed their support.

The A-team used any means to make Sharon smile. Like showing up for dinner in outrageous costumes and masks — usually as aliens.

They started a ritual where each month they would award one of their group the Diane Alexis Trophy — earned by being the one who most exemplified Coach's attributes.

The previous winner's job was to observe, then award.

Sarah had been the most recent winner. She invited part of the A-team over to talk about what was going on in the case.

Jennifer was off for two days from fire duty. She was supposed to be studying for her EMT test. She opened a bottle of wine and poured three glasses. The test could wait.

Sarah said, "Thought you had to study?"

"I do. But I think I'm in good shape for the test," she paused, "and I need a night off."

Melissa opened her backpack and took out a box of Godiva chocolates. She crunched one up in her fist and tossed it into the fireplace. "In Diane's memory."

Each woman gobbled down a Godiva.

Sarah picked up the box. She turned sideways in her chair, cradling the chocolates protectively in her arms. Changing her voice slightly, she said, "These chocolates are mine, mine, mine. Melissa gave them to me. They're mine, mine, mine."

She opened the box, grinned, and flipped a candy to Jenn. Then pretended to guard the box again.

Jenn, Julie and Melissa broke out laughing. Jenn said, "That's Diane right down to a T."

Sarah started to cry.

Jenn, Julie and Melissa looked at Sarah's shattered face and soon all four were sobbing.

Sarah said, "Every time I get happy, every time I forget Diane for a few moments, I feel guilty."

"I know," Melissa sighed. "I feel the same way."

Sarah decided to change the mood, but not the meaning of their get-together. "It might help if we relived moments from the past that were special involving Diane. 'Keeping her memory alive.'"

"That's an easy one for me," said Melissa. "The scavenger hunt last year. On Crazy Dress Day."

* * *

Diane told the lacrosse team they were not going to practice on Crazy Dress Day, they were going to play a game. She told them she didn't care what they wore as long as they arrived in running shoes.

The team showed up early that morning. One was dressed as a clown, another as a Girl Scout, another as a Keystone Cop look-alike.

Some had even worn their clothes inside-out.

They gathered in the gym in front of their coach.

Diane divided them into groups of six.

To each group she gave a Polaroid camera and said, "You're going on a scavenger hunt."

One of the team asked, "Off campus?"

"Of course, off campus."

"Like this?" She pointed at her Girl Scout uniform.

"You picked it, not me."

"Can I change?"

"No." Diane said. "This hunt is a little different than most hunts. You're not to bring back anything. You're to take pictures of certain assignments. Like," she looked at her clipboard, "touch a cow."

Diane ran her finger down the list. "Shake hands with the Dean. Things like that. And remember, I want to see the object and the lacrosse player. For instance, a finger touching the side of what might be a cow doesn't count. I want to see that it is part of a cow and the whole person."

She handed out the list to each team, then added, "One other thing. As you are supposed to be athletes, none of you can use transportation besides your feet. No cars, no skates, no bikes, no skate boards."

"We get it, Coach," Melissa called out.

"The team that wins gets an A in P.E."

"But we *always* get A's in P.E."

A grin appeared on Diane's face. "Maybe not this semester."

"What are *you* going to do, Coach?"

"Play the game and beat the pants off you guys."

The teams took off.

Diane and the Scavenger Hunt

Cows were not exactly plentiful in central Contra Costa County. Years earlier the landscape held many a cattle ranch and farm, but now those same rolling pasture-like hills held homes. Development after development, rows of houses on curving streets feeding numerous cul-de-sacs, malls, now jumbled together from Orinda to Pittsburg, from Concord to Dublin.

Not much room was left for cows.

But there was a farm about five miles away. The teams took off. One headed for the Dean's office, others towards other objects on the list like the Walnut Creek Fire Station. Object: Have your picture taken next to a fire truck and a fireman.

The young women on the lacrosse team knew that the "game" was really just another way to get them to train. Diane was big on conditioning. "Can't eat candy if you don't train," was one of her battle cries.

Melissa's team decided to draw up a map and plot the shortest routes between various objects.

One of her team said, "Coach never said we had to stick together."

Melissa held up the camera. "She only gave us one camera."

"She didn't say we couldn't buy *more* cameras."

"Right, she's always telling us to *think*, think, think a problem through. These throw-away cameras can't cost all that much."

They divided themselves into three teams.

Melissa had a point to make. "Diane didn't say we had to take the pictures ourselves. There are six items on the scavenger list and six people to a team. What if we got other people to take the picture?"

"Like a cow?"

"I'll handle the cow. The rest of you go to the mall and buy five cameras. The firemen won't say 'No' to taking a picture, and neither will the Dean."

Five women headed off to a nearby mall to buy cameras. Melissa jogged south, toward the farm.

279

Pace yourself, she thought, don't rush. No need to if the other teams hadn't figured out that the problem was more than just running madly about the county.

That was Coach. "Lacrosse is not just a game," she'd say, "it's a problem. You have to think."

Melissa ran down a trail that meandered through a grove of trees. The trail led through county and state property, no structures besides maintenance sheds, all the way to the farm.

Melissa was in good shape. But she didn't want to press herself on the hills.

The first hill was steep, but Diane had taught them to handle hills on their cross-country jaunts.

"Personalize them. Give them names. Easier to tackle an enemy when they have a name."

Diane had gone on to name the hills they chugged up. Names like Medusa and Mr. Evil and Dracula.

"Give them antagonists' names," she'd say. "Like Hitler's Hump, Hussein's Horror, or Diane's Drudgery."

Melissa thought, Coach never had a problem teasing anyone, even herself.

She kept a seven-minute pace for the five miles, reached the farm and immediately had a problem.

There was no one there. The cows were there, but no people.

She studied the camera. No delay setting. No setting it on a log, aiming it at a cow, and then walking over and touching the cow.

Her arms weren't long enough to take a picture of herself touching the cow and still get the cow and all of herself in-frame, like Diane had specifically instructed.

She looked around. My team's depending on me. There has to be a solution. She shaded her eyes and scanned the horizon. No farmhouse lay snuggled in a group of trees. Her shoulders sagged.

*   *   *

Sarah, Julie and Jenn listened with rapt attention.

Diane and the Scavenger Hunt

Melissa said, "I got lucky. A guy in a Jeep came by. He took my picture, me touching the cow. Man, are those things big. I ran back to school. I raced across the football field. I saw Diane ride by, standing in the back of a pick-up truck. She called out, 'I said you guys couldn't use transportation. Nothing about me not using it.'"

Tears formed in Melissa's eyes. "Diane won the contest. She cheated like you wouldn't believe."

"How?"

"The picture of her touching a cow? She went to the Safeway meat counter and touched a steak. The fireman and the fire truck? They were a toy fireman and a toy truck."

Sarah started to laugh, then cupped her head in her hands. The tears returned.

Jenn, who was feeling just as sad, saw Sarah's sorrow and said, "Let's think of something happy. Something Diane did that made us laugh."

"Like Fooze Ball?" Sarah said between sobs.

All the women burst out laughing.

"She was terrible at it, wasn't she?" Julie said.

"She couldn't get the hang of it," Jenn added.

"Remember the look on her face?" asked Sarah. "A look that announced that the whole world depended on her winning."

Melissa, wiping tears caused partly from laughter and partly sorrow, looked at her friends. "Diane was the only teacher I have ever had that I wanted to be just like."

The others tearfully nodded.

Melissa said, "I don't mean exactly *like*, I don't look anything like her."

Sarah said, "You mean her personality."

"Right," Melissa replied. "And her humor. Her honesty. Her unbelievable loyalty, her ferocious competitive nature."

"Stop it," Sarah asked, tears rolling down her cheeks.

Jenn added, "You're killing us."

"Sorry."

Sarah removed the trophy from her bookcase and gave it to Melissa. "You have won the honorary Most Like Diane Whipple Award this month."

Melissa hugged the statue to her.

Jenn said, "Sarah and I bought a book on how to handle grieving."

"Like what we're all trying to do for Sharon?" Julie asked.

"No. To alleviate the grief inside ourselves."

"Is it working?"

"Not yet."

Chapter
Forty-two

Flight to Nowhere

From the grand jury room to various locations around Northern California, Tuesday, March 27, 2001.
Hammer meticulously took Marjorie Knoller through the events of January 26, 2001. When she got up. What she had for breakfast.

Step by step, right up to taking Bane to the roof. Then down the stairs. Into the hallway.

Using a diagram, Hammer asked Marjorie to place an X and a M1 next to it to show exactly where she was. Then Hammer placed a D1 down in front of Diane's doorway.

Over and over Hammer asked, "Is that a fair and accurate description?"

Once again the tragic events of the afternoon were related by the one living witness to the whole thing.

When Bane first became interested in Diane, he, "only pulled me a half a foot," Marjorie said.

Hammer marked the diagram again with an M3.

Foot by foot. Six feet, eight feet. Hammer led the witness down the hallway. Bane moves, Knoller restrains. The tug a war marches from Knoller's apartment to Whipple's apartment.

And, once again, Marjorie insisted that she never lost control of the dog.

Hammer asked, "He was pulling you down that hallway. He was more powerful than you?"

"No."

Hammer asked, "Then you willingly went down the hallway?"

"No."

Hammer kept marking the diagram: M4, M5, M6. The prosecutor kept asking, "Are you going where you want to go or where the dog wants to go?"

"I'm fighting with him."

After Hammer led the witness through the entire attack, Marjorie compared controlling a dog Bane's size to controlling a horse. The size of the controller didn't matter, the relationship between the person and the animal did.

Hammer asked her if she had ever seen Bane or Hera lunge, snap, growl or bite another person or animal.

She had not.

Marjorie testified for over three hours.

The grand jury retired to deliberate their decision. They had a few choices to face. They could find that there was insufficient evidence to indict Noel and Knoller on anything. Or they could find that both were guilty of owning a mischievous animal. That was a felony carrying a maximum three-year sentence. They could find that both were guilty of involuntary manslaughter, which, as a felony, carried a four-year maximum sentence. Or they could find one or both guilty of second-degree murder, a felony with a penalty of 15-years-to-life.

Outside the courtroom, Noel and Knoller were surrounded by reporters and cameras. Men and women shouted question from, "How do you think the grand jury will decide?" to, "Do you regret appearing before the grand jury?"

Noel said, "The prosecutors better have a very strong case, or they'll be embarrassed. And Mr. Hallinan will not be elected mayor. The prosecution is going to have its work cut out for it."

His wife added, "You can't be responsible for something you don't know is going to occur."

Marjorie had a dizzy spell. Paramedics at the courtroom treated her. She and Noel left the building.

The couple got into a rented maroon Chevy Impala and drove off. Following close behind was a vanguard of media vans and cars.

Henry Hunter leaned next to the open window of a car and said to his two field investigators, "You know what to do."

Robert Noel pulled into the Opera Plaza garage. Speeding through the underground parking lot, he quickly exited, managing to lose all the media.

One car was waiting at the exit and followed a discrete distance behind the Impala.

From San Francisco to Woodland. 3:15 p.m.
Mike Becker and Rich Daniele were in the undercover car. They followed Noel and Knoller,

The couple left San Francisco via the Golden Gate Bridge. They crossed the Bay again over the San Rafael Bridge and headed north.

They sped up once getting to Yolo County.

Rich maneuvered, trying to stay a few cars behind.

"You're losing them," Becker said.

"They're going ninety. I'd like to make it alive through this."

The car they were tailing was not only speeding, it was meandering back and forth passing slower vehicles, which was everyone else on Interstate 5 except Becker and Daniele.

Mike repeated, "You're losing them."

Rich glanced at the speedometer: 92 MPH.

Mike said, "Where's the CHP? I thought they had helicopters for this kind of stuff."

"Airplanes," Daniele said through clenched teeth.

"What?"

"Airplanes. Haven't you seen the signs? This road patrolled by aircraft?"

"Yeah, I have. So where are the airplanes?"

Daniele swerved, missing a logging truck, swerved again, missing a van. He roared past a RV and caught sight of the couple's car — about a quarter-mile in front of them.

Becker said, "Talk about a flagrant breaking of the law."

"Reckless driving?"

"And speeding. The limit here is sixty-five. They're breaking that by twenty-five miles at least."

Daniele, with one eye on the road and the other on the speedometer, corrected. "Thirty miles an hour over the speed limit."

Becker said, "Where do you think they're headed?"

"Not Mexico. They're headed north."

"Canada?"

"Who knows?"

"We must have extradition treaties with Canada?"

"Who knows?"

The car they were in, a nondescript vehicle meant for stakeouts, not high-speed chases, trembled and shook. Reverberating metal groaned with fatigue. Suspicious dark smoke belched from the exhaust.

Becker said, "I'm calling in."

"To see if the grand jury has indicted yet?"

"No. To tell Hunter to call the highway patrol and get them to slow those two down."

"What about the grand jury?"

"When they indict, we'll arrest them. But we can't do anything until they do."

Daniele muttered, "How about arresting them for speeding?"

"We're not traffic."

"How about a citizen's arrest?"

Ignoring his partner, Becker used the radio in the car and called in to the Hall of Justice. He told Hunter what was going on.

Hunter asked, "What do you want?"

"A cop."

Daniele added, "There's never one around when you need one."

Hunter called the CHP. The California Highway Patrol dispatched a vehicle. Near an exit to Woodland, Noel and Knoller were pulled over.

Daniele parked his vehicle about five car lengths behind. They watched two CHP officers saunter up to Noel's vehicle. They talked briefly with the occupants, then one patrolman walked back to the two San Francisco police officers.

Wearing mirrored sunglasses, he said, "I'm Officer Matt Stuller. We advised Mr. Noel that we were going to arrest him for speeding and reckless driving if he didn't knock it off."

"Why didn't you arrest him for speeding and reckless driving *before* he knocked it off?"

The highway patrolman grinned. "I figured you guys had much bigger fish to fry. Besides, my partner is citing them right now for those misdemeanors."

"How did they react?"

"Not well. Mr. Noel is very obviously upset. He yelled. He got red in the face. Ms. Knoller does not look well." The CHP officer paused, then asked, "Any news on the indictment?"

"Not yet," Becker said and pointed at the police radio. "No news from the grand jury."

The highway patrolman said, "Noel told me they're headed for a friend's house in Corning."

"Which is where?"

"About ninety miles from here."

Becker asked, "How far from San Francisco?"

"About a hundred and seventy miles."

Daniele said, "The way we were speeding, we would have made it in under two hours, including time for rest stops."

"Noel said he would follow my vehicle," the highway patrolman said. He saluted Becker and Daniele, then went back to his vehicle.

A three-car parade ambled up Interstate 5: A highway patrol cruiser, Noel and Knoller's car, and Becker and Daniele's unmarked squad car.

After an hour and a half they reached Corning, took the exit, and proceeded to a single-family residence on a small county lane.

Robert Noel and Marjorie Knoller went inside.

The highway patrol asked Daniele if he needed any more assistance, learned he didn't, saluted again and left.

Becker glanced at his watch. "After six. Why is the grand jury taking so long?"

Daniele shrugged and pointed. A sheriff's vehicle was pulling alongside. The deputy sheriff said, "We're to assist."

"Why?"

"If an indictment comes in, we're to take the accused to Red Bluff."

"Why?"

"They're in our county. Tehama."

Becker sniffed, winced, then inhaled again. "What's that smell?"

"A mixture of olive and goat."

"What?"

"Over there," the deputy pointed at a grove, "are olive trees. And over there are goat farms."

The undercover police car's radio beeped. It was 6:15 in the evening. Becker listened, then said, "You got it."

He turned to his partner and said, "Time to make an arrest."

Daniele asked, "What charge?"

"Mischievous animal and manslaughter for both." He paused, then added, "Second-degree murder for Knoller."

City of Red Bluff, Oak Street Jail House, Tehama County, Wednesday, March 28, 2001.
Knoller and Noel were led into the rural courtroom. They were dressed in orange jump suits and shackled.

Jim Hammer walked over to each and dropped a copy of the indictments on their laps.

Superior Court Judge John J. Garaventa announced that because they had demonstrated a flight risk, bail was set at one million for Noel and two million for Knoller.

They were transported back to San Francisco that day.

Henry Hunter's office, Thursday, March 29, 2001.
Hunter knew what would happen next. Noel and Knoller would appear at an arraignment. Both would plead not guilty.

Then Hammer and Guilfoyle will have to prove the charges. Whether manslaughter or second-degree murder, they don't have to prove they *intended* to kill anyone. But they do have to prove that Noel and Knoller's actions were so reckless and dangerous that those actions would likely result in a person's death.

Hunter remembered the press going nuts over some photos that were purported to have nude scenes between the lawyers and their dogs.

Hunter pulled out a file. Apparently, Joe Atkin, a prison guard sergeant, found a letter disguised as a legal correspondence addressed to Schneider from either Noel or Knoller, regarding sexual activities between Noel, Knoller and the dog Bane.

Also found in the cell were pictures of Knoller posing nude with drawings of fighting dogs. Other photos were of a male dog's genitals.

Apparently not enough evidence, Hunter thought, for a misdemeanor charge of bestiality.

Chapter
Forty-three

Charity and Guilt in the Public Court

Citizen Cake, corner of Gough and Grove, San Francisco, Tuesday, May 15, 2001.

Bad to good to bad to good. So far, the day had held ups and downs for Sharon Smith. She had gone to an arraignment that morning. Another bust. Like all those since Good Friday. Delay after delay had prevented Noel and Knoller from even pleading guilty or not guilty.

This morning, Marjorie had failed to appear, claiming mental distress. Lunch was much better, with former San Francisco mayor Frank Jordan. He and his wife had been very supportive after Alexis was killed.

In the afternoon, Marjorie Knoller again showed up in court in a wheelchair. More lawyer talk, another delay.

Kimberly Guilfoyle and Jim Hammer had explained these tactics to Sharon. Like jockeying for a change of venue.

The DA had made an end-run around that ploy by, surprisingly, allowing a change of venue without a contest.

Public defenders were to be appointed.

Other names came to the attention of the media. Diane Whipple's mother filed her own wrongful-death suit on April 10, 2001.

The mother of the victim, Penny Whipple-Kelly, told the media that if successful she would give the money to promote education and safety for dogs and people.

She told the press, "My heart is broken. Like there is a hole in my heart. Diane had a right to be safe and secure in her home. I do not want this to happen to anyone else, ever again.

Diane was a bright, vibrant, enthusiastic woman who had a zest for life."

Diane's mother had since returned to Connecticut.

Noel and Knoller were still in cells on the seventh floor of the Hall of Justice — still avoiding an arraignment where they would be asked by a judge to plead "Guilty or innocent?"

But now, after another wasted afternoon sitting in a courtroom watching Knoller sit in a wheelchair having, as Henry Hunter had described it, "Another attack of the vapors," she was headed for one of the city's first-class dessert parlors — Citizen Cake.

At five that afternoon there was an auction scheduled by Diane Whipple's friends.

Sharon arrived at the parlor. Nearly three hundred people crammed the bakery, from babies in arms to the elderly. Many of the lacrosse team, like Megan Bryan, were present, as well as their coach Sarah Miller and Jennifer Krusing. Melissa Boyle, who graduated the past year, stood by Julie Duff, sports umpire.

Kathryn Kendall, executive director of the National Center for Lesbian Rights, climbed up on the counter and said, "It is an honor to be here and be a part of the group that is helping Sharon in her fight. On January 26th Sharon's life was forever and tragically altered. The lives of the rest of us were altered when Sharon went public talking about her life, her commitment and her relationship with Diane."

She went on to talk about Sharon's outrage and disbelief when she found out that, under California law, her relationship was not only invisible, but irrelevant.

"What Sharon Smith and Diane Alexis Whipple had," Kendall said, "was a marriage. And the law must be changed to recognize that. Sharon has been an inspiration to all of us who have met her and work with her. "

She introduced Michael Cardoza. He said, "When I talk about Sharon and her relationship with Diane, I truly don't understand what the problem with society is. They were in love. They had a wonderful relationship. When I first met Sharon I can't tell you the feelings I had. I knew the law. But those laws

291

will change — and they will change with this case. Unfortunately, it takes a case like this to show the populace the injustices that go on under our own laws.

"I work with Sharon on a daily basis. And she blows me away. If I went to Hollywood to cast this, I couldn't find a better person to work with. She's done this with dignity, with intelligence. She's represented the gay community. She is a woman that I truly love. The best thing that's come out of this for me is I have a new friend, and I've met so many other new friends through this. I am honored."

Michael introduced Sharon. She thanked the owner of the bakery. She thanked Kendall and Cardoza for their support. She said, "It's amazing how many people are here. I am so touched by this, as I have been by all the cards and phone calls of support. It really does give me the strength to go on."

The raffle began. Items like truffles and cakes and a catered dinner for ten and tickets to a women's soccer game were auctioned off.

The organizers of the auction were not only surprised but stunned when they discovered that in the two-hour party, they had raised over $35,000.

Superior Court, the Hall of Justice, Tuesday, May 29, 2001.
Robert Noel was lead into the courtroom, once again packed with reporters. He wore an orange jump suit.

His wife, Marjorie Knoller, was pushed into the courtroom in a wheelchair.

The judge asked how they pleaded.

Each, in turn, answered "Not guilty."

Henry Hunter watched the two prisoners led out of the courtroom. He thought, back to the seventh floor, where a metal door would again slam behind them, as it had for the past two months.

Two months to get a pleading.

Long time for people sitting in a cell.

Charity and Guilt in the Public Court

Of course it counted as time served, and the seventh-floor jail was a motel compared to the grim surroundings of any prison in the state.

What a case, the cop thought. Most cases revolved around greed, or jealousy, or revenge, or hate.

This case involved love and stupidity, friendship and egotism, courage and arrogance, wrapped together like a spider's web, connecting Noel and Diane and Knoller.

No one's been found guilty of anything yet.

Yet.

The two lawyers certainly have been found guilty in the court of public opinion. Guilty toward their fellow human beings of incredible insensitive behavior.

Chapter
Forty-four

An Angel's Spirit Never Dies

Henry Hunter's home, Sunday.
Hunter opened the newspaper. When he got to the section of the *San Francisco Chronicle* called Contra Costa & Valley he saw huge color photograph showed a team hug by the St. Mary's lacrosse team. The caption read: Team Spirit.

Hunter thought, *Spirit.* The more he discovered about Diane's life, the more the realized that the thing that summed up her life and touched all around her was her *Spirit.*

The newspaper article explained how the team members first found out about the death of their coach, and then how they pulled together as a unit to help fight their collective grief.

Hunter turned to the seventh page of the newspaper. There was a photo of Amy Harms touching Diane's jersey, which had hung in the locker room since her death.

There was a photo of three other lacrosse players: Heidi Elmers, Allison Black and Courtney Nelson. There was a photo of Carrie Moore holding a dove. Next to her was Coach Sarah Miller, also holding a dove.

And there was a huge photograph of Sharon sitting under a tree with Allison Back and Megan Bryan. The two lacrosse players were crying.

Hunter thought, a lot has happened since that photo was taken.

Ezpecially to Sharon Smith's life. Like her being on the cover of the national magazine *The Advocate.* Like being interviewed in the magazine *Glamour.*

Like being on all major network morning shows multiple times. Plus *Rivera Live, 20/20, Prime Time, CNN.*

An Angel's Spirit Never Dies

Hunter knew Sharon hadn't asked for it. She hadn't sought it. But in only a few months she had become a national figure and symbol for gay and lesbian rights.

Her case and cause had transcended a one-goal issue. It was about more than same-sex rights. It was about the reality of love. The public understood her pain. The public identified with such a horrific loss and shuddered at the image of how it happened.

The support had come from all corners; people not concerned with issues, but concerned about the real human elements of the story.

Love lost.

Love lost in a horrible and preventable way.

Hunter read the rest of the article about Diane Whipple's St. Mary's lacrosse team.

The senior players were graduating the next day. They described Diane: a sister, a friend, a role model, and a mentor.

And, as always, Coach.

The Pavilion at Hanaleii Bay, Kauai, Hawaii.
Sharon Smith and her sister Janet were on the island of Kauai. Any time Hollywood needed a primeval setting, like that used in *Jurassic Park* or *King Kong*, it considered this island.

The surf was up. Hawaiians and tourists rode the waves on surfboards, boogie boards, or various inflated rubber devices. Bronze-honed bodies mingled with pasty-white tourists. Families played in the surf.

People were scattered about the sand; small groups enjoyed the sun, the cleanliness of the air, the languid warmth of the water, the invigorating feeling of just being alive.

Diane Alexis wanted her ashes cast on two lacrosse fields, the Atlantic Ocean, her grandparents' front steps, a mountain of Sharon's choice, and the Pacific Ocean.

Janet and Sharon drove along a two-lane road that, occasionally, when crossing the only rivers in Hawaii, shrank down to a single lane. Who had the right-of-way was handled in traditional Hawaiian friendliness. The greeting of a fist with thumb and little finger extended was the sign that not only said "Hello," but, "Your turn."

The road did not circumnavigate the island. The lane stopped at Ke'ee, a large horseshoe-shaped cove. The water was shallow, and very clear. No scuba gear or even a snorkel was needed to enjoy the colorful fish that lived in this serenity.

The sisters got out of the car and opened the trunk.

Sharon took off her shoes, rolled up her pant legs, took one of Diane's trophies, now serving as an urn, and waded out about fifty feet into the Pacific Ocean.

Beyond the coral reef the waves were furious, but here, protected, they gently ebbed and flowed.

Sharon said a silent prayer and tilted the trophy's cup.

For a fifth time she cast forth a portion of Alexis' remains.

The ashes swirled about her, forming a circle. As the water slowly rose and fell, the ashes seemed to dance about her, sometimes luminous, sometimes translucent.

A monster wave crashed over the barrier, white foam and froth came furiously bubbling in.

The ashes disappeared.

*   *   *

Back in her hotel room, Sharon knew she had one more obligation: to scatter Alexis' final remains on any mountain of her choice.

Where?

What mountain?

Why am I having such a problem picking a mountain?

She remembered what she said at the memorial service at St. Mary's for Alexis. She had spoken of Alexis' love for lacrosse — both playing and coaching; of chocolates, always Godivas. And of her love for poetry, especially Robert Frost. And *People Magazine*, vacations in Hawaii, long hikes.

And how she took advantage of every day.

She remembered a letter Alexis had given her. The words were engraved in her heart.

"When you look at your life, what do you see? When you look at your life do you see all those around you, those that you love and those that love you?

296

An Angel's Spirit Never Dies

"Do you see the good, not the bad?

"Life is too short and too precious to waste.

"Never break. Never look back. Move forward. Love the life you are living."

Sharon still had no idea as to which mountain to choose. What am I missing? There are plenty of mountains with meaning for the two of us.

Like Mount Tamalpais. I can see that mountain right out my apartment window in San Francisco.

Or the Cévennes Mountains in France.

What a wonderful vacation that was. The wine. The museums. The laughter.

Think about the joy we shared together.

Remember St. Thomas. The Caribbean.

*   *   *

Sharon won a trip to Puerto Rico — an award from her company. Alexis went with her. After the business part of the trip, they had gone over to the Virgin Islands.

As much as Sharon liked her co-workers, it was wonderful to be alone with Alexis.

They had known this day was coming for three years.

After dating for nine months they had decided to become engaged. They pledged betrothal to each other and exchanged rings. They were both sure, then, that they would spend the rest of their lives together, but wanted to follow the traditional route between the promise and the vows.

Now, three years later, they walked on the white sands of the Caribbean beach. The sun was hiding behind a group of cumulous clouds, its yellow-golden light piercing through far enough to cause the clouds to appear like marbled nuggets.

Commitment, Sharon thought. I'm about to pledge my heart and life to this woman I love. There's never been a doubt. Not since I first saw her.

"We have to talk," Alexis said. "I want to have children."

"So do I."

"I mean I want to give birth."

"So do I."

"We're not talking about adopting, are we?"

"No."

"*Having* isn't adopting." Alexis paused, then continued, "But I have a problem. I think we agree, because you're the major wage earner, that I should go first. "

"I thought the same thing."

"But then, when your turn comes and you have a kid, you'll forget about mine."

"I wouldn't."

The grin was back, wider than ever. "But I have a solution. We take our eggs and mix them up."

"Whatever for?"

"We won't know who the mother is."

"If I'm the one carrying the child, wouldn't that—"

"You would be the vessel. The surrogate. But we wouldn't know whose DNA was being passed on."

"You're kidding?"

Alexis' answer was an impish grin.

They sat under the straw roof and talked. They watched the sun plunge down in its orbit and the illusion of it seeming to enter and drown in the water. They talked about how soon they would bring children into their lives. Sharon reviewed the economics of it, and the practicality of having to move and find two-bedroom accommodations. They discussed whether to wait until they owned a home or still rented.

It would take a few years of preparation to be ready to become parents.

The dim light from an already-set sun grew fainter and fainter. The stars appeared in an explosive burst, like a rocket going off on the Fourth of July.

They went to the edge of the surf and held hands.

And there they promised to love and honor and cherish each other for the rest of their lives.

They pledged their vows before the immense cathedral of the universe and the sacred altar of God.

* * *

Sharon went out onto the balcony of her Hawaiian hotel room.

An Angel's Spirit Never Dies

The sun was going down, caught between the ocean below and bunched clouds above. The scene was breathtaking. Red and crimson and vermilion and scarlet cascaded about, mingling with shades of purple and tints of yellow, and splashes of gold, each challenging the next for dominion in an unbelievably beautiful sunset.

The fiery colors were a tropical version of the frigid Northern Lights — emulating the spectrum of the aurora borealis.

Quickly, the sun went from an orb, to half-round, to a sliver. And then it was gone, just a memory in Sharon's mind's eye.

The closest star was swallowed by earth's largest ocean.

I wish you were here, Alexis, to share nature's greatest show — a sunset with just the right amount of refraction and disposition of clumped clouds.

More beautiful than any rainbow. More gorgeous than any waterfall. More spectacular, because it was so fleeting, than the enduring creations of nature like the Grand Canyon and this verdant island.

Exquisite.

What must heaven be like, if our life on earth is but a moment?

She heard the sounds of the waves thundering on the beach. Palm trees waved in time to the music of the water. A faint breeze tussled her dark hair. The smell of fresh salt mingled with pure air. She could taste a faint hint of brine on her lips.

The splendor of it all, *nature* at its finest.

"Alexis, you are here, aren't you? Part of you will always be here."

Your spirit is part of nature, everywhere.

I promise I will live each day to the fullest.

One last act. To scatter your remaining ashes on a mountain — any mountain.

Now I realize why I'm having such trouble picking one.

The highest mountain won't get Diane Alexis any closer to God than she is right now.

Death of an Angel

She whispered, "Alexis, some angels have sinned and maliciously let their evil into the world; and some angels, like you, have generously left behind the essence of their joyous spirit."

Chapter
Forty-five

Oh, What a Year That Was

Henry Hunter's home, New Year's Eve, Monday, December 31, 2001.
Hunter did not like going out on big days of celebration. Home was where to be on holidays like St. Pat's and New Year's Eve.

He absent-mindedly scratched his cocker spaniel's neck and watched the New Year's Eve celebration in Times Square.

A lot had happened since Noel and Knoller had fled up Interstate 5.

The two lawyers had remained in jail for the past nine months, unable to post bail. No one had stepped forward to assist them financially.

The biggest event, Hunter thought, was September 11th.

He remembered sitting in this very chair, transfixed by the sight of the World Trade Center in flames. He had felt his stomach roil when the buildings plunged down.

He had felt assaulted by wild thoughts of how could he help? What sort of logistical hell were the police and firemen going through?

In the end, he had done what so many other Americans had done as they watched the horror unfold from too far away to help: he had prayed.

The war had gone smoothly, more smoothly than he had imagined. Hunter hadn't bought into some of the columnists' fears that Afghanistan would become another Vietnam. Just because England and Russia and so many other countries had failed over the centuries, did not mean America would. America wasn't trying to occupy or conquer, but merely eliminate a cancerous sore on humanity.

He remembered a few lines from a poem, whose author he couldn't recall for the life of him, that he'd read long ago:

"And when you lie wounded on Afghanistan plains,

"And the women come out to cut up what remains,

"Just roll on your rifle and blow out your brains,

"And go to your God like a soldier."

Fortunately, not many Americans in harm's way had gone to their God.

And like any other year, 2001 had brought happiness to some and sorrow to others.

Prosecutor Kimberly Guilfoyle married San Francisco Supervisor Gavin Newsom.

California joined two other states that allow same-sex couples to file wrongful death law suits.

From what he'd heard through the grapevine, Sharon Smith was fulfilling her promise to live each day to the fullest.

Since going to Hawaii, she has ridden a Harley-Davidson on a weekend trip to the Hearst Castle in San Simeon.

She and some of the A-team went skydiving for the first time.

She had spoken to small, intimate groups and to a crowd of over 40,000 people.

She had tossed out the first pitch at an Oakland A's game in August. The day had been proclaimed Diane Whipple Day.

And, Hunter said to himself, she gave every appearance of having the intention of continuing to live each day to the fullest for as long as her life on earth lasts.

And I have a new grandson — Joshua.

Other things weren't as happy. A month before, the California Department of Correction claimed that Paul "Cornfed" Schneider was a "Shot caller" for his gang.

He was accused, through contact with the Aryan Brotherhood, of putting out a contract on the newlywed Kimberly Guilfoyle Newsom.

Oh, What a Year That Was

The convict's lawyer, Herman Franck, scoffed at the idea, stating that the Aryan Brotherhood revered women.

Despite this, Schneider faced 13 counts under a federal indictment, including the murder of a deputy sheriff.

The indictment further charged that Schneider ordered other crimes outside of prison, using the Nazi low riders to carry out his orders.

Hunter changed the channel on his television. It was reviewing the year with a montage of images: the burning World Trade Center, the last pitches in games five and six of the World Series that led to defeats for the Diamondbacks and jubilation in New York — only to be reversed in game seven.

Tiger Woods winning the Master's Cup and holding all four major at once.

Barry Bonds and the incredible 73 homers.

Gary Condit going from front-page news to no-page news.

Osama bin Laden smugly chortling over sending his own unknowing soon-to-be-martyrs to their deaths,

Jack Lemon dies, and will never play on Sunday at Pebble Beach.

A year with death and a year with birth. A year were Russia became a staunch friend to America. A year were the American flag flew from the top of high-rises to the fenders of tractors.

Hunter watched Rudy Guilliani appear on the huge TV screen that hovered over Times Square. The mayor had only minutes left before he left office. He was smiling. He was wearing a FDNY cap.

And, the cop thought, some doctor at the Mayo Clinic named Jim Levine developed a new lie detector machine. A camera that measures heat patterns on the face, millimeter by millimeter. Warming around the eyes is uncontrollable by the person being tested. The camera shows a thermal image of the face. The computer doesn't need a trained technician to operate it.

No expert needed, and instantaneous results.

Hunter realized, I would have been out of a job. Or in a different one all those years I gave polygraphs.

What a year.

A year when Robert Noel and Marjorie Knoller sat in jail cells on the seventh floor of the San Francisco Hall of Justice awaiting trial.

What would have happened if, immediately after the attack, they had walked down the hallway with genuine tears in their eyes and told Sharon how sorry they were for her loss?

What if they had demonstrated real compassion? Real empathy?

What would have happened if, instead of sending those two letters to the DA — one short, the other eighteen pages — they sent a condolence card, a spiritual bouquet and a dozen lilies to Diane's memorial service?

Who knows? The DA would have hit them with something. But, in all probability, let them plead down to probation.

Sharon probably wouldn't have sued.

She originally went to Michael Cardoza to make sure the DA followed through after the two letters. After the perfume and steroid remarks. It wasn't until almost the middle of March before she became angry enough to file the wrongful death lawsuit.

He knew that his men, people like Mike Becker and Rich Daniele, would still be working on the case off-and-on over the coming months.

He knew that more and more information would be forthcoming.

Information on Noel and Knoller.

Information on Paul "Cornfed" Schneider and his cellmate Dale Bretches.

That's how it worked. The more people that testified, the more information that came out. The more information that came out, the clearer became the truth.

Chapter
Forty-six

Another Super Bowl, Other Letters

Hunter's Home, Super Bowl Sunday, January 27, 2002.
Henry and his wife Cindy went to church. Back home, the Sunday paper was read while brunch was being eaten.

There was a chill in the air. Hunter started a fire, turned on the TV and sat in his easy chair. He watched his dog Babs circle three times and settle down.

He waited for the Super Bowl to begin.

Rams versus Patriots.

St. Louis Rams, big favorites. Not to Hunter. Rams, no matter where they play their home games, will always equate to Los Angeles.

The LA/Niners' rivalry still had memories; some sweet, some bitter.

Son Harry hit the coach and asked, "Who you rooting for, dad?"

"Patriots."

"Dim chance."

"I know." Dim. But the dog mauling case wasn't looking dim. Just the opposite — bright.

A lot had happened in the first month of 2002.

On January 4, Robert Noel requested a separate trial. Two buzz's started: delay tactic; and a rift between Noel and Knoller. There might be truth to each buzz.

While he waited for the game to begin, Hunter decided to review some of the material taken during the search warrants. He opened a file and pulled out a letter.

He scanned a letter written by Robert Noel to Paul "Cornfed" Schneider and locked onto:

...I was involved in defending a c.o...

C.O.? Hunter thought, ah, correctional officer.

...c.o., at the prison, CCC in Susanville on criminal charges completely unrelated to the joint. Standup guy.

Unfortunately, he and his family represented about 99 percent of the non-incarcerated black population in Lassen County.

Lots of white c.o.'s over there running around doing KKK shit. Ever hear of the white knights, a group of KKK c.o.'s at Pelican Bay State Prison? Asked a couple of cops, who were trying to get close to us and whom we had some questions about, that same question. Heard mumbles and replies and they stayed away from us after that.

Anyway, the guy had a daughter who was shacked up with a white piece of shit who was the father of her kid and who is not welcome on the guy's property. The boyfriend got POS...

Hunter wondered, POS? What's that stand for?

Maybe the context of the sentence will help. He read: The boyfriend got POS, the boyfriend got Position Of Superiority?

No. The boyfriend got... Police Officers Security?

No. Before 'boyfriend got' was: *not welcome on the property. The boyfriend got POS.* Ah, Piece Of Shit.

Hunter read:

...POS status because he was a hero. He thought it was to beat up women, including the guy's daughter. POS comes on to the property walking right up to the front door, challenges the guy to come on out because he's going to kill him. The guy had every reason to believe that the piece of shit was packing and comes out with a .357, cranks up a round, what was aimed 20 feet to the side of the piece of shit and tells him to get going or the next one is up his ass and between his eyes. Guy should have been given a medal and made to shut up. Instead, the D.A. overcharges like a son of a bitch looking to put him in for 15 years, ineligible for credit because it was charged as a 245...

245. That's assault. Hunter continued to read:

Another Super Bowl, Other Letters

... offense. Eventually, he got a deal worked out — D.A.,
himself, was not an ass, just his charging deputy — felony but a
wobbler, nine months county jail and given that he had been in
four months, he was out the door after sentencing.

Sentenced to nine months, out in four. Time off for good
behavior, Hunter assumed. Just like Robert Noel who been sitting
in the jail on the top floor of the Hall of Justice for almost a year.
Now, with a matching day of good behavior for each day served,
he's accumulated almost two years towards time served.

Hunter went back to the letter.

When I grew up, that kind of shit would never happen, have
the witness to support the threats and put between his eyes. Only
one side of the story to tell and it was self-defense.

Put between his eyes? Oh, put a round between his eyes.
Interesting. This is advice coming from a lawyer to his client — a
life-without-possibility-of-parole felon.

Hunter glanced at the television. Super Bowl XXXVI had
started. The Rams kept making mistakes and the Patriots kept
capitalizing on them. A commercial came on and Hunter reached
into the file one more time.

Another letter, dated January 11, 2001 was written by
Robert Noel to Paul J. Schneider. It was highlighted by the words:

CONFIDENTIAL LEGAL MAIL.

Marjorie F. Knoller   Attorneys at Law   Robert E. Noel
January 11th 2001

Paul J. Schneider
C-6) 196, D8-211
Pelican Bay State Prison
P.O. Box 7500
Crescent City, CA 95532
Re: "Triad" and various other matters.

Dear Paul.

By the time you get this letter we should have seen you at
least for the first visit on Monday the 15th. Really looking forward

to it — both me and Marjorie. Hope all goes well. Spoke with visiting today and was told that they had us approved for the 15th, 16th, 20th and 21st. We plan on getting to the gate at about 7:30 a.m. or a little later so that we have sufficient time to deal with the b.s. if there is any this time.

Well, Hera has again decided to chew the t.v. remote — just bought a new one a week ago after she destroyed the first. She has given up her attacks on the portable telephone, but at $14 a pop it mounts up. Only thing we can figure is that when she and B'ster are left home, after awhile she gets insecure and looks for something that has our scent on it and the remote dies — little, little pieces.

It has been raining like a two-cunted cow pissing on a flat rock all day. [Marjorie demands credit for the expression.] Really high winds. According to the the weather map the storm moved through Del Norte earlier today. We had to go out to take care of some business downtown and stopped for an early dinner/late lunch at Foley's – had them set 3 pints and 3 places. Calamari and fries and Marjorie had BLT and fires. They have gotten used to us now and set it for 3.

Table for three? Hunter wondered. Three? They set a place for Cornfed? What? A symbolic setting? Did the third pint of beer just sit there and go flat? Was the food left on the third plate uneaten?

He continued to read:

[Marjorie is just venturing out with Hera for the evening walk — miserably cold, blustery wet — figure they are leaving at 7:10 p.m. — would bet they are back by 7:25 p.m.]

Actually back at 7:40 p.m. — report no rain.

This morning's was an interesting one — getting used to the "jail break" approach the kids have, break for the door like horses out to the starting gate, stand next to the elevator shifting from one leg to the other to the other etc., the ferocity of the panting directly proportional to how badly the mutt feels he or she needs to go at that point, elevator opens — hopefully with no one in, otherwise they will knock 'em down rushing in. Once in they know the drill and they have the length of the ride timed — don't start getting *agitated for the exit until the elevator passes the 2nd floor. As the elevator comes to a halt and the gate slides back, the two of them hit the door with their snouts, pushing it open as if a small charge of C4 has just gone off and blown the hatch and they are making to the front door, sliding on the marble floor of the entry way to slide up to the glass. One or the other will then take a paw and hit the door to signal that it needs to be opened. Once the door is opened they hit the sidewalk, turn right and head off.*

This morning was one of those days — we get the elevator after one of our neighbors had been dicking around with it — about a 5 minute wait for the kids. We get on, the panting is now anxious. As we reach the 1st floor I see someone standing by the door through the small view hole and tell them to step back. Just at that point the kids hit the door with their snouts, the door blows open and they are nose to nose with the little sheltie collie and an obnoxious little white piece of shit that one of our neighbors on 4 has. B'ster and H are into a defend mode and I get them back in and we ride back up to 6, send the elevator back down so the dog walker can get the other mutts out of the lobby and home. As soon as the door opens at 6, one of our newer neighbors, a timorous little mousy blond, who weighs less than Hera, is met by the dynamic duo exiting and almost has a coronary — the mutts show only passing interest as she gets in and goes down. Once we get back in the elevator, the scent of the other mutts is everywhere and the two of them searched that 3X4 box repeatedly — without success — looking. When they blew the door in the lobby they had the scent from the door to the elevator and they were off and running for the door. I opened the door and they flew out — with Hera virtually doing a freeze in mid-stride when she hit the first blast of rain. At that point, the ardor for the hunt was caught up in the aversion to rain in all forms. After some coaxing from me and from B'ster she resumed the walk but stayed under any overhanging porches — and she didn't miss any on the route. She would not piss in the rain — waiting until we took her out later in the day — she held it about 15 hours — not because she didn't have the opportunity — she is just picky about where she pisses and poops and under what conditions.

Death of an Angel

The letter went on about a gypsy friend that Noel knew in Baltimore. Then talked about Noel's days in high school.

My Varsity letter in high school was in music — if you think football is a great way to score with the gals, try music — especially classical — gals who love to sing are really into things oral — and the closeness of the working on a great piece of music really intensifies the feelings — not unlike the situation Marjorie and I have with the practice where we work so closely toward the same goal — an amplification — at times I think about what would have been if I had pursued music to the world class level — I know I would have gotten laid a lot — but I would never have met Marjorie and that would have been too great a price to have paid.

I wanted to thank you for the thoughts expressed about your feelings about how comfortable you would feel about Marjorie and I inhabiting your body and mind. The feelings are mutual and I am sure you know what it means to hear those words from you. I agree — inhabiting Marjorie's body — I wouldn't be able to keep my hands off it either!!!

Agreed with your views on the KKK and black racism. Nobody should accept being shit on or abused — black or white — stand up for yourself but get on with life — don't like "whiney black boys" any more than I like "whiney white boys." I also agreed with your analysis of how the incident at the house should have gone — fuck the warning shot — guy at your door telling you you better kill him 'cause he is coming for you — only one way that should end — put it between the eyes and have only one side of the story.

Hunter stopped reading. This was written by a lawyer to a convict? He stared at the last sentence. "Put it between the eyes and have only one side of the story." What a revelation into Noel's thought process. And maybe on why the story has kept changing over the past year.

He went back to the letter:

Poor bastard though didn't get any support from his family — wife sided with the daughter's boy friend and undercut the shooter's defense.

Another Super Bowl, Other Letters

Really, really glad you liked the photos in the letter of 1/1. There were similar ones that I am sure you have gotten from Marjorie on New Year's Eve. On the issue of full frontal — Marjorie says maybe at some point. That is something she reserves for her two husbands alone.

Hunter went into the kitchen and poured himself a glass of water. It didn't change the bitter taste that had pervaded his saliva.

He went back to the living room and glanced at the Super Bowl. The Rams weren't doing well. That should have improved the policeman's mood. It did not. He continued to read.

On the adoption — I believe Marjorie and I do have an appreciation for what it means to you.

Hunter thought, one minute he's referring to Marjorie's two husbands and next the adoption? He sighed and read:

My letters since the one on the 31st go into more of my feelings on the matter. We will have talked about this I think in considerable detail when we are together. It is the one form of legal action which can join the 3 of us in a binding family unit — if it were permitted to be accomplished through a second marriage that would have been the medium — but we have become a family and Marjorie and I are prepared to go as far as possible to formalize that arrangement.

The cop paused. So much for stating that the adoption was to have better access to the convict's medical records.

I didn't think you would have a problem with my religious affiliation and choice. But I don't know what factors you need to deal with in your family life and I did not want to presume to do something that would have placed you in jeopardy or which would cause you trouble in any respect.

Noel wrote about how he became interested in Judaism. Then he mentioned the law.

One of my mentors during law school was an instructor of mine named Harry. Harry was a "Master of chancery." Maryland still clung to the British system of circuit courts [Supreme Courts], people's courts [municipal courts], Orphans' Court [probate] and Equity or Chancery Courts for which there is no equivalent in California. The Chancery courts were the direct

311

descendants of the British Chancery Court where the King's Chancellor could be approached for relief from the strict application of the common law — it was a "court of conscience" and directed to doing what was "right" or "equitable" rather than what was strictly legal. Harry took me under his wing and I would during law school go to his office one day a week and work with him for the experience. Much of the work was listening to Harry expound on matters of equity and a lot of it revolved around Jewish philosophical thought. I have never forgotten Harry and though he was firm in his beliefs he never tried to impose them on others. His view on religion which I came to accept is that organized religion is nothing more than an attempt by one generation to pass on to those that come, some information or belief about life that the sender believes to have universal value. Viewed in that fashion, all religions become books to be consulted but not to be driven by.

Noel wrote about what he liked best about getting married in the Jewish faith. *One thing I really liked about the ceremony is that the words used to join us — "I am my Beloved's and my Beloved is mine" — matched perfectly the way we felt about each other and what we had. They still do and would work equally well with you and Marjorie. No hint of unequal status between dedicated and passionate loving partners.*

Hunter thought, this guy is confusing Judaism with Mormonism — even the Mormons don't allow multiple husbands.

The letter closed with:

Enclosing some shots for Dale that I pulled from Maxim – thought he might enjoy them. Well, going to run. See you if all goes well on the 15th. Watch your backs and keep each other safe. With all of the warmest and best wishes for you and Dale.

Deiner Genossen und Freund,

Robert

Hunter glanced at the top of each page. Written were the words "*Confidential Legal Mail.*"

Another Super Bowl, Other Letters

What, the policeman wondered, does this correspondence have to do with anything legal between Paul Schneider and Robert Noel?

Hunter turned his attention back to the Super Bowl. The Rams had tied it up. Score was 17-17. Then the Patriots engineered a nine-play drive and kicked a field goal with no time on the clock.

Upset. By the underdogs.

Right out of Hollywood On the last play, in the last second, the underdog wins the game. Like Burt Reynolds in *The Longest Yard* — when the convicts beat the guards. Reading Noel's letters you would have to assume he would root for the convicts.

Hunter thought about underdogs. Who were the underdogs in the upcoming trial?

Over the years he had learned that predicting a jury's mind was impossible.

Chapter
Forty-seven

The Torch goes to the Prosecutors

Hunter's home, San Francisco, Saturday, February 9, 2002.
Hunter loved the Olympics — Summer or Winter.

He appreciated the competition. The spirit of excellence and the thrill of victory or the agony of defeat. Plus, there's the lure of the many similarities between a sporting contest and a trial, with tremendous preparation leading to grueling challenges.

He turned on his television. He watched a lone race car speed down a straightaway.

His watch read high noon.

Where are the Olympics?

He had zeroed in on the opening ceremonies the evening before, choking up when the American flag that had once flown over the World Trade Center was brought into the stadium. He had felt both anger and pride at the tattered symbol of his country.

But anger was soon replaced by his anticipation of the upcoming Games. He understood what it took to be the best and appreciated the commitment and devotion to purpose the Olympic Games represented.

Devotion to purpose. Like the devotion to purpose cops put in while amassing evidence for prosecutors.

Hunter thought about the lawyers involved. The face of San Francisco's district attorney appeared in his mind's eye. Terence Hallinan's lineage was splashed across his Irish face. In his mid-sixties, the etched lines of age revealed his humor while betraying his strength.

The DA had fought many battles in his life; from the boxing ring to the courtroom, from being a defense attorney most of his life to being the chief prosecutor of crime in his beloved hometown.

The DA would prefer to watch an hour of Jake La Motta and Sugar Ray Robinson going toe-to-toe at Madison Square Garden, than watch the Olympics.

Hallinan was born on December 4, 1936, the second of five brothers. He was elected district attorney in 1995.

Hallinan was the epitome of opposites to what you would expect in any prosecutor, let alone the top gun in a major metropolitan city.

He was accused of civil disobedience and battery charges when a young man. He had battled on the side of defense lawyers when it came to the right to use marijuana for religious purposes. He had battled for a reexamination of illegal prostitution. He had consistently spoken out against the death penalty, going so far as to appear as an expert witness in capital cases for the defense.

And the head prosecutor of San Francisco — like Diane Whipple — barely missed making a U.S. Olympic team; in his case boxing.

Hunter again looked at his watch. Five minutes after twelve. Still, cars raced around the Daytona Beach oval. A graphic announced that this was a qualifying race for next week's Daytona 500.

What's going on? Is NBC nuts?

His watch read nine minutes after the hour, then ten minutes.

Finally the screen turned from auto racing to Salt Lake City, framed behind the five Olympic rings.

Over three billion people had watched the opening ceremonies and its fire within — fire on ice — fire without theme. And now NBC decides to delay the Olympics with coverage of a NASCAR race in Florida?

The Super Bowl? Sure, delay. The seventh game of the World Series? Delay.

But delay the Olympics for NASCAR? Auto racing may have a huge following, but delay the Olympic Games for a trial run in an auto race?

Hunter settled in his armchair and watched a recap of the images he had seen the night before coming from Salt Lake City. The fire spiraling up a metal structure that looked like a twisted, gigantic icicle. The Olympic flame bursting into sight with the snowy mountains of Utah as a backdrop.

He thought about how that ten-minute delay from the NASCAR race to the Olympic coverage had felt like two hours.

Time. Time and how subjective it was came to mind.

Throughout many of the reports he had turned over to the DA's office, the question of time had come into play. Marjorie and her sixty seconds restraining Bane, then fifteen seconds of being towed down the hallway like an anchor.

On television, cross-country skiers, seemingly linked together like a train, collapsed at the finish line, their anguished faces showing utter exhaustion. Four years training for this one brief moment. And the uncertainty that comes with competition.

Like the DA's office, Hunter thought. For the past year Jim Hammer and Kimberly Guilfoyle had prepared for the trial, and the uncertainty that comes with testimony and cross-examination.

Much had happened in that year, and not all of it involved criminal proceedings. Like Kimberly Guilfoyle marrying Gavin Newsom, rising San Francisco politician.

Then this year began, and with it many memories of what had happened in the past year. On January 26, the one-year anniversary of the death of Diane Whipple, a candlelight vigil was held at Dolores Park in San Francisco. Hundreds showed up to honor and keep alive the memory of the woman who died so horribly. People like Sharon Smith and Sarah Miller and Kate Kendall spoke of the loss of their love, their friend and their associate.

Other events in January included Noel and Knoller requesting a motion to separate their trials. Noel's side felt that their position would be jeopardized by association with Knoller — and because Noel wasn't even in San Francisco at the time of the attack .

The Torch Goes to the Prosecution

Knoller's side felt that Noel's inflammatory statements to reporters a year earlier would hurt her case.

Judge James L. Warren denied the motion, saying, "There isn't anything one way or the other that will show that one defendant is prejudiced by the other. This is a classic case for a joint trial."

The DA and his team won with the denial of the motion to separate, but lost when Judge Warren wouldn't allow introduction of anything regarding Noel and Knoller and the possible inappropriate sexual conduct with the dogs.

That might have helped, Hunter knew, in explaining aberrant behavior in the animals.

He recalled reading something about that in a recent Matier & Ross column. He rummaged around and found the article. He scanned the information:

"Prosecutor James Hammer all but accused defendants Marjorie Knoller and Robert Noel of having an inappropriate relationship with their dogs.

"The defense vehemently denies it, with Knoller's lawyer, Nedra Ruiz, labeling the suggestion as specious filth, backed by zero evidence.

"What prosecutors have are a series of letters that Noel and Knoller wrote to their adopted convict son that allegedly described sex acts involving the two or three of them.

"Investigators searching Schneider's Pelican Bay jail cell found cut-and-paste sexually explicit photos involving Knoller — but those pictures apparently didn't involve the dogs, weren't considered relevant to the case and were never turned over to prosecutors."

Another legal battle was resolved when the dog Hera was finally put down at the end of last month — a year and four days after Diane Whipple was killed.

What a circus that was.

People like Anaperia Aureoles and Cesar Millan got into the act. Anaperia convinced Knoller's attorney, Nedra Ruiz, to hire Cesar — a noted dog whisperer.

317

Death of an Angel

The dog whisperer interviewed the dog Hera and proclaimed she was not vicious.

The judge didn't buy it and the Hera was executed.

The judge had also gotten angry at some of the lawyers.

Hallinan angered the judge less than a month before. He had given an interview to the *Daily Journal*, a professional periodical for lawyers. The DA was asked to comment on the ability of the prosecution to get a second-degree murder conviction against Knoller. DA Hallinan responded, referring to Marjorie's grand jury testimony, "It is full of such blatant lies, and it's clear that she is just making things up."

Judge Warren cited him for contempt of the gag order.

Nedra Ruiz, Marjorie Knoller's lawyer, was called on the carpet for the same thing last year.

Letters between Noel, Knoller and Paul Schneider were allowed as evidence by the judge. The letters were reported to contain statements that the lawyers would have liked to have had a three-way marriage with the convict, but had to settle for an adoption instead.

But the main event was the on-going preparation for the dog-mauling case, to be heard in a Los Angeles courtroom.

Hunter again glanced at the Olympic events as he outlined his thoughts for the looming trial. So many sports involved teamwork, like a prosecution team preparing for trial.

The court date for opening statements in the Noel/Knoller case was set for February 19.

Hunter jotted down names of lawyers involved.

Lead prosecutor: James Hammer. Assistant prosecutor: Kimberly Guilfoyle Newsom.

Every case had to have liaison between the police and the prosecutors. A lawyer who acted like a funnel between the gathering of evidence and the pretrial work regarding the presentation of that evidence.

That was Kimberly. A cop's prosecutor.

Hunter and the personnel in his detail respected her. She had amassed a 97% conviction rate as a prosecutor. She had amassed a 100% conviction rate on adult felonies.

The Torch Goes to the Prosecution

And beyond that, she respected and appreciated the work that the 'thin blue line' did to help her win that 97% conviction overall rate and that 100% adult felonies rate,

Kimberly's job also entailed preparing the prosecution witnesses for trial. A long and arduous task.

Who else is involved in the trial?

Nedra Ruiz: Knoller's defense attorney. She was a member of Tony Serra's law firm — who recently represented Sara Jane Olson. Nedra, like Marjorie, was married to a lawyer. His name was Laurence Lichter. They owned a rottweiller. Their dog tried to attack a plumber working next door to their home. The dog was sentenced to quarantine for 10 days.

Bruce Hotchkiss: Noel's defense attorney. He was 67 years old. He went to Kansas State University and Washburn University of Topeka law school.

Those were the main contenders.

Who else?

The judge. Superior Court Judge James L. Warren. He was the grandson of former Chief Justice Earl Warren. Judge James Warren was born the day after Saint Patrick's Day in 1944. He had a Bachelor of Art, Political Science, from the University of California. He was Juris Doctorate — Hofstra University College of Law, Hempstead, NJ and served as Articles Editor, Law Review in 1973.

James Lee Warren was in private practice as an associate with Pillsbury, Madison & Sutro, in San Francisco, from 1975 to 1980.

He served as senior counsel in complex litigation for Pacific Bell in 1993 and 1994. He was a judge *pro tempore*, Superior Court from 1986-94.

And he was appointed by Governor Pete Wilson on August 23, 1994 to the San Francisco Superior Court.

His most startling case previously was in 1995 when he allowed wrongful death suits against gun manufacturers.

Hunter absentmindedly watched another Nordic skier cross the finish line — oblivious to the country the athlete represented.

He thought about the legal maneuvers that occurred over the past several months, since the end of the grand jury hearings.

In May, Noel and Knoller filed a demurrer. They claimed the indictment was illegal.

The demurrer was overruled.

In June, Paul Schneider and Dale Bretches filed a motion to become defendants in the civil case.

It was denied.

In July, Judge Warren ruled that Hera was to be put down. Noel and Knoller fought back with a mandamus, a court order aimed at dog court, requesting a new dog court hearing.

The judge ruled against Hera.

Noel and Knoller appealed to the California Supreme Court.

The original judge's ruling was upheld.

In August, Noel and Knoller requested a change of venue.

Hunter remembered Hallinan's reaction at the time: fine, change the venue. Anywhere in California would be OK. Like a boxer agreeing to have the fight anywhere and anytime the opponent wanted.

What else?

The trial.

What will the defense put up?

Probably that Noel and Knoller could not possibly believe that their dogs were dangerous. After all, they lived with them in a tiny apartment. How dangerous could *that* be?

Against that will be a long list of witnesses willing to testify that the dogs acted violently in the presence of their owners. That beefed up the manslaughter and mischievous animal charges, but second-degree murder will be a lot tougher.

The defense will assuredly counter with the cops. Almost always happened. The defense lawyers states, "First cops on the scene didn't do anything and the victim died."

The defense would lament about cold-hearted cops who stood by collecting overtime and watching Diane's last minutes, knowing full well that they, because of lack of training, were forbidden to help.

The Torch Goes to the Prosecution

So many of the cops on this case needed trauma counseling for what they saw and what they *could not* do to help

On television, the announcer was going over the Olympic venues for the next sixteen days. Sixteen days, where over 2,200 of the world's finest winter athletes would be tested against others and themselves.

And, thought the cop, the DA and his staff will be entering into a month of grueling work, on the field of the courtroom, doing their jobs to prove Robert Noel and Marjorie Knoller guilty.

Hunter knew the courthouse where the dog-mauling trial was to take place. It was the same courthouse where the Menendez brothers once stood trial for murder. It was the same courthouse where O.J. Simpson stood trial for murder.

The trial should prove interesting, the cop knew. Each of the lawyers involved had their own style, much like a few fictional lawyers in movies he liked.

Hotchkiss' laid back and courtly approach was similar to Charles Laughton in *A Witness for the Prosecution*. Hammer emulated Gregory Peck's more direct and thoughtful delivery as demonstrated in *To Kill a Mockingbird*. Nedra Ruiz's famed dramatics were like Raymond Burr in *A Place in the Sun*, when he smashed the canoe with an oar.

And then there was Kimberly Guilfoyle Newsom. Hard to peg with only one example. In both job and demeanor she was like Demi Moore in *A Few Good Men*, when she played co-counsel to Tom Cruise. In passion and knowledge for her case, she was like Katherine Hepburn in *Adam's Rib*.

And like Demi Moore and Katherine Hepburn, Kimberly Guilfoyle Newsom was gracious, yet strong.

On television, the scene switched to a long-shot of the Olympic torch's flame. The policeman thought about all those thousands of people who had carried the flame across so many states. Each turning the responsibility over to the next to protect that symbol.

Just like this case and the flame of responsibility that now goes to the prosecutors.

Part Two

The

Trial

Chapter
Forty-eight

Prosecution's Opening Statements

Superior Court of California, Los Angeles, Department 26, Division 53, Tuesday, February 19, 2002.
The courtroom was beautifully appointed. Three rows of benches ran parallel to a half-wood, half-glass partition separating the spectators from those behind this new edition of the legal "bar."

The walls were paneled in wood, with sound-control perforations.

A long single table was provided for the attorneys, with the defense to the spectators' right and prosecution to the left — nearest to the eighteen seats that held the twelve members of the jury and the six alternates.

The defendants no longer wore orange jump suits; their attire during the arraignments and hearings and motions. Robert Noel wore a suit, his wife a business ensemble with her hair tied in a bun.

The jury sat with the six alternates nearest to the witness box.

The judge wasted no time in beginning the trial. He said, referring to the lawyers' opening statements, "Bear in mind that this is not evidence, this is a statement by the respective lawyers, if the defense wishes. The prosecution I know is going to make an opening statement. It's a statement by the lawyers to tell you what they anticipate the evidence will be.

"Remember, at this stage, the slate is completely blank. Anything that we discussed in voir dire for purposes of evidence does not exist. We don't know if there is a person named Marjorie Knoller, we don't know if there is a person named Diane Whipple, we don't know if there is a dog, we don't know if there is an Aryan Brotherhood or if anybody is Jewish or anything. Whatever comes into evidence will be what you will decide. Everything else is out of your mind."

The judge nodded toward the prosecution. Jim Hammer went to the lectern and picked up a hand-held microphone. He said, "This case is a about a young woman, Diane Whipple, who was killed by two dogs in San Francisco owned by the two defendants, Mr. Noel and Ms. Knoller, whom the evidence will show had extensive knowledge of the dangerous nature of these dogs and who received repeated warnings about what they could do to protect other people.

"The evidence will show that Diane Whipple was not the first victim of these dogs, but was the last in the line of almost 30 prior warnings and incidents putting them on notice of the danger of the dogs and exactly what they could do to protect other people. The evidence will show that they disregarded all of those warnings and that Diane Whipple is dead as a result.

"So what happened on January 26th, the date Diane died?"

Hammer methodically took the jury, step by step, through what happened the day Diane was killed. Hammer used a series of pictures, enlarged on a huge screen, to show the jury visually what things looked like on the day of the attack. Pictures like the two bags with the groceries strewed about.

He came to the point when the first police arrived at the scene. He said, "The police officers, these two women officers, went up to Diane. They saw her crawling. They could see these wounds all over her body, especially about her throat and the back of her neck, and they told her to stop, stop crawling. She responded. Diane Whipple was still conscious, alive. She responded to the officers when they said, 'Stay still,' and she relaxed and stopped crawling.

"The officers attended to her. And over the next few minutes, Diane Whipple went in and out of consciousness. The paramedics came, tried to treat her. At one point, her heart stopped. They got it back going again, but all this time she was bleeding, you will see in a moment, from all over her body, especially about her neck, the back of her neck, which was pierced so deep it almost went down to the vertebrae, from the throat, you will see, and she eventually died."

Not a sound could be heard in the courtroom. Those that loved Diane, people like Sharon Smith and Sarah Miller, had the memory of their love and friend etching grief on their faces.

Hammer, pointing at a large screen, said, "These are some of the graphic photos showing wounds that Diane suffered at the hands of these dogs. You will hear how deep that wound from the dogs' teeth pierced in the back of her neck and how — you can see, I will show you in a few moments again, on the right side of her neck, you see those marks, the teeth marks? I will show you in a moment the teeth that caused those teeth marks."

He showed the jury pictures of Diane taken during the autopsy.

Sharon, her sister and Sarah left the courtroom.

Hammer took the jury through where the dogs came from. He carefully explained the movement from the convicts to Janet Coumbs ranch to the small apartment at 2398 Pacific Avenue.

The prosecutor told the jury that he would call nearly thirty witnesses who would testify to prior knowledge by the defendant to the violent nature of their pets.

While Hammer spoke, Marjorie Knoller and her attorney, Nedra Ruiz, took notes.

Hammer said that the day Robert Noel was accidentally bitten by his dog Bane, who was in a fight with another dog, Noel had a medical kit on his person. Hammer asked a rhetorical, "Why do you carry a medical kit when you're walking your dog?"

Hammer told the jury that this dog fight occurred five months before Diane died.

Hammer said, "And I want to go over with you briefly now, in light of the issues in this case what they had to say in their own words about the issues in this case, about knowledge, what did they know, were they able to control these dogs and what did they say happened that led up to the death of Diane Whipple.

"I am going to start with Ms. Knoller. Before the grand jury, Ms. Knoller was asked repeatedly about her knowledge.

327

Death of an Angel

This is a lawyer sworn under oath before the grand jury about what she knew about the dangerousness of these dogs and here is what she was asked and here is what she said."

Using the huge screen on the wall, Hammer flashed immense blowups of grand jury testimony. The following appeared:

Question: *Anyone else warn you that these dogs were dangerous?*

Answer: S*pecifically, no.*

Question*: Before April 1st, 2000, had anyone in the world—*

Hammer explained, "April 1st, 2000 is the date that Hera was picked up from Janet Coumbs." He pointed once again at the screen.

Question*: Before April 1st, 2000, did anyone in the world ever warn you about the potential dangerousness of Bane, Hera or any of the other eight dogs?*

Answer*: No.*

Question*: Had anyone ever warned you before April 1st, 2000 that you should not bring these dogs into the City?*

Answer*: No.*

Question*: Had anyone ever warned you that it would be a liability to bring these dogs into the City?*

Answer*: No.*

Question*: Or to your home?*

Answer*: No.*

Question*: Did Dr. Martin, the vet, tell you these animals would be a liability in any household?*

Answer*: No, he did not.*

Question*: Before January 26th of 2001, did Hera ever do anything in your presence that gave you cause for concern that she might be a danger to another person or animal?*

Answer. *That she might be a danger?*

Question*: She.*

Answer*: No.*

Question*: Never?*

Answer: *No, never.*

Question: *Before January 26th, 2000, did you ever see Bane bite another person?*

Answer: *No.*

Question: *Did you ever see during that same period of time Bane ever lunge at another person?*

Answer: *No.*

Question: *Did you ever see during that same period of time Bane be aggressive to another person?*

Answer: *No.*

Question: *Before January 26th, 2001, did you ever see Hera bite another person?*

Answer: *Hera, no.*

Question: *Did you ever see Hera lunge at another person?*

Answer: *No.*

Hammer explained to the jury that he was going to call many witnesses that would swear that Marjorie Knoller was aware or had been told that both Hera and Bane were dangerous.

Then the prosecutor got into the area of control. Again, using the screen he flashed questions and answers from Marjorie's grand jury testimony.

Hammer said, "Referring to the grand jury. And this is about the time surrounding the death of Diane Whipple, What Marjorie Knoller says happens is that she was dragged down this hall towards Diane Whipple and it took almost a minute, she says, that the dog drug her down a few feet and then she pulled him back and he drug her a few feet and pulled her back, and so I asked her…"

Hammer picked up a portion of the grand jury with his left hand and read: "You were unable to control them, correct, since he's dragging you?

"Answer: 'That's not accurate.'

"Do you call that control, he drags you down the hallway?

"This is Marjorie Knoller, the lawyer, under oath: 'Yes.'

"That's what you call control?

"Answer: 'Yes. He overcame my physical ability.'

"Question: You were not able to control him, correct?

"Answer: 'That's not accurate.'

"It's still control," Hammer said, "being dragged down the hallway by this dog. Question: Just your definition is that he's dragging you down the hallway and then knocking you to your knees and dragging you on your face. Is that control in your opinion?

"Answer: 'It's my ability to be able to totally control him and maintain control over him, yes.'

"'That's control, dragging you down, knocking you to your knees, and Ms. Knoller's sworn testimony is that *was* control. Is that control in your opinion?

"Answer: 'Yes.'

"Again on this issue of whether or not she was able to control, she's claiming she was always in control. Here is a letter to Paul Schneider, one of these letters from the search warrants that Marjorie wrote this time. Listen to this, ladies and gentlemen."

Hammer read the letter. "'We do take them out separately for walks most of the time as we trained the puppiness to walk off leash most of the time. And she is a pain in the butt when you keep her on lead for her whole walk.

"'Although I have a decent amount of upper body strength, if Bane really wanted to go after another dog, I don't have the body weight or leverage straddling him as Robert does.'"

Hammer paused and referred to his notes. He cited other witnesses that he would call that would refute Marjorie's statement that she was always in control.

Then he said, "Marjorie Knoller testified at the grand jury that she gave brief first aid to Diane Whipple, put her finger towards her throat and after she did that, she testified this under oath, ladies and gentlemen, that she put both dogs away."

On the screen flashed:

Question: *What did you do with Bane?*

Answer: *I brought him down the hallway to her apartment. Hera, I called Hera. Hera came in with me.*

Hammer said, "The testimony at grand jury from Marjorie Knoller, again under oath, was after the attack, she briefly gave first aid to Diane, then put both dogs away at the same time, secured them in her apartment. And then look at what she says she did next while Diane is still in the hallway, and this is under oath."

On the screen appeared: *I went out of my apartment, I went all the way down the hallway into Ms. Whipple's apartment and found my keys on the floor of her apartment. I came out of the apartment and that's when I encountered the two female officers.*

Hammer said, "After Diane Whipple has been mauled by these dogs, she has seen the wounds to her throat, her trachea is punctured, she can't breathe, she is bleeding from her neck, she's bitten nearly from head to toe, she gives brief first aid, she claims under oath to put both dogs away and then what does she do? She walks down the hallway over or around Diane Whipple's naked body, goes in Diane's apartment and looks for her keys. She says she finds them and encounters the police in the hallway. Now, what would the evidence show on those claims by Ms. Knoller? When the police arrive, Marjorie Knoller is nowhere in the hall. When the police arrive, the dogs aren't secured, one is still running loose with Diane Whipple alone."

Hammer took a moment, then shifted gears. He said, "I want to look at two brief claims with you of what Mr. Noel said to the grand jury, again a lawyer under oath. What did he have to say about knowing about the aggressiveness of these dogs? Listen to these questions and answers:

On the screen appeared the following:

Question: *Did you ever see Bane bite any person?*
Answer: *No.*
Question: *Did you ever see Hera bite any person?*
Answer: *No.*
Question: *Did you ever see Bane lunge at any person?*
Answer: *At a person, no.*
Question: *Did you ever see Hera lunge at a person?*
Answer: *No.*
Question: *Any other incidents, Mr. Noel, where Bane or Hera acted aggressively towards any person?"*
Answer: *No, nothing.*
Question: *Do you remember them ever lunging at a person in your hallway?*

331

Answer*: No. If they were with me, if the two of them were with me, they are under control.*

Hammer turned from the screen and said, "Mr. Noel, in his press conference at Pelican Bay State Prison said after Diane's death. 'Bane was a wonderful mutt. No, he wasn't a vicious dog, but no, Bane had never shown any signs of people aggression.'"

Hammer held up a large photo showing Noel in a hospital bed, then a photo of a bloody finger. "What's this? This is his finger almost severed. According to Mr. Noel at his press conference and under oath, he had no notice at all of any nature of either dog. Remember the first issue was what knowledge did he have about dangerousness? The second issue I talked about with Ms. Knoller was were they always in control. I asked the same questions of Mr. Noel. Again, this is at the grand jury with the lawyer testifying under oath. I asked, 'So October 23rd' the dogs broke free from Marjorie, correct?'

"Look at his answer."

On the courtroom screen appeared: *It's a characterization of it, yes.*

Question: *She lost control of them, correct?*

Answer: *I don't think I would characterize it as lost control but they got away.*

Question: *Besides that incident, did you ever see either one of the dogs break free from or Marjorie lose control of one of those dogs?*

Answer: *No.*

Question: *Did you ever lose control of one of the dogs?*

Answer: *No.*

Question: *Did the dogs ever overpower you so you couldn't hold them back?*

Hammer faced the jury. "What did he say under oath? 'No, never happened.'"

He read directly from the grand jury transcript. "Question: 'Was there ever an occasion where you opened the door to your apartment and let one or both of your dogs go running down the hall towards the elevator without you being in the hall?'

Prosecution's Opening Statements

"Picture that, ladies and gentlemen. You have seen the hallway, at least a diagram and picture of the hallway. Diane lived at one end, they lived towards the other end, and it's a pretty narrow hallway. Imagine what it would be like with one or two of these large dogs running down the hall. He is asked, 'Did this ever happen?' He says, 'No.' I say 'Never?' He says. 'Never.'

"Look what we find in one of the letters. This is from October 6th, well before he testified under oath before the grand jury. 'When I opened the door, two Presa faces were immediately pressed into the gap side by side. Before I could get my body in the doorway to block them, they pushed forward into the hall and took off side by side down the hall toward the elevator in a celebratory stampede. 240 pounds of Presa wall-to-wall moving at top speed. Up against the wall at the other end of the wall bouncing off, turning and running back the other way, bouncing off me and heading to the wall at the other end, turning, running back, Marjorie snagging Hera, Bane taking off to the stairs to the roof door and down and back into the apartment.'

"I ask you, ladies and gentlemen, are those dogs under control?"

Hammer read the letter involving Noel getting used to the 'jailbreak approach the kids have.'

And he asked, "Are those dogs in control?"

Hammer, during his entire delivery, kept the hand-held microphone in his left hand, gesturing with his right. He said, "Ladies and gentlemen, the key issues in this case are what did they know, the knowledge. This is the implied malice. What did they know about the danger of these dogs and what did they do in light of that knowledge? You have heard their version. They didn't know anything about it under oath. You will hear the evidence, you will be able to decide.

"I have covered three points by Ms. Knoller: her claim to not know anything about the danger, to have never lost control even while she is being dragged on her face before the dog kills Diane Whipple, and her claim to have immediately put both dogs away and met the police in the hallway when, in fact, the dog was still running loose with Diane, and she didn't meet them in the

333

hallway. And I have covered two claims by Mr. Noel, he himself too saying 'I didn't know anything about danger, nothing, I never lost control.' You saw the evidence."

Hammer then played the interview that Noel and Knoller gave to *Good Morning America* the year before. Knoller went on about how she had tried to protect Diane during the attack.

Once again, immortalized on video tape, Knoller stated that she was not responsible, never lost control of the dogs, and didn't understand why Diane Whipple didn't just go into her apartment and close the door.

When the video ended, Hammer said, "Her account there, which she repeated at the grand jury and in even more detail when I asked her questions, was that she laid on top of Diane Whipple practically the entire time to protect her and put her own life in danger to protect Diane Whipple from these dogs. I ask you to ask yourselves as this trial goes on, how does Diane Whipple get all of those wounds and every piece of clothing ripped from her body with the waistband intact if that woman was on top of her the whole time? Know what the evidence will show? After her claim of being on top of Diane Whipple the whole time in the middle of this ferocious attack, know what wound she suffered? Marjorie Knoller had small cuts to her hand. As to the black eye you saw there? At the scene when the police interviewed her, there was no indication whatsoever of any injury to her eye and she didn't claim any.

"How about the claim that Diane Whipple just stood there for a minute while she was trying to restrain the dog? The evidence will show, ladies and gentlemen, I have already told you part of it, is that Diane Whipple in early December was bitten by one of these dogs, that she was afraid of these dogs, that she did everything she could to stay away from these dogs. And this defendant says that she just stood there with her door open and grocery bag inside and came back out twice into the hall into these dogs? You decide."

Chapter
Forty-nine

Defense's Opening Statements — Ruiz

Superior Court of California, Department 26, Division 53, Tuesday, February 19, 2002.

Nedra Ruiz said, "My name is Nedra Ruiz and I have the honor to represent Marjorie Knoller in this action.

"The tragic death of Diane Whipple joins us all here today. Her untimely and horrible passing brings us together in a search for justice. In that search each of you will be judges of the facts. You will each determine whether or not the prosecution has met its burden to prove each and every element of the offenses charged beyond a reasonable doubt. In a case involving criminal charges, our system of justice imposes the burden of proof on the prosecution, and so they will make their presentation of evidence first. And this statement is Marjorie's opportunity to outline the evidence that we will present through cross-examination of the prosecution's witnesses and through the presentation of defense witnesses after the prosecution rests."

The defense attorney went through a brief account of the medical history of Bane. The dog was on pain medication which was giving him diarrhea.

Ruiz explained why Marjorie had to take her dog to the roof to relieve himself.

She described the events that happened on January 26, 2001 that resulted in the death of Diane Whipple.

Ruiz went into the center of the courtroom well and got down on her knees and reenacted the scene.

The lawyer said, " Marjorie was very concerned. She had never been in a situation where Bane had pulled her off her feet.

She had never been in a situation where both dogs were not being obedient to her. She had never been in a situation where Hera was barking hysterically as Bane was jumping up on someone. She wanted immediately to take emergency action to protect Ms. Whipple. She wanted to put Ms. Whipple out of harm's way. She wanted to get Ms. Whipple away from these dogs."

Ruiz described Marjorie being pulled off her feet, then said, "The dog is still forcing his way toward Ms. Whipple and starts to grab at her clothing and pull it. Marjorie then flings her body on Ms. Whipple and says: 'Don't move. I think he's trying to protect me. Don't move. I think he's trying to protect me.' Ms. Whipple is terrified, of course. The dog starts to pull at her clothing. Hera is barking hysterically.'

"Marjorie can feel Hera pulling at the clothes of Diane's pants." Nedra Ruiz was back on her feet, facing the jury. "She can feel the dog behind her, who's got her real attention, who's got all of her focus is the dog Bane because, as he's attacking, she's lying on Ms. Whipple trying to keep the dog from biting at Ms. Whipple."

Nedra got back down on her knees. "And for a few seconds she's able to do it because Ms. Whipple is able to be still. And in those few seconds, the dog will pause.

"But then when Ms. Whipple tries to escape to the door of her apartment, the dog commences to attack again and the dog begins to bite Ms. Whipple. Ms. Whipple is flailing, of course;" Nedra waved her left arm about, "she's terrified. She's panicked, as is Marjorie. And in this flailing, while Ms. Whipple is lying face down, she flings an arm up and gets contact with Marjorie's face. It was a backward motion and she hit Marjorie in the face, and Marjorie is stunned for a second and sees, horrified, the dog bite Ms. Whipple on the back of the neck.

"Marjorie is screaming." Nedra Ruiz's voice rose. "'Stop, stop! Get off her! Stop, stop!' She's screaming, she's yelling, she's hitting at the dog. She's trying to keep her whole body around Ms. Whipple to protect Ms. Whipple from the jaws of this berserk beast.

"The dog is pulling at her clothing, even underneath Marjorie. Even though Ms. Whipple is underneath Marjorie, Ms. Whipple is being bitten on her sides, on her back. Marjorie is aware that the dog is biting Diane, scratching at her, and the dog bites Marjorie, as well. Marjorie actually has her whole body on top of Ms. Whipple like this, and the dog is coming over her because she's got the leash. The dog is circling back and forth and even walks on Marjorie's back to try and get at Ms. Whipple.

"Marjorie is screaming: 'Stop! No! Stop! No!'"

Nedra Ruiz's voice quivered with emotion. The rhythm of her delivery rose and fell like she was preaching a sermon.

"The evidence will *not* show that Marjorie loosed the leash and went off to call 911. The evidence will show that Marjorie was screaming at the top of her lungs and knew that someone would call 911, was hoping that someone would come to her aid. No one did. No one did."

Ruiz paused, then continued, still in an extremely emotional voice. "She was lying on top of Ms. Whipple telling her: 'Don't move; stop; don't move.' Ms. Whipple couldn't stop. She was fighting for her life. Marjorie's fighting to stay on top of her. Marjorie was fighting to protect her from this dog. The dog actually bit Marjorie on the shoulder and up here on the upper breast and made bruises.

"Down here on the ground Marjorie was slapping at the head of Bane as it came over to bite and ravage the flesh of Ms. Whipple. And you'll see pictures of the scratches Marjorie got on her hands when, at one point, her whole hand went into Bane's mouth and he lacerated her thumb.

"As Marjorie is trying to cover Ms. Whipple's body, Marjorie is thinking that she has to get to some position of safety and actually thinks: Maybe we can crawl to the elevator. And Marjorie and Ms. Whipple actually are kind of like crawling. Marjorie is actually on top of Ms. Whipple like this…"

Ruiz began to act out the recreation of the scene.

"…and they are crawling like this."

The defense attorney went down on her hands and knees in front of the jury box and acted out what she was saying. "They don't get up. They can't get up on their knees. They are actually lying on the ground and moving themselves down on the floor.

"Marjorie says she gets over by one of the doors and she starts hitting it with all her might with her leg, like this."

Nedra Ruiz again acted out the scene, banging the floor to emphasis each point..

"And Esther Birkmaier hears that. She hears a tremendous thumping. It's Marjorie…"

Ruiz acted out her words, banging on the side of the jury box. "…thumping as hard as she can. She's barely even aware what apartment it is. All she's aware of is she needs help and she's hoping someone will hear this pounding and come to aid her."

Back on her feet and facing the jury, Nedra went on to explain about the neighbor Esther Birkmaier, calling 911; about Esther being afraid; about Esther putting on the chain to her door; about Esther thinking she could run to the bathroom for safety if the dogs broke through her door.

Ruiz said, "This entire time Marjorie never, ever lets go of the leash. The entire time she's trying to pull at Bane, she's slapping at him, she's hitting him, she's yelling at him, she's thinking of whatever she can say or do to stop this attack. But the only weapon she has at hand is her body. And she puts her body on Ms. Whipple and tries to protect Ms. Whipple from the dog with her own body."

Nedra Ruiz's voice rose and fell, in an almost-hypnotic rhythm. Her voice was not dulcet. If anything, it was on the verge of strident. "Ms. Whipple stops moving. Marjorie, by this time, has her fingers on the back of Ms. Whipple's neck. She's applying direct pressure. She's trying to stop the bleeding. She's trying to save Ms. Whipple's life by stopping the bleeding and Ms. Whipple is still. And in those minutes, those seconds, Bane ceases to attack. He's just standing there over Marjorie and Ms. Whipple. They are still lying on the hallway floor, but Bane has stopped. And in that second, Marjorie thinks: 'I've got to get these dogs away from her. Any minute now all hell could break loose again. I've got to get this dog away from her.' And she gets up. She's able to steady herself, grab Bane and start pulling him, now that they've ended up toward the elevator, where Marjorie thought: 'Well, maybe the door will open and somebody will get out and help me, or maybe we will go into the elevator and close the door.' They are lying right by the elevator, and Marjorie gets up and takes the dog back to her apartment.

"And, as she's doing that, she realizes that Hera has not come with her. She wants to put both dogs away. She takes one of the dogs, Bane, and she puts him in the bathroom, and she realizes that Hera is out there and she yells: 'Hey, where do you think you're going?' Hera comes. Hera comes and Marjorie puts Hera away in the bedroom."

The defense attorney explained that the police then arrived. She explained why they saw a dog running loose — because Marjorie was inside securing Bane.

She said, "The police officers are there to give aid to Ms. Whipple. Marjorie is now a witness to this. She's not going to be permitted to give aid. The police officers will testify they assume responsibility of this matter. When they were charging up the stairs, it was them radioing: 'Hey, when we see the dog, we are going to shoot it.'

"And in that second, when someone else assumes responsibility for Ms. Whipple, Marjorie realizes: where are my keys? She realized she has no keys and wonders: Well, where did they go? I had them. I had them here." Ruiz patted the side of her suit. "They are not in the hallway. And she ends up finding them in Ms. Whipple's foyer. When they fell, that's where the keys were. That's where she finds them."

During most of this opening statement Marjorie Knoller kept her head down, only occasionally glancing up at her lawyer.

Ruiz said, "Emergency technicians show up at the scene and they take pictures. They take pictures of Marjorie Knoller. And this is one of the pictures they take. This was taken right there on the sixth floor. This picture was taken within an hour of the incident. This picture was taken because it reflects the condition of Marjorie Knoller."

Ruiz held a photograph blow-up of Marjorie Knoller, whose face looked shattered. Ruiz's voice started to crack with emotion. Almost wrenching. "I know you've seen terrible pictures of Diane Whipple today. You've seen how Bane rent her flesh. But the evidence will not show that Marjorie stood back and let that horrible thing happen to that beautiful girl. Marjorie Knoller tried to save that woman's life with her own body."

Nedra explained to the jury that the blood pattern on her client was the kind of soaking that occurs when you place your body on a victim and try to protect it from a berserk dog.

Ruiz showed the jury pictures taken by the San Francisco police department; pictures of Marjorie's bloody and lacerated hands. She held up a photo of Marjorie's bloody hands.

Ruiz said, "The minutes are ticking away for Ms. Whipple. Marjorie did everything she could for Ms. Whipple. The evidence will not show that she abandoned Ms. Whipple. The evidence will show that she tried to stop Ms. Whipple's bleeding, and the only reason she got up off of Ms. Whipple was to make sure that Bane didn't hurt her more.

"Evidence will show that it wasn't until Alex Cardenas, a medical officer with the SWAT team arrived, that someone tried to stop Ms. Whipple's bleeding again. She went into cardiac arrest, and you heard the prosecutor mention the cause of her death: Massive blood loss.

"Mr. Cardenas was able to reestablish a pulse. Ms. Whipple died that evening at the San Francisco General Hospital after surgery."

Nedra Ruiz's voice choked on emotion, her voice cracking again.

The defense attorney told the jury about Animal Care and Control arriving. About Bane being tranquilized. About the dog Bane being led out with come-alongs.

Then she said, "The police on the scene asked Marjorie if she wanted to make a statement. At first she declined, but before the afternoon was out, before 6:00 o'clock that afternoon as she was sitting covered in blood in her kitchen, she spoke to officers, I think it was Officer Becker, and she gave a statement. I'd like to play it for you."

Jim Hammer said, "Your Honor, hearsay, not admissible by the defendant."

The judge asked Ruiz, "What is this you have, counsel?"

"It's a taped statement that Marjorie Knoller gave that same evening."

The judge said, "There is a question about whether or not its admissibility is an issue. It can be admitted by the prosecution as a statement against interest or confession or an admission. There is a legal issue about Ms. Knoller introducing her own statement. She can testify as to what she said, but no decision has been made yet as to whether she's going to testify. So at this stage of the record, the statement is not admissible."

Nedra Ruiz said, "Very well. Ms. Knoller spoke to the police that very same afternoon and she told the police—"

Hammer again protested with, "Your Honor, this is the same objection, unless it's proffered that she will testify."

Ruiz said, "She will testify, Your Honor."

The judge leaned forward and said, "I don't know what the status of the case is going to be after the People rest, and the Court cannot accept this unless you are convinced, regardless of the status of the People's case, that you're saying Ms. Knoller is going to get up there and testify. You may want to be very careful about waiving her rights in that regard. The jury has been fully instructed that the defendants have a right not to testify at all."

Ruiz said, "Your Honor, I wish to play the statement and I believe that Ms. Knoller will testify, and the statement is completely consistent with her grand jury testimony and any testimony she'd give in this court."

The judge said, "That doesn't make it admissible. It's still hearsay. However, if you are going to make a representation to the Court that regardless of the state of the evidence at close of the People's case she is going to testify and subject herself to cross-examination, then you can relate to the jury what the testimony will be. You still don't get to play the tape, because it's hearsay. And as far as I can tell right now, it doesn't fall within any of the exceptions that the hearsay rule contemplates, but you are permitted to make that representation as to what the evidence will show if you are fully prepared to subject Ms. Knoller to cross-examination on the stand, regardless of the state of the People's case when they close. It's a big decision."

"I'm prepared," Ruiz said, "to make it at this time, Your Honor. Ms. Knoller will definitely testify in this action."

"Do you wish to speak with her first?"

"Certainly."

Ruiz went to Marjorie and spoke briefly, then said to the court, "Your Honor, Ms. Knoller will be testifying in this action."

The judge said, "Ms. Knoller, I want you to understand that if the People were to rest today, having put no evidence on, the representations being made by you and your counsel is that you will, nevertheless, get up on the stand and subject yourself to cross-examination, at least to the extent that it concerns the subject matter of this statement."

Marjorie Knoller said, "I understand that."

The judge said, "Ladies and gentlemen, Ms. Knoller may have waived her right not to testify. That does not in any way affect Mr. Noel's rights. He still has the absolute right not to testify if he wishes not to do so. The same thing, you cannot consider Mr. Noel's decision not to testify for anything whatsoever. His constitutional rights remain intact."

Nedra Ruiz laid out for the jury what her defense of Marjorie Knoller would be.

She explained her client's love of animals and how she cared enough to research how they should be treated.

"I am confident," Ruiz said in conclusion, "that after you hear all of the evidence presented to you, you will conclude that Marjorie Knoller is not guilty of any of the offenses that she is charged with in this action. Thank you."

Chapter
Fifty

Defense's Opening Statements — Hotchkiss

Superior Court of California, Department 26, Division 53, Tuesday, February 19, 2002.
Bruce Hotchkiss was 67 years old. He had an amiable face, a friendly smile and a courtly demeanor. He was representing Robert Noel. He had a reputation of being a fair and honest advocate.

His delivery was in stark contrast to the animated Nedra Ruiz.

Hotchkiss said, "As the judge indicated to you last Friday and again this morning, the purpose of an opening statement by counsel is to allow counsel to tell you what they anticipate the evidence will be. And what I want to do very briefly is to outline the evidence that will show Mr. Noel is not guilty of the two charges against him."

He said, "I have the advantage of being brief. I can be brief because Mr. Noel was not present when this tragedy occurred. The evidence will show that Mr. Noel left the apartment building at 2398 Pacific Avenue, that he shared with Ms. Knoller, who is his wife and who he practiced law with. He left there at approximately 8:00 a.m., somewhere between 8:00 a.m. and 9:30 a.m., because he had court appearances out of county that day or, excuse me, out of the City of San Francisco that day.

"Mr. Noel took care of his court appearances and around 3:00 p.m. was on the way back home when he had a flat tire in Berkeley, California. Because of that flat tire, Mr. Noel did not arrive back at the apartment building until after this tragedy. When Mr. Noel did arrive, the event was already over and the animal control people were taking Bane from out of the apartment building and placing him in their animal control van.

"Mr. Noel was not present at any time during the tragic events that occurred on the 6th floor of 2398 Pacific Avenue."

Hotchkiss reiterated some of the facts that Nedra Ruiz mentioned, then summarized his case. "There will be an enormous amount of evidence that the prosecution will introduce in this case that has nothing to do with the dogs Bane and Hera, and has nothing to do with the events that occurred on the 6th floor hall-way of 2398 Pacific Avenue. That evidence has nothing to do with the guilt or innocence of Mr. Noel or Ms. Knoller. That evidence will be introduced to attempt to convince you that Mr. Noel should be found guilty because he has an unconventional lifestyle.

"Having an unconventional lifestyle has nothing to do with the guilt or innocence of Mr. Noel.

"There will be no evidence that the actions of Mr. Noel were aggravated, reckless, or flagrant in regards to the dogs Bane and Hera, or the events that occurred on January 26th. He was not present at that time.

"There will be no evidence that the consequences of the tragic events on January 26th could have been reasonably foreseen by Mr. Noel. He was not present at that time.

"There will be no evidence that the tragic death on January the 26th was a natural and probable result of an aggravated, reckless, or negligent act by Mr. Noel. He was not present at that time.

"At the conclusion of the case I'll ask you to return a verdict of not guilty as to Mr. Noel on both counts."

Chapter
Fifty-one

From Coumbs Ranch to Pelican Bay

Superior Court of California, Department 26, Division 53, Wednesday, February 20, 2002.
The body of the trial had begun. Kimberly Guilfoyle Newsom knew that a case was brought to fruition much like a home was built. Without a good foundation, the house was in trouble. The trial was part of the process, another stage, a job to be done. All the work over all the months would now be presented.

The foundation was strong. It was time to see what kind of house would rest on top.

Janet Coumbs summarized what had happened to her from her first involvement with Dale Bretches and Paul Schneider, to when Noel and Knoller took the dogs from her.

Then it was the defense's turn. Nedra Ruiz began her cross-examination. Once again, like so many of the witnesses for the prosecution, Janet Coumbs was taken through her statement made to the police and grand jury.

The defense attorney asked, "How long did the dog Bane live at Hayfork with you?"

Ms. Coumbs answered, "From June of '98 until April 1st of 2000."

"Did you consider Bane to be part of your family?"

"He was my dog, yes. We loved him."

"And he loved you?"

"Yes, he did."

"You never feared Bane?"

"No."

"Bane was never vicious to you?"

"No. Bane pulled my wagon. He pulled my wood from the wood pile to the house. He was a big clown."

"Haven't you said he used to dance for people?"

"I did. He would get up and jump and dance."

"And you never saw him be vicious to people, did you?"

"No."

"Bane had a cat, didn't he?"

"Yes, he did."

"What was the name of the cat?"

"Chewy. It was Chewy Chubakka."

"And Chewy Chubakka, the cat, was Bane's personal cat?"

"Yes, it was."

"Didn't they sleep together?"

"They did."

"Did they groom one another?"

"I don't know if they did it, but the cat would rub against Bane's legs and stuff. The cat didn't really like us to pet him. It was Bane's cat."

"You took pictures of Bane and his cat?"

"And the other cats that I had, too, yes."

"Did Bane ever kill a cat?"

"No."

"You never saw Bane kill a sheep, did you?"

"No."

Ruiz took the witness through the dogs being chained, then asked, "Now, when you had him on a chain, did you note his personality would change?"

"No."

"When he would escape, he would slip out of the collar, and was he vicious when he got free?"

"He usually went down, played in the pond for a while and then he would come back and say here I am, I'm free, look at me type thing."

The defense attorney went through what happened when the vet, Dr. Martin, came to the ranch, then asked, "Concerning Hera, did you teach her to sit?"

"Yes."

"Did you teach her to walk and heel?"

"Yes. I had to when we got her."

"Did you teach her to stay?"

"No. You can't. I couldn't do it with her."

"Did you try to teach Hera to stay?"

"Not really. We had them in the pen and we would go and love on them and we would take them for walks and stuff and they would go on a chain or a leash and stuff."

"Did you teach Bane how to sit?"

Janet Coumbs answered, "Yes."

"Did you teach him how to walk at heel?"

"Yes, I did."

Nedra Ruiz concluded her cross. "When Marjorie and Robert came to pick up Bane, did you cry when Bane left?"

"Yes, I did."

After a lunch break, Robert Noel's defense attorney, Bruce Hotchkiss, took over the cross-examination. He asked Ms. Coumbs how she met Paul Schneider, then asked, "Paul was an artist, was he not?"

"Yes, he was."

"Had he sent any artwork to you?"

"Yes."

"Have you seen a lot of his artwork?"

"I would say so."

"It's good?"

"He did a very beautiful picture for me of a cougar coming down a mountain."

"One of the reasons that Paul wanted the dogs was so that you could take photographs of the dogs and send those photos to him; isn't that correct?"

"Yes."

"And he would use those photos to draw pictures of dogs?"

"Yes."

"Paul was very interested in dogs, wasn't he?"

"He was a fanatic."

"As part of this agreement, as you've indicated, Paul wanted you to send him photographs so that he could do his artwork of the dogs; isn't that correct?"

"Yes."

"You entered into this agreement with Paul, didn't you?"

"Yes, I did."

Hotchkiss went through Janet Coumbs' involvement with Schneider, then asked, "You hadn't read any manuals or dog books on what might be required for training of large dogs, had you?"

"No."

"And since you hadn't read anything about how to train large dogs, you didn't train them based on any manuals or anything else, did you?"

"No. Paul wrote to me and told me, 'These are really good dogs. They are companion guard dogs. They will guard your sheep.' That was what I knew about them."

"You assumed there was no training or nothing needed be done with these dogs?"

"Pretty much."

"You didn't feel that you needed to bring the dogs in contact with human beings on a regular basis?"

"After I got the dogs, Paul told me not to allow them around people. Bane was out in the front of my property, in the front area. People would go over and pet him. I didn't take him off his chain. They would go pet him. They loved him."

When Jim Hammer took over, he asked the witness, "You mentioned that at one point you cried in relation to all the dogs?"

"Yes."

"When was that?"

"The day they left."

"That Bane and the dogs left, correct?"

"Yeah."

"Was there any interaction with Ms. Knoller in which you cried?"

"Yes. She called me and she told me that they could take my home, they could take my farm. I've worked a long time to have a home and that they could take my car, they could take any future earnings that I had, even, and it made me cry. And she told me that the dogs belonged to Brenda, and that's not what I understood. You know, I was prepared to give up puppies. We bonded with them in some ways and we loved them, but you know you're going to get rid of them. But Bane and Isis especially, those were our dogs. They were *my* dogs."

"When you cried during this conversation, was Ms. Knoller still on the phone?"

"Yes, she was."

"How did she respond?" Hammer asked.

"She said, 'You can get all this to go away. Just turn over the dogs.'"

"Did you feel threatened by Ms. Knoller?"

"I really did. I felt that they are going to come and take my home."

* * *

The first witness after a lunch break was the veterinarian, Dr. Martin. He testified as he had at dog court.

Mara Lamboy, a front office assistant supervisor for San Francisco's Animal Care and Control, took the stand. The direct examination was conducted by Kimberly Guilfoyle Newsom. The witness verified that Robert Noel had purchased dog licenses for Bane and Hera and signed himself and his wife as co-owners.

After Lamboy, Newsom called Carlos Sanchez, who worked for the special operations division of the San Francisco district attorney's office. He verified the evidence that was seized at Pelican Bay State Prison and at the defendants' apartment. These were entered into evidence.

The last witness called that day was Devan Hawkes. He worked for the California Department of Corrections in the Special Services Unit. It took the few minutes remaining that day to go over his qualifications.

The next morning he would testify about his specialty — prison gangs.

Chapter
Fifty-two

A Hawk and the Aryan Brotherhood

Superior Court of California, Department 26, Division 53, Thursday, February 21, 2002.
The day included witnesses that testified during dog court and the grand jury proceedings. People like John Watanabe, the mailman; the dog-walker, Lynn Gaines; David Mosher, who claimed he was bitten on the butt while exiting the elevator; and the lawyer Neil Bardack.

Their testimony at the trial was the same as at dog court, and Ruiz's cross-examination was essentially "why didn't you complain to anyone?"

Two new witnesses to aggression were Steve and Aimee West, owners of the dog that Lynn Gaines walked. They had an encounter themselves with the dogs. Kimberly Guilfoyle Newsom questioned them. The couple went to Alta Plaza Park where they ran into Bane and Hera. Hera latched onto the snout of a dog named Bacas. Noel and the owner of Bacas tried to separate their animals, but were unsuccessful. Mr. West tossed his keys and hit Hera on the neck — Hera let go.

Newsom asked Aimee West, "Anything else where you ran into Bob Noel?"

"At the park one morning he had his arm in a sling. I asked if he was okay. He told me that he was down at Chrissy Field with Bane on a halter. Another dog, off leash, jumped his dog. He tried to break it up and his finger was seriously injured."

"Did he tell you which dog was responsible for his finger getting bitten?"

"I believe he said that Bane had hurt his finger."

A Hawk and the Aryan Brotherhood

The next witness was Devan Hawkes.

Mr. Hawkes' expertise was discussed. He had testified as a witness regarding prison gangs in courts from San Diego to Santa Clara County. One of his job descriptions was debriefing.

Jim Hammer asked, "Tell the jury, what is debriefing?"

"When a member or an associate of a gang decided to drop out of the gang, then we conduct what's called a debriefing interview. That's an opportunity we have to discuss the gang's activities, history, that person's personal knowledge and involvement in the gang. We do that for the purpose of getting information about the gang and its membership. Also to evaluate the person's sincerity in dropping out of the gang and to identify that person's enemies so that we can properly assign housing away from those enemies."

Hammer asked, "Are reading letters also an important source of information in developing your expertise in this area?"

"Yes. They are a primary source of information."

"Are letters that you look at ever disguised as confidential legal matter?"

"Yes."

Pictures of Paul Schneider and Dale Bretches were introduced and identified by Hawke as being members of the Aryan Brotherhood. He had started his investigation because Mrs. Coumbs had phoned him in 1999.

. Hammer introduced evidence, hand-written documents. He introduced a drawing with the words "War dog," "Bane, Bringer of Death: Ruin: Destruction."

Receipts were introduced regarding the purchase of books by the inmates called *Fighting Dog Breeds, History of Fighting Dogs, American Pit Bull Terriers, World of Fighting Dogs, Gladiator Dogs,* and *Manstopper: Training a K-9 Guardian.*

Hawkes explained that during the course of his investigation he found evidence that Mr. Noel was participating in determining prices for pups for sale. He named other Aryan Brotherhood members who provided funding for the purchase of dogs; people with nicknames like Hillbilly and Blue. A letter showed that Noel was in contact with a James Harris, of Stygian Kennel.

The prisoners formed a business called Dog-O-War Presas.

Hawkes stated, in his opinion Noel and Knoller were involved in a scheme to breed, raise and train dogs with certain members of the Aryan Brotherhood.

The video involving Noel and a TV reporter discussing the book *Manstopper* was shown to the jury.

Hammer asked, "Do you have an opinion whether or not Robert Noel and Marjorie Knoller are associates of the Aryan Brotherhood?"

The witness answered, "Based on the criteria that the Department of Corrections has, I believe this would be enough information to support that they were associates of the Aryan Brotherhood."

Hammer asked, "Are you familiar with an occasion in which Mr. Schneiner stabbed a lawyer?"

"Yes."

"In your opinion, was that activity related to the Aryan Brotherhood?"

"Yes. The weapon that Schneider used to stab the attorney had a symbol of the Aryan Brotherhood on it."

"How did he get the weapon in to the courtroom to stab the lawyer?"

Bruce Hotchkiss objected on the grounds of relevance. The judge overruled the objection.

Devan Hawkes answered the question, "He smuggled it into the courtroom in his rectum."

Hammer introduced a letter written from Robert Noel to Paul Schneider, marked Confidential Legal Material. The prosecutor read from the letter, regarding the stabbing of the lawyer: "'I don't think Marjorie ever told you what my response was, with which she agreed immediately, upon hearing that. Every time we were told that, "If he did, he must have had a damned good reason and the smuck probably deserved it."'"

Hammer looked up from the letter and asked, "Is that relevant in your opinion about whether or not the defendants are associates of the Aryan Brotherhood?"

"Yes. It shows them siding with Schneider. With an act that he did."

Hammer looked at the letter. "Let me read on: 'When someone from the defense side mentioned a possibility of wanting to depose you, Marjorie and I both agreed that we would have no problem being in such a setting with you, but that I would want to make it clear that I was not sitting between you and the door. And if you went for the door, all she and I would do was to wave good-bye and wish you good luck and God's speed.' Is that relevant to the defendants being associates of the Aryan Brotherhood?"

"Yes. Mr. Schneider, by the Department of Corrections, is considered a high escape risk based on a previous escape and his mastery of concealing contraband, weapons and handcuff keys."

Hammer read another section of the letter: "'You asked if I would be surprised to learn that you had a healthy piece on you at the trial.'" The prosecutor asked the witness what a "piece" meant and learned it meant a weapon.

Hammer read: "'Absolutely not. Would not have been surprised in the least. Given that Marjorie and I had heard of you, especially the missing light switch and the a.c. vent cover. I had no doubt that you were carrying.' What is the significance of that?"

"Carrying refers to possession of a weapon."

Hammer introduced another letter into evidence, with Noel and Knoller's letterhead and written to Dale Bretches, Paul Schneider's cellmate. It also carried the words "Confidential Legal Mail."

Hammer read: "'Thought I would pass on some interesting developments. Heard from a source today that (prisoner's name omitted intentionally) is housed in federal custody in Colorado and that (another prisoner's name omitted intentionally) together with a number of other Pelican Bay State Prison inmates housed at the federal correctional facility at Lompoc.'" Hammer asked the significance of the letter.

Hawkes answered: "The letter refers to witnesses and where they are located. One of those witnesses is very much an enemy of Mr. Schneider, having once stabbed him, for having dropped out of the gang." Hammer asked if the locations of the witnesses in Lompoc and Colorado were made public.

They had not.

Hammer asked if this was serious.

"Very serious. Identifying the location of a protected witness has the potential that great bodily harm could come to that witness."

Hammer introduced another letter written by Noel to Paul Schneider with the reference "*The Triad.*"

Hammer read: "'When I grew up, that kind of shit would never have happen. Have the witnesses to support the threat and put between his eyes. Only one side of the story to tell and it was self-defense.' Is this relevant to the opinions you have given today?"

"Because it appears from the language here that he's encouraging getting rid of any other witnesses, to just leave one side of the story."

The judge called for the morning recess.

* * *

After the break, Nedra Ruiz went to the lectern and cross-examined Devan Hawkes. She said the convicts never met Bane or Hera. Then she asked, "During the 70s the Aryan Brotherhood was worried about dying out, weren't they?"

"It was during the '80s."

"And they recruited amongst the Nazi Low Riders?"

"Yes."

"Did they recruit any Latinos?"

"There are a number of Latinos who are members of the Nazi Low Riders."

"Are there any African Americans?"

"Not that I'm aware of."

"And the Aryan Brotherhood wouldn't recruit a lawyer who volunteered to do free work for African Americans in San Francisco, would they?"

"I'm not aware of any attorney being recruited."

"Marjorie Knoller isn't a member of the Aryan Brotherhood, is she?"

"No."

Ruiz took the witness through people who had the dogs, like Janet Coumbs and Brenda Storey, who considered themselves owners of Bane and Hera.

She asked Devan Hawkes if he had ever read the book *Manstopper*.

He had not.

Ruiz said, "So you're unaware that on page 183 of that book the author concluded that a pup exhibiting chronic fear or excessive aggression over a newcomer's arrival would also be inappropriate for being trained to be a guardian?"

"I have not read the book."

"So you wouldn't be aware that the author of the book concludes that dogs with hip dysplasia or other genetic defects of that kind are not fit to be guardian dogs or trained to be guardian dogs?"

"I don't know the contents of the book."

"You are aware that Bane had dysplasia?"

"Yes."

"But you're not aware that Hera had subaortic stenosis?"

"I'm aware she had a heart condition."

"And you know that as a result of Hera's heart condition she wasn't to be bred."

"Bred anymore."

"Bane wasn't going to be part of a plan to breed other puppies. were you aware of that?"

"That was the indication, but not the initial intent."

Nedra Ruiz introduced a magazine called Dog-o-War, pointed at a margin and asked if the witness recognized Paul Schneider's handwriting.

Hawkes answered, "It appears to be, but I'm not a handwriting expert."

Pointing at magazine, the defense lawyer asked, "Doesn't that article indicate that the Presa Canario is a very loving and gentle with the family and animals?"

"Correct."

"Here is a sentence that indicates two Spanish judges have yet to hear a single instance of a Presa Canario attacking unwarranted and the Persas' tolerance with children is legendary?"

The witness agreed.

"And doesn't it indicate on the following sentence that 'socializing them,' meaning the dogs, is mandatory?"

"Yes, it does."

"Doesn't it indicate that training is highly recommended?"

"Yes."

"Doesn't it say that they are very forgiving of strange children, instinctively recognizing them as no threat?"

"That's what it says."

"Do you consider Brenda Storey to be an associate of the Aryan Brotherhood?"

"I consider an associate to be someone who participates in criminal activity knowingly and who aids the gang. I would consider Brenda Storey to be more of an associate than Janet Coumbs. I do not believe that Janet Coumbs knew that Schneider and Bretches were in the Aryan Brotherhood."

Ruiz went through the background of the dogs' connection with Coumbs and Storey. Then she asked, "You know now that Bretches and Schneider aren't into fighting dogs?"

"I believe that to be true."

"Isn't it true that a person could help an individual who might be a member of a gang without ever intending to benefit the gang."

"I suppose that's possible."

Ruiz turned the witness over to Hotchkiss. After exchanging pleasantries with Devan Hawkes, the lawyer asked, "Based on your experience, both within the prison system and as a gang expert, it's not uncommon for somebody in prison to try and develop a relationship with someone on the outside, either someone who is kind or considerate to get something done on the out-side, would not that be a fair statement?"

"That is a common practice."

Hotchkiss asked a series of questions involving the length of time Bretches and Schneider had been in prison, the difficulty of communication because of that length, and the need to use conduits like family and their attorneys.

The lawyer brought up the Madrid decision, which dealt with the validation of one prisoner accusing another of something. Then the defense lawyer asked, "Prisoner X can say prisoner Y is a gang member, can't they. That is one way you validate?"

"Correct."

"If X says Y is a gang member, Y can't find out who is calling him a gang member, can he?"

"If kept confidential," Hawkes said, "that is correct."

"One of the difficulties is that if X has a grudge against Y, he can say he's a gang member and that makes the validation process suspect?"

"Correct."

"Your opinion was that my client was siding or assisting the Aryan Brotherhood because he said that if he was in a courtroom and a guy like Schneider came towards him, he would get out of the way. Would you expect somebody to stop a prisoner if he were trying to escape. A citizen?"

"I would hope any citizen would do what they could to prevent a crime from being committed."

Hotchkiss brought up the letter in which Noel mentioned shooting someone. He asked, "In that letter, Mr. Noel was talking about an individual who had been threatened by somebody who was coming over to kill him. Isn't that correct?"

Devan Hawkes said, "And the response he felt appropriate was not only in defending himself by shooting this guy, but the significance is eliminating the witness. He's having a discussion with an inmate in this, the best thing is to eliminate any other side of the story."

It was almost 4:30. Court was scheduled for only four days a week, it would not meet on Fridays unless absolutely necessary.

This was for the convenience of all those involved who lived in San Francisco, to allow them travel time between their homes and court.

Defense attorney Bruce Hotchkiss finished the day and his cross-examination with a rhetorical question: "Isn't this a discussion between two men, one of them in prison for life perhaps one of them blowing off a little hot air?"

Chapter
Fifty-three

Witnesses for the Prosecution

Superior Court of California, Department 26, Division 53, Monday, February 25, 2002.
On the first day of the week, prosecutor Jim Hammer called many of the witnesses who had appeared a year earlier at dog court or at the grand jury hearings. People like dog-walker Mario Montepeque — whose statement was read into the record at dog court, and Diane and Sharon's neighbor Henry Putek, who testified before the grand jury.

Others witnesses included dog-walker Ron Bosia, who testified at dog court, and Diana Curtiss, who appeared before the grand jury.

Skip Cooley, who lived next door to Noel and Knoller, testified about a series of letters exchanged, cordially, with Robert Noel, regarding barking.

These neighbors also complained to the building manager.

Rhea Wertman-Tallent, who had told the police about an incident regarding the dogs, testified.

On the stand, she described the incident vividly and with great animation. "The two huge dogs were reared up on their hind legs, eyes crazed, baring their teeth, lunging forward trying to break their leashes. They were facing towards me and the school children. The dogs were making the most horrible sounds, like they wanted to kill something now."

She also used phrases like, "The caretakers/owners have to be insane to have wanted to keep these dogs in the city in an apartment."

And, "The landlord has to be retarded, too."

On his cross-examination, Robert Noel's attorney, Bruce Hotchkiss inferred that she might have been swayed by all the publicity regarding the case.

Another dog-walker, Abraham Taylor, testified that the Tuesday before Diane Whipple died, at 7:30 in the morning, he was walking down the street with one of his charges, a Belgian shepherd. Coming toward him were Marjorie and Robert with their dogs. The dog Marjorie had a leash on suddenly broke free and raced straight at Abraham.

The dog-walker grabbed Hera's harness and the back of her neck and forced her to the ground. Then Marjorie got the leash and led the dog away.

Hammer asked, "Did Ms. Knoller apologize to you?"

"No."

"Did you see Ms. Knoller verbally correct her dog?"

"No."

"Did she physically correct the dog that almost attacked your dog?"

"No."

The same series of questions were asked, except this time they regarded Robert Noel.

Each time the answer was again "No."

Abraham told of another incident where he ran into Noel and Bane in the apartment building at 2398 Pacific. In the small elevator Noel mentioned that he was thinking about adopting a third dog, because someone else couldn't take care of it. Noel said, "It's tough enough having two. Could you imagine owning three?"

During Ruiz's cross-examination she asked, "Didn't you pet Bane when you got in the elevator and rode with Robert Noel?"

"Yes."

"How long have you been a dog-walker?"

"At this time, just less than a year."

"Based on your experience as a dog-walker, you would never have pet Bane if you thought he was going to bite you?"

"I wouldn't have gotten on the elevator if I thought he was going to bite me."

Ruiz asked the witness, "Hadn't you seen Marjorie about a half a dozen times in the neighborhood?"

"Probably less than that. Yes, I've seen her in the neighborhood."

"On those occasions, you'd never seen Hera demonstrate aggression to people, had you?"

"No."

Then it was Hammer's turn. "The time when Hera broke away from Marjorie was the first time you saw Marjorie have trouble controlling the dog?"

"That's the first time I've seen the dog test her control."

Hammer asked, "The previous times you saw Marjorie with Hera, the dog didn't test Marjorie's control?"

"Right."

Hotchkiss was very brief in his cross-examination. He asked, "After this incident occurred, both Mr. Noel and Ms. Knoller asked you if you were okay and asked if your dog was okay, didn't they?"

"Mr. Noel asked me if my dog was okay and if I was okay."

* * *

In the afternoon session, Kimberly Guilfoyle Newsom examined a witness named Mary Willard. After fleshing out the witness' background, she asked, "Did something unusual happen to you in late October, early November of the year 2000?"

"I was on Fillmore Street near Jackson Street in my parked car. It was early afternoon."

"What did you see?"

"I saw Mr. Noel come out of the Mayflower and walk down Fillmore."

Newsom asked the witness to identify what the Mayflower was — a market. She asked her to identify Mr. Noel. The witness did. Newsom asked, "Did Mr. Noel have an animal with him?"

"One. He was walking his dog. He started to cross the street. The dog took off. Mr. Noel fell down on his knees and the

361

dog pulled him across the street. When he got to the other side he was able to get back up again."

"Did he yell at the dog?"

"He looked like he was yelling. I could not tell what he was saying. When he was getting pulled across the street he did not look like he was shouting anything, he was just trying to get back up."

* * *

Ruiz's cross-examination was short and to the point. She asked if the witness noticed if Mr. Noel had a bandage on his hand. He did. She asked it there were any people in the crosswalk. There were not.

* * *

The next witness was also a woman, Kelie Harris.

Hammer took over the questioning, bringing up an incident that happened in June or July of 2000. "Were you in the Presidio when you had an encounter with some people and a dog?"

Ms. Harris was in the park with her husband. With them was their dog, a Labrador puppy, and a neighbor's dog, a one-year-old half-husky/half-Labrador.

The Presidio is an old military base on the northern tip of San Francisco, now a park. Old cannons used to cover the entrance of the Bay from foreign invaders. Now they were housed in the old brick fort, a monument to the past.

In the former military base, walking down a trail, the Harris' encountered another couple standing off the trail.

Kelie said, "As my husband and I walked with our dogs, our dogs darted off of the trail and started to circle the couple with a very large dog." She then stated that Knoller asked them to leash their dogs.

Hammer asked, "What was the tone of her voice?"

"She was afraid. She was excited. She was insistent."

"You called your dogs back?"

"Yes."

The Harris' started to walk away, but their dogs again went back and started circling the larger dog.

Hammer asked, "Was this aggressive in any way?"

"Just puppy circling. There was no encounter."

Marjorie Knoller then asked them again to please leash their dogs, adding, "You don't know how serious this is. This dog has been abused. He will kill your dogs."

Kelie said, "I just stood there. I didn't verbally respond to her. I just wanted our dogs back so we could keep walking."

"Did you report this to any authority?"

"No."

On cross, Ruiz asked, "You were asked to leash your dogs. Did you?"

"When they came back the second time, we leashed them."

"Did you put them on a leash immediately?"

"Not immediately. I wanted to move away from the couple with the dog. I did not want to take the time to grab both dogs and leash them up. I wanted to move away."

Nedra Ruiz asked, using her hands to emphasis each word, "During this entire interaction with the dog that Marjorie was with, it never barked at you, did that dog?"

"It didn't bark."

"The dog never lunged at you?"

"The dog didn't move. It was a statue."

* * *

Each day, court reporters Christina Paxton and Joanne Farrell would transcribe the proceedings into verbatims. These were converted into both hard copy and computer discs. Copies were sent each day to San Francisco.

From the trial's first day, Hunter had made a point of following the progress by reading transcripts. He had watched the opening statements on Court TV. Since then, he had depended upon the dailies.

He glanced through the witness list and saw that Kimberly Guilfoyle Newsom had examined Mary Willard.

Hunter knew that Kimberly had prepared almost all of the witnesses that appeared for the prosecution.

He knew what that meant. It didn't mean telling people what to say. That was against the law. It did, however, mean allaying fears, holding hands, assuaging egos, and ensuring that nerves and spouses and scheduling didn't gum up future testimony.

He knew how dedicated she was to her profession, especially when it came to animal cases.

As he usually did, when he found out who was handling the witnesses in a case, the witnesses that his team had dug up, he checked out the prosecutor.

Kimberly had amassed quite a reputation in the few years she had served in Los Angeles, before she moved back to San Francisco and married Supervisor Gavin Newsom.

He had obtained copies of some of her letters of reference. He opened that file and scanned a few of the quotes:

I am pleased to inform you that I have selected Long Beach's trial machine, Kimberly Guilfoyle, as our Prosecutor of the Month. She has a talent to keep jurors on the edge of their seats when she is arguing. After one of her powerful closing arguments I got the feeling that her jurors would really have liked to applaud her performance. Signed, head deputy Steve Kay.

She even got letters from jurors. Mariko Hessig wrote: *I have an overwhelming compulsion to comment on how fortunate I think you are in having Attorney Kimberly Guilfoyle on your staff. Her work on this case was absolutely flawless. I was so greatly impressed by her exceptional ability that my faith in our legal system has been restored.*

Hunter pulled out a letter written by Los Angeles County Deputy District Attorney Steven Graff Levine: *I prosecuted dozens of special circumstances murder cases. I worked with Kimberly. I have observed her in court and in trial. She is smart, dedicated, ethical, a fearless cross-examiner, and she knows how to put a case together and communicate with a jury.*

From colleagues to jurors, Hunter thought, all respected Kimberly.

He mentally corrected himself. Make that from colleagues to jurors to *cops*.

Chapter
Fifty-four

'My Dog is Not Friendly'

Superior Court of California, Department 26, Division 53, Tuesday, February 26, 2002.
The first witness called in the morning was Cathy Brooks. She was examined by prosecutor Kimberly Guilfoyle Newsom.

The witness stated that last summer she ran into Marjorie Knoller while walking Hera. They chatted. Cathy asked what type of dog was Hera. Marjorie answered, "They were bred as guard dogs or attack dogs along the lines of a Rottweiler, or breeds of that nature."

However, the conversation did not lead to a discussion on whether this particular animal had been trained to guard.

A few months later, Cathy Brooks ran into Robert Noel walking Bane. Her dog ran up and Noel said, "You better call your dog, my dog is not friendly."

She asked, "Does your dog have a problem with people?"

Noel answered, "My dog is not friendly."

On cross-examination, Ruiz solicited that neither dog barked, growled or snarled during the two incidents.

Derek Brown was the next witness. He was a former resident of 2398 Pacific. He stated that he had three enounters with the dogs.

He said, "The first incident was fairly typical of the others. My wife and I were walking, had just entered the lobby on our way out to go for a run, I think on a Saturday morning. And it's a very bright lobby; the sun is streaming in. As we came down the stairs into the lobby, a man with two very large dogs was coming in the front door of the building and my first reaction was to position myself between the dogs and my wife, as she doesn't like large dogs.

"We had taken a couple of steps down the landing to the main part of the lobby. The two dogs started lunging at — they were on their leashes — lunging at us and barking. The kind of sound you hear when two dogs get in a fight. It's a very violent kind of a sound and lunging at the leashes, up on their hind legs, their claws are sliding on the marble floor, basically going berserk. And we just kind of shrunk back against the wall and tried to work our way out the door.

"Meanwhile, the man with the dogs continued on the other side of the entryway, the dogs continuing to go berserk at us. I uttered something, probably, 'Holy shit' and that drew the response from the man, 'These dogs are not friendly.'

"He got past us towards the elevator. The dogs then focusing their attention on the elevator and we just kind of were left there stunned and amazed."

Kimberly asked, "How long did this whole incident where a man came in, Mr. Noel with the dogs, the lunging, until they got in the elevator last?"

"Possibly I would guess 15 seconds, 15 to 20 seconds."

*   *   *

During cross-examination, Ruiz asked, "You never complained to management about the dogs in the lobby, did you?"

"They were widely spaced and I wasn't even aware that the dogs lived in the building. After the final incident involving my wife, we did decide to complain to the manager."

"And did you?"

"No, because the incident happened just before my wife went out of the country for two weeks. In the last discussion before she went, we said we really have to complain about this and, unfortunately, we left it to do until after she got back."

This exchange, in one form or another, echoed through all testimony involving Hera and Bane's behavior. Why didn't the witness report the incident? To the manager of the building? To the police? To Animal Care and Control?

'My Dog is Not Friendly'

The next witness was Violetta Pristel, Derek Brown's wife. She collaborated her husband's testimony.

Ruiz's cross of this witness revealed the other line of defense besides failure to report the incident. She asked, "On any occasion that you remember seeing these dogs at 2398 (Pacific), those dogs never touched your person, did they?"

"No. I always moved away quickly."

"And they never touched your body in any way, did they?"

"No."

The next witness was John O'Connell, who had testified to the grand jury about Bane lunging at his small son.

Next came Jason Edelman. He lived at 2398 Pacific. In January of 2001 a dog jumped up on his chest. The dog was on a leash held by Marjorie Knoller.

"Did it seem to you to be a friendly encounter?"

"No."

"At the time that Ms. Knoller's dog is jumping on top of you, did she at any time do anything to control the dog?"

"No."

" Did she pull the dog off of you?"

"No."

"How did you get the dog off of you?"

"I eventually pushed the dog off."

"Did you ever hear Ms. Knoller issue any verbal commands to her dog to get off or to stop what they were doing?"

"No."

"After you pushed the dog off, did at any time Ms. Knoller make any apologies to you for what the dog had done?"

"No." The witness then explained that a very similar incident had happen to an elderly woman in the lobby a few weeks later, again with Marjorie and a dog on a leash.

These two incidents were not reported until after the attack on Diane Whipple.

*   *   *

Jane Lu took Mr. Edelman's place in the witness box. She was a postal worker. She told a story very similar to her fellow worker, John Watanabe. She was rushed by a dog that had just exited a

367

vehicle, with no leash. Jane used her mail pouch to protect herself. And she screamed. Very loud.

On cross, Mr. Hotchkiss asked, "Did Ms. Knoller make any statement to you regarding the dog at any point during that time? Did she say the dog won't hurt you?"

"The dog didn't hurt me, actually didn't touch me."

"I know it didn't, but the woman that was with the dog, did she not say 'The dog won't hurt you?'"

"She didn't say that. She just said, '"My dog is fine.'"

Next, the People called Edward Nahigian. He was the last witness for the day. He owned a boot and repair shop. In the afternoons he would often watch people walk by his shop. He testified that before Noel almost had his finger bitten off by Bane, the dog was never muzzled. Afterwards almost always muzzled.

Chapter
Fifty-five

Paula and Andrea and Esther

Superior Court of California, Department 26, Division 53, Wednesday, February 27, 2002.

In the morning session, the prosecution called the first two police officers that responded to the scene: Leslie Forrestal and Sidney Laws. Each repeated their grand jury testimony

Then Paula Gamick, a San Francisco firefighter and an emergency medical technician who responded to the emergency at 2398 Pacific, testified.

Kimberly Guilfoyle Newsom took the witness through her background, then asked, "Tell us what you observed when you arrived."

Paula said, "We came up the stairs. To the left I saw a bloody carpet and blood on the walls."

Kimberly asked if she went to Marjorie Knoller's apartment.

The witness answered, "The door was open. I announced: 'Fire Department, does anybody need assistance?' I found Marjorie seated at the kitchen table."

Kimberly had the witness identify Marjorie Knoller in the courtroom as the person she saw in the apartment, then asked, "Was there anyone else present?"

"Mr. Noel was to the left of me, standing." She identified Robert Noel.

Kimberly asked, "What did you do next?"

"I squatted down and introduced myself. I took her wrist to take her pulse." The EMT took the jury through her assessment of Marjorie.

The witness said, "I noticed that she appeared to be covered in dry blood and still somewhat moist blood in her hair and on her clothing."

The EMT took Marjorie's pulse. "I asked her if she was okay, because I was concerned with so much blood. I wanted to know where to start, and she mentioned she had a cut on her thumb. And so I went right to the thumb to look at the cut on her thumb, her right thumb."

"Was that injury apparent to you without her pointing it out, or did she point it to your attention?"

"She brought to it my attention."

"And what did you notice?"

"Approximately a one-inch, maybe one-and-a-half-inch gash on her right thumb."

The witness was shown a photo of the right hand.

The prosecutor asked, "Did you notice whether or not the defendant had any other physical injuries?"

"I didn't notice anything else, but I asked if there was anything else because it was just a cut, and she pointed out another small cut on her index finger of her right hand."

"With respect to that injury, did you feel that any other medical intervention or treatment was necessary to treat that cut?"

"That cut, no, not at all."

"Other than the two injuries that you've just identified to us, were you able to make any other observations that you noticed, any physical injury to the defendant's person?"

"I was still concerned because there was so much blood, so I did a cursory head to toe, you know, just touching her head to see if I felt anything, see if anything hurt, grabbed her shoulders, 'does this hurt,' right down to her chest or hips and down her legs, and there was no other pain that was acknowledged to me."

The defendant, while testifying, demonstrated a cursory pat down, physical examination of the defendant starting at the head using both hands and going from the head, shoulders, arms, then all the way down the torso, stopping at the legs.

Guilfoyle Newsom asked, "Did the defendant appear to have any responses or behave in a way that seemed to you to be a problem or indicative of shock?"

"The vital signs were all within normal limits."

Kimberly asked, "What exactly did you do in determining whether or not the defendant was in shock at the time?"

"There are several things that can indicate shock. I checked her pulse. She was extremely calm, breathing. There was no sweating. Her blood pressure was normal. All vital signs were in normal range." Gamick also determined that Marjorie was not in pain anywhere on her person.

Kimberly asked, "Did you inquire as to her emotional well-being?"

"I asked, 'Are you okay?' I was intimating that: Are you emotionally okay?"

"What did the defendant respond?"

"Her response was, 'I've seen this sort of thing before.' I looked at her very questioning, and she added, 'I'm an EMT. I've been in bloody situations like this.'"

"During all this time, did the defendant, Ms. Knoller, inquire at all about the well-being or welfare of the victim?"

"Not once."

Kimberly called Andrea Runge to the stand. She had been a deputy animal control officer for five years.

Prosecutor Guilfoyle Newsom asked, "What did you observe upon entering the sixth floor area?"

The witness put her head down. Her words came very softly. Normally, in a crowded courtroom there is certain shuffling, coughing, movement, that you find in any group of people. As Andrea Runge spoke, movement and sound stopped. The people in the courtroom strained to hear the near-whisper of the witness as she described what she saw.

"The elevator door opened. The victim was lying face up. She was completely naked. All her clothes had been ripped off. I saw blood. Her coloring was blue and she appeared to me to be dead. I walked to my right, I was directed to where the dog owner was and also the dogs. It was my job to secure the dogs and to investigate who the owners were."

"What did you do to fulfill your job obligations?"

"I proceeded to the north end of the hallway. Ms. Knoller was kind of in a crouched position on the floor and Officer Forrestal was with her. I needed to find out who the dogs belonged to. I asked her if she was the owner of the dogs. She stated to me that she and her husband owned the dogs."

"What did you do next?"

"I tried to access the situation. The scene in the hallway was devastating. There was blood 20 to 30 feet in the hallway. And shreds of clothes. The carpet was soaked in blood. There were clumps of hair. It was incomprehensible what I came upon."

The witness paused, then added, "And Ms. Knoller was oddly calm. *Almost cold.*"

*   *   *

Esther Birkmaier, the elderly neighbor of Sharon Smith and Diane Whipple, took the stand, just as she had at the grand jury.

James Hammer took her through the usual background questions, then asked, "You mentioned a woman yelling 'Help me, help me,' correct?"

"Yes."

"A voice that you did not recognize, correct?"

"Yes."

As he had during the grand jury hearing, Jim Hammer took Ms. Birkmaier through what she saw and heard that terrible day over a year before.

Hammer asked, "When you walked towards the peephole to see what was outside, during that whole time you were walking to the peephole, did you hear any other voice yelling anything?"

"No."

"While you looked out the peephole, did you hear any other voice yell anything?"

"No voices."

It wasn't until Esther went to the phone and dialed 911 that she heard a second voice, a voice that she recognized as Marjorie Knoller's, yell "No, no, no!"

Later she heard the same voice shout, "Get off!"

Hammer asked, "About how much time passed before you first heard this other voice?"

"Approximately two minutes."

"About how long were you on the phone to 911?"

"I would estimate two to three minutes."

"During this two to three minutes on the phone, did the dogs keep making noise or stop?"

"The barking continued."

"During any of that time on 911, did you hear the woman who had yelled 'Help me, help me' say anything else?"

"No, I did not."

"This other woman whom you first heard after two minutes or so, did you hear that voice say anything else while you were on the phone?"

"Again, the 'No, no, no' and then that's when I heard 'Get off' for the first time."

"Tell the jury about this banging on your door, please."

"As I approached the door, there was banging on the door and it got progressively louder until it was crashing against my door."

"About how long did the crashing go on?"

"Three to five minutes. Finally, the barking and growling stopped and there was silence."

Esther went on to tell the jury of an occasion, four months before the fatal attack, of running into Marjorie Knoller in the hallway with Hera — off leash.

San Francisco Hall of Justice, General Work Detail, Thursday, February 28, 2002.
As usual, Henry Hunter received the dailies of the trial from the court reporters.

After reading Esther Birkmaier's testimony, Hunter spent a couple of hours going over old files, audio tapes and video tapes involving the dog-mauling case. These would be stored after the trial. He ran across the original 911 audio tape. He remembered, he was right, way back when the 911 call by Esther Birkmaier was ruled inadmissible at trial as hearsay by the judge.

Curiosity took over and the seasoned cop played the tape again.

Esther Birkmaier's voice came over the tape recorder's speakers. "Yes, I'm just a wreck. Please send police..."

Hunter could hear extremely loud barking in he background.

Esther said in a high-pitched voice, "We have two dogs rampaging out in the hall up on the sixth floor and I think they have — their — even their owner cannot control them. They are huge."

The dispatcher said, "OK, the owner knows that the dogs are in the hallway?"

"I think they're attacking the owner, too, I reckon — she's screaming right now, and I don't dare open the door 'cause the dogs are huge. Please hurry! I hear her screaming and I don't dare open the door. These dogs are ferocious."

Hunter took out that 911 tape and slipped in the second 911 call from Esther. She said, "I called five minutes ago; we have two ferocious dogs on the loose."

The dispatcher asked, "So you've already called us?"

"Yes."

"We're on our way, ma'am, you just have to be patient. You only called five minutes ago."

Hunter knew that in less than a minute, the first two officers arrived and called for an ambulance and animal control.

He thought, I forgot about Esther. I forgot about how terrified she must have been. When I saw the Incident Report and the flag EW, all I thought about was the possible effect on her testimony as an elderly woman. Not the possible effect on her from having witnessed part of the attack and heard much of it.

Hunter thought about those two women, Esther and Marjorie. One, an elderly lady with no motive to lie or exaggerate, who states, "The owner has lost control of her dogs." And the other with motive to lie, states, "I never lost control of my dogs."

Paula and Andrea and Esther

One was definitely telling the truth, the other was defiantly telling a lie.

And I'd put my money on the liar being the one who, at the scene, remained oddly calm. *Almost cold.*

Chapter
Fifty-six

Sharon Smith Testifies

Superior Court of California, Department No. 26, Division 53, Thursday, February 28, 2002

On the day that Diane's domestic partner was to testify, there was a warning from the judge involving security. Then, an EMT police officer named Alec Cardenas was called as the first witness.

He responded to the emergency call within two minutes. Hammer asked him what he first saw.

The police officer said, "When I originally knelt down, I noticed right off a large wound to the left side of her neck, she was bleeding profusely, her body was starting to pale a lot. There was blood all over, all around her, up the wall. Some hair clumps had been pulled out. She was in a bad way."

Hammer asked, "What did you do next?"

"With the help of my partner, Officer Whitman, we turned her over, maintaining C spine consideration. Keeping her in position where in case she had further injuries to her neck, her spine, to keep those in line, attempt to keep her breathing in line."

"What did you do after you turned her over?"

"Maintained her breathing, continued to check her pulse and breathing, watching the chest rise, knelt down to hear her breaths. Although her breathing was shallow, I could feel them."

"What did you do next?"

"Continued to monitor, and, at one point, I could feel no pulse and I had no breathing."

"About how long after you got there did you stop sensing the pulse and see that she stopped breathing?"

"It was over five minutes."

"And during that first five minutes, were you able to stop the bleeding about her throat and neck?"

"No."

"Why not?"

"It's beyond my capabilities. Just too much bleeding. I didn't have proper equipment. That would take a doctor or pretty advanced paramedic to do that."

Hammer asked, "Did the paramedics have some equipment that you didn't have?"

"Bag valve mask, some gauze material to put on the wounds, oxygen. I didn't have any oxygen. I had nothing."

"Bag valve mask. What is that?"

"Basically it's a plastic bag. It's squeezed. It's got a mask on it that you put over a person's nose and mouth to assist in breathing. I didn't have that."

"Is this something that a typical patrol officer carries, these things?"

"No."

* * *

When Nedra Ruiz took over the questioning, she asked, "How long were you on the sixth floor before you applied direct pressure to the neck of Diane Whipple?"

"Maybe a minute."

"And you applied direct pressure to her neck area because you could see she was bleeding a lot?"

"Yes."

"And she was bleeding from the neck?"

"Numerous places, yes."

"So you were trying to prevent her from bleeding to death right in front of your eyes?"

"I couldn't cover every wound. I was just trying to work with one wound, one that looked major."

The defense attorney went through the time-frame of how long it took the paramedics to arrive, then asked, "What first aid equipment did you have when you arrived on the sixth floor of 2398 Pacific on that day?"

"I had none."

"After Ms. Whipple was taken away by stretcher, didn't you then encounter Marjorie Knoller on the sixth floor?"

"Yes."

"When you first noticed Marjorie, she had blood in her hair, didn't she?"

"Ms. Knoller had blood from head to foot."

The defense attorney walked the police officer through how Marjorie Knoller not only looked, but how many lacerations she had to her body.

Nedra Ruiz asked, "When you were looking at Marjorie's body, did you see anything that looked to you to be a dog bite?"

"Yes."

"Where did you observe those wounds that appeared to be dog bites?"

"There was two on her forearm of her wrist and I believe there was cuts to her thumb on her hand. She had scratches on her upper arm. I mean still below the elbow, but upper arm."

"Did you ask her if she wanted to go by ambulance to a hospital?

"I offered her ambulance service."

"Ms. Knoller didn't go away by ambulance anywhere?"

"Not to my knowledge, no."

After this witness left the stand the jury was excused for a moment from the courtroom. Mr. Hammer told the judge that the People would not, for forensic purposes, be introducing the skull of Bane. The jury then returned.

The next witness was Gregory Mar. He was a crime scene investigator (CSI). One of his specialties was forensic dentistry.

He did a comparison and analysis from the model and the pictures of Diane Whipple's injuries.

Jim Hammer asked, "Explain to the jury about a 'model.' What did you do to make models and why?"

"We did an impression of Bane's upper and lower teeth, just like when you go to a dentist's office and if you have a crown, use the polyvinylsiloxane impression material. And from that material we were able to pour a plaster cast which will be a fair representative of Bane's upper and lower teeth. We did the same procedure with Hera, but because she was still living at the time, we can only take an impression of her anterior or her front region of her teeth. We couldn't do it in the back."

Gregory Mar testified that he matched the impressions of Bane to wounds on Diane Whipple, but could not positively state that other wounds were caused by Hera.

Spencer Gregory was the next witness called. A San Francisco police officer for 21 years, he was also a crime scene investigator. A series of photographs were shown the witness of the crime scene that he testified were a fair and accurate depiction. These photos were taken to preserve the crime scene before anything was moved, like the grocery bags in front of the open apartment door of Diane Whipple's home.

Part of this witness' job was the original identification and tagging of various parts of clothing — from Diane Whipple.

*   *   *

As news reporters and others in the courtroom fidgeted in their chairs, Sharon Smith was called to the witness stand. It had been over a year, but, finally, she would be speaking to a jury. A resolution was in sight.

As he did with each witness, Jim Hammer elicited the background information — like Sharon moving to 2398 Pacific in 1999. And of her life with Diane Whipple.

Then, without additional preamble, he asked Sharon about the dogs that lived in apartment #604 – referred to by them as "those dogs." And Diane and Sharon referred to the owners as "those people."

Sharon mentioned meeting Robert Noel in the lobby of the apartment building with Bane and reaching out to pet the dog. "Mr. Noel screamed 'No, don't do that. The dog was just in a fight with another dog in the park and he is spooked.'" Hammer asked her about a phone call she received from Diane involving a dog bite.

Sharon said, "I was at my desk. The phone rang and I answered. It was Diane, and in a very panicked voice said 'That dog just bit me.' And I was immediately frightened because of the panic in her voice. After she told me about the bite, I said, 'What

379

did you do?' She said 'I told him, you need to control your dog,' and I said, 'What did he say to you?' She said 'Nothing,' he just stared at her."

"Did you have occasion to look at either one of her hands, to see if there were any injuries you could see?"

"Yes, I did."

"Tell the jury what you saw, please."

"It was her left hand, and on the top of her hand she had a couple of very deep indentations that were red."

Sharon told the jury, after that Diane went out of her way to avoid the dogs, even making sure that Sharon was between her and the animals if they ran into them in the lobby.

She said, "On occasions when we were waiting on the sixth floor for the elevator to come up, I would open the door and she would grab my arm, just grab it right here…"

Sharon demonstrated by grabbing her arm, "…very hard and say 'Don't do that, you don't know if the dogs are going to be there.'"

Sharon went on to relate, "As we were leaving, exiting the elevator, she would look down the hall where Noel and Knoller lived, which is something she didn't do before. She was looking for the dogs."

"And before the bite in early December, had you ever seen her do that?"

"No."

Nedra Ruiz went to the lectern and began her cross-examination. Wasting no time, the defense attorney brought up the day that Sharon was bitten by Bane and how Sharon testified to that event during the grand jury hearings. She said, "At that time, you stated under oath that in the area of her hand were two or three deep indentations that were red. Did you not state that under oath at the grand jury?"

"I think I did."

"Now, subsequent to your testimony at the grand jury, which happened in March of this year, you testified at a hearing in this court sitting in Los Angeles, did you not?"

"Yes, I did."

"And at that time, you were again asked to describe the injury that you observed to Ms. Whipple's hand when she reported to you that those dogs had bitten her; is that correct?"

"Yes."

"And at that time when you testified concerning the injury here in Los Angeles, you stated 'I saw on her hand a few kind of deep puncture marks;' isn't that correct?"

"Yes."

"And that testimony was also under oath?"

"Yes."

Ruiz brought out that Diane took extraordinary measures to avoid meeting the dogs. Then she asked, "Was there someone to whom you paid rent?"

"Yes."

"And who was that person?"

"The owner of the building."

"Did you ever tell the owner of the building that Diane Whipple had been bitten by a dog?"

"No, I did not."

"Concerning the puncture marks that you observed of the wound that Diane Whipple suffered, did you ever seek medical treatment for that wound?"

"No."

"And you entrusted many of the details of your domestic arrangements to Ms. Whipple; isn't that correct?"

"We did everything together as a couple."

"And you took no action to remedy a situation where your life partner lived in fear?"

"No, we took action. What we did was kept ourselves out of the presence of those dogs."

"So you both decided not to make any complaint whatsoever about the fact that Diane Whipple had been bitten?"

"I did not make a complaint. Of course now, I wish I would have made a complaint."

"Do you consider that had you made a complaint, Diane Whipple might be alive today?"

There was a collective gasp that flashed through the court-room, spectators, lawyers, the jury and even the judge.

Sharon Smith looked like she had been slapped in the face.

Jim Hammer leapt to his feet and said, with an outraged voice, "If she is trying to blame Ms. Smith for the death of Diane Whipple—"

The judge, with a stunned look, said, "Counsel, is there an objection?"

Hammer said, "Relevance."

Mr. Hotchkiss seconded, even though he was representing one of the defendants, with, "Yes, yes."

The judge said, "Sustained."

Kimberly Guilfoyle Newsom slumped back in her chair. Bushwhacked, she thought. Sharon was just ambushed.

The accusing question to Sharon Smith, suggesting that Diane might still be alive today if she had filed a complaint, was the beginning of a storm.

Chapter
Fifty-seven

An Autopsy Report

Superior Court of California, Department 26, Division 53, Monday, March 4, 2002.
The final day of the prosecution's case had only three names on the posted witness list: Carlos Sanchez, Steve Murphy and Dr. Boyd Stephens.

Sergeant Murphy testified about how the various search warrants were developed and conducted.

Carlos Sanchez was called to verify certain photos and letters into evidence.

Then Dr. Boyd Stephens was called. He had been the chief medical examiner of the City and County of San Francisco since 1971. He was a Diplomate of the American Board in three specialties: anatomic pathology, clinical pathology and forensic pathology.

The doctor had testified in courts in most of the counties in California, and in Oregon, Nevada, New Jersey and other states. He had testified in superior courts, federal courts, military courts.

During his career, he had personally performed over 10,000 autopsies and supervised another 60,000.

He supervised Doctor Venus Azar, who did the actual autopsy on Diane Whipple.

One of Doctor Stephens' other functions was examining the bodies of Bane and Hera. With Bane, the brain was removed and examined for rabies. There was no evidence of that disease. The body had a great deal of blood on the fur, the muzzle, the teeth, and around the front legs.

Death of an Angel

Prosecutor Kimberly Guilfoyle Newsom asked, "Based upon your review of the paramedic records, the hospital records, your investigation and the autopsy, do you have an opinion regarding the cause and manner of death of Mrs. Whipple?"

"Multiple traumatic injuries, and she had extensive blunt trauma. The manner of death was judged to be a homicide."

Newsom approached the witness and introduced People's evidence numbers 84-A through 84-H, 85-A through 85-J, 86-A through 86-H, and 87-A through 87-H. They were 34 photos taken during the autopsy of Diane Whipple and they were laid out on four huge boards.

Kimberly asked about the photos, "Do they fairly and accurately depict the injuries that you observed on the body of Ms. Whipple at the time you took the photographs?"

"They do as much as the two-dimensional image can."

The prosecutor asked the witness to step down and use a pointer as an aid to relate to the jury what the various photos depicted.

The judge warned the spectators that these were specific photographs. "These are very, very detailed. You may not want to be present."

Some spectators left the courtroom.

The doctor methodically went through photo-after-photo, detailing what was involved in each of the 34 images. Each photo was blown up and shown on the large screen.

Guilfoyle Newsom pointed at the first photo.

The doctor said, "This photograph, the first one you are showing, is an image of Ms. Whipple's body after it was washed and cleaned."

The prosecutor said, "Let me stop you for one second. For the record, this is People's 86-B for identification. Can you tell us if this is the body prior to or after being washed?"

"It's after she was washed. Some of the medical apparatus is still present, and the medical apparatus that was on this lady included a tube into her throat to help her breathe, catheters that were placed in both the groin areas, catheters that were placed in

384

both ankles. She also has had fairly extensive surgical revision about portions of her body."

Over and over, Newsom would point at a photo or identify it by number, and the doctor would, in a dry monotone, explain in medical terms the brutal wounds inflicted on the victim.

In a voice almost like he was lecturing a class, Dr. Stephens began: "Let me start by defining what these injuries are. In medicine, we use the term of blunt trauma to cover all types of injuries that are produced by the transfer of force. A blunt trauma injury is just force that's applied to a surface.

"And it could be caused by any type of object. It could be a blow delivered to a person, it could be a person falling against something.

"The hallmarks of blunt trauma or bruises, that's the lowest level, is just enough force to disrupt vessels. Abrasions is just enough force to scrape the skin. Lacerations is enough force to puncture or penetrate the skin and then, of course, it continues on to fractures and so forth.

"These injuries that we see on Ms. Whipple in all of these photographs are all blunt trauma, and that means they are not sharp force injuries like cuts or internal injuries, they are all forms of blunt trauma.

"The injuries on this photograph include a pattern injury, and that's when blunt trauma reflects something about the surface or contours or features of the object that caused them."

About the photo marked 86-D, the doctor said, "This is a bite mark. There is actually several of them overlapping. And the large canines have literally cut through the tissue in several areas, lacerating down into the underlying muscle. But you see the teeth, front teeth that make this pattern. This is a well-defined bite mark and is one that could be related to a particular animal, at least as a consistent match."

Such dryly delivered words. Words that held behind their meaning the terrible and tragic events that had occurred more than thirteen months earlier.

The doctor said, "This is a large abrasion. This area across the right shoulder is a combination of abrasions. Some of them are somewhat patterned. There are a few lacerations in that area. Again, a laceration is a penetration of the skin. Also, a number of abrasions about the back and somewhat pattern abrasions across the lower and mid-back. There is a total of 77 grouped or named masses or collections of injuries about this patient."

Newsom asked, "Is that throughout the entire body of Diane Whipple?"

"Yes, yes. With all the injuries as far as we can count them, there are 77 discrete areas of injury."

"You can't tell where one begins and one ends?"

"They are. For example, in looking at the neck, there is obviously several applications of force. You can see another application of a similar force just behind this first one," he pointed at the image, "so there are several areas that overlap, and that's true for many of the areas."

The doctor's testimony, so medical, so precise, was mesmerizing to the layman. The jury sat, silent, a few taking notes, as the relentless onslaught of medical testimony continued.

"There is a large area of bruising about what would be the biceps or the inside biceps, series of abrasions, a few lacerations, a number of lacerations in the back of the arm, the triceps. Some of these are small punctures. They could be teeth that produced them, but most of them are just non-patterned abrasions."

As torturous as the testimony was, it was finite. Nearing the end of the list of photos, Newsom pointed at 87-G.

The doctor said, "The surgical staples have been removed. It now shows the gaping injuries about the part of her left neck. Two other wounds are still sutured but it shows an injury that we have not seen before. Towards the back of the neck, as well as a large number of abrasions, some of them line-like which could be caused by claws, tooth or something else. But extensive area of contusion and injury about the left neck, shoulder and extending well into the hairline. The two lacerations of the ear are partly seen. The extensive laceration that runs along the side of the neck is now seen."

The last photo was discussed: 87-H.

The doctor said, "This view shows the back of the head. It displays the extensive lacerations that are part of the pattern extending from the right side of the face. You will see the right ear
off to the right side of the screen, the left ear off to the left, again showing a series of pattern abrasions, multiple lacerations and then some of which are teared."

Newsom asked, "Showing you the top laceration, which appears to be the widest and most extensive, what would that be consistent with?"

"The tissue gapes," the doctor answered, "on the human body because of elastic fibers. It's what keeps us moving and stretching. It allows us then to stretch. If the elastic fibers are torn across the way that they are oriented, the wound tends to gape. If the tear or laceration is between the fibers, it tends not to. So a wound that cuts across the fibers tends to gape fairly extensively. There is not a vertically oriented line, perhaps something like this (indicating) which doesn't gape quite as extensively, but it's also a function of the nature of and extent of the injury."

"And would that top injury be consistent with a canine?"

"Yes. It is consistent with it. When you put together all the other features, this is a bite mark."

With the last photo explained, the jury and spectators assumed this line of questioning was over. But Newsom asked, "Was there anything on the neck injuries, in your opinion, that was consistent with fatal bites by animals?"

"There's several major vessels that have been torn or lacerated, and that's a significant source for the bleeding. But she also has a crushed larynx. And larynx is what we think of as our voice box, where the Adam's apple is. This is composed — this is a structure, obviously, that you breathe through, but it's also impor-tant in speech because that's where your vocal cords are. That structure is totally fractured and has been punctured several times by teeth. It's a crush-type injury, so that the larynx has been crushed literally from side to side, as well as several of the teeth puncturing through portions of the structure.

"There's also quite a bit of injury to the muscle and associated bleeding vessels within the neck along with these areas of laceration, plus the other injuries that we've talked about, that would cause bleeding on the other parts of the body."

"Is that consistent with, specifically, animal attacks that you're aware of?"

"It is in the aspect that it's not uncommon for a carnivore to go for the neck. Carnivores kill by asphyxiating the animal. And if you watch a lion kill an animal, they don't grab the back of the neck, they go for the throat. A leopard, for example. It's a typical way carnivores will kill a large animal."

"By cutting off the air supply?"

"By crushing the larynx and cutting off the air supply. And usually, they will hold that until the animal asphyxiates."

"Based on your external observations and examination of Diane Whipple's body and injuries she received by the dog or the dogs at the time of the attack, could these injuries have been received with anyone between Ms. Whipple and the dogs?"

"Not for a specific injury. Obviously, there's nothing between Ms. Whipple and the dog at the time a specific injury occurs. These injuries cover just about every part of her body, so obviously, injuries may have occurred at one part and they could not be occurring at the same time by the same animal, but another area."

"You specifically identified 77 discrete or defined areas of injury on the body of Ms. Whipple, correct?"

"Yes."

"So during the time that those 77 or so injuries are inflicted, is your testimony that there was no one in between Ms. Whipple and the dogs at that time?"

Defense attorney Ruiz said, "Misstates the testimony of the witness, Your Honor."

The judge said, "Overruled."

The coroner said, "Yes, at the time that these specific injuries occurred, there couldn't be anything between Ms. Whipple and the dog."

An Autopsy Report

The doctor went on to testify that that there were no controlled or illegal substances in the victim's body.

The prosecutor asked, "Were there any conditions or findings of disease that may have contributed in part or in total to the death of Diane Whipple?"

"No, she was in excellent health, a young lady, good physical condition. There's no other pathology that would explain her death."

"And at the time of the autopsy, did you make any observations to determine whether or not Ms. Whipple was menstruating at the time?"

"She was not menstruating."

"Doctor, lastly, with the extensive injuries that Diane Whipple suffered at the time of the attack, would a faster medical response or earlier medical intervention have prevented or saved her life?"

"Counsel," the coroner answered, "I don't think so. Generally, if you lose rapidly a third of your blood volume or more, you're not going to be recovering. In other words, that's typically a lethal injury if you lose a third or more of your blood volume. Based on a review of the scene photos and the injuries that she has, I believe Ms. Whipple did lose more than a third of her blood volume at the scene. Early on she was still described as breathing. The larynx is fractured, so she would have what's called paradoxical breathing. In other words, as she tries to breathe in, the larynx would tend to collapse. It would tend to suck in like sucking through a soft tube. I think those injuries produced a serious and significant injury to her brain, and I don't think that she was survivable, even with earlier treatment."

"And you mentioned the amount of blood. Are you aware of how much blood Ms. Whipple's body would hold?"

"Yes. Based on her body weight, her blood volume and liters would be about four-and-a-half liters. A liter is not quite a quart, but you can think of it as a quart for just our purposes. So her body has about four-and-a-half quarts of blood in it."

"And are you aware of how much blood she may have received through a transfusion?"

"In the emergency room and in the operating room and then in the intensive care unit they gave her about eight to ten liters, or quarts of blood, and about ten quarts of other fluids plus other medications. So her blood volume was exchanged at least twice by just medical therapy. Paramedics also gave her several liters of fluid or quarts during their resuscitation, so exactly how much she had been given is not known in the medical records, but it's in excess of 20 quarts."

That night, after arriving back at her hotel room, Kimberly Guilfoyle Newsom did not sleep well. She was exhausted emotional. And physically. She had not slept well the night before.

The autopsy testimony was crucial to deliver to the jury. They had to know the reality of how Diane died.

And that reality was brutal to anyone with empathy towards their fellow human, both physically and emotionally brutal.

Henry Hunter's Office, Room 411, General Work Detail, Monday, March 4, 2002.
Hunter called in Steve Murphy. He knew the cop had ways of learning things in a hurry. He asked his sergeant, "I know the usual stuff about Kimberly Newsom. But I want to know a bit more on her background."

"Because?"

"She's a good prosecutor, we both know that. She's been inspiring to work with the past year. So, my answer is just curiosity. You have to have a thick shell to handle going over an autopsy as vivid and graphic as the one she had to introduce today."

"I'll have it in a few days."

Chapter
Fifty-eight

They Were Nice Dogs

Superior Court of California, Department 26, Division 53, Tuesday, March 5, 2002.
Bruce Hotchkiss, Robert Nocl's attorney, called the first witness for the defense that morning.

The clerk swore in Dr. Stephanie Flowers, a veterinarian who worked at Peninsula Equine in Menlo Park. She testified that at the end of April 2000, she examined a dog named Hera. The purpose was a rabies exam for a health certificate. The doctor removed a foxtail from one of Hera's ears.

Hotchkiss asked if the doctor had experience in removing foxtails.

The vet answered, "It can be a difficult procedure because it's painful. Most doctors generally don't like necessarily looking down the ears with the ondoscope. Dogs have a vertical and horizontal canal so it's really uncomfortable. And when there is a foxtail in there, it can be painful and so sometimes if you have an exceptional dog that will tolerate it, you can do it with restraints. Otherwise, you usually have to sedate to remove the foxtail."

"How would the dog act if you don't sedate it?"

"They will be very difficult to restrain. You don't want to hurt them in the process. You have to use what we call an alligator forceps to remove it and if they are moving around, you can puncture an eardrum."

"How did Hera tolerate that procedure?"

"Very well."

"Was she sedated?"

"She was not sedated. We did not give her any kind of sedation. She was very calm and allowed us with minimal restraint to remove it."

"Did you make any comment to Ms. Knoller about how she went through the procedure?"

"She was great with the procedure. It's always refreshing when we don't have to sedate the dog to remove foxtails, and I was surprised how good she was."

"You told all that to Ms. Knoller?"

"I am pretty sure I did."

The doctor went on to tell that Hera had a heart murmur.

Nedra Ruiz took over the questioning and brought up the foxtail and asked if it caused a dog pain.

"Yes."

Nedra asked, "During the procedure, did Hera try to bite the technician?

"No."

"Did she snap at the technician?"

"No."

"Did she lunge toward the technician?"

"No."

Nedra asked the same questions again, but in relation to whether the dog did those things towards the doctor.

The answers were all "No."

This refrain of asking witnesses did the dog lunge, bite, snap or act aggressive toward you, was to be a reoccurring theme in Ruiz's line of questions.

* * *

When Hammer took over the cross-examination, he asked, "Can a dog's personality radically change regarding aggressiveness?"

"Yes. From hostile environment, threatened environment."

"Ms. Ruiz went on for 15 or 20 minutes about how many times you didn't see Hera lunge at you and you didn't see Hera bite, and those kinds of questions. Do you recall?"

"Yes."

"Hypothetically, if you learned that Hera, after she left you, repeatedly lunged at people, came close to their face in some cases, bared her teeth, growled aggressively, scampered with her feet to get to people even after being pulled away, would that present a different picture of Hera than you saw?"

"Yes."

"Would it suggest a change?"

"Yes, a change from when I saw her."

"Is it also the case that dogs' personalities regarding aggressiveness could be different in their home environment than in some neutral place like your office?"

"Yes."

"Isn't it true that dogs often are more aggressive and more protective around their home environment?"

"They have an innate sense of being territorial, yes."

"And in fact, their aggressiveness can increase as the dog bonds with its owner?"

The doctor answered, "If they are protective type dogs, yes."

* * *

On redirect examination, Hotchkiss asked the doctor if she was familiar with the concept of dog bite inhibition — meaning that dogs, when at play, don't bite down as hard as they do when they are in an aggressive mode.

The doctor said he was, indeed, familiar with the concept.

Hotchkiss asked, "Assume that in these two bites, that the skin wasn't broken, that there was little, if any, marks and neither people have obtained any medical attention and neither person complained to any — to the Animal Control or to anybody. Would that fact, regarding those bites, have any effect on your opinion?"

"Yes, it would."

"And what effect would that have?"

"Because it did not break the skin," the veterinarian said, "usually these inhibition, where they don't quite use their full force, it's a warning. They are giving us a warning that I want you to back off, I don't want you to do what you are doing or I am basically warning you that I may bite you more."

* * *

On his recross-examination, Hammer asked the vet, "On several occasions Hera and the other dog lunged at people without provocation. Would you consider those clear warning signs that Hera and the other dog were a danger to human life considering the size of the dogs?"

"I would say it's clearly inappropriate and potentially dangerous behavior."

"To human life?"

"It could be harmful, yes."

"And if a dog wants to harm somebody, particularly a dog of Hera's size, they can bite repeatedly and do a terrific amount of damage, can't they?"

"If she wanted."

"And the fact that the dog only bites once and bites very lightly, would that have anything to do with one's opinion about the dog's aggression?"

"Without being there, I cannot make an opinion. I do know dogs that are not aggressive dogs and they will give a warning to someone, and that's about it."

This exchange, first the defense questioning a witness, then the cross-examination, the redirect and recross was repeated throughout most of the defense witnesses testimony.

The next witness was Alan Paul. He owned the San Francisco Brewing Company. Two or three times a week Marjorie and Robert would come in, with Bane and Hera.

Hotchkiss asked how long the dog owners would stay.

The pub owner answered, "They enjoyed a leisurely afternoon very frequently. They might bring work with them or be reading a paper or just might be there for several hours."

"Did you ever make any comment to them about your feelings surrounding the dogs?"

"Yes. We discussed the dogs almost every time I saw them. They loved their dogs and they went out of their way to walk them around town, and they were so happy to have a place where they could sit down and relax with their dogs."

"Did the dogs always get along well with the people that were walking in and out?"

"Always, or I would have asked them to leave, absolutely. They were there at the doorway to my business."

"As a business owner, I take it you are concerned about liability insurance?"

"Definitely. The dogs never misbehaved."

Ruiz established that thousands of people walked by the pub, in this very busy Marina District of San Francisco, near where Hera and Bane would be by their owners. The pub owner also stated that he never saw the dogs misbehave.

Hammer's cross-examination was very brief. During it he asked the witness about the dogs. "You have no idea if they lunged at people repeatedly at 2398 Pacific?"

"I was never at those premises."

The next witness for the defense was Bonnie Seats. She had met Hera a year or so earlier, in front of 2398 Pacific. She said, "I petted her. I put my hand out for the dog to sniff and she gave it a lick, and then I started petting her. And I kneeled down and was talking to them, rubbing her ears and stroking her back."

The witness further stated that her seven-month-pregnant niece was with her and she did the same thing. During this time, Hera was wagging her tail.

Following Bonnie Seats was Antoinette Creyer. She had met Marjorie and Robert four years earlier. She was a waitress at the brew pub. She verified what her employer had said about the dogs never being a problem at the restaurant. She had occasionally even hand-fed the dogs.

Christopher Monica took the stand. He worked at Mailboxes, Etc., a very busy postal store. The two lawyers/ defendants had used that premises for conducting part of their business. The witness had never seen the dogs act aggressive. He would, once in awhile, pet the dogs.

Again, as he did with every witness who had never been to the defendants home, Hammer asked if Christopher had any knowledge of how the dogs acted at the place where they resided.

The witness had no such knowledge.

Chapter
Fifty-nine

Contempt

Fox Network Television, Tuesday Night, March 5, 2002.
The TV show *On the Record* with Greta Van Sustern is carried by
the Fox Network. This particular evening they featured an
interview with Nedra Ruiz.

The host asked, "Nedra, what's your defense? The prosecution paraded a lot of witnesses in the courtroom to suggest
these dogs were dangerous and that your client knew it."

Nedra Ruiz said, "None of those witnesses reported their
complaints or their fear to Marjorie or Robert. And I think it's
going to be very hard for the jury to determine or conclude that
based on no warnings at all, these dogs were dangerous. The
people in the apartment house didn't complain. Even the surviving
partner of the tragically dead Diane Whipple, Sharon Smith, never
complained. There are some folks who have testified that they did
warn Robert and Marjorie that they feared the dogs. And when
Marjorie and Robert found out about that, they kept the dogs away
from those folks."

Van Sustern asked, "Did your client ever see those dogs
being vicious or snarling or—"

"Never."

"—lunging at anyone?"

"Never," Ruiz answered again. "When Marjorie saw the
dogs lunge at anyone, she had them on a leash and under control.
At least three or four of the witnesses that have come forward who
lived at the apartment house testified that sometimes the elevator
would open up, the dogs would lunge, but either Robert or
Marjorie would be there immediately to pull the dogs back. And
so neither dog ever touched these folks."

Contempt

"Let me play devil's advocate," the reporter said. "When you say they're lunging on a leash, that at least that's some indication to Marjorie to have a concern."

"These dogs were lunging," Nedra responded, "because they wanted to go out for a walk. These dogs were excited to see people and felt territorial. But they were under control. Robert and Marjorie had no idea that this tragic juxtaposition of events would take place and that Bane would go berserk, drag Marjorie down a hallway, and begin to attack Diane Whipple. No one regrets the tragic death of Diane more that Robert and Marjorie."

"What did your client do during the attack?"

"Marjorie held onto the leash during the entire attack. She tried to pull the dog away. She tried to stop the dog from getting near Diane Whipple. When the dog began to attack Diane Whipple, Marjorie flung her body on Diane Whipple and covered Diane's body with her own in an effort to protect Diane from this berserk, crazy dog that she had only had since September."

Ruiz went on to explain how Marjorie did everything humanly possible. "And Marjorie didn't run. Marjorie stayed and tried to protect Diane."

"You've taken a lot of heat for your cross-examination of the victim's partner, suggesting she had some responsibility. Do you stand by your cross-examination, or was it poorly worded?"

"I stand by my cross-examination. When I argue this case to the jury, they'll remember that question."

"What exactly were you implying?"

"I'm implying that Sharon Smith did not fear for her… is exaggerating or lying about an allegation that Diane was bitten, in December before the attack. Sharon Smith has described the wound in various ways. First she said it was a welt. Then she said it was a puncture mark. Then she contends that her life partner lived in fear to even use her own elevator, or even go into the hallway."

"Are you saying that Sharon Smith lied about it?"

"That's what I'm saying. Everyone in the apartment building wishes things were different, wishes that Diane was alive. So do we."

Greta said, "All right, let me—"

"And now they come forward and claim that they lived in fear, when as a matter of fact, the dogs were acting normally. Marjorie and Robert were controlling the dogs, No one complained because no one had a thing to complain about. Now, of course, people come forward to say, 'Oh, we lived in fear.' These folks did not live in fear. They lived in complacency."

*   *   *

Network Television, Wednesday morning, March 6, 2002.
When interviewed later by the media, Jim Hammer said "We're not going to take a position on Ms. Ruiz's violation of the gag order. I do know from talking to Sharon Smith that she was personally offended by the public accusation of her being a liar."

Michael Cardoza's image was now on the screen, as he responded to Ruiz and her earlier statements.

"You blame the police, you blame Diane for her own death, and now you blame Sharon and you call Sharon a liar?" The attorney for Sharon Smith paused, then said, "No, you're not going to get away with this."

Michael Cardoza immediately drafted a letter to Judge Warren explaining what he viewed as a violation of the judge's gag order. Part of a gag order was that a lawyer could not comment on the credibility of a witness.

Cardoza wrote that his client was extremely offended by Ms. Ruiz's attack on a nationally televised program.

The storm that began with the question to Sharon Smith when she was on the stand, was now fanned into a hurricane.

Chapter
Sixty

Four Doctors and a Prison Tattoo

Superior Court of California, Department 26, Division 53, Wednesday, March 6, 2002
Four doctors testified that morning, all of them veterinarians. Their names were Dr. Andrew Sams, Dr. Sheila Segurson, Dr. William Thomas, and Dr. Wanda Adams.

Dr. Sams worked for a pet hospital in Madera, in central California, and also for Pets Unlimited. In 2000 he did his standard exam and evaluation on Bane. He diagnosed left knee cranial disruption with hip dysplasia.

Dr. Sams operated on Bane on December 5, 2000 and discharged him on the next day with instructions not to walk him for the first two weeks, other then to go to the bathroom. Bane was also sent home with a pain patch on him that would last a few days and was also given doggy aspirin. Dr. Sams told Noel and Knoller that they should not breed Bane due to the hip dysplasia.

During his cross-examination, Hammer asked, "Who does it list as the owner's name?"

"Marjorie Knoller."

"Does the fact that during your brief visits, he didn't bite or lunge at you, say anything at all about whether or not he bit and lunged at other people, for instance, at the place he lived?"

"No."

Dr. Polly James at Pets Unlimited referred Bane to Dr. Sams for surgery. He did not recall Bane being an aggressive dog during any of these exams.

The next witness, Dr. Sheila Segurson, was a veterinarian at Pets Unlimited. She had a consultation with Noel and Knoller on April 30, 2000 regarding Hera's heart murmur. She examined Hera thoroughly and took blood tests and x-rays. The first time she examined Hera, the dog weighed 69 pounds. On the second visit, Hera weighed 95 pounds. Dr. Segurson referred Noel and Knoller to a cardiologist at UC Davis for Hera's heart murmur.

Her overall impression of the dog was that Hera was in poor condition, but was getting much better and thought Noel/Knoller were taking good care of her. She had no problems taking blood or x-rays on Hera and did not see any kind of aggression, nor did she have to sedate her for these tests.

On cross, Hammer asked, "If she lunged at you and their owners pulled her back and she kept scratching and crawling to get to you, is that aggressive?"

"Yes."

*   *   *

Dr. William Thomas took the stand. A professor at UC Davis, he was certified in veterinarian cardiology. He did not recall much, other than Knoller brought Hera in for an examination in January of 2000 regarding the dog's heart murmur. The notes in his file read that Hera was a happy dog and did not need to be sedated during the echo cardiogram. His diagnosis was congenital heart disease and birth defect of the heart.

Hammer asked, "Do you have any information at all, doctor, about how Hera behaved in terms of aggression in San Francisco around 2398 Pacific Avenue?"

"No, nothing at all."

*   *   *

Next up was Dr. Wanda Adams. She owned the Peninsula Pet Resort in San Carlos, a few miles south of San Francisco, and had owned it for about 15 years. She had an agreement/contract with O'Brien Transportation Services.

On April 1, 2000, Hera and Fury arrived and stayed for approximately six weeks at the Pet Resort. Hera was kept in an indoor/outdoor run. They fed and groomed Hera without any problems. Since Hera was there for so long, the staff would take her for walks and took a liking to her.

Four Doctors and a Prison Tattoo

Dr. Adams testified that Hera was groomed without a muzzle and the dog groomer and staff had absolutely no problems with the dog. The doctor did not feel the animal was aggressive.

Hammer asked if the dogs had lunged at the doctor, would he have considered that aggressive behavior?

The vet answered, "Yes, I would."

* * *

After the testimony from the four vets, the next two witnesses were Angelos Prongos and Eleftherios Prongos, brothers who owned the Mayflower Grocery Store on the corner of Fillmore and Jackson. They had known Noel/Knoller for about five years and would see them almost everyday. Sometimes the two lawyers would come in and shop and sometimes they would just walk by the store. They never saw the dogs show any aggression towards them or anybody else walking on the streets. They also saw people pet the dogs while Noel/Knoller were in the store shopping.

* * *

Ms. Heshe Stark was then called the witness stand. She had known Robert Noel and Marjorie Knoller for approximately ten years and was a personal friend. She also worked with them on a professional level. She was an investigator, and throughout the years had been retained by the married lawyers on behalf of their clients.

During the summer of 2000, Noel and Knoller stopped by to visit and brought Hera with them. They sat on her patio and Hera was a good dog and did not bother her two cats whatsoever.

* * *

The second-to-last witness for the day was Michael Beachnau, general manager for a restaurant called Left to Albuquerque, located in an up-scale area at Union and Fillmore streets. He testified that Noel and Knoller would frequent the restaurant about 3-5 times a week. He said he saw many dogs at the restaurant and the dogs were no different than anyone else's dogs. He never saw the dogs acting aggressive.

* * *

The last witness for the day was James O'Brien. He owned and operated O'Brien Shipping and Transporting. The company arranged and provided shipping or transporting for animals, from mice to elephants.

In March of 2000 he received a call from Marjorie Knoller regarding transporting eight dogs from Hayfork to La Puente, CA and San Carlos, CA. When Knoller told him they were Presa Canario dogs, he had never heard of the breed. After his phone conversation with Knoller, he read about the breed in the dog encyclopedia. It said they were bred for fighting.

Mr. O'Brien arrived at Janet Coumbs' house on April 1, 2000. When he arrived, three dogs were chained to a tree and the others were in dog runs in the back.

Noel and Knoller met them at Coumbs' house about 6:30 a.m. with portable dog cages that were assembled at the house. Although the dogs were barking and lunging when he got there, he evaluated the situation and did not feel they were aggressive.

Mr. O'Brien testified that he had no problems getting the dogs in the cages, other than the dogs trying to back out, which was a normal thing for any dog to do. Neither Bane nor Hera had any bad reactions, nor did they act aggressive in any way.

The dogs were transported to the Pet Peninsula in San Carlos. Mr. O'Brien transported some of the dogs to a residence in La Puente. When he arrived, he was met by Rachel Huguez, who signed for the dogs' release. She told him to unload the dogs and leave them in their crates on the front yard because people would be coming by to pick them up.

Hammer asked the witness, "Tell the jury the scene when you got down to La Puente and dropped off these other dogs."

The witness answered, "Residential neighborhood, dark. It was about 10:00 o'clock at night. And when we found the address, we made contact with the person that was in the house. And then we turned the lights on in the trailer to unload the dogs to put them on the lawn. Several people came out of the dark, because they apparently had been expecting their arrival. But it was a residential neighborhood, well-kept."

"Did you have kind contact with a Ms. Huguez?"

"We told her that the dogs had arrived, and she was expecting us. And we asked her what we should do with them.

She said, 'Leave them on the lawn because the people that are expecting them would be coming to pick them up.'"

"At some point did 10 to 12 people arrive?"

"There could have been that many. We were busy unloading and it was dark. I remember specifically two men arriving earlier. There were more people, but I don't remember. Children, women."

"Anything distinctive about those two men?"

"One of the men had tattoos."

"Where?"

"On his neck."

"Did you recognize them?"

"It's what I would refer to as prison tattoos."

* * *

Henry Hunter had followed the dog-mauling trial like Javert followed Jean Valjean in Hugo's *Le Miserables*. Transcripts were sent up each day, and he would watch both the morning and the evening news broadcasts.

He watched Nedra Ruiz on NBC. She said, holding up a hand creating a circle, "The cops did zip."

Hunter sighed. Any competent criminal defense attorney knew what the cops' guidelines and procedures were.

Nedra said, about prosecutions witnesses, "The minority of people who came forward now are just that, a silent minority."

Huh? Hunter thought. First off, the prosecution witnesses who had come forward were not silent — they testified. And until Nedra calls in more witnesses that the dogs were gentle, then those folks for the prosecution aren't a minority.

Plus, even if Nedra called a thousand witnesses, and everyone of them testified that in their opinion the dogs were gentle, it wouldn't change the immutable fact that those two dogs were involved in the death of a woman.

If Hitler lived and showed up at the Nuerembug Trials and a thousand people testified that he was a swell guy, it wouldn't change thc fact that he was an ego-maniacal, butchering monster.

Chapter
Sixty-one

An Angry Judge, a Terrified Witness and Katie Couric

Superior Court of California, Department 26, Division 53, Thursday, March 8, 2002.
Judge Warren wasted no time getting to the business at-hand, and the business at-hand had nothing to do with the jury — they weren't present.

The judge said, "On January 23rd, this court entered a modified order restricting public comment. That was directed among other things at counsel. That order specified that counsel were able to discuss openly with the media the following: the result of any proceeding held in this case, which may include a brief statement of the results of the day's testimony and the purpose for which such testimony was offered. This exception does not authorize comments regarding the credibility or veracity of any witness, nor any comment regarding the effect such testimony will have on the charges or defenses asserted.

"I don't have the transcript with me right now, but when I entered that modified order, I made it very clear and all counsel indicated they understood that this exception did not authorize counsel to go and hold press conferences in the hall or any other place calling, among other things, witnesses liars.

"It has been reported to me that on Tuesday, March 5th of this week on the Greta Van Susteren Show the following inter-change occurred between Ms. Greta Van Susteren and counsel Nedra Ruiz."

The judge read from a transcript what had happened on the TV show, finishing with Ruiz's inflammatory comment about Sharon Smith.

"Ms. Van Susteren: Are you saying that Sharon lied about it?"

"Ms. Ruiz: Yes, I am."

The judge put down the transcript and said, "This is obviously something that we try very hard to avoid. We are doing everything we can to ensure that the defendants and the People receive a fair trial in this case.

"The jury is partially sequestered to ensure that, but this type of comment — and I do not know whether it did or did not happen — is precisely the type of conduct that is likely to infect the jury if they ever hear of it. Counsel are perfectly free to challenge the witnesses in court, there are privileges that attach to that. They are not free to challenge the veracity of witnesses outside of court in the public media under the circumstances of this case."

The judge ordered Nedra Ruiz to appear before him after the trial to explain why she should not be held in contempt.

The judge told the bailiff to have the jury brought back to the courtroom.

There was seven defense witnesses on the posted daily list: Stephen Tornay and his wife, Galena Tornay; Julianna Jette; Kim Boyd; William Huie; Dave Neville; and David Kuenzi.

The Tornay's owned a kennel in Smith River, California, very near Pelican Bay State Prison. Eleven days before the attack on Diane Whipple, the dogs Bane and Hera were boarded at their premises. They had no problems with the dogs.

The next witness was Julianna Jette. She was in Lodi visiting her best friend, Kim Boyd. When she entered her friend's apartment a large dog stood up. She asked Robert Noel if she could pet the dog. He said sure. She had no problem with the dog.

On cross-examination, Hammer drew out that Kim Boyd's brother was once in Pelican Bay State Prison. While there he was represented by Noel and Knoller.

Kim Boyd took the stand. She testified that her apartment was very small. She said that her daughter, Crystal, who was seven at the time, got along fine with the dog.

Later, Kim met both dogs in the Pacific Heights apartment. At that time she petted the dogs.

Death of an Angel

In December of 2000, again in her San Francisco apartment, she once again, briefly, met the dogs and petted them.

After the lunch break, William Huie entered the witness box. Mr. Huie owned a dry cleaners where Robert Noel took his clothes. When the dogs were brought into his store they would just stand there, no interaction.

Over and over, on his cross-examination, Jim Hammer asked each witness, "You have no idea whatsoever how these dogs acted in their San Francisco apartment building?"

All answered "No."

Dave Neville took the witness stand. He lived a few blocks from Noel and Knoller. In early January of 2001 he saw a white male, Caucasian, 30ish, walking two dogs that looked like Bane and Hera.

Hammer asked the witness, "The dogs you saw that day, were they aggressive in any way?"

"No."

David Kuenzi was called as the next witness. He was in his apartment at 2398 Pacific Avenue on January 26, 2001 at approximately four in the afternoon. He became aware of a woman screaming and called 911.

NBC's *The Today Show*, Friday, March 8, 2002.

On March 8, *The Today Show* interviewed Michael Cardoza. After filling the background on the most recent controversy, Cardoza said, "Sharon said about Nedra, 'She knows I'm not lying.' Then she became very quiet and we talked for quite awhile about it. So it upset her."

Katie Couric said, "So Nedra Ruiz is claiming that Sharon misrepresented the first incident—"

"That's correct."

"—when Diane Whipple was first bitten. And that she also lied about her living in fear, about her being afraid of these dogs before this very fateful incident took place."

Cardoza said, "That's exactly what she's doing. It makes me think of Ronald Reagan when he said, 'There she goes again.' She's done this before. She violated the gag order right in the beginning of this particular trial. I just hope that her antics don't sway the jury and they lose sight of the fact that this trial is about justice for Diane. I hope they keep their eye on that ball."

Couric said, "Before we talk about violating the gag order by doing this televised interview on Fox, this seems to be a continuation of her strategy of recent days, when she questioned Sharon Smith on the stand. She said, 'Do you think Diane Whipple would be alive today had you reported the initial dog bite incident.' Correct?"

"That's over-the-top for any trial attorney. She's just savaging Sharon's psyche right now. She's done it outside the courtroom and inside of the courtroom. This is going to backfire on her. I don't think the jury likes what's going on. We've watched the jury not make eye contact with her. They appear to be very bored when she's doing cross-examination. My opinion is this is working very much against her with this jury."

"If found guilty," Couric said, "Nedra Ruiz could be sanctioned, she could be required to pay a fine, she could even be disbarred. Although I understand from legal observers that they doubt that will happen."

"I doubt that too."

Katie asked, "If it's okay for you to talk to me on this program, why shouldn't it be all right for Nedra Ruiz to talk on another show?"

"Simply, I'm not one of the advocates in the trial. I'm not one of the two attorneys in the courtroom. They arc. That gag order goes to the district attorneys trying the case and to the two defense attorneys defending the case. I'm not the attorney in the courtroom. It's no different than you commenting on the case."

Chapter
Sixty-two

Weaving a Tangled Web

Henry Hunter's Office, Room 411, General Work Detail, Monday, March 11, 2002.
Steve Murphy walked into Hunter's office and said, "Saturday was her birthday."

"What? Whose?"

"Kimberly's. Big shindig. Fund-raiser. She wore a—"

"I wanted deep background." He knew part of Guilfoyle Newsom's history, but partly driven by curiosity and partly by just a cop's nature to want to know, he had asked Murphy to research the prosecutor's past.

Murphy said, "She was born in the Mission District, moved to Westlake. Went to school at Mercy High School. She knows karate. She went to UC Davis and graduated in—"

"Professional background is deep enough."

"Okay. I talked to people that worked with her here and with her for the few years she was in Los Angeles. A reoccurring theme of her personality: commitment, ethics, a workhorse, and the most often mentioned: honest. I heard it over and over."

"I've heard that, too,"

Murphy said, "Her father is Irish."

"Her mom?"

"She was Mercedes Marie Gerena. She died of leukemia when Kimberly was ten."

"How did she feel about them?"

"I quote," Murphy said and pulled a piece of paper from his pocket. "'I have never done anything in my life my mother would not have approved of or been proud of.'"

"Just how did you research that info?"

"I asked her:"

Hunter nodded. Sometimes the most effective research was the most blunt. "Anything else?"

"Yes. Her devotion to her job. She said, 'I believe it is my job to do everything I can so that everyone in our society feels safe; feels that justice is not an abstract concept, but a fact of life for all Americans.'"

"She's an idealist."

"Yes she is. She went on to say, 'Our legal system has its flaws but it is the best legal system in the world.'"

"Anything else?"

"She believes in people. She said, 'Human beings, deep down, are essentially good. Any jury can filter through whatever bull might be thrown their way and use common sense to get to the truth of a case. Juries make the right decisions, almost unfailingly, because people know right from wrong.'"

"If she's right, Robert Noel and Marjorie Knoller are in deep trouble."

Superior Court of California, Department 26, Division 53, Monday, March 11, 2002.
There had not been too many occasions during the trial to celebrate. The lawyers flew home to San Francisco each Thursday night and came back to Los Angleles at the end of the weekend.

Yet, that Mardi Gras weekend was special to Kimberly Guilfoyle Newsom.

Her birthday party was at the Ritz-Carlton, where she was crowned Mardi Gras Monarch for raising the greatest amount of money for pediatric and neo-natal care programs at California Pacific Medical Center.

But now it was back to work.

The first witness that morning was the police officer who was also the judge at dog court, Bill Herndon.

Present among the many spectators, as they were on so many days, were Sharon Smith and her sister, Jennifer Krusing, and Melissa Boyle. Also present were Marjorie Knoller's parents and Diane Whipple's mother.

During the policeman's testimony it became apparent that the questioning was aimed at establishing that in San Francisco there was a method to complain about a vicious animal.

Next, Darrel Sichel testified that he met Marjorie and Robert three years earlier. He was around sixty years old, with a friendly face and demeanor. The defendants had prepared a will for him and incorporated his business. He had gone to their apartment. He had found their dogs to be very friendly.

Then Marjorie Knoller walked to the witness stand. She was wearing a pale-blue sport jacket with a purple sweater.

She became emotional almost from the first moment.

Ruiz asked, "Marjorie, how are you today?"

"I am feeling awful. Just thinking about the horrible way that Ms. Whipple died in that hallway, it causes..."

Knoller's voice cracked. She continued in a trembling voice, "It causes me great sorrow. And I am in pain for everybody who knew her, and my heart goes out to her family and friends." She started the cry, then her voice raised at least an octave to the level of keening, "And she died so horribly, and I couldn't – I couldn't stop him from doing what he was doing."

She took another minute to compose herself, wiping her eyes with both hands.

Ruiz took her client through her personal background, involving education and how she met Robert.

Knoller's responses were measured.

Ruiz's questions were an attempt to put a human face on her client for the jury. A face of a caring person. A real person, who just happened to love dogs. And that her love went beyond dogs, to horses, even turtles and a parrot.

Then Nedra Ruiz, slowly, carefully, detail by detail, led her client through the events that placed the two Presa Canario dogs in her apartment on January 26, 2001.

Throughout her testimony, Marjorie came across as thoughtful.

During much of this testimony Sharon Smith leaned forward in her seat, listening intently.

The trail of the dogs, from Brenda Storey to Janet Coumbs to San Francisco, was detailed.

During this phase of her testimony, Marjorie Knoller was more composed, although her face looked shattered, ready to crumble again at any moment.

Accusations brought up by the prosecution were detailed, like, "Did you choose the name Dog-O'-War kennels?"

"Oh, no."

"Did you ever want to possess a mean dog?"

"No."

"Did you ever train Hera to be aggressive?"

"No."

"Did you ever train Bane to be aggressive?"

"No."

Finally, near the end of the day, Ruiz got to the events of January 26, 2001. She brought her client up to the moment when Bane knocked her off her feet.

Marjorie Knoller said, "He overcame what resistance I was exhibiting and he pulled me off my feet and ran down the rest of the hallway to where Diane Whipple was standing."

"When he pulled you off your feet, can you tell me what happened to the leash?"

"The lead was still wrapped around my hand. I was trying to pull him back and he was pulling me down the hallway."

"Where was Hera when Bane pulled you off your feet?"

"Still in the apartment, but once Bane pulled me off my feet, my recall is that Hera came running down the hallway."

"Can you recall where Bane dragged you to?"

"Down the hallway towards where Ms. Whipple was. I was flat out on my stomach with the lead trying to pull him back, and he was proceeding down to the end of the hallway where Ms. Whipple was standing."

"Can you recall if you were saying anything while he was dragging you off your feet?"

"I don't think I was saying anything."

"Had Bane ever done that to you before?"

"No."

411

"Were you aware that he had done that to anybody before?"

"No."

"Can you recall if Ms. Whipple fell or was struck?"

"Bane has just done something that I've never encountered him doing in a number of ways. First of all, not responding to my commands and pulling me off my feet and jumping up on — well, jumping up on somebody. I'd never seen him do any of that before. I don't know if I answered your question."

"Can you recall Ms. Whipple's position after you fell in her apartment?"

"We were both face down on the floor in her apartment."

"Then what happened, can you recall?"

"I remember saying to her: 'Stay down. Don't move.' And my primary goal was to get me and Bane out of the apartment.

"Why did you tell her not to move?"

"That was what I had learned to do if a dog is acting in a manner that may be an attack mode, that you play dead. You stay down, you don't move, and that's what I had learned as a kid. If an animal attacks you, you just play possum. You roll up and you stay still and you don't move."

"When you said that to Ms. Whipple, where was she?"

"She was prone on the floor in the hallway of her apartment. I kept telling her to 'Stay down. Don't move.' It seemed that any slight movement, any movement on her part, he reacted really violently. You know, any kind of movement on her part he was pulling at her clothing, probably biting her, I don't know. And the only thing I could think to do was to try to get between him and her, because I'm it. There's nothing else that I could do to try to stop him from what he was doing."

"And what did you see Bane do after you got back on Ms. Whipple?"

"He would still be trying to tear at her clothing underneath me, but he seemed to start calming down. It would seem that if there was no movement on either of our parts, even though I was trying to keep him under restraint, you know, holding the lead in my left hand and pulling slightly and trying to grab the other portion of the lead, it seemed as if he would calm down somewhat so that I could grab hold of him and try to pull him back and towards me and away from her."

The witness described getting the dog into the hallway, but Diane followed. Marjorie jumped back on top of her and began kicking Esther's door.

"Were you able to stop Bane's attack on Ms. Whipple?"

"Momentarily, and then he would start again."

"While you were lying on Ms. Whipple, was she crying out?"

"I really cannot recall her saying anything."

"Did you cry out?"

" I started screaming… I was screaming. I was giving him commands. I was screaming at him: 'Bane, no. Bane, stop. Bane, off.' And he wasn't responding to anything that I was saying. He just totally ignored any of the commands that I was issuing and increased his attack on Ms. Whipple."

"How did you move toward the elevator?"

"Basically not crawling, but shimmying down the hallway, moving in a manner where we are not on our knees. It's more like we are shimmying down the hallway."

Knoller related that she felt if she could get Diane to the elevator maybe she could get her inside to safety. She described how she was crawling with Diane to achieve this. "I don't know how to explain that better than I am. You're not on your knees, you're not really high off the floor, you're just moving basically along the floor."

"Did you do anything else?"

"I kept yelling. I seem to remember banging on Hank's door with my legs, with my foot to see if he were home. I vaguely remember hearing Esther saying, you know, something about, and I'm not sure if she said: 'I called for help' or, 'I called 911,' or something to that effect, to let me know that somebody was hearing what was going on in that hallway. I can't really recall a lot of anything that was heard, other than my screaming. I can't really recall anything specific. I've got memories of certain things that I may have heard, but I can't say for sure whether or not I heard them."

"What happened?"

"Bane just wouldn't stop. He wouldn't stop attacking her. I would think that things were settled in terms of him being calmed down enough while I was on top of her trying to protect her from him, and I would think he was calmed down enough where I could grab the lead again and hold on to that and the harness and keep him from moving around her body and tearing at her clothing while she was underneath me. But every time I would try to move off her, restraining him that way on my knees, he would either catch a movement or just basically rip the harness, rip the lead out of my hand and started attacking her again. The best way that I can describe it would be that it seemed as if he would calm down if I were on top of her where I was trying to protect her from any further biting and damage that he was doing, and what would happen would be that he would be doing a lot of damage to her prior to my getting back on top of her and between them. And it kept going on like that and getting worse and worse and worse, and he wouldn't stop. He wouldn't listen. He just wouldn't stop what he was doing. Anything that I was trying, he wasn't listening. He wasn't responding."

Voice rising and falling, cracking and sobbing, Knoller went on. "Every time I think it would be over and I could get him away from her and get him the hell out of there, it would get worse and it would start all over and it just got worse and worse and worse and worse. He just wouldn't stop. Anything that I was trying to do, he just wouldn't stop. He wouldn't listen. He wouldn't respond. He just wouldn't stop what he was doing."

"Did you ever strike at him?"

"I hit him in the face to get him away from her. I put my hands on his mouth to get him away from her. I was pushing him and beating him and he wasn't feeling it. None of that anger was being redirected at me, it was all being directed at her, and it was getting worse and worse and worse."

"Did Bane ever bite you?"

"Yes, he did."

"Where did he bite you?"

"A number of places. He bit me on my arm, he tore at the sleeve of my sweatshirt on my right arm. He was biting my right arm. He was biting my left shoulder and back. He bit me on my chest. I could feel him putting his jaws on me, but he wouldn't — I could feel the pressure, but he would release, he wouldn't complete the bite is the best way that I can describe it. He would stop; for some reason, he wouldn't complete the bite."

It was five o'clock. The judge called it a day.

The people in the courtroom, mesmerized by the last ten minutes of testimony, filed out.

Knoller would take the stand again the following day.

Henry Hunter's home, Monday, March 11, 2002.
At the end of each day, transcripts of the trial were forwarded to San Francisco by email. Henry Hunter picked up a copy, as he did each day, and took it home.

Another chilly evening was attacked with a fire. Hunter settled into his easy chair and began reading.

He got to Marjorie's statement about how Bane overcame what resistance. He read: *I was exhibiting and he pulled me off my feet and ran down the rest of the hallway to where Diane Whipple was standing.*

What? Ran? Down the *rest* of the hallway?

Ran? What happened to the anchor?

He read: *I was flat on my stomach…*

So now Bane pulled her like a sleigh rather than an anchor.

The cop got to the part about Marjorie trying to get Diane to the elevator and safety.

He shook his head.

Not very logical. You have the victim of your dogs' attack halfway into her own apartment and you decide to shimmy, where? Twenty, thirty feet to an elevator?

Then what?

Wait for the door to open?

So some other poor soul can get mauled?

Or stand up, exposing Diane to more attack, while you push the call button?

The cop read on. He came to Marjorie stating: *I vaguely remember hearing Esther saying, you know, something about, and I'm not sure if she said: 'I called for help' or, 'I called 911,' or something to that effect, to let me know that somebody was hearing what was going on in that hallway.*

Wow, thought the cop. Now she knows that not only is Esther home, but that she's called 911,

What is this? ESP?

The only thing worse than a lie is a *stupid* lie.

Chapter
Sixty-three

Marjorie Tells What Happened

Superior Court of California, Department 26, Division 53, Tuesday, March 12, 2002.
The judge announced that a witness was being taken out of order because of scheduling.

A distinguished-looking gentleman, carrying a large white envelope with numerous photographs, took the witness box. Standing next to the witness, Ruiz went through each of the photos. They were shots of various parts of Marjorie Knoller's anatomy: an arm, a wrist, a profile. Time after time the defense attorney asked if the bruises were consistent with dog bites or consistent with a person who had been knocked off her feet and dragged down a floor.

The motive for having the doctor testify became transparent: to collaborate Marjorie's story about being *dragged like an anchor.*

Ruiz introduced large blowups with multiple photos of injuries to Diane Whipple. A photo was shown on the gigantic courtroom screen. Sharon Smith and her sister left the courtroom. Then Penny Whipple-Kelly left.

Using a pointer, the doctor led the jury through the lacerations and contusions.

When Hammer took over the cross, Sharon Smith and her sister returned to the courtroom.

Hammer ascertained from the doctor that Marjorie's wounds were minor or insignificant in comparison to those suffered by Diane Whipple.

At a quarter to eleven, Marjorie Knoller returned to the stand.

Ruiz brought the witness back to approximately where they had left off the evening before, then asked, "What did you do with Bane?"

"I was holding onto him for dear life because I was hoping that he wouldn't go back and start doing what he had been doing so that I could... I could..."

Marjorie started to choke on her own words. She gasped out, "I could finally get him out of the hallway and away from Diane Whipple. I wanted to get him contained if I could. I wasn't sure that I could even do that."

"When you left Diane, could you describe her condition?"

"I know she was breathing. I was pretty sure there was a pulse. I know that while she had been bleeding out for an incredibly long, well, to me an incredibly long period of time. I mean I am covered in blood, there is blood all over. Bane is covered in blood. I knew that obviously it was a grave injury and that she was bleeding out. Bleeding out means to me that there is a severe injury that is or probably can be fatal."

"Where were you when you first observed that severe injury?"

"I just don't recall."

"Did you touch that injury?"

"Yes, I did, or at least one of them."

"When?"

"When Bane calmed down to make sure that... that..."

Marjorie choked back a sob and continued, "...that I could get him calmed down, I put some fingers in one of the wounds in her neck to apply some pressure so that at least I could try to stop the blood from... from flowing... from flowing."

Tears streamed down the witness's face.

Ruiz asked, "How long did you do that?"

"I estimated about a minute while I was trying to get Bane to calm down so that I could get him out of there, get him away."

"Did you stop applying pressure to that wound?"

"I had to," Marjorie's voice became high-pitched, "because I needed to get him the hell out of there."

"Ms. Whipple's wound, can you tell me where that was?"

"It was one of the wounds on her neck. I was applying pressure to the right side of her neck because that's where Bane was situated. So I put my two left fingers in the right side of her neck and I was holding Bane to not start attacking again."

"What did you do with Bane?"

"I finally was able to back him off far enough past Ms. Whipple's body so that I felt that I could, just like I had been trying before, to get to a position where I could stand up and start moving him towards 604 and, of course, locate Hera, because I had no idea where she was."

"Was Bane still on a leash?"

"Yes, Bane was still attached to me."

"What did you do with Bane after you were stood up?"

"I grabbed the lead with as much strength as I had left, or as much as I could muster, and I started pulling him down the hallway. He wasn't really agitated at this point. He seemed to calm down so I could do what I was doing. I didn't know how long he would be in that state because periodically during all this time in the hallway, he would calm down for a bit and then all of a sudden, he would start renewing his attack on Ms. Whipple and I would have to get in between him and her and try to get him away from her, get him off her, but he kept doing that. It would seem like he would calm down and then he would renew his attack."

"Did you take Bane to your apartment?"

"But before I did that, I needed to locate where Hera was because I didn't want her out there."

"Did you locate Hera?"

"Yes. When I got up and felt relaxed enough to look around the area of the floor space, I saw her."

"Where were you then?"

"Past Ms. Whipple's body, on the wall, walking towards 604, not very far. I think it was just past the doorway to 605."

"Were you facing Ms. Whipple?"

"I was still facing Ms. Whipple, and I spotted Hera."

"What did you do then?"

"I was turning Bane around and walking with him past 605, I told Hera to come."

"What did you do with Bane?"

"I walked towards the apartment door to get Bane inside the apartment with me and I turned around and called Hera again to make sure she was coming, to follow us into 604."

"Were you and Bane in apartment 604 before Hera was?"

"By maybe a split second or so. Bane and I were entering and Hera was following behind us. In other words, when I called her, she was moving down the hallway, jogging down the hallway, as Bane and I are moving down the hallway and we entered 604 at approximately the same time."

"After you got Bane in 604, what did you do?"

"Bane and Hera and I got into 604, I shut the door and then I moved Bane in to try to get him into the bathroom, to make him stay in the bathroom and then I closed the door on Bane. I threw Hera's harness in with Bane because Hera's harness had been split. I grabbed Hera by the top of her back and I threw her in the bedroom, I closed that bedroom door and I got back out into the hallway as fast as I could. However long that took to put Bane and get him contained in the bathroom and stick Hera in the bedroom, that's how long it took me to get back out in the hallway."

"Could you describe your physical condition?"

"Covered with blood, exhausted, a mess."

"What were you going to do next?"

"Go back to Ms. Whipple and see what aid I could render and what her condition was, whether she had a pulse, whether she was breathing, what I could possibly do to help her out."

"When you exited your apartment and saw the officers there, did you say anything to them?"

"I can't recall if I said anything to them. I was going to ask whether or not I could help because I would normally do that. I am a biohazard, they are not. I could render aid to Ms. Whipple until somebody arrived. That was what I was thinking of doing but that's obviously not what happened."

"What can you recall doing after you saw the police officers?"

"I recall going to look for my keys. I recall going to look for my keys because I realized that they weren't in my pocket. I closed the door to my apartment, my husband isn't home, management doesn't have the keys, the dogs are inside. They have to break down the door to get through the door to the dogs."

"Did you find your keys?"

"I did."

"Can you recall when you did that?"

"After I encountered officers Laws and Forrestal."

"Where did you find your keys?"

"In the foyer of apartment — of Ms. Whipple and Diane Smith's — I mean Sharon Smith's apartment."

"Was that after you saw the police officers?"

"Yes."

Ruiz carried a blowup to the lectern and held it up at an angle for the jury to see. It was a profile of Marjorie's face. The defense attorney asked, "After the tragic events on January 26th, did you make any statement before the media?"

"A number of occasions, yes."

"After this dog attack that occurred on January 26th, can you describe your emotional state in the days that followed?"

"Abysmal." Marjorie choked back a sob. "I was a basket case. I was having difficulty doing anything. It took all my effort to be able to get out of bed, take a shower and get dressed. I was doing my best to compartmentalize it as well as I could, to get out and function. All I wanted to do was be left alone."

"Why did you speak to the media at all?"

"I was overwhelmed, I was angry at some of the things that had been said and I felt that people should hear or try to hear what my perception was of what had happened."

"Do you blame Diane Whipple for the dog attack?"

"No, not at all. I never have."

"Have you ever claimed you are not responsible for the attack suffered by Diane Whipple?"

"I said in an interview that I wasn't responsible, but it wasn't in regard to what Bane had done, it was in regard to knowing whether he would do that or not." Marjorie started to weep. "And I had no idea that he would ever do anything like that to anybody. How can you anticipate something like that? It's a totally bizarre event. How could you anticipate that a dog that you know that is gentle and loving and affectionate would do something so horrible and brutal and disgusting," the witness started to gasp and added, nearly screeching, "and gruesome to anybody? How could you imagine that happening?"

Chapter
Sixty-four

The Hammer

Superior Court of California, Department 26, Division 53, Tuesday, March 12, 2002.

After lunch, Hammer took over. He went directly to the heart of the matter. He asked, "Ms. Knoller, yesterday morning when you first testified, your lawyer asked you how you were doing and you began to cry and you said you were feeling awful about the way in which Ms. Whipple died, and how sorry you were for everyone she knew and how your heart went out to her family and friends. Do you remember saying that?"

There was a melancholy air about Knoller's appearance. She said, "I remember something. I don't remember the exact words."

"And that's why you were crying, because you were so sorry for Diane Whipple and her family and friends; is that correct?"

"For everybody involved in this tragedy."

"Were you crying for yourself or for Diane and her family and friends?"

"I was crying for her family and friends and the pain they feel."

"After Diane Whipple's death, did you ever once call or try to contact Diane's mother to express any sorrow or responsibility?"

"I didn't think it was appropriate to do that, no."

"Did you ever do that?"

"No."

"Did you ever send a letter?"

"No."

"Did you ever attempt in any way in the weeks after Diane Whipple's death, before you were indicted for murder, attempt to contact Sharon Smith to express your sorrow for her pain?"

"No."

"Did you ever send her a letter?"

"No."

"Did you ever tell her you felt responsible?"

"No."

The prosecutor asked, "Since the death of Diane Whipple over a year ago, have you ever expressed sorrow to either Diane Whipple's mother or her partner, Sharon Smith?"

"Personally, no."

Hammer then did what Nedra Ruiz had done: take the witness through events leading up to the death of Diane. Except this time there was a different edge to the questions.

The relationship with Paul Schneider was delved into. Hammer asked, "Ms. Knoller, you testified that you had no part in the Dog-O'-War business; is that correct?"

"That's correct."

"I'm going to publish this now. This is People's 117. At the top of this fragment is the name 'Paul J. Schneider, September 26th, 2000.' Here, in the upper left-hand corner does it say 'Paul J. Schnieder, September 26, 2000?'"

People's exhibit number 117 flashed on the large screen. It was a letter. A highlighted portion was superimposed on the copy of the entire page with the applicable passage highlighted in yellow. On the screen appeared:

I liked the discussion in your letter of the 19th wherein you mentioned the combining of the kennels. I am partial, as is Robert, to Dog-O'-War or, as you had mentioned, in naming the pups Wardog. The potential problem with `Warhouse' is that many people, including Robert and myself, initially read it as `War-horse,' a montegreen waiting to happen, as in the line from the old Creedence song, `There's a bathroom on the right,' instead of `There's a bad moon on the rise.' People will constantly be making the same mistake Robert and I did and refer to it, as

424

The Hammer

'Warhorse.' What about something not in English, as in Guerrahund Kennels or Guerrahunde Kennels, the Spanish word for war, guerra, and the German word for dog, Hund, masculine; hunde, feminine. The feminine for dog in German goes along with the feminine for war in Spanish, but think it looks better with the male version of the word dog in German.

Hammer asked, "People's 117 is a part of a letter you sent to Paul Schneider, correct?"

"It would seem that way, yeah."

"Aren't you helping pick out names for that kennel?"

"I am expressing my opinions as to names."

"Including German names for this combined kennel?"

"It's the German word for dog."

"This is something you had discussed with Robert Noel?"

"Robert and I discussed the fact that Dog-O'-War was a good name for whatever kennel or business that they were in."

"Because it was appropriate?"

"Because I thought it was a good name."

"How about 'Happy Puppies,' or something more benign than Dog-O'-War? Why didn't you suggest 'Happy' or 'Docile Puppy Kennels'?"

Hammer went on to the book *Manstopper*. He said, "Isn't it true that he read to you the part about a story of a man having his finger bitten off by a dog?"

"Yes, he did."

"And he was laughing about that, wasn't he?"

"Yes, he was."

"You thought it was funny?"

"I thought the comment was funny in terms of how it was expressed."

Hammer asked, "Before you first met Ms. Coumbs, you filed a lawsuit against her, correct?"

"Yes."

"She repeatedly warned you about the danger of Hera, isn't that correct?"

425

"That's incorrect."

"It's your testimony that she's lying?"

"That's correct."

"She told you that Hera had killed a sheep?"

"That's incorrect."

"She's lying about that?"

"Yes, she is."

"Those are all lies?"

"That's correct."

"And in the course of these phone conversations with Ms. Coumbs and the lawsuit you had filed against her, at some point you threatened to take her house away and her car if she didn't give up the dogs; isn't that correct?"

"That's incorrect."

"That's a lie, as well?"

"Yes, it is."

Hammer moved on to the vet, Dr. Martin. "Did anyone else besides Ms. Coumbs warn you about any of these dogs or dogs of this kind being brought into a city like San Francisco?"

"No."

"Do you remember Dr. Martin came here and testified under oath?"

"That's correct."

Hammer introduced the letter from the vet, which was flashed on the large screen, specifically warning that the dogs were dangerous.

Hammer introduced a letter regarding Cornfed stabbing an attorney. Marjorie hadn't written the letter. He brought up the letter stating that Noel and Knoller wouldn't get in the way if the prisoner tried to escape. She hadn't written the letter. He brought up the book *Manstopper*. Knoller had never read the book.

On the huge screen, Hammer put up a portion of the grand jury transcript. He took the witness through the series of questions that he had asked her the year before.

Question: *Have you ever seen Bane lunge?*

Answer: *No.*

Question: *Did you ever see Hera lunge?*

Answer: *No.*

Hammer asked the witness about Kelie Harris, "Do you remember her testifying, that you were in the Presidio in July or so of 2000, that you yelled out: 'Please leash your dogs. You don't know how serious this is. This dog has been abused. He will kill your dogs.' Do you remember that testimony?"

Marjorie answered, "Oh, I remember that testimony."

There was now a very different rhythm and accent on the way she used her inflections. Her words were filled with sarcasm.

Hammer said, in a hash voice, "You have a tone in your voice now. What's that?"

Knoller said in a monotone, "I remember that testimony."

"No, you said it with a tone. What do you mean by that?"

Ruiz said, "Your Honor, argumentative."

The judge sustained the objection.

Hammer asked, "Do you remember the testimony?"

"Yes, I do," Marjorie answered.

"Is that false or true, that testimony?"

"That testimony is false."

Over and over, Marjorie Knoller said, in one form or another, when asked about the more than two dozen witnesses that had testified to the aggressive nature of the dogs, "They're wrong," or, "They're mistaken," or, "They testified falsely."

Hammer took another tack. He said, "Is your memory better now or was it better at the grand jury in March of last year?"

"Overall, my memory is better now than it was in March."

"You remember brand-new things now, don't you?"

"There are things that come and go."

"You now suddenly remembered some things that you say happened on January 26 that you never told the grand jury about?"

"Correct."

"The things you seem to recall now are things that help your case, correct?"

"I don't necessarily know if that's accurate or not."

"Let me ask you about four of them, just four, and I'll go into your version of what happened. Didn't you testify to this jury that you were kicking Hank Putek's door to get help?"

"Yes."

"Did you ever tell that to the grand jury?"

"I don't know."

"Were you here when Ms. Ruiz gave her opening statement?"

"Yes."

"Did you hear Ms. Ruiz tell the jury that you kicked Esther's door to get help?"

"Yes."

"Did you ever tell Ms. Ruiz that you kicked Esther's door to get help?"

"I said I might have, yes."

"Did you tell this jury in your testimony that you kicked Esther's door, or did you say you kicked Hank's door?"

"I said I kicked Hank's door."

"So why did you tell them you kicked Esther's door?"

"Because I believe that I kicked more than one door."

"You didn't tell the jury that on your direct examination?"

"No, I didn't."

"Why not?"

"Because I just didn't."

"When did this new memory first come to your mind, Ms. Knoller, about kicking Hank's or Esther's or someone's door?"

"That's not a new memory. I was saying that I was kicking Hank's door even in March, before that."

"Did you remember, when you were in front of the San Francisco grand jury, kicking the door of someone to get help?"

"Yes."

"Didn't I ask you in front of the grand jury to tell them exactly what you did in that hallway?"

"I couldn't remember everything that I did in that hallway."

"But this detail you say you remembered?"

"I remembered, but I didn't discuss it at the grand jury."

"Did you ever mention to the grand jury that you kicked anyone's door?"

"I don't recall my testimony."

The Hammer

Hammer held up his hand with two fingers extended. "Second, you said you hit Bane in the head during this attack. Did you tell the grand jury that you hit Bane in the head?"

"I didn't hit Bane in the head. I was punching him in the side of the face."

"You told this jury you punched Bane in the side of the face, correct?"

"On more than one occasion going down the hallway."

Holding up three fingers the prosecutor said, "You also told this jury that Esther yelled out to you, you think, or said out loud: 'I've called 911.' Remember that?"

"I don't know if I phrased it that way, but I recall somebody saying that 'I called for help,' or something about help."

"Did you tell this jury that you think you heard Esther say that she called 911?"

"I may have."

"It just happened yesterday."

"I know that, Mr. Hammer."

"Did you say that yesterday?"

"If it's in testimony, then I may have said that yesterday."

"You forget what you said yesterday?"

"When I go through the experience in the hallway, I did. Because of the emotional involvement, I do forget."

"Since yesterday you've forgotten that's your testimony?"

"As I said, what I recall about the testimony yesterday is that I have a memory of someone saying that: I called for help and help was coming."

"Did you ever say that at the grand jury before you were indicted?"

"Probably not, no."

"You didn't, did you?"

"I don't know, I don't know."

"You made that up, didn't you?"

"No, I didn't."

"You made it up in response to a question why you never called 911; isn't that true?"

"No, it's not."

Death of an Angel

Now Hammer held up four fingers. "And finally, the fourth thing, these keys. You heard Ms. Ruiz say in her opening that there would be no evidence whatsoever that you went to look for your keys before the police came. Do you remember her saying that?"

"Yes."

"In fact, you told the grand jury yourself that, after putting the dogs away, you walked past Diane Whipple's body and looked for your keys in her apartment; isn't that true?"

"If that was my testimony at the grand jury, that was my testimony at the grand jury."

"Do you not remember what you testified to?"

"I don't."

"Do you recall saying to the grand jury that you walked down, before the police came, past Diane Whipple's body and looked for your keys?"

"I recall that."

"Was that true or false when you told it to the grand jury?"

"It's inaccurate."

"Was it true or false?"

"It's inaccurate."

"You won't answer my question, will you?"

"It's inaccurate."

"I want to ask you some specific questions. Did you tell the jury, when you were being dragged down this hallway, that Bane would drag you, you'd pull him back, Bane would drag you, you'd pull him back, that you were in control that entire time?"

"I was trying to maintain control."

"Did you say 'trying to' or that you were 'in control'?"

"I'm not sure."

"Were you in control as you were being brought down the hall by Bane? Yes or no."

"I was trying to maintain control."

"You've testified to the grand jury that Diane Whipple simply stood there at the end of the hall for over a minute?"

"Correct."

"That she said nothing at all, correct?"

430

"That's correct."

"She just stood there with her door open?"

"That's correct."

"She never yelled for help?"

"That's correct."

"She didn't move?"

"That's correct."

Hammer had questions from the grand jury transcripts flashed on the screen.

QUESTION: *You were not able to control him, correct?*

ANSWER: *That's not accurate. It's still control.*

QUESTION: *Control? Your definition is that if he's dragging you down the hallway and then knocking you to your knees and dragging you on your face, is that control, in your opinion?"*

ANSWER: *It's my ability to be able to totally control him and maintain control over him, yes.*

QUESTION: *Is that control, in your opinion?*

ANSWER: *Yes.*

QUESTION: *Dragging you to your knees and then dragging you on the ground as he approaches this woman, that's control?*

ANSWER: *Yes.*

QUESTION: *That's control?*

ANSWER: *Yes.*

QUESTION: *Did you ever once, as this dog was dragging you down the hallway, say, `Ms. Whipple, get in your apartment'?*

ANSWER: *I had no idea who she was. She was a complete stranger to me.*

QUESTION: *This complete stranger, this woman, this poor woman, did you ever say to her, `Get inside your apartment. I can't keep my dog back'?*

ANSWER: *No.*

QUESTION: *Not once?*

ANSWER: *Not once. I mean she was standing there. Instead of opening the door, she had watched me for quite a period of time with Bane. She watched me when he was mild-mannered and docile walking to the apartment. She is watching me as I opened my apartment door. She is watching me when I'm battling with him down the hallway and she is in front of her open door. And my concern was more with why Bane was going down there than yelling at her. I did not know who she was. She was a complete and total stranger.*

Hammer turned from the screen, looked at Marjorie Knoller with disgust, and shook his head.

Marjorie Knoller's face held an air of dejection. Her eyes were puffy, and haunted.

The term *hot seat* usually refers to a chair in a police interrogation room. That afternoon it was the chair in the witness box.

Chapter
Sixty-five

The Hammer and the Anvil

Superior Court of California, Department 26, Division 53, Tuesday, March 12, 2002.

Jim Hammer asked, " A few more questions about your version of January 26, 2001. When you testified yesterday, did you give the full version to this jury of everything that happened from the time Bane put his paws up on the wall, according to you, by Ms. Whipple's shoulders, until she was left naked dying in the hallway. Did you give all the details, or did you leave anything out?"

Marjorie Knoller answered, "I probably did not give all the details because I don't know all the details."

"Did you leave anything out that you can think of?"

"There are details I always leave out because I don't recall the whole incident."

"Can you think of any right now?"

"There may be some in terms of the events going down the hallway, because I don't recall all of what went on in that hallway. There are things that come and go in terms of the memories that I have about what happened after Bane bit Ms. Whipple in the neck the first time."

"Have you always given the same version of what happened that day, ma'am?"

"Not exactly, no."

"Have you ever changed your story?"

"I will remember more details."

"And then forget them sometimes and remember them again; is that what happens?"

"That's what happens."

"As you sit here now, are there any details you left out in your story to the jury?"

"There may be details, different details, that I can remember and other details that I can't. The general framework…"

"I'm asking specifics, not general. As you sit here you don't remember any specific details that you've left out?"

"Because of the nature of the incident in the hallway, there are parts of the event that will, at times, seem more concrete than others and it fades in and out. There are things I may have recalled earlier about the incident that I don't necessarily recall later."

Hammer said, "You say Bane put his paws up on the wall by Ms. Whipple's shoulders?"

"Yes," Knoller answered.

"And you've told the grand jury that was not an aggressive move; is that correct?"

"I didn't know whether or not that was an aggressive move or not."

"Between the time he put his paws supposedly on the wall by her and you pushed her into her apartment, tell the jury exactly what happened between those two events."

"Hera was now by Esther's door barking hysterically."

"I just want to know what Bane did."

"Bane came down, stuck his head in the groin area of Ms. Whipple. I pulled him back. I was trying to restrain him. He started moving towards Ms. Whipple. I pushed her into and towards her apartment, and I don't know if Bane jumped on her or pushed her as well into the apartment, but all three of us wound up in the apartment on the floor in the foyer."

"Yesterday when you testified about the events, did you tell this jury, either yesterday or today, that after the paws on the wall, that Bane put his nose in her crotch? Did you say that yesterday or today on direct examination?"

"Yesterday, I don't believe I did."

"Did you say it today?"

"I just said it now."

"On direct examination when you were giving your version to Ms. Ruiz, did you say that?"

434

"I don't believe I did, no."

"Why did you leave it out?"

"It was just part of the event that I wasn't recalling."

"So you forgot it on direct but you remembered it on cross, is that your testimony?"

"Yes."

"So over the course of 24 hours you simply remembered that event?"

"It's part of what I remember occurring."

"After this paws on the wall incident, what you're testifying to now is that Bane put his nose in her crotch?"

"If that's what you're saying my testimony is."

"Do you forget what you told the grand jury?"

"Yes," Marjorie said, "yes."

"Let me read to you this." Hammer read back to the witness her testimony from the previous year given to the grand jury when she said that Bane put his head into Ms. Whipple's crotch and sniffed. Then Diane Whipple said, "Your dog just jumped me." Hammer finished with, "Ms. Knoller then said, 'Agitated, as if there was something he was smelling that was getting him excited.'"

Reading from the grand jury transcript, Hammer continued with, "'Question: How was he acting that was excited? Answer by Ms. Knoller: "My terminology, unfortunately, if I — like a bitch in heat, like he was smelling something that was stimulating to him." Question: Like sexually?'"

Then Hammer read Knoller's answer to his question about a bitch in heat. Knoller had testified, "There's something about any male dog around the scent of a female dog who's coming into estrus where he starts to act differently. He becomes somewhat agitated. In other words, if you're walking a male dog on the street and they are sniffing, their demeanor changes if they scent, or if they smell, the female that's coming into heat or that is in heat. Their body language changes. They start to really sniff and become interested in the scent. It's a change in their demeanor."

Hammer looked up from the grand jury transcript and stared at Marjorie Knoller. He asked, "Yesterday and today when you testified on direct examination, did you mention anything about Bane acting that way around Ms. Whipple?"

"No, I did not."

"Is that something you just forgot?"

"No, it's something that I've come to know that is not an accurate statement on my part."

"What does that mean?"

"My interpretation of his behavior is inaccurate."

"You testified that Diane Whipple hit you during this assault; isn't that correct?"

"Yes."

"Why don't you tell the jury exactly where Diane was and how she was positioned when she hit you."

"Diane Whipple and I were both prone on the floor on the carpet in the hallway in between the door of 606 and 607, and I was covering her and trying to get Bane to calm down. And as I was getting off her, she was trying to get me off her. I don't know if she was panicked, I would assume that she was. We both were fearful and trying to get me off her, she swung her arm back and connected with my right eye."

"Was she face down when she did that?"

"Yes, she was."

"Was she on the ground?"

"She was prone, prone, prone, yeah."

"And you're above her, correct, above her back?"

"I'm starting to move off her back."

"How far are you from her when she supposedly hits you?"

"Not very far."

"How far?"

"I'm bad at that, but maybe six inches."

"And when she supposedly hits you, is the dog biting her?"

"I don't know."

"And it's your testimony that while she's lying face down on the ground, that somehow backwards she hits you hard enough to give you a black eye, is that your testimony?"

"She was moving to try to get out from under me. We are both prone on the ground, she's moving, I'm moving, and she flails back as to get me off her more quickly, and in that movement she struck me in the eye and then Bane went after her."

"That's when Bane really started to attack her?"

"That's when things escalated."

"Before that, he was just pulling her clothes?"

"He was pulling her clothes and I'm not sure whether or not he was biting her at that point, but it would be logical or it could be assumed that, in pulling her clothing, he was also — he may also have been biting her."

"And you testified that you shimmied with Diane Whipple towards the elevator, correct?"

"What I was trying to do with her was keep Bane, it's about a six-foot lead that he was on. I needed to keep him attached to me so that I could hopefully get control of him to get him out of that hallway, and I was trying — we were trying to move down towards the elevator so that she could get into a place of safety."

"From the time Diane was first bitten, ma'am, until the time you left her naked in the hall, what percentage of that time were you on top of the body of Diane Whipple?"

"I can't give you an estimate as to percentage."

Hammer asked, "Were you in contact with her the whole time from when the bite started?"

"No," Marjorie answered.

"You weren't?"

"I was in contact with part of her body, but not on top of her the whole time, no."

"Were you on top of her body most of the time?"

"A percentage of the time. In terms of what I was trying to do, I would be on top of her. And then when I was trying to move Bane away from her, I was on my knees moving off of her body so her upper torso was exposed to Bane. When I would try to release his harness to grab hold of the lead to really pull back on him and try to get myself to my feet is when he would be going and starting to bite Ms. Whipple again."

"And you fought heroically this whole time to save Ms. Whipple?"

"Right. Yes."

437

"You put your hand in his mouth?"

"Not directly in between his jaws, but pushing him away."

"Did you ever put your hand inside his mouth so he wouldn't be able to bite Ms. Whipple?"

"Not inside of his mouth. Not in where his tongue is, but in his mouth in terms of pushing." Knoller demonstrated with her right hand, pushing away toward the jury, "Where his teeth were on the side of his face, yes."

"You ever testify you put your hand inside his mouth?"

"It is inside his mouth. It's not my whole hand in his mouth where he could bite down on it, but it is in his mouth."

"Why didn't you put your hand in his mouth so he couldn't bite Diane?"

"Because I was afraid."

"You cared more about yourself than you did about Diane at that moment, is that fair to say?"

"I was always concerned with Ms. Whipple's safety."

"My question to you was: Were you more concerned about your own safety than about Ms. Whipple's while Bane, your dog, was mauling her?"

"I was always concerned about Ms. Whipple's safety."

"That wasn't my question and maybe you won't answer it, but I'll try one more time. Were you more concerned about your safety or Ms. Whipple's safety during the hall attack?"

"I was more concerned about Ms. Whipple's safety."

"Yet, you never put your hand in his mouth so he couldn't bite Diane Whipple; isn't that true?"

"That's true."

"You knew what could happen if you put your hand in his mouth, didn't you?"

"Yes."

"You knew that before January 26th? If you put your hand in a dog's mouth, the odds are that if he bites down, you might lose your hand. But with a big dog like this, a huge dog like this, you might die if you really got in the way. You knew that, didn't you?"

"Yes, I did know that."

"You knew that before January 26th?"

"If you are involved—"

Hammer interrupted. "I'm talking about these dogs, no other dogs. Did you know with these dogs and their size and their teeth size that if you put a part of your body into Bane's mouth, you could be seriously wounded or die?"

"If you put your hand in any dog's mouth there's always a chance that it's going to be a traumatic and severe injury."

"Ms. Knoller, I didn't ask about any dog. Would you answer my question, please. Did you know before January 26th what could happen if you put your hand in Bane's mouth and only Bane's mouth? Yes or no?"

"Anything could happen."

"You could have been mauled?"

"Of course."

"You could have been killed?"

"Not if I put my hand in his mouth."

"How about if you really got in the way, really in the middle of this feeding frenzy, you could have been killed?"

"Yes."

"You knew with your own eyes what Bane's teeth could do because you saw your husband's own finger almost severed by Bane four or five months before Diane Whipple got killed?"

"What my husband related to me, he said that Bane had done that."

"And you've seen the picture here in court, haven't you?"

"I was the one who saw it on the beach."

Hammer showed her a picture of her husband's arm, in a cast and asked, "He spent three days in the hospital, right?"

"Yes."

"And that was by accident, supposedly, right?"

"It was by accident."

"So you intentionally didn't get in the way of Bane while he was attacking Diane Whipple?"

"That's not accurate."

"The truth is you didn't put your body in between Ms. Whipple and the dog, isn't it?"

"No, that is not true."

"You ended up with two little cuts on one of your hands after 10 or 12 minutes of this vicious mauling of Diane Whipple; isn't that the truth?"

"No, it's not the truth."

"You got some bruises, too, right?"

"I was bitten."

"How many wounds that bled on your body?"

"Not that many."

"Two little cuts on one hand; isn't that correct?"

"No, that's not correct."

"What other wounds bled?"

"The lacerations and puncture on my right arm, the gashes from his teeth and the lacerations on my left hand."

"And your testimony to this jury is you were in the middle of this the whole time?"

"I was in the middle of this the whole time."

"Between Bane and Ms. Whipple?"

"I was not in between Bane and Ms. Whipple the whole time, but yes, I was putting my body on top of Ms. Whipple to stop Bane from doing what he was doing."

"And Bane would bite you and taste you and decided not to bite you the rest of the way, that's your testimony?"

"I would assume there's something about why he released."

"Your testimony's Bane never bit down full force on you?"

"He never punctured me, but there was a lot of force that he was exerting when he would bite and release."

"On your hands he never bit full force, did he?"

"No."

"Your testimony was he sensed it was you, so he stopped?"

"I had my hand on the side of his jaw in his mouth, but I didn't have any hands directly in his mouth or—"

"This went on for 10 or 12 minutes and you actually watched Ms. Whipple get every shred of clothing ripped off of her body, isn't that true? You weren't on top of her when the dogs were dragging the pants off her, were you?"

"The dogs weren't doing that. Bane was doing that."

"Hera didn't do that?"

The Hammer and the Anvil

"Hera did not do that."

"Hera didn't do anything?"

"I don't know what Hera did other than barking in the hallway, because she was not in front of me."

"Did she pull at Ms. Whipple's clothes?"

"She pulled at my pants leg and Ms. Whipple's pants leg."

"So you know she pulled at Ms. Whipple's clothes, right?"

"The only reason I know that is because I was on top of Ms. Whipple and I was dealing with Bane, so if Bane was in front of me, I assume that it was Hera that was doing it."

"Did you watch Hera the whole time, Ms. Knoller?"

"No, I was watching Bane the whole time."

"Then how do you sit here and tell this jury that she didn't bite Ms. Whipple?"

"I said I don't know where she was. I know that she was not in front of me. In other words, I'm on my knees and there is an area where Bane can attack, and he was constantly attacking. Once I was no longer restraining him by his harness, he had almost five and a half feet that he could move on that lead, and that was around Ms. Whipple."

"Do you know whether or not Hera bit Diane Whipple?"

"I don't know whether she did or not."

"She might have because she wasn't in your view, right?"

"She was not in front, she was behind me."

"So you don't know?"

"I don't know."

"Why did you say at the Animal Care and Control hearing that you knew Hera didn't bite Diane Whipple?"

"She didn't bite Diane Whipple from her knees up."

"How about the knees down?"

"I can't answer that question."

"But you told Animal Care and Control at the hearing that Hera never bit Diane Whipple; isn't that true?"

"That was my understanding. That was my belief."

"And that's because you were fighting to keep Hera alive even after she participated in the attack on Diane Whipple?"

"I didn't want Hera put down for something she didn't do."

441

"But you don't know what she did."

"As far as I'm aware, Hera didn't bite Diane Whipple anywhere above, anywhere on her torso above her knees."

"When the dogs were done with Ms. Whipple she had no clothing left on her at all, correct?"

"When Bane was finished with her."

"Hera helped with her clothes, right?"

"Hera did not touch her clothing. My recollection is her pulling at her pants leg and pulling at my pants leg, and that's what she was doing in terms of getting at her clothing. Other than that, I don't have any recall of Hera doing anything other than that."

"My question is: When the dogs were done with her she had no clothes left on her at all; isn't that correct?"

"I don't know if that's completely accurate. If that's what was said and that's how she was found, that's how she was found."

"That's how you left her?"

"I don't know if she was completely naked or not."

"Do you have a doubt about that? You were there."

"I don't recall what she had on. I know that most of her clothing was gone."

"You left her there alone and went to your apartment?"

"I had to leave her, to get Bane and Hera out of that hallway so he wouldn't tear her to pieces more than he already did."

"You swore to the grand jury that in less than 30 seconds you came back out in the hall; isn't that correct?"

"That was my time estimate."

"That was what you swore under oath?"

"That was my time estimate."

"You told the grand jury that you walked back down the hall past Ms. Whipple's body, correct?"

"That's what I told the grand jury."

"And this time you gave no first aid, correct?"

"In my recitation to the grand jury in terms of what had occurred, I did not give any first aid, no."

"Now, to the grand jury you said that you gave a minute or so of first aid and left Diane alone to go to your apartment to put the dogs away?"

"That's correct."

"You said in less than 30 seconds you left your apartment and came jogging back down the hall?"

"At the grand jury I said that."

"You swore a year ago to the grand jury that you passed Diane Whipple's body a second time?"

"That's what I said at the grand jury."

"And gave no first aid?"

"That's what I said at the grand jury."

"And went into Diane Whipple's apartment to look for your keys?"

"That's what I said at the grand jury."

"And you never told the grand jury that you had any problem with your memory of the event; isn't that correct?"

"I didn't say that. I did say that I had problems with my memory."

"Did you tell the grand jury you had any problem with your memory of what happened after you put the dogs away?"

"I said that I had problems remembering the incident in the hallway, yes."

"On these facts did you tell the grand jury you had any problem at all remembering what happened after you put the dogs away?"

"That was my best recollection of what I did."

"That wasn't my question. Did you tell the grand jury in your sworn testimony, that you had a hard time remembering what you did after you put the dogs away? Yes or no."

"I said I had a hard time remembering what happened in the hallway."

It was four-thirty in the afternoon. Jim Hammer turned to the judge and said, "Your Honor, I have another 40, 45 minutes."

The judge told the jury, as he had at the end of every day since the trial began, "Please, again, bear in mind the admonition; do not discuss the case. It's very important that you not form any opinions until after you get all of the testimony, until I have given you the law, and the lawyers have argued the case to you.

"Again, there will be press reports, I anticipate. Do not

read, look at, listen to, talk to anybody about coverage in this case. The system functions because you only listen to and make decisions on the testimony in this courtroom."

Chapter Sixty-six

A Hammer Becomes a Bludgeon

Superior Court of California, Department 26, Division 53, Wednesday, March 13, 2002.

For the third straight day Marjorie Knoller took the stand.

Sharon Smith leaned forward as the court was called to order. She placed her chin on her left hand.

Jim Hammer used the large screen to project pages of the grand jury testimony.

Marjorie Knoller sat with her head turned away from the screen.

Hammer reminded her that during her testimony she had stated that she had placed her hand in Bane's mouth. Using the blowup of her own testimony, Hammer walked her through her grand jury testimony, about when and where she put her hand in Bane's mouth.

Then he said, "When you testified yesterday that you never put your hand in Bane's mouth to this jury, was that false or true?"

"Putting my hand in Bane's mouth is exactly what I was doing. I was pushing him away from her and that's how I got the gashes on my hand."

"Yesterday, I asked you if you put your hand in Bane's mouth and you said no. Do you remember that answer?"

"Yes."

"Was that true or false, Ms. Knoller?"

"Putting my hand in Bane's mouth was doing what I was doing."

"You mentioned yesterday that you remembered a number of new things since testifying to the grand jury. Remember saying that?"

"Yes."

"That you had forgotten a number of things, remember that?"

"I do."

"Did you remember anything new last night?"

"No."

Hammer asked, "You knew Hera was more dangerous than a Chihuahua, didn't you?"

"I said it was situational. She is a larger dog."

"You knew that Presas had been bred to be guardian dogs on January 26th, didn't you?"

"Yes."

"They had been bred to be protective; isn't that correct?"

"That's what a guardian dog is about."

"During this whole time that your dogs were attacking Ms. Whipple, where were their muzzles, Ms. Knoller?"

"In the house."

"You had muzzles for both of them, didn't you?"

"Yes."

"And you didn't put them on that day, correct?"

"Hera wasn't— no."

"You intentionally didn't put it on Bane; is that correct?"

"There is no intent."

"You intentionally did not put it on Bane?"

"No, that's not correct."

"You accidentally didn't put it on him?"

"I had no reason to put it on him."

"You didn't put it on him on purpose. You chose not to put it on Bane, correct?"

"There was no reason to put it on Bane."

"Did you choose not to put it on Bane?"

"I didn't have any reason to put one on him."

"I didn't ask you about a reason. Did you choose not to put it on Bane?"

"Yes, I chose not to."

"And when the police arrived, you came out of your own apartment and never offered to give first aid to Ms. Whipple; isn't that true?"

"No."

"Your testimony is that you asked the police if you could give first aid?"

"Yes."

"Who did you ask?"

"I believe it was Officer Forrestal."

"When the police arrived, the only complaint you made about your own injuries were some small wounds to your hand and arm; isn't that correct?"

"I said I didn't now what I had."

Hammer took the witness through the injuries she sustained during the attack. Then he asked, "Did you tell any police officer or paramedic that you had an injury to your head?"

"I don't think so."

"Two days later, you went for the first medical treatment for these minor wounds; isn't that correct?"

"Yes."

Hammer reminded the witness that she never received stitches, or even prescription pain pill. Then the prosecutor asked, "After the attack on Ms. Whipple but before you talked to your husband about what happened, you talked to Officer Forrestal?"

"Yes."

"You told Officer Forrestal that you took the dogs, plural, for a walk; isn't that correct?"

"That is incorrect."

"You told Officer Forrestal that you came home after taking the dogs for a walk; isn't that correct?"

"That's incorrect."

"That you started to enter your apartment is what you told Officer Forrestal; isn't that correct?"

"That's correct."

"That you saw Diane down the hall with groceries?"

"That's correct."

"That Bane then ran down the hall?"

"That's incorrect."

"Never told Officer Forrestal that?"

"I said that Hera ran down the hall."

"Did you tell Officer Forrestal that Bane ran down the hall and attacked Ms. Whipple?"

"It would be a misstatement, but it wouldn't be false."

"You then told Officer Forrestal that you attempted to control Bane after the attack had begun?"

"That's correct."

"You told this jury that Ms. Whipple kept coming out of her apartment, correct?"

"She did come out of her apartment."

"After you told her to stay inside, correct?"

"Correct."

"Did you ever tell Officer Forrestal that Bane slowly pulled you down the hallway for a minute or minute and a half while you fought him the whole way?"

"Probably not."

"Did you ever tell Officer Forrestal that Diane Whipple just stood there for a minute or a minute and a half while you were being dragged down the hallway?"

"Probably not."

"Did you ever tell Officer Forrestal that Diane Whipple struck you in the face and that's what led to the first serious bite by Bane?"

"No."

"After talking to Officer Forrestal, you talked to your husband, correct?"

"Yes."

"And you got a story together, didn't you?"

Ruiz objected to the word "story."

The judge sustained her.

Hammer asked, "You didn't get a story together with your husband?"

"No."

"Isn't it true that you gave a number of different versions to your husband about what happened?"

"I am not sure."

"You don't know if you gave different versions to your husband?"

Ruiz said, "Objection, Your Honor. Argumentative."

Hammer shot back, "That is the least argumentative word I can think of."

Judge Warren said, "Overruled."

Hammer asked Marjorie Knoller, "Did you give different versions to your husband about what happened?"

"I was trying to recall the events."

"My question is, did you give different versions to him?"

"I don't know."

"You don't know if you gave different versions?"

"I was trying to recall the events as accurately as possible. There are things that I can recall and I don't recall. There are things that I can recall and there are things that I don't at different times."

"On the day of the attack, did you ever give him a different version of what happened or did you always tell him the same version?"

"I was trying to figure out exactly what happened."

"Did you tell your husband, in that first conversation with him, that Diane Whipple punched you in the face?"

"I believe I did."

"So did you always tell Mr. Noel the same version?"

"He was asking me to try to remember as much as I could about what happened in the hallway."

"In the first version you told him, did you tell him Diane punched you in the face?"

"I don't know."

"Was that a significant fact?"

"Yes, it is."

"You told this jury that's what led Bane to finally seriously attack her for the first time; isn't that correct?"

"That's correct."

"Did you tell Mr. Noel that in your first version?"

"I don't know."

"You might have just left out that important fact?"

"I don't know."

"Ms. Knoller, you testified that in the weeks after the death of Diane Whipple, you were a basket case, correct?"

"Yes."

"Couldn't even get up," Hammer said, "had a hard time doing anything, including showering, correct?"

"That's correct."

"Yet you found time to get up really, really early in the morning to go on *Good Morning America* and talk about what happened. What time did you have to get up to go on *Good Morning America*?"

"I don't remember."

"Wasn't it about 3:00 in the morning?"

"I don't know."

"Did you put that ahead of getting sleep and recovering from these terrible wounds you talked about?"

Hotchkiss said, "Objection, Your Honor. Argumentative."

The judge said, "Sustained."

Hammer said, "You got up early, early in the morning to go on *Good Morning America*, correct?"

"I got up early. I don't know what time."

"And that's only one of many interviews you gave to national and local media; isn't that correct?"

"I gave interviews. I don't know how many."

"So many you can't count?"

"No, not so many I can't count."

"A lot, fair to say?"

"A fair number."

"February 8th, you went on *Good Morning America*?"

"I don't recall the exact date."

"I am going to show you something and ask you some questions."

Once again the video from the *Good Morning America* show was run. Marjorie Knoller watched herself on the courtroom screen. Then she turned away and looked at her lap. When her husband began speaking, she looked back at the screen. Occasionally, she would glance at the jury then stare back down.

When the video-taped interview finished running, Hammer asked, "Did you have any visible injuries as of February 8th?"

"Yes, I did."

"The black eye was gone already?"

"Pretty much. I had some makeup on."

"Did you look sad there?"

"I looked awful."

"You looked sad?"

"I do."

"Are you crying there?"

"No, I wasn't."

Hammer said, "You were asked specifically whether or not this dog had ever shown signs of aggression before and you said no, not toward people. That was a false statement, wasn't it?"

"No."

"You also were asked about these other witnesses who had come forward saying the dogs tried to attack people and you called it a total fabrication. That was a lie as well, wasn't it?"

"That misstates what was on—"

"It's a quote. 'Total fabrication' were your words, correct?"

"Those were my words, yes."

"Was that true?"

"Yes."

"And finally, you were asked, and Ms. Ruiz asked you this herself, if you ever denied responsibility and you said 'No, I have never denied responsibility.' Remember that question and answer from Ms. Ruiz?"

"Yes."

"This interview," Hammer pointed at the screen with the *Good Morning America* logo on it, "when Ms. Vargas asked you 'Do you think you bear any responsibility at all for this attack,' you said, 'Responsibility, no, not at all.' Do you still feel that way?"

"No."

"You changed your mind?"

"No."

"You blame Diane for her own death?"

"No."

"You did in this interview, didn't you?"

"No."

"You said she should have gone inside her apartment, that is what you would have done?"

"Yes."

"So it's her fault?"

"No, it's not her fault."

"Is it Sharon Smith's fault?"

"No."

"Is it Sharon Smith's fault for not complaining to the police?"

"No."

"Is it the police's fault that Diane died?"

"No."

"Is it true or not that on January 26th, you took the dogs for a walk?"

"No."

"That you went out of your apartment with one or both dogs without a muzzle. Is that true or false?"

"That's true."

"Did you do that intentionally?"

"I did it all the time."

"When you approached the door to your apartment, you saw Ms. Whipple down the hall?"

"That's true."

"You had been specifically warned before January 26th that he should wear a muzzle. Is that true or false?"

"That's false."

"You owned muzzles?"

"Yes."

"You left them in the apartment?

"Yes."

A Hammer Becomes a Bludgeon

"After the death of Diane Whipple, you or your husband removed them from the apartment?"

"That's false."

"Never did that?"

"Never did that."

"Once you got to the front door," Hammer continued, "Bane ran down the hallway and attacked Ms. Whipple. True or false?"

"False."

"At some point, you got your sweatshirt torn a little bit by reaching into the attack?"

"No, that's not how that happened."

"You didn't get involved because you knew you might be killed if you did?"

"That's false."

"You didn't say that yesterday?"

"No, I didn't say that."

"You knew you couldn't control the dogs on January 26th?"

"That's not true."

"You had lost control several times before January 26th?"

"It depends on what you mean."

"You knew you weren't strong enough to control Bane?"

"I knew he was powerful."

"You knew Bane almost cut your husband's finger off before January 26th?"

"I knew that my husband had put his hand in Bane's mouth."

"And Bane almost bit his finger off before January 26th?"

"Yes."

"After the attack on Diane, you left her lying in the hallway naked, correct?"

"I had to leave."

"Covered from head to toe in bite marks?"

"That, I didn't know."

"Bleeding profusely?"

"That, I knew."

453

"You went into your apartment and you waited several minutes before even coming back out?"

"That, I don't know."

"When the police arrived, you never offered to give Ms. Whipple help?"

"That's not true."

"You never asked how Diane was?"

"I don't recall doing that."

"For an entire hour, you never asked how Diane was?"

"I don't know."

"You never called 911?"

"I didn't have an opportunity."

As Hammer released the witness and took his seat, the courtroom was deathly still.

Chapter Sixty-seven

Nedra's Turn

Superior Court of California, Department 26, Division 53, Wednesday, March 13, 2002.
Nedra Ruiz stood for redirect cross-examination. She said, "Marjorie, the district attorney has made reference to your testimony before the grand jury. When you testified before the grand jury, did you make any statements about your ability to recall the events that happened on the sixth floor?"

"Yes."

"And what were those statements?"

"That I wasn't sure what happened, that I couldn't tell you exactly what happened in the hallway because I don't have complete memory of it. I can't tell you exactly what happened in that hallway. I will never remember everything."

"Who asked you about your memory, about things that happened in the hallway?"

"I believe Mr. Hammer did."

"Did Mr. Hammer ask you about your recollection of what happened in the hallway, limiting it to a certain point in time?"

"Yes, he did."

"When you were asked about your ability to recall those events, what did you say?"

"That I don't have a complete memory of what went on in that hallway. I still don't."

"When you testified at the grand jury that you recalled being in Ms. Whipple's apartment when you first saw the police, was that a lie?"

"That's what I recalled then."

"Subsequent to those proceedings before the grand jury, did you change your mind about where you were when you first saw the police?"

"I found out where I was when I first saw the police."

"How did you find out?"

"From the testimony of officers Forrestal and Laws. Both officers were saying that the first time that they saw me, encountered me, is when I am stepping out of my apartment."

"Do you recall any of their testimony about a dog?"

"Officer Laws testified about a dog going by."

"Why would that testimony about Officer Laws seeing the dog, why did that have any significance to you?"

"That meant that she was on the stairwell watching Hera go by her so that they were on the sixth floor, near the sixth floor."

"Can you recall whether or not before you saw the police on January 26th, where the dogs were?"

"As far as I know, I was moving Bane towards the apartment and I called Hera and Hera was following me in. That was the last time I was out in the hallway. I was moving Bane into the apartment and Hera was following me in."

Once again, the defendant was taken step by step through what her recollection was of the events that had happened almost fourteen months earlier.

Nedra asked, "When you testified before the grand jury, did you talk about hitting or banging on the door to the hallway?"

"I was never asked that question."

"When you testified before the grand jury, did you talk about hearing someone say they called 911?"

"No, I did not."

"Here on direct examination, you testified you recalled hearing Esther Birkmaier tell you she called 911. Why do you recall that?"

"Because I have known Esther for about ten years. She had obviously heard what was going on in the hallway. I couldn't imagine her not letting me know or letting us know that help was on the way. I seem to remember that I heard someone say something about help, get help."

"At the grand jury, you testified you put your hand in Bane's mouth, not more than ten times. Could you describe what you meant by the grand jury testimony, putting your hand in Bane's mouth not more than ten times?"

Demonstrating with her right hand by making a pushing motion, Marjorie said, "It was the movement that I was trying to show to everybody yesterday, and I continued to show everyone. I was trying to push him away from her and I was sticking my hands because his jaws are open or slightly open, and I am pushing him away from her and I have my hands on his teeth and in his jaw area, and I don't have my hand in between his jaws but I have my hand in his mouth so that if he moves, or I move wrong, he could probably take my thumb off or my other finger off. That's what I mean by putting it in his mouth. I didn't stick my fist in his mouth or I didn't stick my fingers all the way between his jaws, but I had my hand on his teeth and I was trying to keep him away."

Again, the witness was taken through the various bites she sustained and the medical attention given her on the spot in the hallway.

Ruiz brought up an event that happened a few weeks after the attack, where Marjorie's 1969 Cougar was spray painted, tires slashed, and the windshield smashed.

Then the defense attorney asked, "What statements and publicity prompted you to go on *Good Morning America*?"

"There were numerous statements and publicity that prompted my consent to go on *Good Morning America*: starting with statements that I believe Ms. Smith was making; statements that were attributed to information received from C.D.C. that was disseminated to the public about the dogs, about confidential information that they had leaked to the press; and Mr. Hallinan's statements about a personal matter being the break in the case."

"What kind of statements?"

Marjorie answered, "Statements that Mr. Hallinan were making were that the adoption was a break in the case, that I hadn't been injured, that those were the two statements that were particularly bothersome to me because he is saying he had information, he had photographs. What he was saying was putting me in a false light, and he revealed confidential information from sealed records in the State of California that should not have been released to anybody."

"Were you aware before you testified at the grand jury that the grand jurors could believe you but still have to issue an indictment based upon receipt of any evidence?"

"My understanding was that yes, I mean they could believe me and still issue an indictment because the district attorney doesn't have to have anybody come and they don't have to listen to anybody that had any kind of positive experiences with the dogs or what would be positive for us. All that the grand jurors would need to hear would be negative evidence. It doesn't have to present anything positive."

"Were you aware before you went on *Good Morning America* that people were picketing your apartment building, demanding justice for the victim Diane Whipple because she was a lesbian?"

"I was aware that there were protests at the building and other places around San Francisco regarding this incident."

"Why did you go on *Good Morning America*?"

"Because it seems that with everything that was going on, all the publicity, all the statements that were being made, the fact that there was so much misinformation, there was so much antagonism going on, that there was such an uproar about what had happened so…" Marjorie's voice began to rise and fall. "…it was so horrible and so negative and so grotesque in terms of how… not only how we were… Robert and I were being portrayed but about what the nature of Hera and Bane had been and that those — just so much misinformation, so… such a… such a… an amount of horrid negativity. I mean the horror was always there, but there was nothing in terms of letting anybody know that… that this was a totally unexpected horrible event."

Marjorie's voice broke, she choked back a sob, her voice became high-pitched, "I mean I never… I wanted the people to know that I — that I never in a million years would ever have imagined that Bane could do anything like that, that he would… he would hurt anybody like that…"

Marjorie Knoller's voice now neared a scream, "...and that he was even capable of doing something like that to a person."

She wiped her eyes with both hands.

Her attorney asked her one more time, what had happened in that hallway so many months before. Then Marjorie said, "I was having trouble trying to sort out anything that went on in that hallway. That was the best that I could do at the time. I am not sure what went on, I am not really sure what happened. I am not sure I want to remember. I am just not sure because everything was so horrible and everything is still somewhat confused. That was the best that I could do at the time. It was the best that I could remember. It's still the best that I can remember."

On re-cross, Hammer reminded the witness that she was given every opportunity during the grand jury hearing to bring in witnesses and evidence. And that the grand jury chose not to call one single witness that she submitted.

Superior Court of California, Department No. 26, Division 53, Wednesday, March 13, 2002.

After Marjorie Knoller left the stand, one last witnesses was called by Bruce Hotchkiss: Jean Wright.

Ms. Wright, a few weeks before the attack on Diane Whipple, ran into Robert Noel walking his dog on Fillmore Street. She had never seen the breed before. She asked the owner if it was okay to pet the dog.

Noel said, "Sure," and Ms. Wright petted the dog. Bane wagged his tail and looked like a happy dog.

After Jean Wright was excused, Nedra Ruiz called her last witness, Peter Barnett. He was a criminalist with the firm of Forensic Science Associates. He had examined the clothing that Diane Whipple and Marjorie Knoller were wearing the afternoon of the attack.

He stated that there were primary and secondary transfers of evidence, such as blood, and that some blood had to come from direct contact between the victim and Marjorie. There was also a transfer of evidence between the two women involving hair. That meant they *had* been in contact with each other.

Death of an Angel

Henry Hunter's Home, San Francisco, Wednesday Evening, March 13, 2002.

Henry Hunter turned over the last page of the three-day transcript involving Marjorie Knoller's testimony.

Ever since he first began administering polygraphs, he had been fascinated in people who lied. He had researched the weakness in St. Thomas Aquinas and his works on variations — like lies of commission, omission and embellishment.

And he had researched falsehood in the great literary works. Over the years he had developed a few favorites.

Ralph Waldo Emerson: *Every violation of truth is not only a sort of suicide in the liar, but it is a stab at the health of human society.*

Socrates: *False words are not only evil in themselves, but they infect the soul with evil.*

Mark Twain: *One of the most striking differences between a cat and a lie is that a cat only has nine lives.*

Chapter
Sixty-eight

I Demand Hammer Take the Stand

Superior Court of California, Department 26, Division 53, Thursday, March 14, 2002.
The last day of the trial before closing arguments would feature the prosecution's rebuttal witnesses. There were only two: police officer Leslie Forrestal and Dr. Randall Lockwood.

Before these rebuttal witnesses were called, Nedra Ruiz spoke to the court without the jury present. She demanded that the judge put Jim Hammer on the stand so that she could cross-examine him on how the grand jury was conducted.

She said, "What did the grand jury mechanism mean to these two individuals?" She pointed at Robert Noel and Marjorie Knoller. "It meant that they were without counsel, it meant that they were unable to cross-examine the witnesses against them. The decision to proceed by indictment, especially when it is impelled by great public outcry, always results in tremendous prejudice to the rights of defendants. They are placed in a situation where they have no rights, they have no opportunity to cross-examine the names of witnesses who are called against them."

"But they knew that when they went in there," responded Judge Warren.

Ruiz said, "Your Honor, that makes no difference whatsoever. The fact that they felt in their innocence and in their naivete that their lack of malice in this action would be evident to all only evidences how easily they were victimized and stripped of their rights in these proceedings. Your Honor, we have a right to call an expert in criminal procedure to analyze the decisions that were made by this prosecutor to go before a grand jury, to ignore all of the positive evidence of witnesses that were clearly placed before him and to shortcut and circumvent, to cut off inquiry when he knew he had a duty under the law of the State of California and the Penal Code to call witnesses that were favorable.

"Especially, you would think in a case where the district attorney of the county has declared that this event that happened on January 26th was a tragic accident and that there was no evidence of training for viciousness of these dogs and there were no prior complaints. It was against that background and the public pronouncements of a district attorney of the county, it was after the district attorney of the county declared that the coroner and the chief inspector of the case had consulted, they had concluded it was a tragic accident and so investigation would have to be ongoing. It was against that background that this case went before a grand jury.

"And to allow the excerpts from the grand jury transcript that have been selected by this prosecutor is to allow this prosecutor to stand as a witness in this case without our ability to confront him as to each and every decision he made in the process of the grand jury in this case to determine if it really was fair and if Marjorie and Robert really had their rights protected when they were the subject of such horrid and prejudicial publicity.

"Your Honor, it's the things that I am alluding to today are a matter of public record. It's a matter of public record that after Ms. Whipple's death, Sharon Smith met with the District Attorney Hallinan. It's a matter of public record that after those meetings, Mr. Hallinan felt compelled to make statements about this case and about the state of the evidence because Marjorie and Robert were un-arrested, to the great clamor and dismay of the many supporters of Diane Whipple. People came forward because they were afraid that because of Diane Whipple's sexual orientation, she might not receive the justice that a heterosexual victim might be accorded, and such a state of affairs is scandalous. And, of course, they had a right to their perception of the failings of the criminal justice system.

"But certainly the decision of this prosecutor to seek an indictment in this particular case cannot be fully elucidated by the sections that he proposes to put forth in an unanswered rebuttal. There is no way for us to confront Mr. Hammer about the decisions that he made in this grand jury, there is no way for us to explore his decisions regarding the evidence in this case and the rights he afforded Marjorie and Robert unless Mr. Hammer takes the stand, Your Honor. And that's what we are demanding now, not that—"

The judge interrupted her with, "You made your point, counsel."

Ruiz said, "Thank you very much."

The judge pointed at Jim Hammer.

Hammer said, "If I may have just two minutes to respond to that. I am proud to join the company of Diane Whipple and Sharon Smith, the San Francisco police department and district attorney and everybody else Ms. Ruiz blamed for the indictment and for her client's plight.

"Ms. Ruiz was attempting to rehabilitate her client for why she went on *Good Morning America*. She started by attacking Mr. Hallinan. That is the first time that issue came up. And then she attempted to attack the grand jury.

"What followed then was her attack on the process of the grand jury, which I objected to. She went on about how unfair the grand jury was. She wants to attack the grand jury as an excuse or reason for going on *Good Morning America* and blaming Diane for her own death.

"Having said that, Your Honor, I tried to cross-examine Ms. Knoller about it but she claimed that, as she does about so many things, not to remember what happened.

"It is fundamentally unfair to allow the defendant, herself, to make allegations about the district attorney's office but, more specifically, about the grand jury process, and then to leave that in a false light.

"All we seek to do is to read to the jury short portions of the record. They aren't hearsay, they aren't offered for the truth of the matter, simply that words were spoken to the grand jury informing them of their duty. I am sure the Court knows words that have a legal effect, an operative effect by being said are non-hearsay. But even if that weren't the case, again they are not offered for a hearsay purpose but simply to show that the words were spoken.

"What is most telling in the passages, Your Honor, against Ms. Ruiz's spurious and false allegations against me and the district attorney's office is one passage where I actually cut off a grand juror who wants to stop Mr. Noel from speaking because they are tired of listening to him and his speeches, and I instructed the grand jury that that would be improper and that in the spirit of fairness, they should let him say whatever he wants to say regarding guilt or innocence. That is in the record.

"Since these aren't being offered for the truth of the matter, I don't know how my veracity is at issue, first of all. Secondly, we have the luxury of the grand jury proceeding, of everything that has been said being on the record. So there is a legal third party, namely the transcript.

"The issue here is brought up by the defense, the fairness of the process and whether or not the grand jury or the DA somehow abused it during this process. The record is what the record is, and the record has, I think, close to 30 specific admonitions to the grand jury, words that are spoken reminding them to be fair, reminding them of their duty sua sponte by the prosecutor what is required by the law with that initial admonition.

"For the defendant to raise this issue, to attack the DA and attack the grand jury process, to allow some limited response for a non-hearsay purpose in the record and then Ms. Ruiz's own expert, is not only appropriate but in fairness, if you don't do it, Judge, then Ms. Ruiz, I promise you will get up in closing argument and this jury will have a completely false light about what happened having opened the issue herself, and then using it to her own end.

Hammer said, "That would be a problem for the jury."

The judge apparently decided that it would, indeed, be a problem for the jury, because they never heard either side's argument.

Nedra Ruiz would not be given a chance to put Jim Hammer on the stand.

Chapter
Sixty-nine

Devastating Testimony About Carnivores

Superior Court of California, Department 26, Division 53, Thursday, March 14, 2002.

For the first time, there were more people in front of the glass partition, including the jury, than spectators and media *behind* the partition.

After the fireworks between the prosecution and the defense, the first rebuttal witness was called.

Officer Leslie Forrestal testified that the first statement made to her by Marjorie Knoller, in the hallway of the apartment building, was made before Robert Noel arrived at the scene. She reiterated that Marjorie had used the plural, dogs, that her male dog Bane ran down the hallway and attacked Ms. Whipple. Knoller then stated to the police officer that she followed and attempted to intercede in the attack.

Hammer asked, "So that we are clear, she said Bane would renew his attack when Ms. Whipple went towards what?"

"Towards her apartment."

"During the whole time you were with Ms. Knoller, did she ever ask about the condition of Ms. Whipple?"

"No."

"During the whole time you were with Ms. Knoller, did she ever ask to render first aid to Ms. Whipple?"

"No."

Hammer had no more questions.

Ruiz asked if the police officer took notes when she first entered the hallway. The officer had not. She had her gun drawn and was trying to ascertain what had happened.

Ruiz accented, as usual, each and every one of her words by using her hands. "When you saw Marjorie, your gun was out?"

"Yes." The police officer looked directly at the jury as she answered the defense attorney's questions.

"Did she hold up her hands?"

"No."

"Did she scream?"

"No."

"When you saw Marjorie, was she gibbering hysterically?"

"No."

"How far away were you with your gun drawn from Marjorie when you saw her?"

"Maybe eight to ten feet."

"So was she walking toward you?"

"No."

"Did she run back in her apartment?"

"No."

"Did Marjorie talk compulsively about the scene?"

"No."

"When Marjorie and you had this encounter in the hallway, did she beg you for mercy?"

"No."

"When you first saw Marjorie, you were standing just a few feet from the bloody body of Ms. Whipple; isn't that correct?"

"Yes."

"You could tell from Marjorie's appearance that she had something to do with this horrible scene?"

"Yes."

Ruiz asked if the officer had audio-taped her interview.

Forrestal had not.

Hotchkiss asked a few questions, establishing that his client arrived after the attack.

* * *

The last witness to appear before closing arguments was Dr. Randall Lockwood. He was vice president for research and educational outreach with the Humane Society of the United States in Washington, D.C. He had been with them for about 17 years.

Devastating Testimony About Carnivores

His educational background included a bachelor's degree in biology and psychology from Wesleyan University in Connecticut; master's work in ecology and evolution at University of California Irvine; and a Ph.D. in physiological and comparative psychology from Washington University in St. Louis, Missouri.

The doctor's professional history focused on dissertation research in the area of animal behavior, particularly canine dog behavior like the social structure and aggression in the wolf pack, based on studies of wolves in captivity and in nature.

The doctor went on to explain, "That was watching wolves interacting with each other, seeing basically how they used aggression in the course of both their social structure and in other interactions."

Hammer asked, "Have wolves or dogs changed in the last 25 years, or do they still act the same way?"

"Some dogs are quite a bit different from wolves. Primarily, in my view, dogs tend to be more aggressive than wolves because that's what we've chosen them to be. That's what we've selected and bred them to be. Wolves tend to play very fair and have a high degree of bite inhibition. We've often selected our dogs to be quite a bit more aggressive than wild canines normally would be."

"What is bite inhibition?"

"Wolves and dogs use their teeth to communicate when they bite. In the context of a social interaction, they can bite to various degrees. They can bite to hurt, to kill, in the case of prey, or they can bite to warn. I believe that when canines initiate a bite, when they begin to bite, they usually know what they want to bite and how hard they want to bite, depending on the context of that bite. Within the context of most dog interaction, many of the bites are inhibited. They might be playful, they might be a warning, they might be bites that are basically designed to say: I'm in charge, I'm the boss, or: Stay away. So most dogs show a good degree of bite inhibition unless highly aroused or in some other way disturbed."

"Or they want not to be?"

"Or their intent is to cause harm, which is something we often do see in fighting dogs and guarding dogs that traditionally have been selected to have less bite inhibition."

"And you've studied that regarding dog bites?"

"With relevance to my involvement here, I've spent about the last 20 to 25 years looking at dog bites, dog bite prevention, and specifically looking at fatal dog attacks since about 1972."

"You mentioned wolf studies. Do they have any relevance to understanding dog aggression and dog bites?"

"They do. All dog breeds ultimately trace their origins to wolves. A great deal of dog behavior has its roots in how wolves interact with each other and interact with their prey. So my focus has been in looking at how wild carnivores, particularly wolves and coyotes, interact, and how they use aggression and seeing how this might relate to dangerous dog issues."

"Carnivore is what, a meat eater?"

"Right."

Hammer went into the areas that the doctor had studied involving the Diane Whipple attack, noting that he was not charging for his services.

"Did you read a claim by her," Hammer pointed at Knoller, "either at the grand jury or trial testimony, that during the fatal attack on Diane Whipple, Bane would bite her, taste her, and then stop biting and redirect his bite?"

"Yes, I did."

"Based on your training and experience and all the work you've done in this field, is that a reasonable assertion? Do dogs work that way?"

"I don't think so, no," the doctor answered. "Bites can occur very rapidly. The decision to bite is made quickly. Taste is a rather slow process. If a bite is hard, usually it's because the animal chose to bite hard. If a bite is soft, that's a bite that I believe would show bite inhibition. We have many instances of dog bites where skin is not broken. There may be a bruise. And in most cases, we would interpret that as the dog giving a warning, not necessarily wanting to hurt. If a dog, particularly a large dog, wants to hurt you, it will."

"Is it the way dogs work? Do dogs sort of bite and then halfway through the bite, decide if they want to make it a hard or soft bite, or is it a decision made by a dog before he bites?"

"The decision is usually made by the time the dog first begins lunging, jumping, or initiating a bite. And many of the bites we see to children from family dogs I think are actually highly inhibited bites. The dog is snapping. Sometimes there's not even direct physical contact. It's fortunate that many of the millions of bites we see each year are not that serious, are not deep puncture wounds."

"Another way to ask this: If a dog is going to give you what you call an inhibited bite, is that a decision a dog, in the dog's mind, makes before he or she bites?"

"Yes. The message the dog usually wants to send: Move back. Get away from my stuff. Stay away from my prey. It's very common in the wolf pack. When you see wolves at a kill, the dominant wolf may be one of the main animals that's delivering the serious blows. If others come in, perhaps in feeding and interfering too soon, they will receive bites from more dominant animals basically telling them to back off until they are needed, or back off until the dominant animal is done."

"Have you studied the pictures of the wounds on Diane Whipple's body that was suffered in the hallway of her apartment January 26, 2001?"

"Yes, I have."

"Do those bites show what you'd call bite inhibition or not?"

"A few might. Some of them were bruises, but many of them are very deep puncture wounds and lacerations. Some were obscured by scratches and others, but certainly, the more damaging of the many, many bites were clearly not inhibited."

Hammer asked the doctor if he had read Knoller's account about being on top of Diane Whipple.

"Yes, I have."

"Do you have an opinion," Hammer asked, "about whether or not, if that were true, assume that claim is true that she's on top of Ms. Whipple much of the time or in contact with her almost the whole time, whether or not she would have suffered more severe wounds? I'm focusing now on dog behavior."

"What we often see in other dog bite cases I've reviewed, in many of them, maybe up to a third where there's intervention or interference with a dog bite in progress, let's say trying to break up a dog fight, a situation you often get, there is redirected aggression. In the frenzy of an attack, the dogs will bite people nearby, other dogs nearby, because in a very energetic, sustained attack, there is much less bite inhibition. Many of the injuries we deal with, I think with children and with dog owners, involve bites that are delivered in the context of trying to break up a dog fight or interfere with a dog attack on someone else. In one study we looked at specifically of severe bites, I believe about 30 percent of them were within the context of interfering with an attack on another. So in a situation where there's close physical proximity between one victim being bitten severely and another person who is close at hand, I would expect at least some redirected bites that were equal in severity to the severe bites that the victim received."

"In your review of all the evidence in this case, and not just the attack, is there any kind of evidence that would exemplify what you're talking about in terms of redirected aggression?"

"I believe the bite sustained by Mr. Noel is an example of the kind of redirected bite, again, interfering or intervening in a fight between dogs where there's an overflow of the aggression to another target nearby. Again, we see that very often in dog-on-dog bites and dog-on-human bites. And one interpretation I find is consistent with Mr. Noel's injuries as a redirected bite from Bane."

"Did you see any evidence, from what you saw of the injuries allegedly suffered by Ms. Knoller, of that kind of full-force, redirected aggression towards her?"

"The one bite to her hand, if that is a bite injury, might be one of those, but I felt that the injuries that she had described to her forearms in particular were inhibited. If Bane had wanted to cause damage, he would have. I think they suggested to me that she was probably at some distance, at least a few feet at the time and basically, Bane was giving her inhibited bites to get her to back off and let him do what he felt was his job."

"So explain that scenario that you've just mentioned."

"Bane," the doctor said, "in my view, as a guarding and protecting dog, was doing what he felt was his job of attacking a stranger, intruder, whatever. He, according to the testimony presented, was not being persuaded or commanded successfully to back off. I believe he would have interpreted Ms. Knoller's actions primarily as interference and was essentially telling her to leave him alone until he was done. And, in fact, had she been striking him or putting her hand in the mouth, as was indicated in some of the testimony, I believe she would have suffered injuries at least as severe as those that Mr. Noel received."

"So based on that, do you have an opinion whether or not she was literally physically in the middle of Bane while he was chewing on her, biting on Ms. Whipple the 77-some-odd times?"

"I believe she may have been nearby, but she was not in very close proximity."

"This is the last area I want to ask you about ⬜ do the good dog witnesses, someone pet him, someone was nice, the dog didn't attack them, in your mind, do those undercut the dog bites? How do you explain that?"

"On the one hand, if a dog licks ten children in the face and then bites the finger off the 11th, those ten prior acts are irrelevant in terms of telling me what standard of care needs to be exercised in supervising that dog. In terms of specifically understanding how you might have that, it's helpful to understand that guardian-type dogs like these breeds are often very tuned in to the wishes of their handlers. Guard dog trainers and others talk about a dog's ability to read the leash to understand what the context is they are in. If the owner is comfortable and conveying a relaxed mood, the dog will echo that. If the owner is hostile or tense, the doggies will pick up on the body language and mood of that. And if there are no signals being given, if the dog is on his own, essentially, then he has to make the decision what his job is to do. And without proper training to make the right decision, to inhibit aggression, he may decide this is a situation that requires aggression."

"Putting all these instances together, doctor, but he could pet the dog, the dog was friendly, and on other occasions the dog lunged, was aggressive and all the rest; is there any discernible pattern you can make out of all that evidence together over a time, in other words?"

"The pattern of the incidents, that seemed to me, just looking at the time line, to be of increasing frequency, indicated the dogs were clearly bonded to the owners, clearly protective of them, but also clearly increasing their instances of challenging those who they interpreted to be a risk or needing to be threatened."

Hammer asked his last question. "Finally, did there seem to be some pattern regarding location about this increased aggressive and, as you put it, protectiveness of the dog?"

"Many of the instances in the immediate area that the dogs regard as their territory, in and around the building."

"Does that make any sense to you as a dog expert?"

"That's what these dogs were bred to be; very protective and territorial."

Chapter
Seventy

The Prosecution's Closing Arguments

Superior Court of California, Department 26 Division 53, Monday, March 18, 2002.
Judge Warren wasted no time in getting to his jury instructions. He said, "This case has had a lot of emotional excitement in it. Reading the law may not reach the heights that counsel have attained earlier. You have got to focus. I have to read it the way it is, no histrionics, no gyrations, simply the law. So focus.

"You must not be influenced by pity for or prejudice against either defendant. You must not be biased against either defendant simply because he or she has been arrested for the offenses charged, that they have been charged or that they have been brought to trial. None of these circumstances is evidence of guilt and you must not assume from any or from all of them that either defendant is more likely to be guilty than not guilty.

"You must not be influenced by sentiment, by conjecture, sympathy, passion, prejudice, public opinion or public feeling. Both the People and each defendant have the right to expect that you will conscientiously consider and weigh the evidence, apply the law and reach a just verdict regardless of the consequences."

The judge took his time, almost an hour, to carefully explain the law to the jurors. There were five counts; two against Robert Noel and three against Marjorie Knoller.

He said, "Homicide is the killing of one human being by another. Homicide includes murder and manslaughter."

When the judge finished his instructions, Jim Hammer went to the lectern. It was time for the attorneys to make their final appeal to the jury. It was time for closing arguments.

Death of an Angel

Hammer said, "I have watched you and one thing that is clear is you have paid very, very close attention. We have done our best to put our case in focus on the real issues in this case. Other evidence, about how many people liked these dogs, is really not relevant to the issues in the case.

"What I want to focus on this morning is the law that applies to this case. I am not going to repeat everything you have heard, that would be a disrespect to you, but I am going to briefly summarize the relevant evidence as it relates to the law.

"What this case boils down to is a young woman ripped to death from head to toe in the hallway of her own apartment. That is what this case is about. Seventy-seven wounds from head to toe, ladies and gentlemen, 77, everything except her scalp and the bottom of her feet in front of the owner of the dogs, who ends up with two small cuts.

"That's what this case is about. And what makes it so sad is that it didn't have to happen. Diane Whipple didn't have to die in the hallway of her own apartment by the beasts owned by these people. She could be alive today and she should be alive today. What makes it horrible, though, and a crime, is that they knew with their own eyes what these dogs could do.

"They read about it, they heard about it. They had not just notice, they had *certainty* before them. People told them what would happen and they willfully ignored it, arrogantly."

He pointed at Robert Noel. "Who could imagine such a case, that one of them writes a letter mocking her, mocking a woman, big brave Mr. Noel. Hey, Mr Schneider, buddy, guess what happened today? This timorous — you know what that means? Frightened, scared — timorous, mousy little blond almost had a heart attack. Big, brave Mr. Noel, big, brave lawyer 200 some odd pounds. This timorous mousy little blond almost had a heart attack today, dogs paid her passing interest. What would it have been if it wasn't a passing interest?

"And you know what he said about it after she was dead? After she died, in front of the grand jury under oath, that she almost had a heart attack, this woman who is now dead: 'Did you care she was having a heart attack?' You know what his answer was? I don't know how you could forget this ever for your lives. 'No, not particularly.' 'Did you care that you had a woman living in your hallway who was terrified of your dogs?' What was his answer under oath by a lawyer? 'No, not particularly. I didn't know her.' That's the defendant's real world. That's his sworn testimony under oath.

"What makes it sick is he did that two weeks before she died and those were his answers after she died. And what makes it sick is that woman over there, Ms. Knoller, went on national television and there is not a tear in her eyes. And after all the evidence that you know now and that they knew then, she was asked by that reporter, 'Do you accept any responsibility as a human being for what happened,' and cold as ice, she said 'No. She should have closed the door. That's what I would have done.' Those are the real faces of these defendants.

"And Ms. Knoller can take the stand and she can cry the first 45 seconds and try to appeal to your sympathy and try to convince you that she is so filled with sorrow for Diane Whipple. But before these charges were filed, ten days or so after Diane is dead, when she says she is a basket case, she goes on *Good Morning America* and blames Diane Whipple for her own death."

Hammer lifted a plastic impression of Bane's teeth. He opened the jaws and held them toward the jury. "This is what they saw everyday, often lunging at people. By the time Marjorie Knoller walked into that hallway intentionally without adequate restraint, no choke collar, nor anything else she had been told to use, and no muzzle, by the time she went into that hallway and the dogs broke loose like they had done many times before, it was too late."

Again Hammer waved the plastic teeth at the jury, "Knowing what it would do, the crime was complete."

Hammer put down the teeth.

He said, "Under the law, if you find that Marjorie Knoller acted in conscious disregard when she left that day without muzzles, knowing what these dogs could do, then you find implied malice and under the law, implied malice equals second-degree murder. None of these crimes requires intent to kill."

Death of an Angel

Hammer listed the elements of each crime. He stated that one element in one crime was unusual, that the victim, herself, had to take all reasonable precautions.

"You can start to understand why the defendants concoct this Diane-just-stood-there story. If they can convince you that Diane had a chance to get out of the hall but just stood there, in other words, was negligent herself, then that would defeat 399, owning a mischievous animal, the least serious of the charges. They are trying to shift the blame to the victim to create a defense. The truth, ladies and gentlemen, and you have heard it, is that Diane Whipple was terrified of these dogs, that she had been bitten, herself, by them.

"Diane's keys were in the door. She almost got inside, but the dogs were too quick. And Ms. Knoller's own first story, remember that story to Officer Forrestal that she gave before she had time to talk to her husband and concoct her story, confirms this. Remember, Officer Forrestal said that Marjorie Knoller told her that the victim was crawling towards her apartment, not away from it, crawling towards her apartment and that is when the dog attacked. There was nothing in that version at all about Diane standing there for a minute and a half, this terrified woman. Only later, like when she was on *Good Morning America,* did Ms. Knoller say 'She should have just gone inside, that is what I would have done.'

"The second crime is the involuntary manslaughter. Notice this is the next one with negligence, criminal negligence, and it has two elements: a human being was killed and, secondly, that the killing occurred in the commission of an ordinarily lawful act which involves a high degree of risk of death or great bodily harm without due caution and circumspection."

Hammer went on to the most serious of charges. "The third crime that you will be deliberating on is a charge against Ms. Knoller only and that's the implied malice murder. Notice here, again no intent to kill, but this is the highest level of negligence or recklessness, a known danger and conscious disregard of that danger. Three elements. First, that the killing resulted from an intentional act. What's that act in this case, ladies and gentlemen?

476

Going into the hallway with two dogs without muzzles, without proper restraint on the dogs. Second, the natural consequences of that act have to be dangerous to human life. And, third, the act was deliberately performed with knowledge of the danger. Not just that you should have known but that you did know the danger and you acted in conscious disregard for human life.

"Couple of points here. When the killing is the direct result of such an act, it is not necessary to prove that the defendant intended that the act would result in the death of a human being. Once again, no intent to kill required.

"I want to make three points I think will be helpful to you in your deliberations.

"The first point we talked about already is that no intent to kill is required, so put that off the table.

"The second is that phrase 'malice aforethought,' unlawful killing with malice aforethought. That is what murder requires. And there are two points in this instruction I think that will clarify what that means because it's a legal term. Malice aforethought does not necessarily require any ill will or hatred of the person killed. When you hear 'malice,' you might think oh, do they have to prove he hated her or something like that? That's not the case. It's a legal term that talks about this knowing danger and acting in conscious disregard.

"And, finally, how about that word 'aforethought'? The word 'aforethought' does not imply deliberation or the lapse of considerable time. It only requires that the required mental state precede rather than follow the act. So you knew of the danger and acted in conscious disregard. That's the mental state before you went out into the hallway. So, again, no need to prove hatred or ill will, and no need to prove planning or deliberation.

"I think this boils down the task before you: the difference between manslaughter for Ms. Knoller and implied malice murder, and I will read it.

"There are many acts which are lawful but nevertheless endanger human life. If a person causes another's death by doing an act or engaging in conduct in a criminally negligent manner without realizing the risk involved, he or she is guilty of involuntary manslaughter. If, on the other hand, the person realized the risk and acted in total disregard of the danger to life involved, malice — malice doesn't require meanness or hatred — is implied and the crime is murder.

"What is the issue? What were the state of minds of the defendants? Did Marjorie Knoller, through all of those prior incidents, realize the risk involved from everything she had seen or heard?

"What did the evidence show on that?"

Hammer went through the evidence that he had presented. He traced the events from Pelican Bay State Prison to 2398 Pacific. He went on to list the prosecution witnesses who had testified, from Janet Coumbs to Dr. Randall Lockwood. He reminded the jury that Marjorie Knoller had testified that each of the witnesses who had said that Bane or Hera had lunged, snapped, growled was mistaken.

Aggression after aggression was mentioned.

Hammer said, "With this evidence in mind, ladies and gentlemen, by January 26th, it was not a question whether someone was going to be mauled or killed by these dogs. The only question on January 26th was when and who and where?"

Hammer told the jury that when Robert Noel left his apartment the day of the attack, he knew with one hundred percent certainty that there was a problem with these dogs and that he himself couldn't control the dogs and his wife couldn't even control one. "And it didn't mean a damned thing to them."

The prosecutor said, "Marjorie admitted in that first story that after Bane ran down the hall, she ran after him. I submit that's true, but it was too late.

"After Diane had been ripped to death from head to toe and ripped of every piece of clothing on her body, that woman," he pointed at Knoller, "left her alone in the hallway and when the police arrived, one of those dogs was still running down the hall.

"And what else do you know for a fact, uncontroverted, ladies and gentlemen? In the hour that the police are there, how many times does Marjorie Knoller ask about the poor woman who is dead now? Zero.

"And her little cry here — I am just going to say it. Her little cry for 45 seconds when she hits the stand. 'How you doing today, Marjorie, how do you feel?' If you don't think that was a concocted little speech for you like on TV to try to get you to feel sympathy, then I don't know what it was. 'I feel such sorrow for Diane and her family and friends.'

"Then why didn't you write a letter or call her partner?

"I ask you, whatever else you do here, to say no to her. You don't come into this courtroom and do this little act for us and cry and pout on command when your lawyer gets up and then when Mr. Hammer asks you questions, go all over the place and 'oh, I can't remember.' The heart of this case is what she knew before January 26th."

Hammer went on to list what he thought the five basic defenses would be.

One: No one ever complained about our dogs. Rebuttal: But the witnesses knew how Marjorie and Robert were. They knew that people were afraid of them.

Two: This was just an accident. Rebuttal: an accident is something happening without warning. Here there were warnings.

Three: People like our dogs.

Hammer said, "Dr. Lockwood dealt with all that evidence when he said if a dog licks a child ten times in the face and then bites it once, the ten are irrelevant."

Four: Noel wasn't there.

Hammer said, "If you gave your keys to a drunk driver knowing that he's drunk and having seen him in an accident before, it's not a defense to say ah, it happened ten miles away, I wasn't there. I wasn't there isn't a defense."

Five: What a hero Marjorie Knoller was.

Hammer said, "First aid is not a defense, even if she gave it. The heart of implied murder is knowledge; what did you know before January 26th when you *intentionally* went out into that hallway, you *intentionally* didn't put a muzzle on them, you *intentionally* didn't have adequate restraint on those dogs. It's not a defense, but then why lie about it? I am going to save that for the last issue. Why lie about it?"

Hammer said, "There is one instruction that I think is very important in evaluating Ms. Knoller's testimony and it's Witness Willfully False. A witness who is willfully false in one material part of his or her testimony is to be distrusted in others. You may reject the whole testimony of a witness who willfully has testified falsely as to a material point unless, from all the evidence, you believe the probability of truth favors his or her testimony in other particulars."

Hammer listed lies, saying, "Who would ever have thought that on the stand you would see a lie developing?" He reminded the jury about Marjorie testifying that she didn't call 911 because she *knew* her neighbor Esther had done so.

He brought up the keys. "I submit to you, ladies and gentlemen, Marjorie Knoller never entered the apartment of Diane Whipple at all. She didn't push her in, she didn't get close enough to that dog. As Dr. Lockwood said, from the evidence it's clear, and from her own wounds she never got in the middle of the thing. But if she wants you to believe that she acted heroically and violently by pushing Diane into her apartment, she's got to put herself in that apartment and the way she chose to try to convince you of it is, look, I even lost my keys in her apartment and I went looking for them. The only problem is, it's a lie and we proved it.

"She didn't come out of the Diane's apartment. And guess what? You know it's a lie. No one ever let her in Diane's apartment after the cops came. That didn't happen. Laws and Forrestal didn't let Marjorie go and look in Diane's apartment for any keys. It's a lie, and under the law you can reject everything she said. The law also says that if someone lied about the crime before they testified, you can consider that as consciousness of guilt. People lie for a reason and smart lawyers who know the law lie for specific reasons.

"When you analyze their lies; his lies to the grand jury, her lies to the grand jury and to your face, you will see that they aren't lying about their middle names or where they go shopping or what color their car was. They are lying about all those elements I have laid out. We didn't have knowledge, we never lost control, our dog never bit, lunged or attacked, we are not even the owners, we are the caretakers.

"It's on the key elements that they have lied to you about, and I ask you to say no, don't walk into this court and take an oath and look us in the eye and lie and get away with it."

The prosecutor pointed at the immense screen. On the left appeared a photo of Marjorie's hand, forefinger extended showing two cuts. On the right side began a slide show featuring image after bloody image, the slides flashing as quickly as an MTV video, of the 77 wounds that Diane sustained.

Hammer finished his closing argument. "What do you get, a free mauling? Is that what the law requires? Ah, now we know. They killed Diane Whipple. Is it not enough to read about the boy being mauled or to get mauled before you are on notice? You don't get a free mauling. You don't get a free death "

Chapter
Seventy-one

Defense's Closing Arguments

Superior Court of California, Department 26 Division 53, Monday, March 18, 2002.
After the lunch break, Bruce Hotchkiss offered his closing argument..

First thanking the jurors for the attention they had shown throughout the trial, Robert Noel's lawyer then said, "Please recall in the opening the district attorney talked about Mr. Noel's connection with two prisoners, and he talked about statements in Mr. Noel's letters. And he wants you to believe that Mr. Noel is a bad person, and this explains what happened in this case. A tragic accident occurred. Unforeseeable. Nobody could expect it. Then things came out about Mr. Noel that upset people.

"And as a result of that, the district attorney has had to cobble together a case.

"It's a case full of passion and prejudice. You saw a lot of passion here this morning. And the reason you saw a lot of passion was because that's all there is to this criminal case.

"This case illustrates why we have a jury. You're not here to determine if Mr. Noel writes letters to prisoners that may say some things that maybe you or I would not write. You're here to determine if, on January the 26th, Mr. Noel did a lawful act that involved a great risk of death in a criminally negligent manner that did cause the death of Diane Whipple.

"All the rest of this stuff is bluster.

"The district attorney mentioned some of the things that Mr. Noel said in his letters. He said: 'The schmuck deserves to be stabbed.' Ask yourself what that's got to do with whether or not

Defense's Closing Arguments

Mr. Noel did a lawful act on January 26th that involved a high degree of death in a criminally negligent manner that caused the death of Diane Whipple.

"Mr. Noel in his letter said if he tried to escape, 'I'd get out of the way.' Ask yourself what that's got to do with Mr. Noel's criminal liability, if any, on January the 26th.

"He quoted all of the profanity that Mr. Noel has used. Ask yourself what that's got to do with Mr. Noel's criminal liability for January the 26th."

Robert Noel's lawyer went into burden of proof. "Proof beyond a reasonable doubt. It's that state of the case which, after the entire comparison and consideration of all the evidence, leaves the minds of the jurors in that condition that they cannot say they feel an abiding conviction of the truth of the charge.

"And that's the standard that you have to apply in this case. What that means is when you go back to the jury room and you start deliberating, you do not determine whether Mr. Noel and Ms. Knoller are guilty or not guilty. You determine: Has the prosecution proved their guilt beyond a reasonable doubt. Even if you have a strong suspicion that they are guilty, you've got to return a verdict of not guilty."

Hotchkiss went into the incidents involving the supposed viciousness of the dogs. "These are not dogs that were taught to be killers. The district attorney has talked a lot about the stuff at Pelican Bay and what Mr. Schneider and Mr. Bretches may have wanted, but there's absolutely no evidence that Mr. Noel treated these dogs as anything other than the family pet.

"The prosecution's relevant evidence to prove that Mr. Noel knew they were killers, consists of what I call bad-dog witnesses. I'd like to set the bad-dog witnesses' testimony in context. Nobody filed or made any complaint about these dogs. No police report was filed. No Animal Care and Control report. No complaints to the landlord. No insurance claims. No lawsuits.

"Why is that? You've got people down here testifying about events that occurred prior to January the 26th. At the time those events occurred, they were events that were in the normal human/dog interaction. People didn't think enough about them to make any report. Ask yourself if the situation, as testified to down here by every one of those individuals, was as bad as they say it was, why didn't they file? Why didn't one of them file a police report, an Animal Care and Control report, report to the landlord or insurance claim or a lawsuit?

"Now, they weren't down here lying. They were testifying to what they believe happened. They are honest people. A horrendous, horrendous event occurred after each one of these individuals had an interaction with the dog. Diane Whipple was killed in the hallway of her building by a family pet. The absolutely unthinkable happened.

"And everybody says: *My God, how could that happen*?

"And then what occurred next? As the district attorney said, they begin to see the secret life of Robert Noel. He begins to be portrayed as a bad person. This event is exactly the same on a very, very, very small scale as the morning of September 11th, 2001, when the planes went into the Twin Towers. Prior to that, if you would ask anybody would a plane purposely fly into the Twin Towers, you'd get a resounding no. After that happened, if you'd ask anybody do we have a danger of planes flying into buildings, they'd all say yes. And after that happened, you have people reporting incidences and wanting to blame somebody.

"Immediately after this happened the CIA was to blame, the FBI was to blame; looking around for somebody to blame. And Mr. Noel was the bad person to blame because he wrote letters that are offensive to many people and he had an interaction with a prisoner that is offensive to many people. And it made it easy for the people who had interactions with these dogs prior to the event to say: *My God, I had an interaction with this dog*, and they start searching their minds. *I should have known. I should have been able to see something.* And they start, in their own minds, making things up that didn't actually happen on a perfectly reasonable and for a good-faith reason. They are not down here lying to you today. They are telling you what they actually believe happened, but they are telling you that through the filter of January 26th and through the filter of the subsequent bad things that have been said about Mr. Noel.

Defense's Closing Arguments

"The type of people that you would expect to have enough experience to complain if, at that time, it was a really disturbing dog incident, would be the postal workers, and that's Janet Lu and John Watanabe. They didn't make any complaint. Others you think would complain would be the dog trainers. That's Ron Bosia, Lynn Gaines and Abe Taylor. None of them made any complaints."

Hotchkiss finished his closing arguments.

"This will be a significant event in your lives. And the concept of 'beyond a reasonable doubt' I think is best exemplified by down the line, a year from now, two years from now, five years from now, when you're by yourself and looking at yourself in the mirror, ask yourself: *I did the right thing. I applied the law and I did what was right in this case.* I think that's the best standard I can give you for beyond a reasonable doubt. I ask you to return a verdict of not guilty on both counts as to Robert Noel. Thank you."

*　　*　　*

Nedra Ruiz replaced Bruce Hotchkiss at the podium. She said, "Marjorie and I would like to thank you for the time, the attention you have brought to this task, all of your lives have been disrupted, to hear the witnesses and decide the important and material facts in this case.

"Earlier today you heard the district attorney in this case accuse Marjorie of being a liar. He pointed to the grand jury testimony and said that it was inconsistent with testimony that she gave here in this action. Nothing about the grand jury testimony that Marjorie gave is hidden. It was a proceeding that was written down. It was taken and transformed into a transcript and it's part of a public record.

"Marjorie testified repeatedly at that grand jury that she couldn't recall all the events that had happened in that hallway on January 26th. And she testified here that because of the shock, the horrible trauma, that she had endured trying to save Diane Whipple's life, that she couldn't recall every single bite. She couldn't recall exactly how the attack progressed down the hallway. She remembered that she called out, that she screamed.

485

She couldn't recall hearing Diane scream, but she recalled then that the voice in her ears that she remembered was her screaming over and over again.

"I think Marjorie has a reason to be a little confused about what happened on January 26th. She was traumatized. She was dragged through blood. She was dragged down a hallway.

"I understand why Marjorie might not be able to recall every detail. Hey, she looked like this after January 26th."

On the screen appeared a picture of Marjorie Knoller taken the night of the attack.

Knoller's defense attorney took the jury one last time through how the dogs went from Coumbs Ranch to her client's apartment. She went through the letters written to Paul Schneider.

Then Ruiz accused the prosecution of hiding evidence. She went to the clerk of the court, got a plastic bag, returned to the jury, held it up and said, "This evidence was never shown. It is a torn sweatshirt. Why did Mr. Hammer hide this from you?"

Nedra Ruiz explained how Marjorie came into contact with the dogs in a very pure way: she was rescuing them.

She noted the care and attention that the dogs were given by various veterinarians. She spoke of how the only reason Dr. Martin was on the scene was because Marjorie wanted the dogs vaccinated.

Then she ran through the litany of the people that the dogs *did not* harm or intimidate.

Ruiz said, "If Marjorie disregarded human life, would she have approached the task of rescuing these dogs in the manner that she did? No. She did not approach the task of rescuing these dogs in a wanton, negligent, reckless manner. She took this as a very serious, very thoughtful endeavor. She wasn't about to do it without information.

"She ascertained that the Presa Canario was a guardian-breed dog."

The defense attorney said that it was a tragic accident that put Diane in that hallway fumbling for her keys. Each step from the moment Bane saw Diane, to the end of the attack, was gone over and called a tragic accident.

486

Defense's Closing Arguments

Then she turned to the law. "I'd like to refer now to the law regarding murder. In this case you will be assessing whether or not the intentional act, the intentional act, which is in this case, walking the dog Bane up to the roof, whether that intentional act was dangerous to human life, and you'll have to decide beyond a reasonable doubt that this act was deliberately performed by Marjorie Knoller with knowledge of the danger to and with conscious disregard for human life.

"Sharon Smith testified that there was this bite, this incident, that made Diane so terrified that she hesitated to use her hallway. That she didn't want to use the elevator. And why is that significant? Sharon Smith was introduced to you as a regional vice president of Schwab. She's an executive. Would an executive allow the love of her life to live in fear? Wouldn't that executive draw a line in the sand and say: This beast bit my girlfriend and I'm not having any of it? Wouldn't an executive complain?"

Ruiz said, "You cannot decide that Marjorie's guilty of murder because Diane Whipple died. It's kind of an ironic thing. It's a necessary element for the murder charge that Diane be dead, but in order to find Marjorie guilty of murder, you must be certain beyond a reasonable doubt that these instances that happened before the 26th gave her sufficient notice that she knew that that dog was liable to kill.

"But if we look at these instances and we see there's no complaint, there's a reason why. These people didn't think enough about these instances to complain."

Ruiz moved on to the testimony of Esther Birkmaier. "She testified that it was very quiet that day. She didn't have a TV on, but she could hear barking. And she didn't even pay it any mind. But then she heard someone say: 'Help me, help me,' and she didn't recognize that voice. But she did recognize the voice of Marjorie, and this is even before she made the 911 call. She heard the voice of Marjorie and she told the dispatcher—"

Jim Hammer said, "Your Honor, I'm going to interrupt. I think your instructions limited not for the truth of the matter and Ms. Ruiz is arguing for the truth of the matter."

The judge said, "It appears to be so."

Ruiz said, "Your Honor, this is the testimony that Esther Birkmaier recalls."

The judge called for a pause while he studied a sheaf of papers. Then he said, "Ladies and gentlemen, there was an order by the Court that stands. Ms. Birkmaier was allowed to tell you what words were used for the purpose of hearing the words, but not for the truth of the matter asserted. She can testify in court as to what she saw, but this is a conversation that happened outside of court. And, as I told you at the time it was admitted, you may not consider that conversation for the truth of the matter asserted, rather for the fact that certain words were spoken which may have an independent significance, but not for the truth of the matter asserted, and that will remain the case. Counsel's instructed to argue in accordance with the Court's ruling."

Instead of relating what Esther told the dispatcher, Nedra changed tactics and referred to what Esther told the jury. She spoke of when Mrs. Birkmaier went to her peephole, then called 911: "Marjorie couldn't abandon Diane to go and call 911, but from what she recalls someone said: 'Help's on the way.' She knows Esther Birkmaier. She's known Esther Birkmaier for ten years. She knew that someone would call 911, and she knew that Esther wouldn't call twice and not let her know."

The defense lawyer went through the injuries sustained by her client during her defense of Diane. Ruiz said, "Marjorie doesn't call herself a heroine. She doesn't think what she did was heroic. She told the police, who arrived immediately at the scene, that she was responsible. They were her dogs.

"When it counted, when it could save Diane's life, Marjorie was there taking full responsibility for the animals and trying to prevent injury to Diane. When it counted. And when Marjorie barely knew what was going on.

"She was convinced she encountered the police coming out of Diane Whipple's apartment. What material difference does it make? Does it make her less responsible?

"No. What's the motive for that discrepancy, that tremendous inconsistency? What's the reason? Her trauma. That she was so confused and traumatized by this event, that at the end she thought she was down the hall when she was really in her own apartment, because the police officer said that when they arrived on the scene, Marjorie was still putting the dogs away. One of them was loose, and Marjorie remembered: *I was trying to stop Diane's bleeding. Bane had stopped. I had to get him away.*"

Ruiz went on to what her client's reaction was. "She never dreamed, even when the dog was hauling her down the hallway toward Diane, that the dog meant to kill. And she certainly had no idea of even knowing Diane was going to be in the hallway at that hour. She certainly had no thought, based on what she knew about the dog, that this dog was liable to kill. That if he got out of control, that he would kill. And she certainly had no conscious disregard for life.

"All the evidence concerning Marjorie's interactions with these dogs has shown you that Marjorie respects life. That she acted to rescue these dogs and not for any purpose of fighting them or encouraging them to be mean.

"If, after you review these facts, you discover that you are not persuaded, that a majority of people oppose you, then you must remember that we are not here for consensus. We are not here for compromise. We are here for justice, and the justice that we seek are 12 verdicts, 12 individual verdicts.

"The powers that you bring to your individual determinations, your individual deliberations, will make your justice particular and will give us 12 individual verdicts that will demonstrate your courage, your sincerity, and your commitment to your oath to render impartial and fair verdicts. I am confident that you will acquit Marjorie of these accusations of murder and manslaughter. I am confident that you will render justice to Marjorie."

Chapter
Seventy-two

Rebuttal

Superior Court of California, Department 26 Division 53, Tuesday, March 19, 2002.
In criminal cases, the prosecution always has the last word. This slight edge is granted because the burden of proof is on the prosecution; the burden to convince all twelve jurors of guilt.

Hammer said, "Mr. Hotchkiss claimed that I used Mr. Noel's profanity against him. I didn't put the words in his mouth. But as you heard from the instructions yesterday, one of the key issues you will have to decide is whether or not these people, these lawyers, acted in such a way that they showed disregard for human life. And I ask you what more telling evidence could there be that when prior victims to Ms. Whipple experienced violence from these dogs, either actual in the term of a bite like Mr. Mosher, or threatened violence like lunging into the face of a little boy, or at the stomach of a pregnant woman, or when someone warned them put a muzzle on that dog, please look what your dog could do, how does he respond? We don't have mind readers, we have people's words and what they write and then you can infer things from their actions. But you have their own words how they treated victims.

"David Mosher, from Marjorie Knoller, is an idiot. From Robert Noel, he is an asshole.

"That's how he reacted to an accusation his dog had done something. More than once, yeah, more than once. Why? *He's an asshole.* Why not? That is the state of mind of Robert Noel well before Diane Whipple died.

"That other woman that warned them (the dogs should) wear a muzzle, be careful, what does he call her? *A fucking bitch.*

Rebuttal

They sit here polite with their tie on and it's hard to believe as you sit there there are people like this, but the truth on the streets before they were facing murder and manslaughter is this is how they treated victims. And I cannot imagine more powerful evidence, direct evidence of their state of mind and who they thought were more important, their dogs or the people around them.

"There are only two ways of looking at these witnesses. Either Jill Davis was really attacked in that lobby and almost got her pregnant stomach bitten or she didn't. There is no gray. Either Jill Davis, that nice woman who came in who has, you heard, no motive to lie or anything else or to fly to Los Angeles to get these people, either Jill Davis is telling the truth or she's not. Black and white, and that's it. Either Dave Mosher got bitten in the behind and got a welt or he didn't, and so on with all the rest of the witnesses.

"Each one of these incidents alone, if you looked at it, if it happened to someone, one lunge, one snarl, one bite, one minor bite might not be enough for you to call 911, you know, in the middle of robberies and murders and all the rest and say a dog just lunged at me. The police might say, well, call our business line.

"That's one explanation. And how many people did you hear say to you ladies and gentlemen, nice ordinary citizens, I wanted nothing to do with these people from their cold attitude and the way they wouldn't even apologize and even while their dog was snarling and trying to get at me and he would just say *Oh, they are fine.* One witness stood up there and said when Ms. Ruiz pressed her, why didn't you complain, why didn't you say something to Mr. Noel, remember that? And she said he's got 240 pounds of dogs on him, you want me to walk up to him, and he can't control them. You want me to go up and complain and show you—"

Nedra Ruiz stood and in a firm voice said, "Misstates the evidence, Your Honor."

The judge said, in an equally firm voice, "Counsel, this is closing argument. There will be no further interruptions or you

491

will be out of the courtroom." He pointed at Jim Hammer. "Please continue."

Hammer said, "You heard the evidence, ladies and gentlemen. Do you expect those people to walk up to nice Mr. Noel while he's got these beasts that he can barely control — and that's the evidence. Ms. Ruiz wants to spin it. Oh, he would jerk the chain and that's control. If that is control, ladies and gentlemen, then they are free to go back out into San Francisco or Los Angeles with big beasts like this again and act exactly the same way, and they are free to have their dogs lunge at people's faces, at little boys' faces and pregnant women and say that's okay because look, I am in control. That is ridiculous.

"So you decide about this great conspiracy to frame, as Ms. Ruiz put it yesterday, to frame poor Marjorie Knoller."

Hammer went on to warn the jury not to listen to Nedra Ruiz suggestion to examine each piece of evidence by itself. Rather, look at it as a whole.

In rebuttal to the circumstantial evidence flag that Marjorie Knoller's defense attorney raised, Hammer said, "So did she know that she couldn't control them? Yes, one hundred percent, because she experienced it herself. It didn't require inferences or circumstances. She felt it, she saw it, she experienced it. This is not circumstantial evidence, ladies and gentlemen, this is direct evidence and nothing has contradicted those three events."

He continued, "This is the most powerful. She denied it to you but then I read her her grand jury testimony. She had read her dogs were meaner, tougher than pit bulls. They were used to hunt down pit bulls. Now, who doesn't know how dangerous pit bulls are? She knew they were tougher, meaner than pit bulls.

"And how about the dogs' teeth? I showed you. You can look at them in the jury room. Frankly, just from the teeth alone, in a violent or aggressive or lunging dog, you don't have to be a six-year-old to tell looking at those teeth whether or not they could inflict serious damage upon someone."

Hammer switched his attack to Robert Noel. "Mr. Noel's recklessness, I submit to you, began the day he brought these dogs into San Francisco.

Rebuttal

"It culminated on January 26th when he intentionally left his house with these two huge beasts in the company of a woman he knew one hundred percent could not control them.

"And are you really telling me the law is such that if he's delayed one hour coming home, he's not guilty, all of his recklessness shifted to his wife?

"I want to talk briefly now about Ms. Ruiz. The best she could come up with on attacking the witnesses against her client was one alibi on one person and that was Mr. Bardack. And what was the alibi? A taxi cab record with no times on it which is supposed to be proof that Marjorie Knoller must have been at the hospital and therefore Bardack is a liar.

"Isn't it quite likely that Ms. Knoller came home to take the dogs for a walk like they always did around four o'clock, fed them and went back to the hospital and came home again that night?

"That's the whole defense case on the attack on all these witnesses; a taxi cab record without a time, and that's it.

"The most troubling charge, though, by Ms. Ruiz is the attack on Sharon Smith. She calls her a liar and I guess wants you to believe she's lying — well, not guess. She said to frame Marjorie Knoller. She said something else, though, which I will never forget, while Sharon Smith was on the stand a year after her partner's death: 'Don't you think it's your fault that she's dead because you didn't complain?' I guess that's a defense strategy. I am not going to attack her integrity or her.

"You saw Sharon Smith testify. You decide, you are the judges of that. Is there any evidence that three little marks on the hand left a scar? You can use your common sense. There is certainly no evidence that three little marks on the hand would leave a scar months later but, ladies and gentlemen, if you have no evidence but your client to rest on, what are you left to do? Call everybody a liar, including the victim's partner, and accuse the police of killing the woman by not giving first aid, and accuse the grand jury of impropriety and accuse the district attorney.

"I am not going to give Ms. Ruiz the dignity of a response to her charge and I am not going to attack Ms. Ruiz. I thought about it a lot last night and thought about attacking her, but I won't.

I think it's all a diversionary tactic. She wants to suck me into some fight with her to protect my integrity. I will stand on my own two feet with my integrity. You heard the evidence in this case and that is what this case is about."

Hammer told the jury that he had one more bit of Knoller's testimony he wanted to show them. He said, "I pointed all her lies out to you yesterday. I stopped counting. Maybe you have other memories than I have. This is what I think is the most striking: Did you notice how she testified when Ms. Ruiz questioned her as opposed to when I questioned her? When Ms. Ruiz questioned her, her memory was quite good and she cried occasionally and had a pouty face. When I questioned her, she couldn't remember the simplest thing if they hurt her case.

"And not just that. You saw a bit of Marjorie Knoller, the lawyer, and this is the part I want to point out. Remember one of the key issues in this case? Was there an intentional act? That is the first element we have to look at in implied malice murder."

On the screen appeared a portion of the trial's transcript involving Hammer's cross-examination of Knoller.

HAMMER: *During the whole time that your dogs were attacking Ms. Whipple, where were their muzzles?"*
KNOLLER: *In the house.*
HAMMER: *You had muzzles for both of them, didn't you?*
KNOLLER: *Yes.*
HAMMER: *And you didn't put them on that day, correct?"*
KNOLLER: *No. Hera wasn't — no.*
HAMMER: *Did you put it on Bane?*
KNOLLER: *No.*

Hammer said, "Watch this question, this is in the law."
HAMMER: *You intentionally didn't put it on Bane; is that correct?*

"Look at the answer." Hammer pointed at the screen. "That's a lawyer talking."
KNOLLER: *There is no intent.*

Hammer faced the jury. "Where did that come from, *there is no intent*?" Then pointed at the screen.
HAMMER: *You intentionally did not put it on Bane, correct?*

Rebuttal

KNOLLER: *No, that's not correct.*

Hammer said, "Simple English answer is 'Yeah, I intentionally didn't put it on.' No, that's not correct. That would get me convicted."

HAMMER: *You accidentally didn't put it on him?*

KNOLLER: *I had no reason to put it on him.*

HAMMER: *You didn't put it on him on purpose. You chose not to put it on Bane, correct?*

KNOLLER: *There was no reason to put it on Bane.*

Hammer said, "How many times did this happen, where she wouldn't answer the question? Finally, I come back:"

HAMMER: *Did you choose not to put it on Bane?*

KNOLLER: *I didn't have any reason to put one on him.*

Hammer said, "Again she wouldn't answer."

HAMMER: *I didn't ask you about a reason. Did you choose not to put it on Bane?*

"And finally an answer," Hammer said as he again pointed at the screen.

KNOLLER: *Yes, I chose not to.*

"These are not accidental lies, ladies and gentlemen, they are not accidental evasions, they are done with a purpose, and if you study the lies in this case, you will see that they all go to the elements of the crimes. And on that issue, the law says if you think someone intentionally testified falsely, you can reject their own testimony. That's the first step, ladies and gentlemen. But the next step is to ask *why* are they lying, what do they have to hide? If this is just an accident, you don't have to lie about it. If something is just an accident and you have nothing to hide, you don't have to lie about it. You lie when the truth cannot set you free, you lie when the truth will convict you.

"I am going to go one last time, after talking about Ms. Ruiz's diversions, to the law of implied malice. And I want to say this before I do: I didn't hear the defendants arguing mischievous dog statute yesterday. Sounds like they are kind of conceding that. I heard them talk quite a bit more about the involuntary manslaughter. I think what's going on here is an attempt by the defendants to get you to compromise. Oh, murder, God that sounds so serious, let's just do that nice middle charge and feel good about ourselves. I urge you not to fall for that, to look at each of these crimes, all of the evidence and decide is this not the most serious level of negligence where people consciously disregard warnings, and that's implied-malice murder."

"The evidence, and it's uncontradicted, is that time and time again they were warned, use a muzzle, put a choke collar on and they said, in Mr. Noel's words: *I can do whatever I goddamn please, I can go to any park I want with the dog off-leash.*"

Ruiz rose to her feet. " Objection, Your Honor. The dog was on-leash at all times."

"Counsel," Judge Warren said, "there will be no further objections. The jury will recall the evidence. Ladies and gentlemen, it is improper and counsel's conduct is improper by standing up in closing argument and objecting to her recollection of what the evidence was. The jury will recall what the evidence is. Arguments of counsel are not evidence and it is improper.

"Ms. Ruiz, please take your seat and not get up again or the next objection will be made from the holding cell behind you."

Nedra Ruiz sat down. Two sheriff's deputies moved directly behind her.

Hammer continued his rebuttal argument.

"There is no doubt, ladies and gentlemen, from the evidence about his statement, which is: *I can do whatever I goddamn please.*

"Then there is the death of Diane Whipple. This is a murder case involving two defendants, by a dog."

Hammer stepped back from the podium, crossed his arms, then stepped forward again. "Ms. Ruiz came up with this new theory that I am hiding evidence from you about Marjorie's torn sweatshirt. Well, I did such a good job of hiding evidence that I put it in a sealed secret bag, marked it for evidence. Not a very good hiding job."

Jim Hammer finished his rebuttal argument.

"Ladies and gentlemen, if not this case, on these facts, with over 31 witnesses, when is it a murder case? And if not these defendants, then who?"

Chapter
Seventy-three

Another Battle in the Media

Henry Hunter's home, Wednesday, March 20, 2002.
The case was now in the hands of the jury. Normally, this was the time when the lawyers involved went into seclusion and asked themselves if there was anything else they could have done? Or asked? Or presented?

It was also a time when the police involved in the gathering of evidence asked themselves the same questions.

Trail lawyers and police do not like to feel helpless. They want to know that their work is complete.

But now was the time, with the door closed on the jury's deliberations, that they *were* helpless.

Hunter roamed around his front room. It was seven in the morning. He knew that somewhere down in Los Angeles Jim Hammer and Terence Hallinan and Kimberly Guilfoyle Newsom were doing the same thing.

A time of pacing, the cop thought. Pacing and wondering.

He had followed the action in LA with great interest, as did all the police who had worked on the case. Nothing was more depressing than working to the best of your ability and then watching the judgment of others overturn that effort.

He had read an article the past Monday in the *Los Angeles Times* about Sharon Smith. She was interviewed by Ann Gorman. The column had covered Sharon's becoming an activist for gay and lesbian causes.

It also mentioned that Sharon had finally picked the sixth place to scatter Diane's ashes: Mt. Tamalpais.

Hunter nodded. Good choice. That mountain in Marin County was visible from many places in the Bay Area.

The cop quit pacing and turned on his TV. A picture of the dog Bane greeted him. Then the image turned to Nedra Ruiz, who said, "When the prosecutor interrupted my argument he was never greeted by a threat from the judge to go straight to jail. The prosecutor was then able to finish making his arguments."

He flipped the channel. Ruiz again appeared on the screen. "There was a drumbeat on the prosecution, in this case, by the gay community. They didn't want Diane Alexis Whipple's death to be swept under rug. They did not want her to not receive justice just because of her sexual orientation."

Again the channel was changed. Bryant Gumbal appeared with Nedra Ruiz. He said, "Is it your feeling that the longer the deliberations go, the better off it is for you?"

Nedra answered, "Considering that many people feel the case is open and shut, this is not a whodunit. Marjorie took responsibility for the two dogs from the inception of this tragedy. Many people have presumed that Marjorie is guilty."

Gumbal said, "It seems that both you and the prosecution's strategy was to blame others for the attack. Was that part of your strategy, to shift the blame?"

"Marjorie has always accepted responsibility."

"That's not quite true. Marjorie, for a time, blamed Diane Whipple. What can you tell us about the emotional state of your client?"

"She's very anxious. She faces fifteen years to life. She's been incarcerated for over a year on these charges."

Gumbal asked, "If the verdict goes against you, do you feel you have grounds for appeal?"

"Certainly. The immense bail issue itself. The decision not to sever the trials. The decision to admit totally extraneous evidence about prison gangs."

Hunter changed channels to NBC's *Today Show*. Jim Hammer appeared. He said, "The question I put to the jury was, hey, if thirty's not enough, what do you need, fifty? Do you need a hundred prior warnings?"

Another Battle in the Media

Matt Lauer asked about the personal attack, that Hammer was gay and prosecuting a case involving a victim who was gay.

Hammer answered, "That's usually a sign of desperation. Any kind of notion that I can't fairly prosecute a case because I'm gay is like saying to a black person that they can't be a fair prosecutor if the victim was black, or that a woman can't prosecute when the victim is a woman. It's outrageous."

Matt Lauer then introduced Nedra Ruiz.

She said, "I don't think the jury will buy that Marjorie acted with conscious disregard for the safety of other people."

Hunter hit the remote again. He saw that they were playing the Knoller tape on *Good Morning America*.

Nedra Ruiz was asked about claiming that the prosecution caved to the gay community.

Again, Ruiz mentioned the outrageous bail for her client.

Hunter thought, outrageous? She and her husband were deemed a flight risk. For fleeing up Interstate 5 at over ninety miles an hour.

Kimberly Guilfoyle Newsom appeared on the screen.

She said, "There has never been a murder conviction in California in a dog-attack case. We felt from the beginning that this was a murder case. Implied malice is about the subjective knowledge that they had. The conscious disregard towards those warnings that resulted in the death of a human being, Diane Whipple."

The successful prosecuting attorney was asked to respond to Ruiz's claim of pressure from San Francisco's gay community.

Kimberly answered, "As a prosecutor I know both myself and Mr. Hammer were offended by those remarks. To suggest that we would not give equal justice to any victim and their families is offensive. We committed our resources and worked very hard because we believed this was a murder case."

Hunter turned off the television.

He put on his fedora, adjusted his suspenders, kissed his wife good-bye and went to work.

Very seldom do the men in blue have an opportunity to actually witness a verdict on a crime they have worked. They

499

usually are out working on another crime. Few trials are televised. The results of most of the cases they worked on were relayed by the liaison attorney, like Kimberly Guilfoyle Newsom was on the dog-murder case.

Hunter knew he would let his men watch television when the verdict came in. He wanted his team, together — Rich Daniele, Mike Becker, Steve Murphy — and he wanted to be with them when the verdict was read.

Chapter
Seventy-four

The Verdict

General Work Detail, Room 411, San Francisco Hall of Justice, Thursday, March 21, 2002.
Once the dog-mauling case had been turned over to the jury, Henry Hunter's men began dropping by his office with increased frequency. A TV was in the corner, tuned to a network news channel. Mike Becker or Rich Daniele or Steve Murphy took turns poking their heads inside Hunter's office to see if there was an update.

Finally, a voice from the TV set spoke the words Hunter and others had been waiting for: "We interrupt this program for a special announcement."

Hunter listened to the report that the jury had come to a decision on all five counts. This would be televised live, by all major networks and some not-so-major networks at 1:30 p.m.

Soon, Hunter's office was crowded with members of his General Work Detail team.

There was a short delay as spectators were seated, the jury seated and lawyers seated.

The judge entered. All rose, then returned to their seats.

Judge Warren turned to the jury. "It's my honor to face you today for the last time as a judge in this case. I understand, Mr. Foreperson, that you have reached a verdict on the five counts that are before the jury."

"Yes, your honor."

"Ladies and gentlemen, let me explain to you the procedure. I am gong to ask the floor person to hand the envelope that has the verdicts in it to the deputy, he will give them to me. I will review the verdicts only to see if they have been properly filled out."

The judge went on to explain that his clerk would then come forward, he would hand the verdicts to her, and she would read the verdicts aloud. Then the verdicts would be entered and that, technically, was the end of the case.

The envelopes were retrieved from the jury foreperson by the deputy and handed to the judge. He carefully reviewed each document, then gave them to his clerk.

The judge said, "This is a court, when the verdicts are read it is very important that you maintain respect for these proceedings. Please, let there be no outbursts in the audience."

He told his clerk to read the verdicts.

She read: "Verdict as to Marjorie Knoller, count three: We the jury in the above entitled action find the defendant Marjorie Knoller guilty of the crime of being an owner of a mischievous animal who killed in violation of section 399 of the California Penal Code."

There was no apparent reaction from Marjorie Knoller, except her head nodded slightly.

The clerk said, "Verdict as to Robert Noel, count three: We the jury in the above entitled action find the defendant Robert Noel guilty of the crime of being the owner of a mischievous animal who killed in violation of section 399 of the California Penal Code."

There was no reaction from Robert Noel.

The clerk said, "Verdict as to Marjorie Knoller, count two: We the jury in the above entitled action find the defendant Marjorie Knoller guilty of the crime of involuntary manslaughter in violation of section 192.B of the California Penal Code, a felony."

Marjorie Knoller's hands were folded and on the table in front of her. She stared straight ahead. Still, no obvious emotion.

All counsel on both sides maintained composure. Jim Hammer sat with his hands in his lap. Kimberly Guilfoyle Newsom's hands were clasped together on the table. Bruce Hotchkiss' face remained impassive. Nedra Ruiz scribbled notes.

The Verdict

The clerk said, "Verdict as to Robert Noel, count two: We the jury in the above entitled action find the defendant Robert Noel guilty of the crime of involuntary manslaughter in violation of section 192.B of the California Penal Code, a felony."

Still no reaction from Noel. His face remained stoic. Yet, the façade began to crumble slightly. There was an aura about his eyes — eyes that stared straight ahead and were very hard to read — that seemed to emote either rage or shock or disbelief. But the eyes also looked haunted.

The clerk said, "Verdict as to Marjorie Knoller, count one: We the jury in the above entitled action find the defendant Marjorie Knoller guilty—"

There was an intake of breath — not only from Marjorie Knoller, but from most of the spectators.

"—of the crime of murder in the second-degree in violation of section 187 of the California Penal Code, a felony."

Marjorie Knoller's face looked like it had just been hit by a baseball bat. Nedra Ruiz put her right hand on her client's back, then leaned over and began to whisper to her.

The words, whatever they were, seemed ineffective in removing the shocked and shattered look on her client's face.

Robert Noel sat rigid — eyes fixed straight ahead. Not even a hint of recognition to his wife, now convicted of second-degree murder.

Marjorie turned to the glass partition and searched. She found her mother and father. With a look that was absolutely beseeching, she mouthed the words *help me*.

Sharon Smith, holding a picture of Diane Whipple, began to weep. Her sister held her.

The jury was asked to individually support each verdict with an audible roll call. Twice, each of the twelve jurors repeated the word "guilty" as to the counts charged against Robert Noel.

Three times they did the same thing as to the counts against Marjorie Knoller. It was as if 36 lashes had been delivered to her psyche.

A first in California criminal justice was entered into the record.

The jury had deliberated eleven and a half hours to reach their five verdicts.

The entire verdict proceedings took just under fifteen minutes, about the length of time Bane and Hera attacked and murdered Diane Whipple.

The next step for both Noel and Knoller was to return to jail in San Francisco and await a report from the Probation Department. On the involuntary manslaughter charges the sentencing could be two, three or four years. In California there is a low, medium and high range. Judge Warren would have to use findings of aggravating or mitigating circumstances. If those two inputs balance, then Robert Noel would face three years.

Marjorie Knoller faced a sentence of fifteen-years-to-life.

*   *   *

After most of the media had raced out of the courtroom to file their stories, and after the friends and loved ones of Diane Whipple left, a few of the jurors returned to the courtroom to talk. Court TV remained to televise the juror's explanations. Terence Hallinan also remained, as did James Hammer and Kimbely Guilfoyle Newsom.

The jury foreman was a 64-year-old man named Don Newton. He repaired sewage treatment equipment for a living. A few of the jurors joined him on-camera and a few stayed off-camera to deliver their remarks.

He was asked about Nedra Ruiz.

Newton said, "Ruiz is an amazingly dramatic person. She's an incredible actress. I think, to some extent, she was counterproductive. But I really feel she tried to do the best she could for her client. Ruiz tried to seem like she wasn't organized, but every time she rustled all the papers she would come up with the right answer."

About Marjorie Knoller, he said, "Her testimony was not believable. That was crucial in coming to our decision."

The jury discounted Marjorie Knoller's testimony. Yet, they did try very hard not to hate the defendants.

The jury foreperson was asked in what order they debated the charges.

The Verdict

He answered, "First we discussed the mischievous dog. Then manslaughter, moving up on the seriousness of the charges."

When asked about the letters Robert Noel had written, Newton answered, "They showed an attitude, a general approach. They showed Noel as not a very nice person."

Newton went on to say that the jury felt Dr. Randall Lockwood was very credible.

The jury was asked why they reviewed some of Robert Noel's testimony.

Newton answered, "It was necessary for us to investigate whether or not he had set up a pattern of contradictory information which made us unable to believe his explanation. It made it clear that he was not any less responsible in this than Marjorie Knoller. They were equally responsible."

Jeanne Sluiman, a bank operations manager, said about Nedra Ruiz, "With what she had to work with, I believe she did a good job. She is very dramatic. But we had to go underneath all that and actually just take what we felt were the facts and not her theatrics."

Following the verdict, Robert Noel reportedly said, "After 34 years of trying cases, nothing a jury or judge does surprises me."

Nedra Ruiz and Bruce Hotchkiss left the courthouse without comment.

The television coverage moved to the other participants in the trial.

Sharon Smith said, "I am very grateful to the jury and to Judge Warren. Jim Hammer has done an absolutely amazing job in getting the evidence in. There is no real joy in this, but certainly some measure of justice for Diane was done today. I'm glad the jury didn't buy some of the smoke screens that were put in front of them."

Terence Hallinan was next. "When Jim was finished with his argument, he told me he was at peace with himself because he had done everything that could be expected of him. It was a case that went in so perfect. You couldn't ask for it to go in any better. The correctness of that was the verdict of the jury. They didn't hold any prejudices against the defendants They gave the defense attorney her due. They gave everybody their due. It was a painful process for them, but they tried to follow the law and to do justice here. I am proud of my prosecutors, Jim and Kimberly, and everybody else that was involved. This was a year-long process for everybody involved; teamwork that combined with the extra special effort that Jim put out."

The San Francisco district attorney had one final thought. "Today is a vindication of the criminal justice system. This is going to be an example to everyone in the country. If you have a big, dangerous dog, you'd better supervise them, or you're going to be held accountable."

Hammer said, "This has been over a year-long fight to bring to justice the people responsible for Diane Whipple's death."

Hammer gave thanks to all those who helped in the case, from the police to the LA DA's office. He added, "I'd like to thank Paul Cummins, who suggested I close my rebuttal argument with, 'If not these defendants, who; if not this case, when?'"

He paused, then continued. "Nothing will bring Diane back, but, hopefully this will send a message across the country, across the world, about how people should regard other people."

The lead prosecutor took a ring out of his pocket and held it up for the television cameras to zoom in on. "Sharon Smith, before we started this trial, gave me this ring. It was Diane Whipple's favorite possession. This is the lacrosse championship ring she had earned while a student at Pennsylvania State University in 1989."

Hammer said, "I carried it in my pocket every day of this trial. I told Sharon Smith over a year ago that we would fight and fight and fight to bring justice to this case.

"This jury has done that."

Justice had prevailed in the San Francisco dog-mauling case.

Chapter
Seventy-five

An Appeal

Hall of Justice, San Francisco, Friday, April 12, 2002.
On March 25, four days after the jury verdict, Marjorie Knoller's parents, Harriet and David Knoller, hired Dennis Riordan, a California appeals specialist.

Dennis Riordan had handled more than 100 murder-case appeals.

Tony Serra, the colorful defense attorney with a now-high-profile associate, Nedra Ruiz, explained what had happened.

"This was Nedra's desire. We contacted Riordan. He is the best appellate lawyer in the West. This was a joint effort of all parties to bring the best appellate case possible."

Many pundits had offered possible appeals: the prejudice of allowing the Aryan Brotherhood connection into testimony; Nedra Ruiz's theatrics; and, as usual — when one has time to go back and pore over transcripts to analyze, at leisure, calls made by a judge on the spot — certain rulings made by Judge Warren.

Defense attorney Bill Fazio, a former prosecutor who twice came within a percentage point of becoming San Francisco's DA, offered his insight.

"It's almost a buffet of appellate issues that are present in this case," observed Fazio.

Riordan had asked the judge for an opportunity to present his motions. The judge had picked Friday, April 12, back at the same courtroom in San Francisco used during preliminary hearings..

Inevitably, many cameras were in the courtroom, plus spectators and reporters.

Henry Hunter left his office and took a seat in the last row of the courtroom.

Hunter watched the two defendants as they were escorted into the courtroom. They were now back in the orange jumps, standard San Francisco jail house garb.

Dennis Riordan argued that he would need time to research and read all material involved in the case.

The judge postponed sentencing indefinitely on both Robert Noel and Marjorie Knoller. The judge called the case unprecedented in California history. No one had ever been found guilty of murder in a case of a dog-mauling fatality, unless they intentionally released the animal with motive to injure.

The judge granted Riordan's request to delay sentencing.

"At this point we will have a hearing on June 7, even if we have to work nights and weekends to get there."

The judge went on to say that, depending on the outcome of that hearing, sentencing for both Noel and Knoller might be moot if a new trial was determined to be in order.

The courtroom emptied. Hunter followed the crowd.

Outside the courtroom, Nedra Ruiz stated: "If I made mistakes, I'm happy to admit them. Perhaps, my mistakes contributed to a false understanding of the evidence. If that is the case, then I certainly want Marjorie to have a new trial."

Jim Hammer was ready with his counter: "The defense has to prove that if a different attorney had done the case, Marjorie Knoller would have been found not guilty. And that's weighed against the enormity of the evidence."

Because of the wrongful death suits brought by Penny Whipple-Kelly and Sharon Smith, and the appeals for a new trial by both defendants, the case was not over; it would go on.

And, Hunter thought, it will go on for me until I talk to one more person, a professional of the law; and get some answers to a few questions..

No matter what a future appeals ruling might bring, however, a jury of their peers had found Robert Noel and Marjorie Knoller guilty on all five counts.

Chapter
Seventy-six

Unanswered Questions

General Work Detail, Room 411, Hall of Justice, April 15, 2002.

Henry Hunter reviewed his taxes, signed next to his wife's name, and promised himself to drop it in a mail box on his lunch hour.

He decided that he wanted to talk about the case with Kimberly Guilfoyle Newsom.

Kimberly was married to Gavin Newsom, an odds-on front-runner to be next mayor of San Francisco. She and her husband Gavin were high society in San Francisco's upper crust, yet both seemed unaffected by the glamour.

Hunter remembered what Gavin had said about his wife:

She is passionate about so many different causes, goes after things with absolute commitment, and still has the ability to pause and reflect on herself, on the world, on any given situation. She is just remarkable.

Kimberly is so grounded, so secure in who she is and what she is, that it is just a joy to watch and listen to her. She understands the difference between significance and success.

She's got her feet on the ground, Hunter mentally added.

He rode one of the elevators in the Hall of Justice from his office on the fourth floor to the third. He walked down a long hallway and stood at the entrance to the DA's offices. The receptionist, behind a thick glass partition, nodded and waved him to a door on his far left. He was buzzed in.

He entered Kimberly Guilfoyle Newsom's office.

She smiled.

He returned the smile. He liked the prosecutor. She was dedicated; a workhorse who understood the importance of the police in the cycle of preparing a case.

She waved him to a chair and said, "I was just finishing a letter regarding your team and the case." She handed him the letter. It was to Fred Lau, the San Francisco Chief of Police.

He read:

*I recently had the pleasure and the privilege of working with Sergeant Steve Murphy, Inspector Mike Becker and Inspector Rich Daniele in the case of **People v. Noel and Knoller**. Their 14 months of dedication and service, despite their own large case loads, resulted in the conviction of both defendants. They wrote a multitude of search warrants and served them. While in Los Angeles with the prosecution team their assistance during trial was an invaluable part of a team that could not function without total cooperation from all members.*

Everything requested of Sergeant Murphy, Inspector Becker and Inspector Daniele was taken care of. The word "no" was not part of their vocabulary. For giving unselfishly of their time, support and understanding to both the witnesses and the Assistant District Attorneys, I thank them. When witnesses needed transportation, they were there. When follow-up of some sort was necessary, they were there. When I had questions, concerns or worries about an issue is a case, however big or small, they were there, unhesitatingly and without exception.

Hunter looked up from the letter. "Thank you. This will go into each man's file."

She grinned. "But you came for another reason."

"Yes," Hunter said, "I have some questions regarding the dog-mauling trial."

"Shoot."

Hunter smiled an inward smile. She was a respected criminal defense attorney. She was gorgeous. Yet there was no façade about her. What you see, the cop knew, is what you get.

Straight foreword, honest.

Just what the dog-mauling murder case could have used a lot more of, from the defendants.

He asked, "You became so personally involved in this case. I know how much you throw yourself into all your cases, but this one seemed…"

She finished for him, "Different. Lot's of reasons. And beyond the brutal aspects of the death. When I was in second grade I wanted to play soccer. The team was boys only. My mom went to bat for me and confronted the coach. She said that if I was good enough, I should be on the team. I made the team. But, more importantly, I learned that everyone should have an equal chance to show their ability. So Diane being an athlete was a connection."

And Diane, Hunter thought, had many of the same qualities as Kimberly. And maybe the most endearing of all was their mutual spirit and love of life.

She said, "You didn't come to talk about my preteen sports."

"No, I didn't. Why wasn't the 911 call from Esther allowed in?"

"We decided that her personal testimony would be more powerful and inclusive. There's nothing like hearing it directly from the witness."

The policeman said, "A personal question. I know why I love being a cop. Why—?"

"I love being a prosecutor because it gives me a chance to help people. A chance to have an impact on my own community in a positive way." Again the infectious smile. "Much like your job does."

Hunter asked, "The Aryans, and keeping out some of that connection?"

"We got part of it in. But the idea of an Aryan connection has prejudicial effect versus probative value."

"A lot of us on the fourth floor would have liked to see Robert Noel charged with the same thing as his wife."

"Sure. But as you well know, we *would* have charged Bob Noel with second-degree if the grand jury had asked for it. We would have prosecuted him on that charge, too."

"What difference did it make, under implied malice, that he was in Oakland?"

"Marjorie was in control of the dogs and did the intentional act of taking the dogs into that hallway. It was her choice."

Hunter asked, "I heard you had two death threats."

"One was on an unrelated case, the other from the Aryan Brotherhood." She smiled. "I had to wear a bulletproof vest for a few weeks before my wedding in early December. And I had protection from both the police and the DA's office."

"Where did you go on your honeymoon?"

"Hawaii. Kona. Except only for a few days, then I had to get back for the trial preparations."

Hunter thought of an old military compliment: *Above and beyond the call of duty.* He asked, "Who set up the order of the witnesses?"

"That was discussed as a team. Suggesting the order and preparing the witnesses was part of my job."

"How about the graphics used?"

"That was Emily and myself. They were produced by a company named Focal Point."

"Who's Emily?"

"She's my law clerk. She has a law degree from Texas. Her last name is Negley. She also helped me with the witnesses. She was invaluable."

Hunter said, "I talked to some people who were there. Very impressive the way the graphics were used to make it simple to see the growth of the attacks from mid-year in 2000, to the actual attack at the end of January 2001."

"Thank you."

"I was told you employed a huge screen to make it easier for the jury to read things, like grand jury testimony. Did that come from here or—"

"We had to pay for all the computer equipment, the big screen, all that came from a company called On the Record."

"That wasn't supplied by LA?"

"No. That stuff was our responsibility."

"Were you able to fly home during the trial?"

"I was down there almost a month, but I did come home for my birthday."

"Being away from Gavin must have been hard."

"I'm a newlywed. I love my husband. It was very hard. But it goes with the territory of being a prosecutor."

Hunter nodded. "How much rehearsing did Hammer do on opening and close?"

"He rehearsed before both opening and close. For instance, the night before his rebuttal, Jim rehearsed at the hotel, in front of Hallinan, Cummins, and myself. Very important to organize not only your delivery, but your thoughts."

"What goes through a good prosecutor's mind when they're getting ready to examine a witness? When you stood up to examine Andrea and Paula and Dr. Stevens, what were you thinking?"

"Exactly what I did when I interviewed them before. Answer carefully. Tell the truth. Don't be nervous. Tell the truth. If you don't understand a question, ask to have it repeated. And tell—"

"The truth," Hunter completed. "Sounds like we both believe in the same mantra."

The policeman paused, carefully formulating his next question. "This case affected me tremendously. And you were involved from the very beginning. How…"

She put her head down and said in a voice that was almost a whisper, "From almost the very first moment of becoming involved, I knew my life would never again be the same."

"Why?"

"As a prosecutor in both Northern and Southern California, I handled numerous animal abuse and animal attack cases as well as violent felonies, ranging from robbery and arson to homicide. Since I was a child, I have had a fascination with and an appreciation for the relationship we humans have with animals in our care. When we act irresponsibly in that relationship, or choose to ignore warning signs, tragedy may ensue. When serious injury or death results from criminal negligence, we as a society are rightly outraged."

Hunter thought, I couldn't have put it any better.

He thanked Kimberly for her time went back to his own office. He thought, what a team it took to bring Noel and Knoller to justice. Law and order, working together. It took a huge team effort to have "guilty" verdicts brought in on all five counts.

In the policeman's mind, he knew they were guilty of far more than that, but not in the court of man.

He remembered what Robert Noel had written in one of his letters to Paul Schneider: *The Chancery courts were the direct descendants of the British Chancery Court where the King's Chancellor could be approached for relief from the strict application of the common law — it was a "court of conscience" and directed to doing what was "right" or "equitable" rather than what was strictly legal.*

The cop knew that there was another court even higher than the Chancery Court — the Court of the Angels with the Supreme Being as judge.

A proverb came to Hunter's mind, one of his favorites from when he first began administering polygraphs.

Proverbs 6, 17 to 19, listed the seven things that the Lord hated and felt an abomination:

A proud look;
A lying tongue;
Hands that shed innocent blood;
A heart that devises wicked plans;
Feet that run rapidly to evil;
A false witness who utters lies;
And one who spreads strife among others.

The head of General Work Detail thought, Noel and Knoller: guilty in Heaven's court — seven out of seven.

Chapter
Seventy-seven

Ground Zero

Henry Hunter's office, Hall of Justice, Tuesday, April 23, 2002.
The policeman glanced at the Chronicle's metro section. He read:
Pit bull mauls boy.

The eleven-year old had gone to his neighbor house, a lady who worked with a veterinarian, to ask help for his limping dog.

He was attacked.

Other neighbors had complained on eight separate occasions about the pit bull who hospitalized the boy. An animal control officer responded and shot the animal to death.

Two days earlier a 5-year-old girl was seriously injured by a Doberman pinscher. The day before another 5-year-old was killed as she was with two family pets — two rottweilers.

Dear God, Hunter thought and sent a silent prayer heavenward for God's innocents.

Time, the policeman thought, to wrap up some unanswered questions about my own dog-mauling murder case. He phoned and asked Steve Murphy to come into his office. Murphy, he knew, had contacts all over the city. The amiable Irishmen's job took him into every level of power and area of expertise, and he knew how to network and connect.

Murphy asked him what he wanted.

"I need information on abnormal behavior."

"For yourself?" asked Murphy with a grin.

"No."

Murphy saw that his boss was serious. He thought for a moment and said, "There's a doctor of psychology out at San

Francisco State University. She's been there for at least twenty years. I assume you want to talk to her about Noel and Knoller."

"I do."

"Then she's what you're looking for."

"And she is?"

"Dr. Iline Kroll Kittredje." Murphy excused himself, and, a few minutes later, returned with a printout of the doctor's educational and professional background.

Hunter scanned the information. The doctor received her B.A. New York University, Washington Square College, English Literature; M.S. — San Francisco State University, Counseling. Then onto her Ph.D. in Counseling Psychology.

She had been a counselor or psychotherapist for over 20 years, as well as Adjunct Professor/Instructor/Lecturer in Counseling for over 20 years at San Francisco State University's graduate Department of Counseling, teaching courses in "abnormal" human development, theory, practicum/process.

Her piece, "Standing Up for Myself" had been published in Radiance magazine. She was the editor of the Western Association for Counselor Education newsletter

After making an appointment, Hunter left his office and drove out to the university. Located in San Francisco's Stonestown neighborhood, the campus was nestled between Harding Park public golf course to the west, the exclusive San Francisco Golf Course to the south, and Sigmund Stern Grove — with its outdoor performance center — to the north.

Hunter loved the city of his birth. He loved driving through the many areas that made up the diverse town. During his career he had worked so many of the different and diverse districts.

He drove onto the campus. Good cops, by nature, are observant. He hadn't been to the university for awhile. He noticed that the architecture was a hodgepodge of different architectural style and eras. A reflection of continued growth.

He found Dr. Kittredje's office and entered. The doctor was on the phone. The professor mouthed "sorry" and pointed at a seat.

Ground Zero

Hunter settled into a chair and waited for the phone call to end. The academic's office held the usual: floor-to-ceiling bookcase, coffee table blanketed by periodicals, knickknacks scattered about.

One picture caught the policeman's attention. It was a framed poster of Tenniel's drawing of Alice and the Cheshire Cat, with the quote:

Would you tell me, please, which way I ought to go from here?

That depends a good deal on where you want to get to.

Hunter knew exactly where *he* wanted to get to: Answers to questions about abnormal people.

The doctor hung up the phone and said, "Sorry about that. When part of what you do deals with students, there's always an emergency happening."

Hunter nodded and said, "Have you followed the dog-mauling murder story?"

"Who hasn't?"

"I would like to ask you a few questions." Hunter paused, organizing his thoughts. "Can psychology answer questions about the horrific, needless death of Diane Whipple?

"You want a psychological autopsy? Sure. Psychology is the offspring of philosophy; it evolved from the centuries-old study and conjecture about the meaning of existence. Both disciplines attempt to help us make order out of seeming chaos.

"In journalism there's a model called the inverted pyramid. Reporters use it to organize their material. By addressing five points when writing articles, readers know what happened to whom, as well as when, where, why and how it occurred.

"The one difference between psychology and reporting is that journalists, we hope, report only facts. Psychology, however, labors under a severe handicap: We don't know capital 'T' truths about the inner workings of the mind, about human motivations and behaviors."

"Sounds like a standard disclaimer."

She smiled. "Close. We constantly try to amass more concrete, scientific knowledge about the psyche, but, frequently, the best we can do is generate hypotheses."

Hunter asked, "Are you saying that you can't answer questions about Noel and Knoller and their actions?"

"No. I am saying, however, that interpretations about people and their actions need to be defined as speculations, not definitive, provable statements of fact."

"Then what's wrong with those two?"

The doctor answered, "Given the bread crumb trail that they left for us to follow, my unofficial, off-the-cuff diagnoses of Knoller and Noel would be that they are individuals with not one, but two personality disorders — antisocial and narcissistic."

Hunter frowned. He dredged up some of his schooling from so many years ago and said, "Those aren't mental illnesses."

"No. They're personality disorders. And, unlike traditional mental illness or disease, personality disorders reflect ways-of-being-in-the-world. They describe an overriding state of mind that's reflected in one's demeanor and behaviors. Imagine that you're baking cookies. If you add orange or vanilla to the basic sugar cookie recipe, you haven't changed the composition of the cookie per se, but you've added a definitive, detectable flavor. Personality disorders are like that; you can *taste* their influence in someone's character and make-up."

"I saw a lot of that giving polygraphs."

The doctor nodded. "Most of us were told by our parents something along the mines of, 'The world doesn't revolve around you.' Narcissists don't believe this. Instead, they're positive that they are both the rising and setting sun. They are the center of their universe. Other people exist merely as pawns for and reflections of them. They have utter disregard and disdain for others' feelings and thoughts; empathy and insight are beyond their ken."

"That's narcissism. You mentioned antisocial."

"Not only are Knoller and Noel narcissistic, we can make a strong case for them being antisocial personalities as well. A total absence of guilt and overwhelming denial of responsibility for their actions are hallmarks of the antisocial individual. They exist to satisfy their own needs and desires; their means always justify their ends. They can be charming and beguiling, if they choose, but only because it gets them where they want to go."

"It got them in jail, is where it got them," interjected Hunter as he digested the clinical insight of a veteran psychotherapist.

The doctor continued. "The worst thing that can happen to them is that their cover is blown and they are seen for how and what they really are... which has happened in the Whipple case. Hannah Arendt wrote a book describing the banality of human evil. Some of her theory applies to Knoller and Noel, too. Their actions, and inaction, are appalling and perplexing to us, but standard operating procedure for them."

Hunter asked, "Does this disaster have anything to do with the fact that those two are both lawyers?"

"I think we have to examine why Noel and Knoller might have chosen the law as their vocation. As I see them, lawyers have a propensity for black-and-white thinking and an affection for definitive yes or no answers."

"Cops have the same affection."

Again, she nodded. "The reputation of the legal system has taken some hard hits in the past few decades. Currently, lawyers seem to define the law as the ability to justify someone's actions, explain it away, and to use situational ethics rather than morality as their foundational touchstone. However, another quality that many attorneys develop is the ability to dissemble. Some can and do utilize sins of omission, innuendo, obfuscation, sleights of tongue, misdirection, and lying upon occasion."

"I've seen that many times as a witness on the stand."

"It wouldn't be surprising if Noel and Knoller acquired the facility to consistently present themselves in the best possible light, facts notwithstanding. They would eliminate and erase anything that might blight their image. It's like putting a shiny new coat of paint on a junker car on blocks in the backyard."

"What about the dogs and the Aryan Brotherhood?"

"The dogs-of-war and the white supremacists, I believe, serve as symbols. People may use such animals and groups to compensate for their own insecurity, immaturity and fears. By affiliating with things seen as powerful, strong and formidable, the person's ego is bolstered simply by the association."

"Bolstered by associating with dogs and Aryans?"

"A psychological explanation for the draw to the dogs and Aryans is called identification with the aggressor. It's the equivalent of 'if-you-can't-beat-'em, join-'em.' You won't and/or can't hurt me, the twisted thinking goes, if I look or sound or act like you in some way. By consorting with these menacing forces, Knoller and Noel were, in essence, able to forge new identities for themselves."

"Any other insight into their personalities?"

"We also need to consider the rage that both Noel and Knoller have. More than likely, it was rarely expressed overtly. But make no mistake, it is there. Keeping fury bottled up and buried makes it all the more deadly. One might ask if Bane's attack on Diane Whipple could have both horrified and intrigued the onlooker. It was, after all, a raw, unadulterated manifestation of might and unbridled instinct. It may well have been fascinating to Knoller, dreadful as that sounds."

"How come," Hunter asked, "Knoller and Noel only reacted authentically when they were found guilty?"

"Before the guilty verdict, they had something going between them that is referred to as 'folie `a deux,' which literally means madness for two. They built this illusional, delusional, world together and comfortably dwelled there, feeling that they were impervious to the rules and regulations that apply to others.

"They shared a sense of entitlement. For example, how could anyone confine and trap those huge dogs in an apartment? It was cruel and unusual punishment for the animals. But Knoller and Noel, with their narcissistic tendencies and shared world view, thought nothing of it."

Hunter found himself nodding in agreement as Dr. Kittredje continued.

"Their own desires, not the health needs of the dogs or the safety of the building's other residents, were paramount. In a sense the dogs, like the Aryans, were unreal and existed only to serve Robert Noel and Marjorie Knoller's more-than-likely-unconscious psychological motivations."

"Again, why did it seem to me that they only reacted authentically when they were found guilty?" asked Hunter.

"Receiving a guilty plea shocked them, first and foremost, because they didn't believe that the jury was made up of their peers. Instead, they may well have considered the jurors inferior beings who would not and could not dare cast stones upon them. They were above the law."

Hunter nodded in agreement, then asked, "But none of this amounts to a defense of diminished capacity, does it?"

"No. Also, it seems likely that Knoller and Noel never fully matured; their psychological — not physical or intellectual — growth was arrested, possibly in their early teens. As adults, we know there is a thinking period between registering an impulse and trying to fulfill it. Kids will frequently go from the want to the get, so to speak. We adults will, sometimes at least, wait until after dinner for the cookies. Knoller and Noel, one might guess, hungered to be unconstrained in their desires, no matter what those desires were, no matter what the price to be paid."

Hunter thought, this helps validate, in professional terms, what I've felt from the beginning.

The doctor concluded, "With entitlement and immaturity, narcissism and insecurity, warped world view and unexpressed anger, we can see that these people were like time bombs, waiting to be detonated."

Sadly, Hunter realized that the doctor was correct. Noel and Knoller *had* been time bombs, as had Bane and Hera — a fatal combination of explosive ingredients that eventually shattered the lives of innocent people.

Henry Hunter closed his eyes for a few seconds. Images of the bloody hallway at 2398 Pacific Avenue flashed by; images of a senseless, preventable and gruesome death. of Diane Alexis Whipple — the ultimate target at ground zero.

Epilogue

The subtitle of this book is: *How Justice Prevailed in the San Francisco Dog-Mauling Case.*

How did *justice* prevail in this case?

Before this tragedy same-sex couples had very few rights under the law.

The California Legislature has passed into law AB 25, giving certain limited rights to same-sex couples.

Justice has prevailed in extending these rights — which were brought to the attention of the lawmakers by Assembly-woman Carol Migden.

Sharon's inability to legally marry Diane Whipple should not be used to make her loss irrelevant, her pain insignificant, or her relationship invisible, anymore than that of a married couple — or those that wish to be married but are prevented from doing so because of the laws of our country.

Sharon must now fight another battle — to give expanded meaning to the wrongful death statute.

Did justice prevail in this case through the verdict of the jury?

Robert Noel and Marjorie Knoller have been found guilty on all felony charges. If their felony convictions are sustained on appeal, they will lose their right to practice law. They have also lost their right to freedom.

Will justice still prevail if, through the appeals process, or a new trial, the verdicts are reduced?

They will serve out whatever remains on their sentences and then once again be able to walk the streets. But they will forever be labeled by our society for their arrogance, their egotism, their lack of sympathy and remorse.

Part of pride is arrogance. Part of pride is egotism. A prideful person cannot admit error, therefore cannot be remorseful

Arrogance, egotism and lack of remorse are not, under our laws, illegal. Yet, under that ancient concept of the Court of the Angels, Robert Noel and Marjorie Knoller will, because of their own prideful seeking of fame through the media, have an indelible mark of shame branded on them by the general public.

Emily Dickinson wrote: "Fame is a bee / It has a song / It has a sting."

Society has, through all of time, either formally (as in the English concept of Coventry) or informally, shunned those whose actions placed themselves in a repulsive position with their fellow citizens.

Those who are without heart are condemned to live without the heart of others.

Justice prevails when the guilty are punished.

When the author started this project he knew very little about the lesbian community. During the course of his research he was able to observe many things. What he saw was deep love, great loyalty and enduring friendship.

Diane Alexis Whipple died a monstrous death, an appalling death, a horrific death, a preventable death.

But was it a useless death?

Her death created an awareness of an injustice, and, because of this awareness, her death was a platform to catapult California's Assembly Bill 25 through committee review and the legislature, establishing a new law in less than a year.

Because of Diane's death an enormous amount of people in California enjoy more legal rights.

How wonderful this world would be if each of our deaths resulted in consequences that brought rewards and responsibilities to people in love.

Author's End Note

*If you are interested in ongoing details involving this story,
i.e. Robert Noel and Marjorie Knoller's appeals and
Penny Whipple-Kelly and Sharon Smith's wrongful death suits,
send an email to __QEangel@Netshel.Net__ and
this information will be sent to you free of charge.*

*If you have any comments regarding this book feel free to email
them to __jhh@Netshel.Net__*

*The trial transcript for the Diane Whipple murder case is 5,445
pages of verbatim – over two feet thick. In addition, the author
combed through hundreds of pages of dog court and grand jury
testimony. Perforce, all three legal proceedings have, by
necessity, been abbreviated. No motive was involved in this
abbreviation beyond controlling the length of this book.*

Publisher's Note

**Quantum Entertainment is actively seeking
short story submissions involving inspiring tales
about the human spirit.
Any *true* story of approximately 5,000 words about
the enduring spirit of human nature
— in any context and involving any age —
will be considered.
Send submission to QEangel.Netshel.Net
Attn. L. Ann, Submissions Editor.**